Private Sins,
Public Crimes

Private Sins, Public Crimes

Policing, Punishment, and Authority in Iran

FARZIN VEJDANI

Yale UNIVERSITY PRESS/NEW HAVEN & LONDON

Published with assistance from the Kingsley Trust
Association Publication Fund established by the Scroll and
Key Society of Yale College, and from the foundation
established in memory of James Wesley Cooper of
the Class of 1865, Yale College.

Yale University Press books may be purchased in quantity for
educational, business, or promotional use. For information,
please e-mail sales.press@yale.edu (U.S. office) or sales@
yaleup.co.uk (U.K. office).

Set in Minion Pro by Westchester Publishing Services.
Printed in the United States of America.

Library of Congress Control Number: 2024933049
ISBN 978-0-300-27568-1 (hardcover : alk. paper)

A catalogue record for this book is available from
the British Library.

This paper meets the requirements of ANSI/NISO Z39.48-1992
(Permanence of Paper).

10 9 8 7 6 5 4 3 2 1

For Bayan and Safaa

Contents

Acknowledgments

The spark for this book came as I was rifling through Princeton University's voluminous Persian newspaper collection for my first book project and stumbled across a previously unknown local police newspaper. While I eventually wrote an article based primarily on that newspaper, the theme of crime and punishment stuck with me as I searched for a new project. This marked the beginning of a nearly decade-long obsession with Qajar legal history, of which this book is the culmination.

I owe an enormous debt of gratitude to Jairan Gahan, who generously shared archival documents and helped me access archival collections in Iran. My research assistant, Sayeh Khajeheiyan, worked diligently on cataloging and transcribing archival sources, which sped up the research process. She also obtained a rare manuscript for me through her contacts in Iran. The staff at the libraries of Harvard University, Princeton University, the University of Toronto, and Toronto Metropolitan University were very helpful in tracking down rare books and articles. Several colleagues were instrumental in pointing me toward and/or providing me copies of sources during my research. These include Abbas Amanat, Assef Ashraf, Peri Bearman, Nandini Chatterjee, Farhad Dokhani, Robert Gleave, Sholeh Quinn, Intisar Rabb, and Mohamad Tavakoli-Targhi. Assef kindly brought to my attention a collection of recently published primary sources that helped shape the second chapter of the book. I am indebted to Farhad for patiently tracking down a rare photograph and several newspaper articles in the later stages of this book's composition. Abbas continues to be not only a mentor well beyond my graduate years but also a good friend, for which I am grateful. I have also benefited and learned from conversations with close colleagues, including Dominic Brookshaw, Farshid Kazemi, Arash Khazeni, and Janam Mukherjee. Dominic graciously took the time to help me with the intricacies of translating medieval prose and poetic texts. I am especially appreciative of Arash's friendship, as he has shared my enthusiasm for the project since the beginning.

Several colleagues read draft chapters of the book and provided useful critical feedback. These include Serpil Atamaz, Aomar Boum, Andrew Bush, Houchang Chehabi, Jairan Gahan, Kristen Stilt, and Nathan Wilkinson. Serpil, in particular, deserves thanks for reading and commenting on significant portions of the manuscript. I would also like to thank the two anonymous reviewers for their thorough and helpful feedback. It has been a pleasure to work with Jaya Chatterjee and Amanda Gerstenfeld of Yale University Press, who have been professional, efficient, and prompt in responding to my queries at all stages of the publication process. I am also grateful to Andrew Katz for expertly copyediting the entire manuscript. Meridith L. Murray efficiently prepared this book's index, which was supported with a grant provided by the Office of the Dean of Arts, Toronto Metropolitan University.

Portions of my research were presented at Harvard University, the University of Exeter, Yale University, the Association for Iranian Studies conference, and the Middle East Studies Association conference. I would like to thank the participants and audience members for their thoughtful questions and feedback. This book benefited greatly from the intellectual stimulation afforded by a fellowship at Harvard Law School's Program on Law and Society in 2019–20 and a Massey College fellowship during my sabbatical in 2021–22.

I would have been unable to write this book without the support of my family. I would like to thank my parents, Ehsan and Farzaneh, for their unconditional love. I owe my deepest gratitude to my wife, Safaa, and son, Bayan, and it is to them that this book is dedicated. Writing this book required precious time away from them. Safaa kindly walked me through some of the trickier Arabic passages used in this book. As I completed this manuscript, Bayan asked what I was doing one morning. When I explained, he remarked that he was writing his own book. May he always remain curious and tenacious.

Note on Transliteration and Dates

This book adopts a modified version of the *International Journal of Middle East Studies* transliteration guide without the use of diacritical marks. Diphthongs are transliterated *aw* and *ay*. Names with assimilated vowels are generally left separate, except names with *Allah* in them, such as, *'Abdullah* instead of *'Abd Allah*. Dates in the lunar Arabic calendar (*hijri*) are abbreviated as *H*. Most Persian and Arabic personal names have been transliterated except if the author has written a work in a European language.

Private Sins, Public Crimes

Introduction

In the summer of 1852, the village headman (*kadkhuda*) of Mahyar, a village just under fifty kilometers from Isfahan, stood accused of murdering Mashhadi 'Ali, a man seen as a potential rival to his post. The unnamed bereaved wife of the slain man found it necessary to travel to Isfahan in order to seek justice from the governor, Chiragh 'Ali Zanganah. Through the course of the investigation, which included the accused being interrogated at the governor's court and brought before a shari'ah court, damning evidence came to light: the coconspirators to the murder confessed that the headman had strangled the victim with their help before cutting up his body and hiding it in the desert. In the face of such evidence, the *kadkhuda* confessed to the murder but sought to pay handsome compensation both to the heirs of his victim and to the governor. The wife and daughter of Mashhadi 'Ali refused and insisted on their Islamic right to retribution, or *qisas*. Since the main adult heirs were women, they approached the city executioner to carry out the execution for thirty tumans, but he declined to do so, possibly because he had been paid off by the headman. Undeterred, the two women exercised their right directly when the governor handed over the headman to them in plain view at the Naqsh-i Jahan Square in Isfahan. Seizing two ends of a rope, they ritualistically re-created the manner of their loved one's murder by choking him to death before a crowd. As people walked by the corpse, they cursed the *kadkhuda* and addressed the mother and daughter of Mashhadi 'Ali, saying, "This is imperial justice: it carries out *qisas* like this for your husband."[1]

On the surface, this appears to be a rather straightforward account of crime and punishment in nineteenth-century Iran. But a deeper investigation of its details raises certain questions about the nature of crime, legal procedure, authority and jurisdiction, and the meanings of punishment, which form the topic of this book. By what criteria did an act become a crime subject to punishment? Who had the authority to investigate and issue a ruling on a crime, and who had the duty to carry out punishments? Finally, what forms did punishments take, and what were they meant to convey?

In weaving together the complex threads that run through this and similar cases, this book addresses the socio-legal history of crime, policing, and punishment in nineteenth-century Iran. First, it examines the theoretical and official state documents that defined crimes and punishments and delineated the jurisdictional authorities responsible for trying and punishing different types of crimes. Islamic jurisprudence, advice literature, reformist texts, policing and penal codes, and imperial decrees constitute the legal corpus for such definitions and delineations. The overall narrative arc of the first section of the book starts with the ideals embodied in Islamic jurisprudence and advice and reform literature, before turning to how these ideals were synthesized, modified, and supplemented in nineteenth-century decrees, administrative manuals, and codes. Second, it switches to the lived experience of everyday crime and punishment to explore how authorities both applied and deviated from norms and laws in practice. Drawing on case studies from three major Iranian cities—Isfahan, Shiraz, and Qum—it examines neighborhood dynamics in explaining the selective punishment of certain crimes, the moral policing of private residences suspected of illicit activities, the use of sanctuaries by criminals to evade punishment and the efforts of government officials to bring an end to the practice, and the recurring employment of public spectacles of punishment.

Beyond Legal Modernity and Modernization

Writing a legal history of nineteenth-century Iran poses a range of methodological and conceptual challenges, given Iran's relationship to modernity and an increasingly interconnected world. With regard to modernity, this period saw dislocations from greater European presence and integration into the world economy, new technologies and commodities, and experimentation with a standing army, schools, and police. Yet most historians dealing with Qajar law have viewed it through a lens of failure and absence: failure to modernize, codify, define jurisdictions, and provide meaningful redress; absence of modern prisons, courts, policing, and the rule of law. Reforms were "abortive" or "ineffective." Violence was "arbitrary."[2] A related approach taken by Hamid Algar has been to reduce the sum of nineteenth-century advocacy for legal reform to the single figure of Mirza Malkam Khan, only to claim that his proposals were inauthentic because they were supposedly not in harmony with Islamic law and thus destined for failure.[3] Broadly speaking, the Qajars are treated as a prelude to the modern Pahlavi nation-state, not sufficiently "medieval" or "early modern" to be understood on their own terms. If this historiography of failure is to be believed, it is miraculous that the Qajars survived not only foreign meddling but also their own maltreated masses.

Qajar interactions with the rest of the world are also more complex than often portrayed. Several historians have been at pains to characterize Qajar Iran in light of the colonial experience, which affected jurisprudence across Asia—yet Iran was never colonized in the nineteenth century. While colonialism offers a paradigm for discussing developments in many places, to speak of Iran as "semicolonial" confuses the fact that it had no colonial officers codifying laws or building institutions, nor was there a "colonial archive" through which to understand Iranian legal history.[4] A more current perspective looks at the regional networks that inform a country's legal processes: Ahmad Faiz has done this for Afghanistan by tracing Ottoman and colonial Indian interactions.[5] Such a framework can only go so far for nineteenth-century Iran, however: many Shi'i jurists were trained in Ottoman Iraq and engaged with scholars residing there but were by and large uninterested in contemporary Sunni scholarship produced in India and Central Asia. Iranian reformers were impressed by Ottoman Tanzimat reforms—alongside the better-known story of European models—which did inspire draft translations of Ottoman penal codes and other codification efforts but not necessarily alongside legal professionalization and institutionalization. Here again, comparative geographical accounts tend to reflect a historiography of failure: the Qajars "fell behind," while the Ottoman Tanzimat "succeeded"; they were "backward" in comparison to Europe.[6] Furthermore, excessive focus on imported innovations risks neglecting the enduring influence of Iran's local modes of lawcraft. Such reductive comparative approaches cannot succeed in describing the internal social dynamics of crime and punishment in Qajar Iran or explain their durability.

This book draws methodological inspiration from scholarship on crime and punishment in Muslim societies and Europe. At one level, it draws on scholarship from Muslim societies—medieval, early modern, and modern, irrespective of whether they were Sunni or Shi'i, Iranian, Arab, Turkish, or South Asian—to make sense of nineteenth-century Iran. At another level, it looks to innovative scholarship on medieval and early modern Europe for frameworks to understand vernacular legal systems. Because formal institutions were less vital than processes in nineteenth-century Iran, I focus not on the *what* of penal law—police, court, prisons—but on the *how*: policing, issuing rulings, and imprisoning. Throughout, sociology and anthropology contribute terminology ("contagion," "pollution," "danger") that helps to move beyond banal discussions of crime as endemic to Iranian society and punishment as an expression of arbitrary despotism or solely as sovereign power. Contrary to characterizations of the Qajars as a failure, a prelude to a nation-state, or a classic patrimonial society, this book argues that the Qajars created a legal system that was fascinatingly coherent on its own terms.[7]

Private/Public and Sin/Crime

This book proposes an alternative, sociocultural conceptualization of Qajar-era legality and morality as these were lived in public versus in private, different from theories defined against the supreme legal or moral authority of God or of the state. Representing theories ascribing authority to God, Wael Hallaq writes that any offense, including adultery, theft, or even murder, is answerable only to God's shariʿah (not simply "Islamic law" but an ethical and moral system that binds Muslim societies without the need for force) and cannot therefore be labeled a "crime," because "crimes" instead presume sanctions defined under a particular Western conception of the state. To Hallaq, all acts are moral rather than legal.[8] Mohammad Kamali also understands the state as having little to do with definitions of legality but understands law and morality on a spectrum of "the five categories of legal value: obligatory (wājib), recommended (mustaḥabb), permitted (ḥalāl), reprehensible (makrūh), and prohibited (ḥarām/maḥẓūr)." In Kamali's schema, the obligatory and prohibited constitute law, while the recommended and reprehensible are moral in nature.[9] This compares with Max Weber's notion that it is the prospect of "physical or psychic" sanction (in this world or, in religious worldviews, the next) that is at the core of the definition of law.[10]

At the other extreme, scholars such as Carl Schmitt hold that the state, embodied by the sovereign, is the ultimate arbiter of legality.[11] Moral considerations in such a worldview are largely irrelevant. In Qajar Iran, this perspective was reflected in advice literature such as mirrors for princes, which maintained a long-standing tradition that the sovereign had the prerogative to carry out shariʿah functions, such as forbidding wrongdoing and implementing fixed mandatory punishments (hudud), in ways often at odds with Islamic jurisprudence and whose legal sensibility was also informed by non-Islamic thought from ancient Greece, Persia, and even India.[12]

Throughout this book, I argue that acts were not inherently legal or illegal, moral or immoral, under criminal law in Muslim societies but rather that their *public* or *private* character determined whether they might be, respectively, a *crime* or a *sin*. A crop of recent studies by Roy Mottahedeh, Kristen Stilt, Baber Johansen, Intisar Rabb, Michael Cook, and Ahmed El-Shamsy have explored the same distinction in Islamic legal texts and manuals.[13] Although there were many gray zones between public and private, crime and sin, this lens helps to illuminate otherwise-obscure points related to nineteenth-century Iran.

I should stress that I use the words "public" and "private" not as direct translations from the Persian or Arabic but to approximate a cultural translation for clusters of relevant concepts, practices, and principles that had no single analogous terms. To be clear, I am *not* using "public" in the sense of Jürgen Habermas's concept of the "public sphere," in which individuals in civil society gather to rationally debate issues of common concern.[14] Nor do I use "public" to mean commonly or state owned, or "private" to mean individually or not state owned (as in "private property").[15] Even the common contemporary usage of "public law," to mean laws pertaining to individual-state relations and encompassing administrative, tax, criminal, and constitutional law, fails to capture what I mean by "public" for the purposes of this book. Rather, "public" encompasses meanings associated with the *manifest, profane*, and *debased*, while "private" encompasses the *secret, sacred*, and *inviolable*. This distinction is crucial to understanding how and why certain acts came to be thought of as punishable crimes. Two brief examples, one from the Islamic tradition and the other from medieval Christianity, are useful for what is meant here. According to hadith, a hidden wrong, not known by anyone, harms only the wrongdoer and is thus exempt from the duty to command right and forbid wrong.[16] As in medieval Christendom, "private or hidden sins could be atoned for in secret," but "public and notorious sins" required public punishment.[17]

This "public"/"private" framework provides a vocabulary to interpret differences between Islamic jurisprudence (*fiqh*) and government jurisprudence. Under *fiqh* criteria, sins that lacked consistent public testimony, a confession, and the like would go unpunished (or less punished). In general, the government respected household privacy and refrained from punishing offenses committed out of the public eye (e.g., drinking, adultery, or prostitution), but in others (e.g., theft, assault, or murder), it relied on differing investigatory standards to make the private public: active collection of circumstantial evidence, which was strictly prohibited for *hudud* and *qisas* convictions; spying, prohibited in *fiqh* but sometimes encouraged in mirrors for princes, which was carried out in public venues where covert vice or sedition might occur; and judicial torture, condemned in both *fiqh* manuals and mirrors for princes but widespread and paralleling Roman canon law, which was

used to close an evidentiary gap and legitimize punishment by expos-
ing secret crimes, criminal networks, or locations of stolen goods.[18]
Punishments for murder confessions obtained in this way were usually
distinct from their shari'ah equivalents.

The idea of the "public" as the general population also appeared
in Qajar-era legal texts, most often under the term 'amm (in contrast to
khass, "elites") in codes and mirrors for princes.[19] Maslahat (common
good) was another relevant word that denoted policy for the welfare of
the public rather than specific elites or individuals.[20] Within fiqh discourse, criminal law for the protection of the public was described as
Huquq Allah (Rights of God), as opposed to law governing claims between parties, or Huquq al-Insan (Rights of Humans).[21] That public
Rights of God included hudud crimes, which by definition occurred in
plain sight, is a further link between this connotation of "public" and
the manifest in legal conceptions of the period.

In order to understand the private/public distinction, it is crucial
to understand how often unarticulated fears of contagion, pollution, and
danger informed crime and punishment.[22] This book therefore draws
on sociological and anthropological concepts of contagion, pollution,
and danger in its study of crime, following on insights from historians
of Europe and authors who have applied these concepts to Muslim
societies more broadly. Émile Durkheim's theory of "sacred contagion,"
which describes a belief that ritual uncleanliness can pass through
contact, thereby polluting the social organism and spreading moral danger, sheds light on conceptions of crime in Qajar Iran as well.[23] Crimes
were considered not only dangerous in a material sense but also as having a morally polluting effect. This pollution could occur either via the
communication of ritual uncleanliness (those who knew ruffians, prostitutes, and thieves could be found guilty by association, without proof of
crime) or via mimesis of criminal acts through the body of the population ("like produces like").[24] Where René Girard has discussed the mimetic potential of violence, the same assumption seems to lie behind
Islamic prohibitions against drinking, gambling, and illicit sexual behavior.[25] This reading suggests how private sin, which only harmed the
doer of the act, could be categorically different from public, contagious
crime, which required a public ritual of punishment.[26]

Sovereignty and Jurisdiction

Within political and legal theory, sovereignty has been understood as the authority with which to use violence in the name of the law. At the core of coercion used for policing or punishment was an underlying claim to the legitimate use of violence, as per Weber's definition of the state.[27] Building on Weber's insights, Carl Schmitt considered the sovereign to be the one capable of making decisions over life and death and determining exceptions to the normal operation of the law.[28] The sovereign's position outside the law enabled them to create law. While some scholars have framed the sovereign claim to legitimate violence as a Western legal form of thinking peculiar and foreign to Muslim societies, this is precisely what the mirrors for princes genre and later Iranian reformist texts considered to be the prerogative of the sovereign.[29] Sovereignty entailed the responsibility to make rulings on crimes and enact punishments. This is perhaps why the term *siyasat* not only meant "politics" or "policy" but also "punishment" in Persian and Ottoman Turkish, in much the same way that "justice" in a range of European languages could mean authority tied to lordship, holding and trying courts, and capital punishment.[30]

Alongside the sovereign, other actors made complementary and sometimes competing claims to the legitimate use of violence. Shiʿi jurists typically ascribed divinely sanctioned violence to the Imam and/or to jurists acting as deputies. In this reading, God's juridical sovereignty was delegated to competent jurists who alone had the competency and capacity to enact legitimate violence, either by forbidding wrong or issuing rulings to punish. A third and often neglected legal nexus of authority, however, was the community itself. When crowds carried out violence on people deemed to be criminals, they saw themselves as agents of the law, either as shariʿah or abstract justice. When the crowd enacted the shariʿah, it was often in accordance with a jurist's ruling or responsum (*fatva*) but without the approval of the governor or shah. At other times, the crowd instead employed more abstract notions of fairness and justice embodied in E. P. Thompson's notion of moral economy.[31] Beyond violence toward notables accused

of hoarding during bread riots, neighborhoods and local communities employed rough justice toward those who were regarded as immoral,
criminal, and troublesome.[32]

In contrast to theories of sovereignty derived from modern
European historical experiences, jurisdiction is an illuminating concept
through which to understand sovereignty's multifaceted dimensions in
Iran. Jurisdiction is commonly used to speak of law's territory, in other
words, what court had authority over which sharply defined territory (often cartographically), and the hierarchical arrangement of courts to
resolve legal conflicts and address apparent contradictions among and
between courts.[33] It is often this very modern and relatively recent (even
in the European and American context) understanding of jurisdiction
that is applied anachronistically to nineteenth-century Iran to highlight
its supposed legal deficiencies. As recent scholarship has demonstrated,
however, in earlier understandings of jurisdiction, a plaintiff could bring
a similar case to multiple courts without it being seen as a sign of arbitrariness or legal chaos in early modern England and elsewhere.[34] Scholarship on jurisdiction in Muslim societies has primarily focused on
mazalim, or courts of redress typically associated with the sovereign,
since it appeared to resolve contradictions, injustices, lack of implementation, and complaints about lower courts in a hierarchical manner
akin to the modern sense of jurisdiction.[35]

Jurisdiction in the Qajar context has been described as a dual system of authority divided between government (*hukumat*) and shari'ah,
embodied by the sovereign and the religious scholars ('ulama), respectively.[36] And yet the daily operation of governance often involved at least
three juridical poles: the shah and his imperial court, which was referred to as *dawlat* or *divan*; the governor's provincial, city, or local authority, typically referred to as *hukumat*; and the shari'ah authority of
the Islamic jurists (*mujtahids*) at their courts.[37] This book argues that,
while on the surface *hukumat* and *dawlat* appeared to be interchange-
able, there was as much conflict as there was cooperation between imperial and provincial courts in criminal cases, especially when governors
found creative ways to subvert the shah's rulings. The overlapping nature of jurisdiction created opportunities for the central government to

amplify its legal authority vis-à-vis the provinces or the local 'ulama but also for the local governor and 'ulama to challenge the shah's involvement in local affairs. That a single criminal case could receive three or more rulings by the shah, a governor, and one or more *mujtahid* is a testament to the fact that Qajar legal jurisdictions were not tightly defined territorially or hierarchically in the modern sense, despite the best efforts of Qajar-era reformers to move in this direction; instead, they were jurisdictions in the sense of courts capable of issuing rulings on similar types of cases.

Shifting analytical lenses, how did jurisdiction appear from the perspective of ordinary subjects, especially marginalized women, slaves, apostates, non-Muslims, lower-status groups, criminals, prostitutes, and beardless youth, who made use of various courts as plaintiffs and petitioners? Marginality certainly had legal ramifications, insofar as there was often differential treatment, processes, and punishments depending on one's category of personhood.[38] At the same time, advice literature and, to some extent rhetorically, imperial decrees (*farmans*), codes, and other written government edicts, stressed the equality of Qajar subjects in being able to access justice and receive due process. Distinctions were made according to not only differences between elites and the masses, gender, or free status but also the crucial issue of public reputation: Were the accused respectable or notorious? Despite the marginalized status of such individuals, they deftly navigated various jurisdictions assertively. Costas Douzinas has argued that "the function of jurisdiction is to bring the sovereign to life and give him voice, and then, by confusing the person who speaks and the subject who states, to conceal sovereignty by confounding its creative, performative aspect with the declaration of the law and by excepting or excluding the sovereign's power of exemption."[39] Seen in this light, even marginal figures had a role in "bringing the sovereign(s) to life" by invoking their jurisdiction through the act, oral or written, of petitioning, even if this did not necessarily guarantee an equitable or favorable outcome. Often when there was tension among all three jurisdictions, marginal actors found opportunities to seek a measure of redress in unexpected ways.

Formal, Religious, and Neighborhood Policing

Mirroring the complexity of jurisdiction, policing did not fall neatly into a single institutional form in Qajar society since it encompassed formal and informal modalities carried out by government appointees, religious leaders and their followers, and even community members. It was justified by a concern with the spread of vice and the upholding of public morality and enacted through guarantorships and collective liability.

Like many Muslim societies, Qajar Iran had government officers, such as the police magistrate (*biglarbigi* or *kalantar*), police chief (*darughah*), and upholder of public morality (*muhtasib*), tasked with policing.[40] Governors and police magistrates often employed their personal stewards (*farrashs*) to act as their personal police.[41] Below these city-wide officials were those who were tasked with policing functions within a specific neighborhood. Since the Qajar urban landscape was administratively broken up into neighborhoods (sing. *mahallah*, pl. *mahallat*), a neighborhood headman (*kadkhuda*) represented his quarter in citywide affairs. When it came to matters of policing, surveillance, and criminal activities, the *kadkhuda* was responsible for his neighborhood and often reported to the *biglarbigi/kalantar, darughah*, or governor.[42] Officials tasked with patrolling, guarding, and surveilling urban spaces often combined military and policing duties, such as the night guard (*qaravul*), who had their own barracks in many cities, and the mounted police (*qarasuran*), who protected caravans and roads outside the city walls. Patrolmen (*gazmah* or *pa gard*) complemented the *kadkhudas* in surveilling neighborhoods.[43] Beyond formal policing figures, religious leaders, such as prayer leaders and *mujtahids*, mobilized their followers, including sayyids (descendants of the Prophet Muhammad) and seminarians, to police and monitor cities for illegal activities. Even ordinary residents of a neighborhood actively policed suspicious activities.

Policing involved such a broad cross-section of Qajar society precisely because there was widespread concern with the spread of immorality, danger, and violence. Since the local government's surveillance capacity was limited (and potentially expensive), the community played a key role in the early detection of immoral and dangerous activities.[44] These ordinary subjects justified their involvement, especially in the face of government inaction, by framing crime as morally polluting and potentially contagious.[45] Manifest moral crimes that had the potential to be mimicked by others out of temptation, such as ecstatic music, lewd sights, and heretical ideas, had to be expunged from the neighborhood.[46]

The sovereign, governors, the ʿulama, and ordinary subjects all invoked the Islamic duty of forbidding wrong and upholding public morality (hisbah/ihtisab) as justifications for policing.[47] But this duty was tempered by the equally significant principle of the domicile's inviolability: the duty to police usually covered manifest crimes occurring outside the domicile, except in extreme circumstances such as an impending murder. Therefore, the domicile, as a locus of sanctity, was theoretically protected from the reach of government and religious authorities or even neighbors.[48] Put another way, the domicile might be thought of as within God's jurisdiction insofar as any sanctions for moral and ethical violations in the form of sin and vice were distinctly otherworldly.[49] It was precisely the domicile's strong inviolability that made it the site of underground parties, where entertainment music, dancing, alcohol, and illicit sex occurred in major urban centers in Iran. The boundaries between the privacy of the domestic residence and the public of the streets became blurred, however, when one or more actors decided that private sin crossed the threshold into public crime, either by virtue of sounds—musical or alcohol induced—spilling into the streets or through knowledge (or, more likely, suspicion) of illicit acts. The ambiguous nature of such a sin/crime often triggered a raid into the domicile by the ʿulama and their supporters, concerned and moralizing neighbors, and/or, more rarely, local policing authorities in a manner that lays bare the tensions between various understandings of public and private.

This brings us to the socio-legal concepts of guarantorship (zimanat or iltizam) and collective liability, which stimulated and gave form to communal policing. Guarantor documents made particular individuals and groups responsible for the criminal actions of others to whom they were connected through financial and other penalties.[50] Official codes regularly included guarantorship, while in practice, local governors employed it to ensure communal policing and embed their authority within society. Thus, guarantorship linked the sovereign to the governors, the governors to their subordinate policing and administrative officials, and ordinary subjects to people in authority over them and to one another in such a way that makes it difficult to draw firm lines between state and society, between authority and subject, and even between religion and government.[51]

Punishment, Ritual, and Expiation

In light of what has been said so far, we are well positioned to understand the underlying rationale for policing (to monitor and prevent the spread of crime) and punishment (to collectively expiate the harm done by sin and to ritually restore balance in the community). If crimes were defined and proven by their publicness, so too were punishments, whose visual lessons were oriented toward the community.[52] Punishment functioned as a form of containment and was meant to isolate the dangerous, polluting, and mimetic potential of crime by removing the vector of contagion from circulation.[53] While some containment techniques involved a living criminal's spatial exclusion through imprisonment, banishment, and/or public shaming rituals, others were permanent: execution, the most extreme solution, eradicated the locus of crime.[54] At times, shaming was tied to an event, but in others, its visible marks reminded the community of the criminal's ejection from normal society: disfigurement, in the form of dismemberment or branding, constituted a means of expiation for the crime but also a means of permanent social marginalization.[55]

The rich, anthropologically informed scholarship on ritual and expiation elucidates how public punishment brought an end to the cycle of disorder instigated by crime in a given community. E. P. Thompson's observation that "publicity was the essence of punishment" until the nineteenth century in England holds true for Qajar Iran, where it was similarly "intended, for lesser offences, to humiliate the offender before her or his neighbours, and in more serious offences to serve as an example."[56] The deterrent lesson, known as 'ibrat in Persian, was an often-repeated rationale for public punishments in Qajar Iran. Rituals of infamy "imparted a moral and cautionary lesson to the public" and were intended to restore balance by ensuring "each one got his due."[57] In a sense, public punishments were "communicative acts," signaling the law's application and the strengthening of the social fabric.[58] By fulfilling the ritual requirements of punishments, the community cleansed itself of the polluting potential of crime.[59] Phillip Smith understands punishment as meant to "destroy and cleanse that which is evil, restore order from chaos, and celebrate the moral and sacred authority of the law."[60] Failing to publicly punish a known criminal had the opposite effect: it emboldened the immoral, the violent, and the thief to act with the "audacity of impunity."[61]

The process of "making someone public," which was known as *tashhir* (literally "publicizing") or parading around town (*shahr gardandan*), drew on a formidable and rich repertoire of scripts, which could include inversion, bestialization, and/or social exclusion. The ubiquitous punishment of being paraded backward on a donkey around town was one such example: the criminal was associated with a beast of burden while inverted, signaling both their nonhumanity and bestialization (figure 1).[62] Other common Qajar punitive parading techniques, which could include being led through town in a bridle, having one's hair shaved off, or being paraded bareheaded or with a silly hat, signaled humiliation and further social marginalization (figure 2).[63]

While nineteenth-century Iranian cities have been examined as sites of religious ritual processions, ceremonial displays of sovereignty, commerce and economic exchange, and interaction between tribes and city dwellers, their legal significance, and their significance in the history of crime and punishment in particular, has rarely been accounted for.[64] As Esther Cohen has demonstrated with respect to medieval France, "the symbolic spatial arrangement of a city as a microcosm, merging through other public city rituals as well, was both enunciated and used in public executions."[65] In Qajar Iran, a ritualized parade through the city's streets and bazaars culminated in executions in the city square (*maydan*), sure to garner and support a large audience. Executed corpses of the condemned were hanged from a city gate as a warning to both residents and people entering the city that

Figure 1: Depiction of a criminal being punished by being
paraded around the city in a bridle sitting backward on a donkey.

(Source: Undated poster [possibly from the 1910s], reproduced in Amir 'Ala'i, *Mujazat-i I'dam*, 38)

Figure 2: Depiction of a criminal being paraded through
the bazaar in a bridle while an executioner collects money.

(Source: Undated poster [possibly from the 1910s],
reproduced in Amir 'Ala'i, *Mujazat-i I'dam*, 41)

this was a city of law.[66] In this urban theater of punishment, it was the "master of wrath" (*mir ghazab*), the Persian term for executioner, who was often the orchestrator of ritual ceremony. As in policing, ordinary subjects had a claim over a portion of the law: in legal retribution cases, the family of the murdered individual could opt to publicly carry out the sentence with their own hands instead of hiring an executioner.

Paralleling the relationship between the domicile and policing, the inviolability of sanctuaries led to the spatial suspension of punishments. The practice of taking sanctuary (*bast, tahassun, panah*) in Qajar Iran stood outside regular norms of punishment and retribution, much as it did in medieval and early modern Europe.[67] George Duby observes that there was a "sacred significance to privacy" in medieval Europe through peace regulations that made churches and the villages in which they were housed a "zone of immunity where violence was prohibited."[68] Similarly, sanctuaries in Mecca and, to a lesser extent, Medina were spaces in which violence was prohibited, including the implementation of otherwise-mandatory punishments and retributions. In Qajar Iran, the shrine of an Imam or a descendant of an Imam (*Imamzadah*), a mosque, a royal stable, a telegraph office, or even the home of a respected Islamic scholar (*'alim*) or notable could act as a sanctuary for someone accused of committing a serious crime.[69] A running debate throughout the nineteenth century was the degree to which this inviolability should be observed, such as in the case of murderers, thieves, and other criminals, and the methods for policing the sanctuary space.

Return to Qajar Persian Sources

Whereas past studies on Qajar-era crime and punishment have relied heavily on European-language sources, this book draws mainly on an array of printed and archival primary texts in Persian, Arabic, and Ottoman Turkish, which include Islamic jurisprudence, advice literature, reformist tracts, legal codes, administrative manuals, letters and correspondences, government and police reports, local and official newspapers, and *farmans*. Taken together, these sources capture both the theoretical and formal dimensions of criminal law while also shedding light on its daily operation in ways that depart from previous studies that rely almost exclusively on European sources to do so.[70]

In past studies, European-language sources have been prioritized, with scholars arguing that there are few Persian sources or that Persian sources are somehow less "objective."[71] This study pushes back against these characterizations by delving into a plethora of Persian primary sources from Iranian archives, including the Ayatullah Burujirdi Library, the Kakh-i Gulistan Archive, Majlis Library, the Malik Library, and the Sazman-i Asnad va Kitabkhanah-i Milli Archive, and printed primary sources culled by scholars in Iran. Iranian historians who jump to European archival sources either ignore the Saidian critiques of Orientalism or, at best, seek to recover subaltern voices by reading them "against the grain."[72] Such approaches are bewildering when one considers that Iran was never a European colony during this era, so official European sources neither reflect official state policies nor exclusively address the lives of ordinary people in legal contexts.

This study takes a fresh look at a variety of Shi'i juridical works outside of conventional laws to establish a background on Qajar legal theory and ethics: what was considered a crime (and cases when violence might be justified), under whose jurisdiction crimes fell, what proof was needed for convictions, and what punishments were appropriate. Advice literature—mirrors for princes (*andarznamah, nasihatnamah*) and the reformist tracts that succeeded them—provides a neglected competing theoretical legal corpus, which emphasized the sovereign's authority in criminal matters over that of Shi'i jurists. Moving to formal law, imperial decrees of the shahs, administrative manuals (*dastur al-'amal*), and a host of documents that may be termed laws, codes, and regulations (*qanun, qarardad, takalif*) provide us with a rich understanding of official policing, imprisonment, and punishment in Qajar Iran. This corpus demonstrates the influence of the aforementioned Shi'i jurisprudence and advice literature on formal laws; the extent of Qajar lawmaking in the realm of policing and penal matters, despite widespread assumptions to the contrary; and the Qajars' legal responsiveness to dynamics on the ground, however temporary or unevenly implemented.

Alongside the preceding sources, diverse Persian sources, such as diaries, local government and police reports, newspapers, and telegrams, offer a fuller appreciation of how crime and punishment operated day-to-day in cities such as Isfahan, Shiraz, and Qum. Governors occasionally wrote narrative reflections on particular tenures that boasted of their strategies to police and punish crime while providing detailed examples. The *ruznamah*, which could mean a government report, diary, or newspaper depending on context, stands out as another rich source for understanding Qajar-era crime and punishment. The Persian word *ruznamah*, literally "daily letter," evolved a series of meanings that mirror developments in Iranian crime reporting. *Ruznamah*s in the sense of "diaries" were rich sources for everyday accounts of crimes, which by the mid-nineteenth century, became a preferred label for government and police reports issued by date and neighborhood.[73] Finally, shortly after this period, *ruznamah* in its current usage as "newspaper" came to draw detailed accounts of provincial crime and punishment from governors' reports to the capital. Alongside the governors' narratives and *ruznamah*s, ordinary Iranians used petitions (*'arizijat, tazallumat*) to voice their objections about how criminal cases were being handled, often addressing the central government to intervene at the local level against a governor or religious authority.[74] With the advent of the telegraph, petitions, reports, and rulings could be sent between the provinces and Tehran at increased speed; most telegrams used here were of the administrative "question and answer" (*su'al va javab*) form, collected into books by city and date. Court officials in Tehran would wire inquiries to governors or other figures in the provinces (sometimes a prominent Shi'i jurist, occasionally a regular subject) regarding the handling of specific cases, thereby providing us with glimpses into the interactions between Tehran and provincial centers, jurisdictional issues in criminal cases, and the management of policing across the empire (figure 3). Rather than viewing this diversity of source material as evidence of administrative and legal failure and underdevelopment, I see it as an opportunity to creatively juxtapose otherwise seemingly disparate primary sources to come to a multifaceted understanding of crime and punishment in Qajar Iran.

In considering the complex relationship between crime and punishment, policing and liability, authority and jurisdiction, I do not limit myself

Figure 3: Nasir al-Din Shah in the Telegraph Office.
(Source: *Vaqayi'-i Ittifaqiyah*, n.482 [21 Rabi' al-Sani, 1276 H./(November 8, 1859)])

in this book to a single approach or paradigm. Instead, I aim to demonstrate why the seemingly arcane passages of Shi'i jurisprudence and the legal dimension of political treatises and advice literature are as important as detailed government reports on the minutiae of everyday crime, policing, and the spectacle of public punishments in nineteenth-century Iran. Within Islamic studies, there has often been an undue emphasis on normative and prescriptive texts, particularly those of Islamic jurisprudence, with little attention paid to the degree to which such texts were implemented in actual cases. By contrast, more empirically grounded studies of crime and punishment in the field of Iranian and Middle Eastern studies give pride of place to lived experience, to the exclusion of prescriptive texts.

I argue that one must understand everyday legal practices alongside the norms, ideals, and symbols derived from such prescriptive and formal textual reservoirs. If crime involves the violation of the law, then it is crucial to understand what that law was in the minds of those who articulated it and how they justified its punishment. Only then can we start to address the crucial question of why, by whom, and how an act was determined to be criminal. To neglect such normative and state-produced texts would be to fundamentally misread the processes undergirding the everyday life of criminal law in Qajar Iran, especially because there were no highly formalized legal codes or legal court structure through which to process criminal cases, nor was there a clear procedural mechanism for processing such cases. Ignoring such processes will lead to reducing crime and punishment to yet another chapter in the supposed long, "barbaric" history of "Oriental despotism," in which arbitrary violence, wanton arrest, imprisonment, or, worse, torture and execution were rampant. Similarly, reducing the social history of crime to subaltern "resistance" to an extortionist state or a premodern "prelude" to modern social mobilizations tells us only part of the story. In fact, most histories of social movements neglect or ignore the legal underpinnings of arrests, detentions, and punishments of individuals as watershed moments in which legal counternarratives were harnessed to decry injustice.

Instead of choosing one method exclusively over another, I use a blended methodological toolbox in this book. The study of the normative and prescriptive texts of the first part is meant to provide a blueprint, not of how law was implemented in practice but of the deeply ingrained assumptions about what constituted illegal behavior and why, the presumed meaning of certain punishments, and their intended social function. The specific spatial set of assumptions about when a vice constitutes a crime or why a crime must be punished publicly and often through highly ritualized spectacles runs throughout many of these texts. It is these same assumptions that provide a crucial piece of the puzzle of the dizzying complexity of criminal cases in this dynamic era of Iranian history, which will shed light on its contemporary relevance for understanding underground private parties, invasive policing of vice, the codification of Islamic penal law, and the enduring practice of public punishments under the Islamic Republic.

Sin, Crime, and Punishment
in Shi'i Jurisprudence

I n Islamic jurisprudence (*fiqh*), criminal law does not fit neatly within contemporary understandings of private and public law. While many crimes may be categorized as part of public law, injuries and murder are generally classified as the equivalent of torts and therefore within the scope of private law. Crimes that warranted fixed mandatory punishments (*hudud*, singular *hadd*) included theft, highway robbery, fornication (*zina*), the false accusation of fornication, drinking wine, and apostasy.[1] *Hudud* crimes were public in two specific ways: first, the crime had to be manifest insofar as it was witnessed by a prescribed minimum number of witnesses who could provide consistent testimonies or was confessed to before a judge and court witnesses; second, the crime was also public insofar as it had the potential to harm the entire Muslim community. And yet, *hudud* punishments were rarely meted out in Islamic history because of the countervailing significance of privacy in Islamic jurisprudence: these same acts committed in private, such as in an inviolable domicile away from prying eyes, were not subject to punishment so long as it did not become public knowledge. To violate this privacy, even in the pursuit of uncovering such an act, was considered sinful insofar as it constituted a form of spying (*tajassus*) and a violation of sanctity (*hatk-i hurmat* or *pardah-dari*).

Crucial as well to understanding this private/public distinction is the Islamic principle of commanding good and forbidding wrong (*al-amr bi'l-maʿruf wa al-nahy ʿan al-munkar*), which for certain jurists was also considered a part of the *Huquq Allah*.[2] While a *hudud* punishment was the outcome of a trial with a high burden of evidence, forbidding wrong was an immediate response to ongoing public wrongdoing. Who was authorized to forbid wrong, especially with violence, was a topic of fierce debate historically. In medieval Sunni Islamic polities, the *muhtasib* was authorized to forbid wrong in public urban spaces.[3] Forbidding wrong covered a wide range of public acts that violated the shariʿah, although the duty to carry it out ceased if the act was done privately.[4]

This is not to say that Islamic jurisprudence condoned private vice; it merely had an ethical rather than legal status. Thus, those who engaged in a prohibited act committed a sin (*maʿsiyah*) for which one could repent (*tawbah*) or take on an act of expiation (*kaffarah*).[5] Muslims were encouraged not to publicize their sin to others, much less to the broader public, since sin committed privately limited its harmful effects to the sinner alone. Once committed in public or made publicly known, however, the same act legally became a crime subject to moral regulation or punishment.[6] There was, in other words, an underlying concern with the public transmission of sin: witnessing the flagrant violation of laws made it potentially contagious through mimesis. The question of when an act was a private vice or a public crime was, at times, ambiguous and subject to debate.[7] For instance, when unrelated strangers gathered at a private party where drinking, sex, or music was involved, was this a private vice or a public crime? And who had the authority to make this determination, and by what criteria?

Along related lines, the issues of jurisdiction authority and visible crimes were closely connected in *fiqh*. The translation of *huquq* as "rights" is somewhat misleading in relation to God since God in Islamic theology did not litigate and was not in need. Instead, according to Anver Emon, the phrase "rights of God" in jurisprudence represented "a term of art to represent social good that must be effectuated by the *imam*."[8] *Huquq Allah* was thus "public" in a jurisdictional sense because it affected the *entire* Muslim community. As upholders of the "public interest" (*masalih al-'ammah*), political authorities were expected to up-hold and champion these interests in most strains of Sunni legal thought.[9] Several scholars have pointed out that the upholder of God's rights, which in certain Sunni legal texts was the sovereign (*sultan*) and the judge (*qadi*) while in Shiʻi jurisprudence was the Imam and/or his representative (i.e., the ʻulama), had the authority to punish the *hudud* crimes as part of the public interest.[10] Tellingly, punishments for such public crimes were to be carried out in public. These punishments were justified in numerous ways, including public order, deterrent examples, rituals to expiate sin and restore community solidarity, and spectacles demonstrating God's sovereignty.

In order to examine the norms, ideals, and principles informing the definition of public crimes, the necessary punishments for these crimes, and the mechanisms for policing prohibitions in Shiʻi jurispru-dence, I rely in this chapter largely on understudied works of Shiʻi ju-risprudence from the Safavid and early Qajar period. The two Safavid-era works were Persian legal compendia: one, by Shaykh Baha al-Din al-ʻAmili, was a comprehensive work written for Shah ʻAbbas I that en-joyed wide circulation, while the second work was written by Muhammad Baqir Majlisi for Shah Sultan Husayn on the specific topic of *hudud*, dis-cretionary punishments (*taʻzirat*), lex talionis (*qisas*), and compensa-tion (*diyat* or *diyah*).[11] What both these Persian works shared was a clear and accessible writing style, which probably made them attractive to seminarians, low-ranking ʻulama, and ordinary believers with a tenu-ous grasp of Arabic. Legal compendia also generally omit hadith justi-fications and past authorities' differing positions about a given rule, only adding to their accessibility. Three other Shiʻi works from the early nine-teenth century used here were of a more comprehensive nature. Chief among them was Muhammad Hasan Najafi's comprehensive work of Shiʻi jurisprudence *Jawahir al-Kalam*, a work that became a standard textbook for seminarians since it summarized the majority and minor-ity opinions on a host of issues with copious citations throughout.[12] In the unique *Iqamat al-Hudud*, Muhammad Baqir Shafti argued that the ʻulama should carry out *hudud* punishments even in the absence of the Hidden Imam, the twelfth Shiʻi Imam who was believed to have gone into occultation in 873–74 (260 H.) and whose return would usher in the Day of Judgment.[13] Finally, Abu al-Qasim Qummi's responsa *Jami' al-Shitat* included illuminating sections on forbidding wrong as a largely public-oriented duty.[14] Although the rules outlined in these texts pertaining to crime were rarely implemented in everyday practice, they are a fruitful starting point for understanding the motivations, justifications, and maneuverings involved in the social history of crime and punishment. They further illuminate why and on what grounds certain Shi'i jurists in the Qajar period took a proactive role in punishing certain public crimes despite the existence of government figures claiming a similar prerogative.

Sight and Sound as Vectors of Privacy

Within Islamic legal texts, there was a recurring preoccupation with the licit and illicit as they pertained both to the visibility of the body and to sound.[15] While certain acts were licit in private and between related individuals, they were rendered illicit when done in public and/or between unrelated individuals. The protection of privacy and the domestic sphere was closely associated with reputation and modesty. The issue of visual intrusion was often highly gendered, with jurists concerned with protecting visual access to women's bodies to a degree that differed substantially from that for men.[16] Sound was similarly gendered: certain jurists considered the sound of a woman's voice as a private part that was meant to be protected from unrelated men. They also viewed sound of another variety—entertainment music without a specifically religious end and libertine lyrics—as a potentially corrupting influence on the public.[17] Even the visibility of certain prohibited instruments triggered the duty to forbid wrong. Sound, whether of a woman or of music, embodied the possibility of sexual incitement. Both sight and sound constituted crucial vectors of knowing and witnessing in Islamic jurisprudence and were therefore at the heart of epistemologies for differentiating between private and public acts.

According to Michael Cook, three basic principles lay at the core of an Islamic notion of privacy: the "prohibition of spying and prying," "the duty not to divulge what would dishonour a Muslim," and the "sanctity of the home."[18] Privacy was connected to the domicile (*harim*), the part of the house rendered inaccessible to unrelated outsiders, and to the body's "valorization" in Islam through the shielding of zones of shame (*'awrah*).[19] In the domicile, a woman's sense of privacy was stronger since she could be less covered, while in public, her privacy was transportable.[20] Yaron Klein argues that privacy in Islam was not a completely territorial (or spatial) idea but rather that "the conflicts between private and public spaces exist . . . between people and the space they inhabit," which explains "the preoccupation with keeping female bodies out of men's sight."[21] Eli Alshech, in explicating the notion of the private sphere in the early classical period, notes that it included "information about immoral behavior, illegal acts, intimate body parts, etc."[22] Muslim scholars called for modesty restrictions partly out of a concern for the visual intrusion of women's bodies.[23] These were not purely motivated initially by fear of sexual arousal, since Muslim women had to cover up in the presence of non-Muslim women (but not other Muslim women) and slaves were not bound by the same restrictions. After the tenth century, scholars began making an explicit connection between sexual immorality and modesty.[24]

Shi'i jurists elaborated on the legal implications of vision and sound along similar lines.[25] The main prohibition was against looking at private parts, encapsulated in the expansive term *'awrah*, by people without clearly defined kinship relations. A married couple, for example, would not be subject to such a prohibition within the domicile.[26] If a man intended to marry a woman, then he could look at her entire body except her private parts, including her face, hands, hair, and her "beauty."[27] A man could not look at anything but the face and hands of a woman he did not intend to marry (and, according to some jurists, not even that). These principles essentially created an obligation for the woman to cover herself but not for the man to do so.[28] In Shi'i *fiqh*, the intermingling of people of the opposite gender through speech and song was prohibited on the grounds that this involved transgressing a woman's *'awrah*, which included her voice. Najafi therefore argued that a man was prohibited from listening to a woman's voice, even in a devotional context, for fear of sexual temptation.[29] Instead, women should only make the call to prayer for other women and for men to whom they were related (*mah-*

ram) but not for unrelated men. Very old women whose voices did not incite (*hizz*) men were exempted from this rule.[30]

Music, whether licit or illicit, similarly reveals the contours of public and private in *fiqh*. For the medieval jurist Ibn al-Jawzi, sound was a danger when it produced a state of rapture (*tarab* or *wajd*).[31] Permissible music had much to do with its intent: Did it promote morality and religiosity, or did it steer people toward frivolity, illicit sex, drinking alcohol, gambling, theft, and murder? Jurists also grappled with the issue of who was involved in musical gatherings. Certain Islamic thinkers permitted hearing a woman's voice in mixed-gender Sufi *sama* gatherings but prohibited entertainment music (*ghina'*) that incited sexual temptation.[32] Musical instruments, such as stringed instruments, wind instruments, and certain bells, were also thought to incite rapture, which could easily be exploited for corrupt purposes and lead to immoral behavior. Therefore, the public display and sale of prohibited musical instruments were considered illicit. According to the medieval theologian Abu Hamid Muhammad al-Ghazali, loud music from wind and string instruments or the boisterous bellows of a drunkard were instances in which the sound was the same as the activity itself (entertainment music in the first case and drinking alcohol in the second).[33]

Aware of al-Ghazali's position on music, Najafi provided a detailed discussion of *ghina'* in relation to "frivolity, nonsensical speech, and falsehood" (*al-lahw wa al-laghw wa al-zur*), which were all forbidden in the Quran.[34] He argued that *ghina'* was similar to false testimony (*qawl al-zur*).[35] He made a distinction, following al-Shafi'i, between a "sweet sound" (*tahsin al-sawt*) that would be used for the Quran, prayers, poetry, sermons, and devotional purposes, on the one hand, and *ghina'*, on the other. As a result, mourning lamentations (*ta'ziyah*) for Imam Husayn, the Shi'i martyrs, the Prophet Muhammad, the Imams, and even the 'ulama were licit.[36] He invoked "custom" (*'urf*) as the criteria by which to distinguish entertainment music from devotional music.[37] Najafi also mentioned that certain 'ulama had argued that music could be used for battle purposes.[38]

What made entertainment music so threatening was that it could incite false feelings in a way that violated an ideal of self-control and cultivation of the senses.[39] If *ghina'* impeded a person's ability to avoid forbidden acts, such as sodomy (*liwat*), *zina*, lying, and the like, or if it led to doubt, then it was considered defective.[40] Najafi stated that "the prohibition on *ghina'* is akin to the prohibition on fornication" insofar as it could lead to corrupt sexual practices.[41] He also noted that mourning music (*al-nawh*) was not automatically licit since lovers could use it to lament their beloved in a manner consistent with delight leading to *fasad*, or it could be used to promote other forbidden acts.[42] Najafi argued that prudence dictated avoiding all forms of *ghina'*, dance (*raqs*), and trilling of the voice (*al-halhulah*) whenever there was doubt as to where it could lead.[43]

Illicit profit was also a legal matter related to *ghina'*.[44] Najafi argued that *ghina'* was permissible so long as income was not derived from it. When income was earned through the use of instruments like the *sarnaj*, *rubab*, and *zimar*, then it became forbidden.[45] Shi'i jurists typically agreed that "the female wedding singer" was the only person who could profit from singing, but only within certain restrictions: she was not to "speak nonsense," perform with instruments other than a *daff* without plates or bells, or have men at her gatherings.[46] Najafi argued that as soon as men entered the party, these became "frivolous parties" (*majalis al-lahw*); in other words, private became public according to the gender and kinship relationship among those who were present within a shared space.[47] *Fiqh* placed restrictions on the spaces connected to entertainment music. Since the production of lutes (*al-barabit*) and reed instruments (*al-mazamir*) was forbidden, property owners should bar renters who produced them.[48] Similarly, they should bar renters who were musicians, except for female wedding singers who matched the previously mentioned licit criteria.[49] These restrictions were intended to make it difficult for entertainment musicians and those who produced their instruments to live among other Muslims.

The *fiqh* penalty for playing music was not always clear-cut, although there were legal repercussions. These repercussions were sometimes defined negatively as lifting liability for what would otherwise be a crime. If someone stole an instrument of play (*lahv*), such as a *tanbur*, with the intention of breaking it, then they would not be subject to the *hadd* punishment for theft since they were forbidding wrong.[50] Enter-

tainment music also affected the moral standing of a Muslim. If someone listened to the "songs of the drunks" (*surud-i mastan*) and sang "in
their manner," they ceased to be a believer (*mu'min*).[51] The entertainment
musician (*mutrib*) and their audience members were both considered
corrupt and therefore unreliable witnesses.[52] Those who attended a party
with entertainment music sinned since a believer should avoid places
where sins such as drinking wine, listening to entertainment music,
dancing, and playing '*ud* occurred.[53] Someone who even greeted a frivolous person (*al-lahi*) engaged in an act of disbelief tantamount to "looking at the vagina of one's own mother."[54]

Fiqh demanded that individuals cover their '*awrah*, in the sense
of both visual and aural nakedness, depending on the relationship
among the individuals involved and the nature of the space in question.
Privacy and publicness were often defined through the vectors of vision
and sound; while certain forms of '*awrah* were permissible in private,
once they occurred in public, they were subject to prohibition and regulation. *Ghina'*, as a rapturous form of sound, was a particularly striking example of a potentially morally compromising threat that needed
to be contained and prohibited in public.

Burden of Evidence and the Knowledge of the Judge

In Islamic jurisprudence, the evidentiary burden for *hadd* conviction
was quite high. First, someone had to notify a shari'ah judge of the crime
to initiate a trial since even the judge did not have the authority to do
so. Next, proof required the consistent testimony of a number of witnesses or a confession by the suspect, which had to be publicly proclaimed before the judge and court witnesses.[55] Consistent testimony
assumed that the witnesses had seen the prohibited act in plain view,
an unlikely scenario given the social stigma of a Muslim believer being
in a public place where their drinking alcohol, fornicating, and the like
could be seen by strangers. Furthermore, confessions extracted through
torture were inadmissible at a shari'ah court, making conviction even
more unlikely. Contrary to most Sunni schools, Shi'i jurisprudence allowed for a third form of evidence for a *hadd* conviction: the knowledge
of the judge ('*ilm al-qadi*). The knowledge of the judge entailed his direct

witnessing of a crime, and, in the case of the Imam, a special form of innate knowledge.

Muhammad Baqir Majlisi provided a succinct summary of the forms of evidence required for convictions for crimes through consistent witness testimonies, confessions, or, in certain cases, oath. Four consistent male witness testimonies or confession by the guilty party on four occasions were required to convict for sodomy (*livat*).[56] For alcohol consumption, two male witness testimonies or confessions on two occasions were needed.[57] Apostasy only required a single confession or the testimony of two male witnesses.[58] The single confession of a murderer was typically sufficient for a conviction, although certain ʿulama argued that this should be done twice. Torture rendered such a confession invalid.[59] If one person confessed to intentional homicide, then a second person confessed to it, and then the first person renounced their confession, then neither was liable for *qisas* or *diyat*; instead, the treasury (*bayt al-mal*) provided the funds for compensation to the heirs (*ʿaqilah*) of the family.[60] Credible witness testimony had to be from morally upright Muslim males, without contradiction between individual testimonies. A minority opinion held that the testimony of one upright man and two upright women could prove intentional homicide.[61] Finally, homicide could be proven by an oath procedure (*qasamah*) when evidence was circumstantial or insufficient and if the accused did not deny the accusation made in the oath.[62] In all of these circumstances, the crime had become publicly known, by testimony, confession, or oath.

Shiʿi jurisprudence atypically allowed for the knowledge of the judge (*ʿilm al-qadi* or *ʿilm al-hakim*) to serve as the basis of conviction. The judge's knowledge of the details of the case allowed him to rule without the usual forms of evidence.[63] The knowledge of the judge was, as with so many other legal concepts in Shiʿi *fiqh*, a reflection of his delegated authority on behalf of the Imam.[64] Majlisi provided an anecdote based on a Shiʿi hadith, which he saw as an illustration of how *ʿilm* operated in criminal cases. In the hadith, the ʿAbbasid caliph Abu Jaʿfar al-Mansur (d. 775) was circumambulating around the Kaʿba when a man approached him with a criminal case: two men went to his brother's house, requested that he join them, and then never returned him to his home. When the caliph questioned the two suspects, they responded that they had merely spoken with the missing man and that he had returned home alone. The next day, the caliph asked the Shi'i Imam Ja'far al-Sadiq to make a ruling on the case. Al-Sadiq heard testimony from both sides. After the day had passed with questions and answers, he told the caliph's scribe to write that "the Prophet of God . . . has commanded that whoever takes someone out of the house is his guarantor [zamin] unless there is testimony that he has returned to his house." He then commanded a slave (ghulam) to seize one of the two men and behead him. At this point, the man proclaimed, "I did not kill him! I just held him down, and my companion stabbed and killed him." The Imam then said, "O slave, remove your hand from him and take his companion and kill him." The companion then interjected, "I did not torture him! I killed him with one blow." Al-Sadiq then turned to the brother of the murdered man and said, "Behead this one as qisas for your own brother," while ruling that the other man should be given life imprisonment and lashed fifty times a year for the rest of his life, the prescribed punishment for being an accomplice to murder.[65] Majlisi remarked that this case was on the basis of 'ilm since procedurally it did not follow the standard rules of fiqh evidence: "In this instance, [al-Sadiq] apparently acted according to his own knowledge ['ilm] because based on Imami knowledge [bih 'ilm-i imamat], he knew that he [the murderer] had killed him [the murdered], and, through this contrivance, he made him confess."[66]

Beyond this innate knowledge, Shi'i jurists also elaborated on the judge's knowledge as a basis for hudud crimes. Both Majlisi and Shafti argued that the judge could implement the hadd punishment "solely on the basis of knowledge."[67] Shafti saw no difference between the knowledge of the Imam and the judge in making rulings in hadd cases and that of the father, husband, and master in carrying out the hadd penalties on their respective domestic subordinates (children, wives, and slaves).[68] For Shafti, the Imam/judge held the extraordinary authority to punish hadd crimes occurring in public on the basis of knowledge, just as the patriarch could do so in the domicile. The issue of the judge having the ability to make a hadd ruling based on his knowledge alone (mutlaqan) was not necessarily universally accepted, with some jurists restricting this to the Imam and only allowing the judges to use their knowledge for the "Rights of Humans" (Huquq al-'Ibad or Huquq al-Insan), which included murder or injury, commercial transactions, and other legal obligations of individuals to one another.[69]

Najafi established what the Imam could do in order to extrapolate the scope of the judge's delegated authority. The Imam's knowledge, and by extension the judge's, was also fundamentally visual. Najafi found that everyone agreed that the Imam judged on the basis of his knowledge alone in both the *Huquq Allah* (which included *hudud*) and *Huquq al-'Ibad*. If the Imam saw a man fornicating or drinking wine, then he could carry out the *hadd* punishment without further proof beyond what he saw (*nazar*) because he was God's trustee in deputyship (*khilafah*). The rationale for this was that *Huquq Allah* had to be implemented by the Imam, while for *Huquq al-'Ibad*, he would have to wait to see how the heirs wanted to proceed.[70] Even if someone guilty of a *hadd* crime confessed before the Imam alone (i.e., without further witnesses), this was sufficient for him to carry out the punishment. Najafi thus affirmed that the judge could rule according to his knowledge alone.[71] Najafi believed that this was true even if the judge's knowledge was somewhat more indirect in cases of *zina* and *liwat*, in which "the knowledge of a judge for the cause of injury was sufficient" for judgment after an examination (*mu'ayyinah*).[72] In Shi'i jurisprudence, the Imam's eye was generally the organ of knowledge; witnessing was tantamount to a visual form of knowing.

Najafi fleshed out the connection between knowledge, the visual, and the aural in his discussion of apostasy. According to him, God granted the Prophet knowledge of who was outwardly a Muslim but secretly an infidel (*kafir*) by virtue of their manner of speaking (*lahn al-qawl*). Despite having this knowledge, he did not expose these individuals' inner condition to the greater Muslim community since this would have deprived them of marriage, eating lawful food, and inheritance. This was ultimately out of concern for the public interest (*maslahah*).[73] Unlike apostasy, *zina*, drinking wine, and theft bound "the concealer and the revealer" (*mubtin wa muthhir*) meaning that the Imams and judges were obligated to expose and rule on the basis of their knowledge. If they failed to do so in these non-apostasy cases, it would lead to "the corruption of the judge" (*fisq al-hakim*), "the abandoning of judgments" (*iqaf al-hukm*), "the loss of the necessity to forbid wrong" (*inkar al-munkar*), and negligence in "revealing the truth" (*izhar al-haqq*).[74] So long as someone held secret beliefs that publicly conformed to orthodoxy, the Prophet, Imam, and/or judge should not reveal them; by contrast, if they had knowledge of other visible *hadd* crimes, they were obligated to punish them to preserve moral and legal order.[75]

The Authority to Implement Fixed Mandatory Punishments

Shi'i jurists agreed that the Imam had the prerogative to forbid wrong and implement fixed mandatory punishments, but whether anyone else did in his absence was up for debate. Most agreed that no one did, not even the jurists.[76] Muhammad Baqir Shafti made the most forceful case for jurists having such authority (figure 4). In his unique treatise, he justified the jurists' authority to carry out *hudud* punishments because God's laws were eternal and immanently applicable in any age rather than being contingent on the presence of the Imam or the Prophet.[77] Building on the idea that the Shi'i 'ulama were the vicegerents of the Hidden Imam in his era, he argued that they had the authority to carry out this duty on his behalf in the name of public order.

According to Shafti, the jurists had the authority to implement the *hudud* punishments on the basis of consistent testimony, confession, and/or knowledge. His conclusion about the jurist's wide scope of authority was encapsulated in the following passage: "And we say, just as it is permissible for the jurists of this era [*li-fuqaha fi hadha al-a'sar*] ... to issue legal responsa [*al-ta'arud li'l-fatwa*], [settle] lawsuits [*al-murafa'ah*], and make rulings [*al-hukm*] among the people, it is permissible for them to implement the fixed mandatory punishments [*iqamat al-hudud*]."[78] Shafti further argued that jurists, and not worldly sovereigns, had the authority to issue rulings during the occultation, or the absence of the twelfth Shi'i Imam, on the basis of a hadith to that effect.[79] He concluded that "the jurist [*faqih*] is from among those who have [authority to make] rulings and so he is authorized to carry out *hudud* punishments."[80]

Shafti believed in the immediacy of implementing God's laws; otherwise, this would render Quranic injunctions meaningless and permanently in abeyance.[81] He viewed the *hudud*'s purpose as being

Figure 4: The Shiʻi jurist Muhammad
Baqir Shafti, author of a work on the necessity
of implementing *hudud* punishments.
(Source: Jabiri Ansari, *Tarikh-i Isfahan* [1999], n.p.)

multilayered and one that held true "in all times," not just the Imam's
time on Earth. The *hudud* was meant to "protect the honor of the shariʻah
[*namus al-shariʻah*]," to prevent people from engaging in forbidden acts,
to avoid "the cause for the destruction of lives [*halakat al-nufus*], and
the imbalance of [public] order [*ikhtilal al-nizam*]."[82] Contrary to purely
ritualistic readings of *hudud* punishments, Shafti viewed it as having a
publicly oriented utility, such as the protection of lives and the promo-
tion of public order.[83]

Shafti employed parables to illustrate his point. He asked readers to imagine a sultan who wrote a book (*daftar*) that stated, "whoever does such-and-such abominable crime [*fahishah*] from among the people will be punished," and then sent a copy of this book to a governor (*hakim*) who was his deputy among the people. Then, after the governor died, the subjects no longer had access to the sultan but only to the book. Shafti then argued that reason dictates that a religious scholar (*'alim*) should carry out the aforementioned punishments to prevent people from dying and to protect public order. If time passed and the sultan returned to ask the *'alim* why he did this, the *'alim* would respond that the punisher was unspecified and that the failure to punish might result in reproach. The sultan would react positively to the response, knowing full well that the action was done with an honest heart.[84] In this parable, the sultan was a metaphor for God, who left a book (the Quran), while his governor, the Prophet and/or the Imam, disappeared, leaving the people only with the book that spelled out the punishment for certain crimes. Even in the absence of the Hidden Imam, therefore, the jurist had a categorical imperative to implement God's punishment.

In another parable, Shafti imagined a sovereign who addressed a people and provided them with a law book. This "people's law book" (*dustur al-ru'aya*) addressed them in the following manner: "O people of Isfahan—for example—It is incumbent on you to do such-and-such and forbidden to do such-and-such." Shafti argued that the people of Isfahan in this example were not just the ones living at the time of the law book's composition; instead, it was all dwellers of Isfahan who considered this text to be true, regardless of the age.[85] He then compared this to passages in the Quran that state "Oh people" (*ya ayyuha al-nas*) or "Oh you who believe" (*ya ayyuha al-ladhina amanu*) as being addressed to all individuals until the Day of Resurrection and not just individuals living during the time of the Prophet Muhammad.[86] Divine laws were meant to be implemented, even in the absence of a prophet and/or Imam, by authorized jurists.[87]

While the Imam was hidden from plain sight, his authority to punish public crimes found expression in the jurists. Shafti made public-order arguments for such authority without any reference to contemporary Qajar government officials or the shah. Instead, he imagined a world in which the jurists' authority, delegated by the Imams and ultimately God, made them autonomous juridical actors on Earth.

The Authority to Forbid Wrong in Public

Closely related to the authority to implement the *hudud* punishments was the issue of who had the authority to forbid wrong. Forbidding wrong entailed bringing an end to public wrongdoing. The clash of competing public and private values made the duty to forbid wrong complicated because, as Michael Cook has observed, "while it is a good thing to stop wrongdoing, it is a bad thing to violate privacy."[88] In order for the duty to forbid to be initiated, "a wrong must in some way be public knowledge."[89] This did not generally apply to "wrongs that are private" since this only harmed the wrongdoer.[90] Cook characterizes Imami doctrine as lacking the "concrete and colourful detail" of Sunni *fiqh* when it comes to describing the application of this principle.[91] Adding further complexity to the issue of application was the question of who had the right to carry out this duty: Was it something restricted to the Prophet and the Imams? In the absence of the Hidden Imam, could it be carried out by qualified 'ulama or by ordinary Muslims? Much like *hudud* crimes, these questions point to the intersection of legal jurisdiction and the private/public dimensions of such crimes.

Commanding good and forbidding wrong were at their core about regulating public behavior through a form of religiously sanctioned moral policing. Of all the early nineteenth-century Shiʻi jurists, Abu al-Qasim Qummi provided the most concrete examples of this duty in his mixed Persian and Arabic responsa *Jamiʻ al-Shitat*. In outlining the necessary conditions for forbidding wrong, Qummi stressed that the person must have knowledge of the necessary (*vajib*) and the forbidden (*haram*) either through the application of independent reasoning (*ijtihad*) by a qualified jurist or emulation (*taqlid*). In other words, the person had to know the law before acting against its public violation. Qummi gave the example of women using a frame drum (*daff*) during weddings: if the act was not publicly known (*ta maʻlum nashavad*), it was not necessary (*vajib*) to forbid it.[92] He further elaborated that the duty was enacted "whenever it became visible [*zahir*]" but ceased as soon as "the sin

stopped" (ma'siyat bardashtah shavad), at which point it might not even
be permissible (ja'iz) to forbid wrong.[93]

While this example indicated why and when a public illicit act
should be forbidden, it did not comment on how. The answer to the
"how" question rested on hadiths that pointed to three modes of commanding or forbidding: by the heart, the tongue, and the hand.[94] The
last of these three modes entailed physical violence and was therefore
of direct relevance to understanding a justification for the legitimate
(and thus lawful) use of violence to prevent or stop a crime.[95] In Shi'i
fiqh, the Imam generally had the sole prerogative to forbid wrong, although jurists proposed a series of justifications for the use of violence
by others when sin became manifest. One move was to redefine forbidding wrong as a defense of the community; injury and death that resulted from such defense were thus rendered lawful and without liability.
Another move was to view commanding or forbidding as being akin to
carrying out hudud punishments and declaring a jihad, which some jurists understood to mean that it could be carried out by a well-qualified
deputy of the Imam (i.e., a Shi'i 'alim).

Shi'i jurists typically did not endorse the use of violence in forbidding wrong, although some articulated novel ways to deploy community defense as a justification for legitimate violence in related contexts.
Baha al-Din al-'Amili aka Shaykh Baha'i (d.1621) only spoke of Muslims
forbidding wrong through speech; the Imam's permission was required
for doing so with violence.[96] Abu al-Qasim Qummi argued that an individual should strive to end the forbidden act by telling the offender to
"stop this action" rather than causing "disfigurement and injury" (qat'
va jazm).[97] However, he claimed that if, in the course of a nonviolent forbidding, an altercation ensued and the sinner was injured or killed, the
killer was not liable. Violence's permissibility was tied to an escalation
of forbidding wrong. The person should start with soft and nice words
before moving on to harsh ones. If this did not work, Qummi suggested
using the hand through light beating (zadan), pulling the ears (gush mal-
idan), and finally hard beatings (zarb-i sakht). Up until the point of injury and death, he considered such actions as warranted; once forbidding
wrong moved into the realm of causing injury and death, then there was
disagreement (ishkal va khilaf) among the 'ulama as to its permissibility.

Qummi appealed to the view of the early Shi'i authority Sayyid Murtaza (d. 965) to claim that the use of the hand was permissible and that injuring and killing in such a context was dissimilar to fixed mandatory and discretionary punishments (*hudud va ta'zir*); instead, it was akin to murder and injury in the course of a defense (*difa'*).[98] Qummi implied that this defense was of the community and not the self since it was intended to protect the community from moral corruption (*fasad*). He reasoned that since community defense did not require the permission or authority of the Imam, it was not, strictly speaking, a case of injuring or killing while forbidding wrong. This argumentation paralleled how early nineteenth-century Shi'i jurists in Iran justified the jihad against the Russians as being a defense (*difa'*) rather than a jihad in the strict *fiqh* sense.[99]

Other jurists explicitly viewed forbidding wrong and carrying out *hadd* punishments as forming a continuum. The jurist Kashif al-Ghita (d. 1812) viewed forbidding wrong that entailed wounding and killing as having shifted to the domain of *hudud*.[100] The biographer Muhammad Tunakabuni described Muhammad Baqir Shafti as being diligent in forbidding wrong and carrying *hudud*, suggesting that the authority to carry out physical violence in response to the violation of God's law was the same.[101] Najafi considered the Imam the only one authorized to forbid wrong, engage in jihad, kill rebels, carry out *hudud* and discretionary punishment, and provide redress (*radd al-mazalim*).[102] In discussing forbidding wrong leading to injury or death, he cautiously allowed for exceptions to the rule. He stated that, in general, Imami jurists saw this as the prerogative of the Imams and their deputies; it could not be transferred to "other people" for fear that it would result in disorder and chaos, including in "times such as these in which strife has overtaken people." He therefore cautioned against authorizing anyone to forbid wrong since this would lead to a "breakdown of order" (*fasad al-nizam*).[103] The authorized deputy (meaning a qualified jurist) had to fulfill all of the requirements (*ma' fard husul shara'itihi ajma'*), which included safety from loss, corruption, and disorder (*fitnah wa fasad*), to forbid wrong and implement the *hudud*. But he concluded that "in these times," such qualities were rare (*nadir*) and perhaps nonexistent.[104]

Forbidding Wrong as Private *Hudud* of the Patriarch

So far, forbidding wrong and *hudud* crimes had a public component. But
what happened when someone witnessed a sin in private? This question
has received little attention. Cook briefly discusses the duty of people to
forbid wrong within the home, such as a wife rebuking her husband or
a son admonishing his parents, noting its limitation especially with respect to violence.[105] He does not address the more likely scenario of a
male patriarch rebuking his family members and slaves. In certain Shi'i
legal works, the father, husband, and master had the authority to forbid
wrong and carry out the *hudud* in the domicile without the usual high
burden of evidence.[106] This idea may have developed historically in Shi'i
jurisprudence precisely because Sunni sovereigns and 'ulama held
political and legal authority; this left only the domicile as a place where
the Shi'i patriarch could act as an analogue to the Imam. The implications of this private authority are crucial for understanding why, especially in cases of fornication, Qajar authorities rarely punished a male
for killing a female family member accused of sexual impropriety.

Some jurists, like Abu al-Qasim Qummi, provided few details
about a patriarch's legitimate use of violence in the domestic sphere while
forbidding wrong. Asked about the husband's duty to forbid wrong on
his wife, he responded that a husband had an individual responsibility
(*vajib-i 'ayni*) to do so if his wife overstepped "matters that concerned
her" and had no one else to "instruct her" about her limits.[107] Elsewhere,
he stated that a child could "forbid wrong" in relation to their father
with "soft words" only.[108] The same principle presumably applied to a
man's wife or slave when they witnessed the patriarch engaging in forbidden acts.

In other works of *fiqh*, the patriarch's authority to carry out *hadd*
punishments on his wife, child, and slave was explicitly tied to the issue
of violence in forbidding wrong. In fact, this specifically private form of
legitimate violence was often classified as both forbidding wrong and
hudud. For example, Shaykh Baha'i and Najafi discussed the patriarch's
hudud authority in sections dealing with forbidding wrong.[109] Shaykh
Baha'i concluded that there was no consensus on this matter since some
jurists argued that only a well-qualified jurist (*faqih-i jami' al-shara'it*)

was authorized to carry out this peculiar form of *hadd* in the domicile. He argued that this form of *hadd* by the patriarch could be carried out so long as it did not require execution or injury (*jarh*).[110]

In contrast, Muhammad Baqir Shafti brought the public and private forms of *hudud* under a single rubric. His position was maximalist: although he acknowledged differing opinions in major classical *fiqh* works, he came firmly down on the side of authorizing the patriarch to carry out *hudud* on the wife, child, and slave. Significantly, many of the passages that he cited on the permissibility of the patriarch enacting *hudud* were taken from sections of *fiqh* works dealing with forbidding wrong.[111] This may explain why the patriarch could act spontaneously upon witnessing an act deserving of a *hadd* punishment. Shafti bolstered his position by citing *fiqh* discussions that stated that the permission of the Imam was necessary for a patriarch to injure someone except in the case of the patriarch's slave, wife, and child.[112] Shafti argued that an individual male Muslim could carry out all manner of punishments directly on those who committed *hadd* crimes within his realm of authority, which included whipping (*jald*), stoning (*rajam*), and even execution (*qatl*).[113]

Shafti elaborated on the patriarch's authority most fully in his discussion of the master and the slave.[114] He argued that there was a consensus among the early Shi'i companions that the Imam granted permission to a master to carry out *hadd* punishments on his slave.[115] In support of his argument, he cited hadiths stating, "Beat your servants for sins [against] God" (*idrib khadimaka fi ma'siyat Allah*) and counseling masters to beat slaves "according to the degree of his crime [*dhanbihi*]" but not in excess.[116] This authority extended to *hadd* punishment for drinking wine (lashes), theft (cutting off a hand), and apostasy (execution).[117] Shafti addressed the issue of how someone carrying out the *hadd* could do so without the comprehensive knowledge of a capable jurist.[118] He argued that the master only needed knowledge of the punishment for a crime: "He who is capable of carrying out the *hadd* is he who knows the punishment of the crime. It is clear that he does not require comprehensive [knowledge]."[119] Closely related to this was the issue of evidence. Typically, confession rose to the level of evidence (*bayyinah*) when the confessor was mature, rational, acting with intent, and free, which would appear to disqualify a slave. Despite this, Shafti considered the slave's confession admissible within the domicile: "The master is legally obligated to carry out *hadd* on his slave when he is presented with what makes him obligated to do so. So the confession of the slave before his master to having committed fornication, for example, four times, is a path of knowledge for the master of their legal obligation."[120]

In a separate chapter, Shafti argued that husbands also had the authority to carry out *hudud* punishments on their wives.[121] He considered the Quranic verse about a lewd woman (*fahishah*) to be a reference to the *hadd* punishment of imprisoning a fornicating woman in rooms (*buyut*) until she died.[122] According to Shiʿi commentators on the Quran, this verse referred to a *jahiliyah*-era punishment for fornicating women, which was abrogated by another Quranic verse that set the punishment for fornication at one hundred lashes.[123] Since the husband was assumed to be the agent carrying out the punishment in the first verse, he was also the agent capable of carrying out the *hadd* punishment.[124] While the second verse abrogated the first, the agent of the punishment remained the husband.[125]

Shafti differentiated between the proof needed in the domicile and that needed in a trial before a judge.[126] He argued that the knowledge of the master, husband, and father of a fault (*ithm*) was sufficient to attain the required certainty for a punishment.[127] He gave the example of a husband being allowed to carry out the *hadd* when he was certain that *zina* had occurred.[128] In support of this claim, he cited a prophetic hadith in which the Prophet Muhammad was asked what he would do if he found a man inside the womb of his wife, to which he replied he would strike her with a sword. When asked how he could do so without four witnesses, he responded that his eyes saw it and so God had knowledge of it, meaning that the knowledge of the immediate witness of fornication (the husband) was sufficient to carry out the *hadd* punishment.[129]

Shafti treated the husband carrying out the *hadd* punishment on his wife as a part of forbidding wrong.[130] Contrary to the medieval Shiʿi jurist Ibn Idris's position that it was impermissible for the husband to kill his fornicating wife if she was caught in the act while in her husband's home, Shafti argued that the husband was justified in carrying out *hudud* punishments in the domicile on the basis of a hadith that stated that a man could kill both his wife and the male adulterer.[131] In his final chapter on the domestic patriarch, Shafti briefly addressed the question of the father carrying out *hadd* on his son (and, by extension, children).[132] Lacking the same details and evidence as other chapters, he claimed that what was permissible to be carried out on the wife was permissible on the son as well.[133]

According to Shafti, the patriarch, as head of household, enjoyed certain prerogatives in the private realm that the Imam and judge had in the public. There were even parallels between the knowledge of the patriarch of the crime and the knowledge of the judge as a basis for *hadd*, with the difference that the patriarch's knowledge was limited to the domicile while the judge's was limited to public events. The patriarch's *hadd* punishment was therefore more akin to the spontaneous act of forbidding wrong than to the outcome of a trial based on conventional evidence required before a judge.

Zimmi Regulations between the Private and the Public

The private/public dimensions of forbidding wrong and *hudud* crimes also encompassed protected non-Muslim communities (*zimmi*s), such as Jews, Christians, and Zoroastrians. *Zimmi*s were subject to regulations of their public behavior in certain facets that were prohibited in Islamic law but not necessarily in Jewish, Christian, or Zoroastrian laws. In Shi'i *fiqh*, the legal foundation of these regulations was the *zimmi* pact, ideally contracted between the Shi'i Imam and the non-Muslim communities. Non-Muslim communities were afforded protection, autonomy in community affairs, and the ability to practice their religion within certain limits. In exchange, non-Muslims had to differentiate themselves in clothing, hairstyles, and the height of their buildings. Shi'i legal articulations of the ritual impurity of non-Muslims likewise took on public and private dimensions with respect to physical proximity between communities.

The status of non-Muslims in Shi'i jurisprudence has received relatively little attention when compared to studies of the same communities in Sunni jurisprudence.[134] Scholars such as Janet Afary therefore discuss the Pact of 'Umar, a distinctly Sunni text, when trying to understand popular Shiʻi attitudes toward Jews in nineteenth- and twentieth-century Iran.[135] It is doubtful, however, that the Shiʻi ʻulama of this period in Iran would have considered the Pact of ʻUmar as a guide for their understanding of Muslim-*zimmi* relations. Instead, as Daniel Tsadik has demonstrated, a Shiʻi equivalent of this text, which appears in various forms in a number of nineteenth-century Shiʻi works of jurisprudence, probably informed the ʻulama's attitudes toward non-Muslims throughout the Qajar era.[136] Building on the scholarship of Tsadik, these same works of jurisprudence may be productively read as a useful starting point for understanding the private/public distinction in crimes committed by *zimmi*s. Before doing so, it is important to understand how the *zimmi* pact underwrote the legality of such punishments. Although the *zimmi* pact was ideally contracted by the Imam, it could also be contracted by an Imam's deputy, a competent person, or even an unjust sultan, who promised Muslim protection of non-Muslim life and property in exchange for a poll tax (*jizyah*) and respect for Muslim laws. Negligence or violation of the pact entailed punishment.[137] Protection required *zimmi*s to vow not to spy for polytheists, shelter them, or have illicit sexual relations with Muslim women or boys.[138]

When *zimmi*s committed a *hadd* violation, the issue of jurisdictional authority emerged and depended largely on who was involved. For instance, if a *zimmi* male committed adultery with a *zimmi* woman, then the Imam could turn the *zimmi* over to their own community for punishment according to their own laws. Alternatively, the Imam could punish the offending *zimmi*s according to Islamic law.[139] The same principle held true in the case of a *zimmi* man engaging in sodomy with another *zimmi*.[140] If a *zimmi* male fornicated with a Muslim woman, then this was punishable by death, even if the relationship was consensual.[141] The case could not be transferred to the *zimmi*'s own community because it involved "violating the sanctity of Islam" (*hataka hurmat al-Islam*).[142] The same principle applied if a *zimmi* sodomized a Muslim male.[143]

Some of the regulations had a clearly spatial and visual dimension: *zimmi*s were not to display publicly what was illicit to Muslims. For example, *zimmi*s were not allowed to drink wine, consume pork, commit adultery, or engage in consanguineous marriage publicly, even if it conformed with their own religious laws.[144] In cases where an individual, whether Muslim or infidel, illegally seized and destroyed the wine of a Muslim, they were not liable for these actions. But if anyone seized a *zimmi*'s wine or pork that was found in a *zimmi*'s private sphere (*mutasattir*), then they were liable for their actions.[145] Similarly, if non-Muslims had hidden wine and the instruments of amusement (*lahv*) and a Muslim destroyed it, then the Muslim was liable for the price of it. On the other hand, if the non-Muslim showed these unlawful things publicly (*agar i'laniyah izhar kunand*), then they had violated the conditions of protection (*zimmah*) and so the Muslim who "killed or destroyed" it was free of liability.[146] Similarly, if someone stole musical instruments, such as *tanbur, surna, daff, nay*, or similar illegal instruments (*alat-i haram*), with the intention to destroy it, they were not liable. But if they took these objects for purposes of pure theft, then they were subject to *hadd* punishments.[147] These punishments and moral regulations, rooted in the principle of forbidding wrong, were fully consistent with the public regulation of vice described thus far. The difference between Muslims and non-Muslims was that non-Muslims were allowed to do certain activities in private that Muslims were barred from doing altogether. The public prohibition of acts that were otherwise permissible privately for *zimmi*s appears to have been for fear of contagion: by seeing alcohol, pork, and illicit musical instruments, Muslims might be tempted to imitate the forbidden actions.

Shi'i jurisprudence also placed architectural restrictions on non-Muslims. *Zimmi*s were not to build new houses of worship, nor were they to construct dwellings that were equally high or higher than those of Muslims.[148] *Zimmi*s' access to certain holy structures was also restricted; Jews, for example, were not allowed to enter the Masjid al-Haram in Mecca or any mosque.[149] Finally, *zimmi*s were not to ring bells (presumably from churches) in a manner that was audible to the broader public. This restriction points to the aural dimension of defining public and private.[150]

If Muslims were both entitled to and expected to maintain a level of bodily privacy in public spaces and situations, non-Muslims were expected to adhere to a distinctive visual set of bodily and sartorial markers in public. Clothing and hairstyle regulations were meant to render non-Muslims immediately identifiable. Jurists prescribed that *zimmi*s wear an item of clothing made of a color distinct from the rest of their dress and wear a red and a white shoe. With regard to hairstyles, *zimmi* males were expected to clip their forelock (*maqadim*).[151]

Finally, the Shi'i *fiqh* concern with the ritual impurity of non-Muslims entailed avoiding certain forms of physical contact, which was a tangible rather than moral articulation of the contagion principle.[152] Impurity was believed to transfer from unbeliever to believer through physical contact. Therefore, jurists like Abu al-Qasim Qummi argued that a Jew who took a bath and whose feet came in contact with a bench polluted the spot.[153]

Zimmi regulations, on one level, highlight the importance of criminal jurisdiction because the Imam had the final say in whether to handle violations himself or refer them to the relevant community. At another level, these regulations demonstrate that non-Muslims were allowed to engage in certain acts that were deemed impermissible for Muslims so long as this was done privately; once done publicly, however, they were subject to forbidding wrong. In cases of *hadd* violations, *zimmi* punishments were sometimes intensified if the case was interconfessional since the "sanctity of Islam" was at stake. Other prohibitions regulated the public presence and comportment of non-Muslims, including distinctions in clothing, shoes, and male hairstyles; banning access to Muslim sacred grounds; and avoiding physical contact between Muslims and non-Muslims for fear of ritual impurity.

Punishment as Ritual, Deterrent, and Containment

If crimes were public by definition, so too were punishments. As we have seen, sins, when made public, became crimes. Punishments, such as *ta'zir, hadd,* and *qisas,* all had public dimensions that included communicating a message to the general population, often in ritualized form. First, such punishments usually occurred in a public place in full view of locals in order to function as a deterrent lesson (*'ibrat*).[154] As Robert Gleave has argued in his study of the seventeenth-century Mughal Hanafi legal compendium *al-Fatawa al-'Alamgiriyyah,* punishments assumed the presence of the community, either as participants or indirectly as an audience to the ritual.[155] Some of the punishments even mentioned the specific ritual for "publicizing" through punishment, such as a parade through local areas or exposure in a public space during crucifixion. Jurists' discussions of the ideal outdoor weather conditions for *hadd* punishments—not at times of the day that were too hot or cold depending on the season—similarly indicate a public setting for these staged rituals.[156] Second, punishments were public by virtue of their participants. For instance, the stoning punishment for *zina* included three categories of participants: the Imam, the witnesses to the *zina* (if the conviction was based on testimony), and the rest of the people present at the trial. Third, certain punishments, such as dismemberment or shaving of the head, were public insofar as they physically marked a person as having committed a grave crime, which was immediately visible to others. Encountering a person with a shaved head, outside of ritually sanctioned contexts such as the hajj, or someone missing hands and feet, outside of a known disability, would therefore instantly mark them as a convicted criminal. Finally, certain punishments were public insofar as they were concerned with the general well-being (moral, legal, and religious) of the population. These punishments, such as banishment and imprisonment, neutralized the danger posed by a criminal to the community by removing or containing them. Majlisi elaborated on this logic by describing imprisonment as a means of protecting the "body, property, and religion of the people."[157] Much like the sin or crime itself, these punishments seem to have been concerned with contagion: only by containment or ritualized lashings, stoning, disfigurement, or execution could collective harm be extirpated and symbolic harmony be restored to the community.

One of the most striking forms of public punishment in Shi'i *fiqh* was the parade since it involved, as Christian Lange has argued, "making someone public" (*tashhir*) and the closely related punishment of shaving one's head.[158] The crimes warranting such punishments were not, on the surface, related to one another: many were of a sexual nature, such as unmarried fornication and pimping, while others had to do with false public statements, such as bearing false witness and a *zimmi* making a false accusation of *zina* against a Muslim. Underlying all of these crimes was a violation of public honor and the need to rectify it through a deterrent spectacle of punishment. According to certain Shi'i authorities, the *hadd* punishment for pimping (*qiyadat*), which meant gathering men and women for fornication or two men for sodomy, was to shave a person's head, to parade them around the city (*shahr*) or tribe (*qabilah*) so that they would be publicly dishonored (*rusva*), and finally to banish them.[159] Other jurists argued that this punishment was reserved only for male pimps, presumably because a woman's hair was part of her nakedness, so shaving her hair and publicly parading her would force unrelated male spectators to engage in the prohibited act of gazing on an uncovered woman, while banishing a single woman without a male guardian might force her into a sexually compromised position in her place of exile.[160] The *hadd* punishment for a non-*muhsan* man—meaning a man who was a minor, never married, or a slave—who engaged in *zina* was receiving a hundred lashes, having his head shaved, and being exiled from the city for a year.[161] A person who gave false testimony would be paraded around the neighborhoods or regions (*mahallat*) of a city, village, or tribal settlement in addition to a discretionary number of lashes so that the locals would not accept his testimony.[162] Finally, a *zimmi* who made a false accusation (*fuhsh*) against a Muslim of having committed *zina* would receive eighty lashes for the accusation and sixty-nine lashes for violating the sanctity of Islam, his head would be shaved, and he would be paraded among the people of his religion "so that others do not engage in such acts," a clear reference to the deterrent function of the parade.[163]

Another unambiguously deterrent public spectacle (*bara-yi 'ibrat*) was the *hadd* punishment of crucifixion for rebels (*muharibs*) against Islam, especially those who had stolen belongings.[164] Majlisi differentiated this form of crucifixion from hanging, which was associated with the "style of [punishment] of kingdoms" (*bih ravish-i muluk*). Instead, *fiqh* crucifixion involved tying up the criminal with a rope to a piece of wood in the ground for three days while depriving them of food and water until they died.[165]

Like crucifixion, stoning to death was a public spectacle of punishment associated with fornication by *muhsans*—those who were mature, free, of sound mind, and married—and also, according to some jurists, with sodomy, lesbian sex, and sex with an unrelated corpse.[166] Stoning was generally a punishment for someone who was a *muhsan* when they engaged in *zina*. Jurists distinguished who should stone the person. If the *zina* was proven by testimony, then the witnesses cast the stones first, then the Imam, and then the other individuals present at the trial. If conviction was by confession, then the Imam cast the stones first, followed by the spectators.[167] Some authorities argued that if a *muhsan* engaged in sodomy or a *muhsanah* engaged in lesbian sex, then they should be stoned in the same manner as those convicted of *zina*.[168] If a *muhsan* engaged in necrophilia with the corpse of an unrelated (*bi-ganah*) person, this also carried the stoning punishment.[169] There were also certain *hadd* punishments for sodomy that were not found for any other crimes, such as being thrown from a mountain, having a wall fall on one's head, or being set on fire.[170]

Unlike the *hadd* punishments, retaliation (*qisas*) for intentional injury and homicide generally operated according to a logic of equivalences, although jurists disagreed as to what constituted an appropriate equivalence. One position held that the injury or execution should generally replicate the initial crime: "kill him in the same way that he killed, unless it was in a manner that is prohibited."[171] Najafi provided exceptions to this logic of equivalences for acts prohibited in normal circumstances, such as execution by "magic" (*al-sihr*), "vaginal and anal" (*qubulan va duburan*) penile penetration, or force-feeding wine (*bi-ijar al-khamr*). For some of these executions, he suggested suitable substitutions: "an instrument of sodomy" (*alat al-liwat*), presumably a dildo, could be used instead of an actual penis, while force-feeding water was a substitute for wine. Najafi conceded that the retaliation did not have to replicate the crime itself.[172] In fact, the preferred retaliation for intentional homicide was beheading.[173] Beyond *qisas*, beheadings were prescribed for sodomy, having sex with one's close relative (*mahram*), rebellion, being a non-Muslim man who engaged in *zina* with a Muslim woman, and being a man who forcibly had illicit sex with a woman.[174]

Dismemberment was a punishment most commonly associated with theft, although in certain cases, it was used for sodomy and rebellion.[175] In addition to being carried out in public, dismemberment permanently marked someone visually. In Shi'i *fiqh*, a convicted thief would have the four fingers of their right hand cut off while their palm and thumb would remain intact, the rationale being that the thief could still do their ablutions and obligatory prayers thereafter.[176] Upon their second conviction, the thief would have their left foot dismembered in a manner that left their heel intact so that they could stand during prayers.[177] This fixed scale of punishment continued with repeated offense: after the third conviction, the thief would be thrown in prison for life, and if the thief managed to steal in prison, then they would be executed.[178]

Among the most widely used public punishments were beatings and lashings. While beatings were largely generic and unspecific, lashings were often distinctive insofar as they were quantifiable. As such, lashings reflected a calculus of corporal punishment that paralleled the duration of imprisonment. Most *fiqh* punishments that included beatings were of a discretionary nature, such as for someone who urinated or defecated in the Masjid al-Haram.[179] A man claiming to have had a sex dream about another person's mother would either have their shadow lashed, because sleep was a place of shadows, or receive a harsh beating.[180] Finally, if someone masturbated to the point of ejaculation, presumably in full view of witnesses, they would be punished either according to the judge's discretion or by having their palms beaten until red.[181]

Lashes, more than any other punishment, were clearly identified with *hadd* punishments for *zina*, the false accusation of *zina* (*qadhf*), and drinking wine (*khamr*). Two non-*muhsan*s who engaged in *zina* were subject to the maximum number of lashes, one hundred.[182] A *muhsan* who engaged in *qadhf* received eighty lashes.[183] Finally, those who were convicted of drinking wine received eighty lashes, whether they were man or woman, free or enslaved.[184] Outside of these punishments, lashes were considered discretionary punishments (*ta'zirat*), which encompassed beatings, imprisonment, reproach, and rebuke, that were left to the judge's understanding of the public good (*maslahat*).[185] Jurists disagreed as to the limits of discretionary punishments: some argued that it had no limit (*haddi nadarad*), while others claimed it was between ten and twenty lashes, three and ninety-nine lashes, or no more than half of a *hadd* punishment for a comparable crime.[186]

The number of lashes often varied according to the status, capacity, and volition of the offender and the nature of the crime. For instance, a person who was not mature (*baligh*) could receive a few lashes, accord-ing to the judge's discretion.[187] A male or female slave, whether *muhsan* or not, who engaged in *zina* would receive only fifty lashes.[188] When a free person and a slave ganged up to kill a free person, then the heir could ask the Imam to kill the free person and lash the slave on his sides.[189] Many jurists argued that it was reprehensible (*makruh*) to beat a slave or a child more than ten lashes.[190] If the *hadd* conviction was based on the testimony of two men and four women, most 'ulama commuted the stoning punishment to one hundred lashes.[191] The *hadd* punishment of-ten increased for non-Muslims. If a non-Muslim falsely accused a Mus-lim of *zina*, the non-Muslim would be punished with eighty lashes for defamation (*fuhsh*), and an additional sixty-nine lashes for violating the "sanctity of Islam" (*hurmat-i Islam*).[192] If two men called each other "a crazy boy," each would receive twenty lashes.[193] If someone was sick, then the number of lashes they should receive would be converted into the same number of switches (*tarkah*), or branches used for corporal pun-ishment, that they would only be beaten with once.[194]

When the evidence was below the standard of *hadd* conviction, discretionary punishments involving lashings came into effect. A man and a woman who were caught naked and conjoined in bed under the same sheet were to be punished with between ten and ninety-nine lashes.[195] Similarly, two mature men who were caught "playing" (*mula'abah*) in between the thighs without the penis entering the anus would receive one hundred lashes.[196] If two unrelated men were caught under the sheets, they could receive between thirty and ninety-nine lashes at the judge's discretion.[197] A man who kissed a boy with sexual desire could receive up to ninety-nine lashes.[198] Lesbian sex (*musahaqah*), meaning the rubbing of two vaginas, would be punished with one hundred lashes.[199] If two women were caught naked under one sheet, some authorities argued that they were subject to punishments accord-ing to the judge's discretion; on the third offense, they received one hundred lashes, and on the fourth offense, execution. Others argued that they only received discretionary punishments and never *hadd* punishments.[200]

Other non-*hadd* crimes typically received lashings. For instance, a convicted pimp (*qurumsaq*) received seventy-five lashes.[201] Bestiality involving the transfer of semen resulted in twenty-five lashes, while other authorities said it deserved one hundred lashes.[202] A man who had sex with his wife during the day in the month of Ramazan was subject to twenty-five lashes and to carrying out an act of expiation.[203] A man who deflowered a girl with his fingers received eighty lashes as discretionary punishment.[204] A storyteller practicing his craft in a mosque received a single lash and would be kicked out of the mosque.[205]

Imprisonment was a versatile form of punishment applied for crimes including theft, apostasy, corruption, personal injury, and murder.[206] It, unlike the punishments discussed thus far, was not so much a public punishment but a means of protecting the public from the moral pollution represented by the criminal's acts. A thief convicted three times received life imprisonment. Some jurists argued that a thief with a limp hand (i.e., someone who would not lose much from dismemberment) should be imprisoned instead.[207] The *hadd* punishment for a female apostate (*zan-i murtadd*) also involved imprisonment for as long as she refused to repent: she would be beaten at the time of prayer each day and be imprisoned until she either repented or died. As part of her imprisonment, she would be forced to wear heavy and old clothing, be given barely enough food and water to keep her alive, and be tasked with hard labor that would pressure her to change her ways.[208] Majlisi cited a hadith in which God called for the imprisonment of ignorant physicians, bankrupt tricksters (*makkariyan-i muflis*), and corrupt (*fasiq*) 'ulama in order to protect the "body, property, and religion of the people." This rationale for imprisonment clearly rested on an understanding of the public good.[209]

In the realm of bodily injury and homicide, imprisonment was regularly deployed as a discretionary punishment, a mode of detaining suspects, and a punishment for accomplices and individuals who ordered an assassination. According to some hadith transmissions, a person who shaved the hair of a woman would be badly beaten and imprisoned. If her hair grew back, then she would receive the equivalent of a bride price (*mihr masal*); if not, she would receive the compensation due for the intentional homicide of a woman.[210] When an individual was accused of murder, a judge could order the suspect to be imprisoned as a way of ensuring that they did not flee. There was, however, a dispute as to how long a person accused of homicide could be imprisoned: some said three days, others six days, while others denied that they could be detained at all so long as the case was not proven.[211] The punishment for someone who ordered a successful assassination or someone who held down a victim while someone else murdered them was life imprisonment.[212] Imprisonment reveals a diverse set of logics, ranging from applying pressure to change behavior to a concern for public safety, property, and morality.

Banishment rested on a similar principle: rather than containing the threat that the convicted criminal posed, it removed them from the locality altogether. This punishment has already been mentioned in relation to certain cases of *zina* and pimping. The most elaborated-on version of it, however, was the punishment for a *muharib*. The shari'ah judge ordered the banishment of the *muharib*, while the local authorities wrote the judge of the next city, telling them not to feed and give drink to this person or to allow their daughters to marry him or to permit anyone to engage in commerce with him. This would force the *muharib* to travel from city to city without the opportunity to settle anywhere so long as they lived, including in non-Muslim lands.[213]

Conclusion

What constituted a punishable crime within Shi'i jurisprudence depended on the private/public distinction. Within the domicile, the individual was granted a degree of latitude to engage in sin: drinking alcohol, illicit sex, and entertainment music were frowned on but tolerated so long as they were not publicized. The visibility (and sometimes audibility) of a prohibited act, particularly to unrelated strangers and in a public space, transformed it from a private sin to a public crime. Forbidding wrong similarly relied on the manifest nature of the prohibited act as a prerequisite for instantiating an obligation to stop it. The specific social category to which one belonged—gender, religious community, and free/slave status—shaped the specific prohibitions to which one was subject in public and in private. Those who were charged with the authority to punish such public crimes, the Imam and/or the judges, were cast as the upholders of God's rights, a shorthand for the public good of the entire Muslim community. This authority allowed them to bypass the regular rules of evidence, such as confessions and consistent witness testimonies, if they had direct knowledge of the acts. Within the domicile, some jurists argued that the patriarch had similar authority to punish on the basis of his knowledge of prohibited acts within the domicile. When sins became public crimes, their punishment required similarly public acts of collective expiation. Punishments operated on multiple levels: as deterrent lessons for public spectators, as acts reaffirming the moral order of the community, as rituals marking the containment of the polluting effect of immorality, as a spectacle publicizing the sinner and their acts, and as a removal of the sinner from social circulation.

T • W • O

Sovereignty and Law in Advice and Reform Literature

Sovereignty is like a seedling and punishment [*siyasat*] like water.

It is thus necessary to refresh the tree of sovereignty with the water of

punishment so that it may bear the fruit of security and peace.

—*Husayn Va'iz Kashifi,* Akhlaq-i Muhsini

According to Wael Hallaq, the shari'ah constitutes a legal universe in which a worldly authority is incapable of establishing new laws through sovereignty; thus, the state, in the Western sense, was "impossible" in past Muslim societies because sovereign violence was not generative of law, as per the formulations of Carl Schmitt and other theorists.[1] Such an argument conveniently ignores the theoretical articulations found in Perso-Islamic mirrors for princes, or advice literature, regarding the legitimacy of sovereign violence and its relationship to law and order. Despite claims to the contrary, Shi'i jurisprudence was not the only consequential textual genre in the Qajar era to address legal issues, including public crimes and jurisdiction.[2] Mirrors for princes were a major source for government understandings of law that operated on distinct, though at times overlapping, assumptions from Shi'i jurisprudence.[3] Instead of examining advice literature solely as a genre of statecraft and legitimation, this chapter explores the crucial nexus between sovereign authority and legitimate punishments.

Fiqh and mirrors for princes shared similar definitions of crimes insofar as vice made public became a crime. Crimes were punished to serve as a deterrent example to others, to maintain order, to facilitate a life of piety, and to safeguard public good by containing the ill effects of crime. Both genres also included punishments of increasing severity for recidivism. There were also clear limits on violating one's privacy, whether it was physical, spatial, or visual. Contrary to *fiqh* formulations, however, such texts made an almost Weberian claim that the sovereign had a monopoly on the legitimate use of violence within a given territory. Advice and later reformist literature were also almost universally categorical in stating that the worldly sovereign had jurisdictional authority (often exclusive and sometimes shared with the 'ulama) in forbidding wrong and implementing *hudud* punishments. Advice and reformist literature therefore included an alternative reading of the shari'ah to that of Shi'i *fiqh*. Ironically, even jurists wrote mirrors for princes in which they echoed the sovereign's authority in implementing and safeguarding the shari'ah, including in the realm of criminal matters.[4] Robert Gleave argues that jurists who wrote in multiple genres, such as *fiqh* and mirrors for princes, strictly obeyed each genre's respective conventions, thus explaining why they often made contradictory statements.[5] While this is certainly the case overall, there were other jurists, like Sayyid Ja'far Kashfi and 'Ali Shari'atmadar, whose works defy straightforward categorization.

Advice literature also included certain universal themes, such as the sovereign's justice (*'adl*) and the need for skilled administration or policy (*siyasat*). Failing the existence of a just sovereign (*sultan-i 'adil*), an unjust sultan was still preferable to chaos and anarchy (*harj u marj*). The emphasis on justice made the religious identity of the ruler irrelevant, as evidenced in frequent references to the justice of the pre-Islamic Iranian king and unbeliever (*kafir*) Anushirvan.[6] The ruler was also expected to be skilled in *siyasat*, meaning both politics and punishment.[7] *Siyasat* as punishment was the sole prerogative of the sovereign and was not bound by the procedures and rules of evidence of the shari'ah court, which opened the way for the use of circumstantial

evidence and judicial torture. Despite this, many advice texts counsel against the use of torture and arbitrary death sentences against
criminals.

By the 1840s and 1850s, a new critical genre emerged that spoke
boldly about government injustices in handling crimes. At roughly the
same time, authors began writing administrative and legal reformist
tracts, which differed from mirrors for princes by looking to contemporary modern states (mainly in Europe) as a model alongside past
golden ages of justice (Islamic and non-Islamic) for inspiration on how
to tackle penal issues. Out of these reformist efforts came a diverse array of texts, ranging from draft penal codes and penal code translations
to adaptations of Islamic legal compendia as codified law.

Sovereign Legitimacy and Punishment
in Advice Literature

During the first half of the nineteenth century, Sayyid Ja'far Darabi
Kashfi, Muhammad Hashim Rustam al-Hukama, Ibn Damavandi, Hajj
Mirza Musa bin 'Ali Riza Savuji, and a number of others wrote mirrors
for princes that justified the sovereign's legitimacy by appealing to Islamic and universal notions of kingship. The sovereign, by acting as the
protector of the shari'ah and the implementor of its ordinances, created
the conditions for people to attain salvation and perfection. The just sovereign (sultan-i 'adil), whose justice was universal irrespective of religion, made him legitimate both in the past and in the present. In contrast
to Shi'i jurisprudence, which took the just sovereign to mean only the
Prophet or the Imams, mirrors for princes understood it to be an attain-
able ideal for current sovereigns.

Most scholars have argued that the concept of shari'ah-based policies (siyasah shari'yyah), articulated most cogently by the medieval
theologian and jurist Ibn Taymiyyah, was a particularity of Sunni
thought, especially from the medieval period onward. This concept legitimized Sunni state discretionary punishment (ta'zir) of criminals
without relying on an Islamic judge's formal rulings or abiding by the
strict rules of evidence required for hudud.[8] Saïd Arjomand has critiqued
those who use siyasah shar'iyyah in a general manner for assuming that

a tendency common in western Muslim polities, such as Mamluk Egypt, held true for Persianate Muslim polities further east.[9] While it is true that in Shi'i contexts, jurists and authors of advice literature did not use *siyasah shar'iyyah* to mean shari'ah-bound policies of the state, they did use it to mean shari'ah-bound punishments.[10] In advice literature, the sovereign was typically concerned with public crimes, meaning both manifest crimes and those that harmed the public good through instability. The sovereign's use of punishment was based not on an exact code but on a general rule of thumb: punishments should follow an increasing scale of severity commensurate with the crime, with imprisonment and expulsion being preferable to disfigurement and the final resort of execution.

The *'alim* Sayyid Ja'far Darabi Kashfi wrote an ethical treatise, *Tuhfat al-Mulk*, in 1817/18 (1233 H.), which fused the languages of mirrors for princes with Shi'i jurisprudence.[11] In it, the sovereign is responsible for providing order (*intizam*) and removing chaos in a way that embodies the maxim "religion and kingship are brothers."[12] Kashfi's reinterpreted the Shi'i notion of vicegerency (*niyabat*) of the Imam to mean not only the vicegerency of the jurists (*mujtahids*) in the absence of the Hidden Imam but also the vicegerency of sovereigns in the realm of politics:

> Therefore, in the hadith they are referred to as the just Imam [*imam-i 'adil*] and the just sovereign [*sultan-i 'adil*] and those other than this as the unjust [*ja'ir*] Imam and sovereign.[13] And it is clear that the *mujtahids* and sultans both have one station [*mansib*], which is the station of the imamate that has been transferred through deputation [*niyabat*] from the Imam to them. It has two pillars [*rukn*]: one is knowledge ['*ilm*] about the Prophetic conditions, which they call religion [*din*]; and the other is implementation of that same condition, which also means ordering the world [*nizam dadan-i 'alam*], which they call kingship and sovereignty [*mulk va saltanat*]. And these two pillars are what they call the sword and the pen, or the world and knowledge. Both pillars are brought together in the Imam.[14]

Unlike Shiʻi jurisprudence, Kashfi's text legitimized worldly sovereigns, such as the Qajars, as deputies of the Imam in the realm of politics by breaking up the Imam's authority into two separate yet equally valid spheres. Kashfi further delineated a jurisdictional separation between the ʻulama and the sovereign by insisting that they were not to interfere in each other's realm of authority, such that the former were not to deal with issues pertaining to "disorder" (*fitnah*), "chaos" (*harj u marj*), "kingship," and "the sword," while kings were not to pursue or claim religious knowledge but instead pursue "the knowledge of [political] order" (*ʻilm-i nizam*).[15]

Kashfi held that the sovereign's authority to punish criminals contributed to the public good and to the ideal context for worship. Kashfi crafted a tripartite discussion of "knowledge-based and practical wisdom" (*hikmat-i ʻilmiyah va ʻamaliyah*), the third part of which was reserved for "shariʻah-bound punishments" (*siyasat-i shariʻyyah*), which were to be carried out by the sovereign.[16] Kashfi's usage of *siyasat-i shariʻyyah* in this manner was broadly consistent with early modern Ottoman authors, who used it to mean "capital punishments in Islamic law."[17] He further justified punishments with regard to their public good insofar as carrying out the *hudud* "removed corruption [*mafasid*]" and "generated public good [*masalih-i ʻammah*]" while "the punishment of sinners" (*hudud-i muʻasi*), "lex talionis of individuals" (*qisas-i nufus*), "compensations, discretionary punishments, and shariʻah-bound punishments [*siyasat-i sharʻi*]" facilitated worship.[18] In his section on politics (*siyasat-i mudun*), Sayyid Jaʻfar Kashfi dealt substantially with the sultan's duty to punish with reference to the notion of the ideal city (*madinah-i fazilah*), a concept elaborated on by philosophers such as al-Farabi and Nasir al-Din Tusi in medieval advice literature.[19] Among the main duties of the kings and sultans was that they were to protect "the laws of justice" (*qavanin-i maʻdilat*) in dealing with subjects and ensure that they were treated equally.[20] Rulers should also prevent subjects from being oppressed and robbed (*sirqat*) and "repel oppression and evil" through punishment (*ʻuqubat*).[21]

Kashfi articulated a scale of increasingly harsh punishments, depending on the crime's potential harm to the community and the likelihood of the criminal's recidivism. If criminals were capable of reform, then the sovereign should use "chastisements" (ta'dibat). If not, then their evil would have to be destroyed through "repulsion and hindrance." So long as their evil deeds did not lead to an uprising (balva), then they were to be tolerated. When their evil became widespread, criminals should first be imprisoned to prevent them from mixing with the general population. Next, they were to be bound so they could not gain control of the city. If problems persisted, the sovereign should expel and banish (nafy va ikhraj) the evildoers from the city and prevent them from reentering it. It was only if someone's evil deeds rose to the most extreme level (afsad) that they should be dismembered. This measure was to avoid executing anyone, since destroying God's creation was the utmost "impolite act" (bi adabi) against the "decree of reason" (hukm-i 'aql). Reason and revelation dictated that only the evilest of leaders who opposed universal reason ('aql-i kull) and the Imam should be executed.[22]

Shortly after Kashfi, the government official Rustam al-Hukama wrote *Shams al-Anvar* in 1835/36 for Muhammad Shah. Rustam al-Hukama reiterated several themes found in medieval advice literature regarding the purpose of government and its legitimacy. First, government was meant to protect "property, life, religion, and honor ['irz]" of the people, which had resonances with similar justifications for punishments carried out by the Imam or his deputies in Shi'i jurisprudence.[23] Second, Rustam al-Hukama interpreted the Quranic verse referring to people in authority (ulu al-amr) broadly as inclusive of "heirs [awsiya], caliphs [khulafa], kings, sovereigns, shari'ah judges and governors [hukkam-i shar' va 'urf], and other leaders" whom the people should follow, an interpretation that was common in advice literature but not in *fiqh* since the latter saw the verse as referring to the Imams.[24] Third, he cited the common advice literature maxim that highlighted the universal significance of justice as a prerequisite for rule: "The kingdom will continue to exist with infidelity [kufr], but it will not continue to exist with oppression [zulm]."[25]

Rustam al-Hukama broached the topic of crime and punishment more directly and concretely than Kashfi did. Although not a jurist, Rustam al-Hukama distilled what he understood to be the core shari'ah principles governing crime and punishment to demonstrate their correspondence with the rationale for government. He viewed crime and punishment as being based on five commandments (*amr*) and five prohibitions (*nahy*) found universally in the Torah and Quran.[26] Among the "eternal prohibitions" (*haram-i mu'abbid*), he included fornication, killing without just cause, telling a lie causing loss, theft, giving false testimony, slander, calumny, illegally taking people's property (especially that of an orphan), and making promises but not following through on them.[27] Rustam al-Hukama expected kings, shari'ah judges, and governors to possess knowledge (*'ilm*) about drinking wine, fornication and sodomy, gambling, and theft, despite these being "ugly, blame-worthy, and prohibited acts" (*'amal-i qabihah-i shani'ah-i manhiyah*), so that they could "forbid and prohibit" them.[28] The use of the Islamic terminology of commanding and forbidding was not incidental since the sovereign often had to act with violence in carrying out this duty in advice literature.[29]

Rustam al-Hukama elsewhere justified entertainment music and organizations akin to brothels as licit. He encouraged the shah to have entertainment musicians and singers (*arbab-i tarab va ghina'*) perform for a range of both private and public events, including weddings, ban-quets, circumcision parties, celebrations, gatherings (*mihmaniha*), happy occasions, holy days, and other festivities.[30] He did so on the grounds that the Quran and hadith attributed to 'Ali promoted music, but so did great Islamic thinkers such as Shaykh al-Ra'is and Davud 'Ali.[31] He viewed providing men with access to sex with women in an organized fashion as a powerful way to avoid social disorder caused by sexual frus-tration. While he did not endorse brothels per se, he did advocate "tem-porary marriage houses" (*mut'ahkhanah*) that were to be filled with beautiful women who did not have any shari'ah restrictions (*mavani'*) on having sex with men. Such houses were to be open to customers of all backgrounds, whether elite or commoners, and were to cater espe-cially to soldiers in the shah's army and those overcome by drunken-ness and sexual passion, for fear that the alternative would be bestiality, sex with dammed sewage canals, or frequenting unveiled, coquettish beardless youths (*shahidan-i tannaz*) or prostitutes.[32]

Rustam al-Hukama made a clear distinction between private sins and public crimes consistent with *fiqh*; however, he differed insofar as he viewed the sovereign as the legitimate punisher of these public crimes. He described drinking wine as the mother of ugly acts (*umm al-khaba'is*) and the worst of "the gravest sins" (*kaba'ir*).[33] But it was "public" drunkenness—literally, with "unveiled nakedness" (*makshuf al-'awrah*)—in the bazaar among the "generality of people" (*mala al-'amm*) that required sanction.[34] Rustam al-Hukama laid out the conditions under which someone who was drunk should be seized for punishment, and these embodied the multiple connotations of a public crime: if an individual was drunk while being "profligate and screaming" (*badmasti va hay va hu'i*) in public spaces (such as in the side streets and bazaar) and "in plain sight" (*'ala ru'us al-ashhad*) among the people, they should be seized. Rustam al-Hukama placed a limit on authorities collecting evidence through spying or smelling someone's breath and accusing them of drinking, since both spying and revealing the faults (*'uyub*) of others were forbidden in the Quran. In so doing, his arguments echoed those made in medieval *hisbah* manuals and the works of al-Ghazali.[35]

Otherwise, Rustam al-Hukama neglected to mention standards of evidence or court procedures, nor were his suggested punishments consistent with Islamic jurisprudence: he argued that the intoxicated person should be forced to drink the postwash filth (*ghazurat*) of a beautiful child before being bastinadoed five hundred times, fined as much as possible, loaded on a donkey backward, and paraded around the bazaar to the tune of instruments and singing so that others would become aware of how such acts would give them a "bad reputation and [make them] infamous" (*badnam va rusva*).[36] Three elements of this prescribed punishment were strikingly consistent with the spectacle of punishment as practiced in Qajar Iran: the bastinado, the parade on a donkey in the bazaar, and the use of music to bring attention to the public punishment.

Rustam al-Hukama elsewhere moved away from using the Islamic terminology of forbidding wrong and toward the Turco-Persian military terminology of prohibition (*qadaghan*). This form of prohibition presumably rested on the discretionary *siyasah* authority of the sovereign and those who were delegated to act on his behalf. He recounted a very specific ritual of punishment that was reminiscent of actual practice and of practices common across medieval Islamic societies, especially those carried out by the *muhtasib* in Mamluk Egypt.[37] He argued that if someone broke the prohibition of government officials, such as the shah, governor, *kalantar*, *darughah*, or *muhtasib*, then they should be put in a "wooden board wearing a hat with a bell and paraded around the bazaar to the tune of musical instruments" playing.[38] In addition to this ritualistic parade, the guilty person would pay a fine and sign a guarantor document (*iltizamnamchah*), which presumably outlined the conditions for their release.[39]

Rustam al-Hukama proposed a series of fixed punishments for physical injury, murder, and slander that reflected certain *fiqh* principles but employed a different language. He suggested that the shah issue a "clear prohibition [*qadaghani*]" on fighting with weapons among subjects, which if violated would result in both sides being executed.[40] If both sides fought only with their fists and feet, then they should receive one hundred lashes (*taziyanah*), a fine, and a forty-day prison (*zindan*) sentence.[41] Finally, if individuals slandered each other and it was proven through testimony, they would each receive fifty lashes and a fine.[42]

Rustam al-Hukama counseled sovereigns to curtail the use of torture and avoid capital punishment. While Shiʻi *fiqh* banned judicial torture, its use by sovereigns was historically commonplace.[43] Rustam al-Hukama argued the shah should not resort to torture if he wanted to seize someone's belongings because of treachery or crime (*khiyanat va jinayat*), reasoning that the criminal would not give up the property even if on the verge of death, nor would they confess to a murder. Instead, he recommended a less violent approach to garnering a confession: the suspect would be taken to a bathhouse (hammam) and bathed and have forty to fifty beetles (*susk*) thrown down their tied-up pants while their hands were bound, after which they would confess without the need for execution.[44]

Rustam al-Hukama similarly wanted to avoid capital punishment, even if lex talionis or disfigurement were warranted. When the shah issued a death sentence (*farman-i qatl*), he should delay its implementation for forty days because "unnecessary execution that was in contravention of the shariʻah" should be avoided. Rustam al-Hukama preferred that the victim's heirs forgive the murderer and take compensation (*diyat*) instead of insisting on *qisas*. In the case of other punishments, such as lashing, branding (*dagh nihadan*), enchaining the neck, and taking fines, the criminal should not be rendered physically disabled (*naqis al-a'za*) except by God's command (*hukm-i ilahi*), a clear reference to the *hudud* penalties. Rustam al-Hukama concluded that "the point is that there should be the utmost care [*ihtiyat*] in execution and disfigurement [*nasaq*]."[45] He counseled the shah to avoid killing anyone, even in cases of rebellion, and instead to seek reconciliation (*musalahah*), except in cases of *qisas*.[46]

Published in 1848 (29 Ramazan, 1264 H.), the Sufi Ibn Damavandi's *Tuhfat al-Nasiriyah* echoed similar themes to those of Kashfi and Rustam al-Hukama in legitimizing the Qajar monarchy.[47] Ibn Damavandi straddled the two ideals of justice, one universal and the other Shi'i. He referred to the commonly cited hadith regarding the Prophet being born during the time of a just king, namely, the "infidel" Sasanian Anushirvan, suggesting that justice was not a trait specific to any one religious tradition.[48] He simultaneously considered the shah to be the protector of the shari'ah.[49] Making apparent reference to Muhammad Shah, Ibn Damavandi's boldest claim was that the "just sovereign" was also potentially "a perfect *mujtahid*" (*mujtahid-i kamil*).[50] He also employed the language of *siyasat* to describe the shah's authority to punish pleasure seekers, such as adulterers (*zaniyan*) and wine drinkers (*maykhuran*), in addition to thieves, murderers, and other impure individuals. He recommended that the sultan "smash their heads with the mace of punishment" (*sarash ra bih gurz-i siyasat kubad*) in order for the people to live in peace. Along these lines, he claimed that "a well-timed punishment [*siyasat*] is among the necessary aspects of leadership [*riyasat*] and kingship," as was "spilling blood with the aim of justice."[51] In proven murder cases, however, the heirs could reach "an amicable settlement by taking compensation" (*diyah musalahah namayand*).[52] Like other mirrors for princes, Ibn Damavandi advocated caution in making the decision to take a life, citing the Quranic verse about killing someone being akin to killing all of humanity.[53]

An anonymous contemporary of Ibn Damavandi penned a work, possibly from the Muhammad Shah or early Nasiri period (ca. 1834–50?), titled *Mishkat-i Muhammadiyah*, stressing the sovereign's authority to implement *hudud* punishments.[54] In the seventh chapter of the treatise, the author endorsed the implementation of *hudud* punishments in cases of moral corruption (*fasad*). He questioned the value of execution and proposed dismemberment, life imprisonment (*habs-i mu'abbad*), and banishment as alternatives. While he claimed that *hudud* punishments included all of these possible options, he also suggested economically productive forms of punishment, such as having criminals work in agriculture (*zira'at*) and engage in labor.[55] This was a significant departure insofar as it introduced the logic of economic productivity to the calculus of punishment.

In 1848/49 (1265 H.), Ja'far Kashfi wrote another mirror for princes, *Mizan al-Muluk*, which, consistent with his earlier work, preferred to call the sovereign's authority to punish "shari'ah-based punishment" without questioning the legitimacy of the sovereign to forbid wrong and implement *hudud*. Kashfi stated that it was the duty of the sultan to "implement the *hudud* punishments on sinners and assaulters and to enact retaliation [on murderers]" and that these could not be enacted without sovereignty (*saltanat*).[56] More so than previously, Kashfi stressed that the Islamic injunction to "command good and forbid wrong" was a shared duty between sovereigns and the 'ulama.[57] As evidence, Kashfi cited the Quranic verse referring to the three commandments and three forbidden things (*nahy*) as a duty incumbent on sovereigns. He further put this into the language of jurisprudence by arguing that the command (*amr*) was legally necessary (*vajib*), while the forbidden (*nahy*) was prohibited (*haram*).[58] His framing of the issue in such terms was clearly intended to deal primarily with law rather than ethics since it did not include legally ambiguous categories such as preferable (*mustahabb*), permitted (*halal*), or reprehensible (*makruh*).[59] In Kashfi's elaboration of the sovereign's duty to command and forbid, the sovereign had the duty to forbid lewdness (*fahsha*), prohibited acts (*munkar*), and rebellion (*baghi*), as well as infidelity (*kufr*), slander, backbiting, obscenity, fornication, vice and immorality, tyranny, enmity, and illegal property seizure (*ghasb*), among other things.[60] Although many of these were *hadd* crimes, Kashfi counseled the sultan to carry out "shari'ah-bound punishments" (*siyasat-i shar'*) on these "forbidden acts" (*manhiyat-i mamnu*) after having attained knowledge of the shari'ah, which it was his duty to protect.[61]

In *Siyasat-i Mudun* (ca. 1851–58), Hajj Mirza Musa bin 'Ali Riza Savuji argued that obeying the "just sovereign" was legally obligatory because he was God's shadow on Earth.[62] Drawing on an image taken from al-Ghazali's *Kimiya-yi Sa'adat*, he compared the state to a body and the shah to its heart.[63] Savuji repeated the common maxim that a kingdom lasts despite infidelity but not oppression to demonstrate how the shah was bound by justice.[64] Combining Islamic themes, he argued that a just king could establish a "felicitous city" and attain perfect leadership (*riyasat-i kamilah*) during the present time of the Hidden Imam's occultation if he implemented shari'ah rulings (*ahkam*) and forbade wrong.[65] The shah had the duty to ensure that God's commandments and prohibitions (*avamir va navahi*) were carried out, that the shari'ah was protected, and that "the laws of punishment" (*qanun-i siyasat*) were implemented.[66] Savuji considered the Quranic injunction to act with justice (*'adl*), to be bountiful (*ihsan*), and to give charity to those who are close (*ita zi qurba*) as referring to the sovereign.[67]

Savuji recounted the types of punishment that the shah should use to stop evildoers in the city, which paralleled earlier schemas for containing moral danger. He considered evildoers to be a class of people "for which there was no hope of reform [*salah*]." Punishment hinged on a private/public distinction: the shah should tolerate this class of people so long as their evil was "not encompassing" (*ghayr-i shamil*), meaning that it did not harm others. But if their evil was widespread (*'umumi*), then the shah should take measures against them based on shari'ah and reason. Savuji then posited an increasing scale of severity for punishments. First, the shah should imprison the evildoers and "block them from mixing with the people of the city," to contain vice. Second, he should have the evildoers bound (*qayd*) so that they "lost control over their own bodies." Finally, the shah should banish the evildoers and block them from entering cities. If these measures failed, then the sovereign should resort to "cutting the body part that is the instrument of evil"—such as the hand, tongue, or nerves—since the shari'ah allowed for it. He added, however, that the shah should avoid doing this too often and invoked the *fiqh* maxim on avoiding *hudud* as justification.[68]

Savuji argued that the shah should carefully consider whether disfigurement as a punishment was consistent with the public good (*maslahat*).[69] Turning to murder cases, Savuji argued that the heirs of the murdered should have sovereignty (*tasallut*) over the murderer such that they could choose either retaliation or compensation.[70] He suggested that the shah run the following thought experiment: he should consider himself a subject and someone else a shah to determine the limits on the sovereign.[71] Similarly, he counseled the shah to avoid acting with "violence and wrath" toward his subjects; instead, he should act with justice toward those who were seeking redress and forgiveness toward those who were seeking mercy.[72] In general, the shah was to treat "the various classes of people" (*asnaf-i khala'if*) equitably.[73]

Qajar-era mirrors for princes justified the sovereign's authority by invoking both universal notions of justice and specific injunctions to protect and uphold the shari'ah, and they deployed government and shari'ah terminology to justify his duty to punish criminals during the Imam's occultation. The types of crimes falling under the jurisdiction of the sovereign mentioned in such texts were usually distinctly "public," in the sense of both being manifest and affecting the general population. Similar to certain *fiqh* punishments, mirrors for princes proposed an increasing scale severity for repeat offenders and the use of spatial techniques of confinement and banishment before moving on to harsher measures such as disfigurement and execution.

Critiques of Government through Law and Order

In contrast to advice literature, Mirza Mahdi Navvab Tihrani *Dastur al-A'qab* and Mirza Shafi' Qazvini's *Qanun-i Qazvini* had substantive critiques of contemporary Qajar administration alongside legal proposals. Both men reported on everyday events in an official capacity and were thus well positioned to critique government penal policies (or lack thereof): Navvab Tihrani was a "chronicler of wondrous events" (*badayi'-nivis*), while Qazvini was a "secret reporter" (*khufyah-nivis*).[74] The two drew on near-contemporary rather than historical examples, unlike most works in the mirrors genre. As Saïd Arjomand has observed, the critical edge of these works made them some of the earliest texts written for an emerging public sphere.[75]

Dastur al-Aʿqab, which was written in 1844 and apparently updated four years later, was mostly an amalgam of anecdotes about contemporary governors, officials, shahs, and ordinary people. These anecdotes were generally critical of the government and, at least implicitly, of the shahs themselves. Navvab Tihrani did, however, invoke sweeping arguments about human nature requiring an authority capable of carrying out punishments (*sahib-i siyasat*).[76] He provided the example of people who had been murdered deserving to have their rights realized through the punishment of the guilty party, a right that only a sovereign could guarantee.[77] Turning to everyday practice in Iran, Navvab Tihrani denounced how troublemakers and ruffians (*mufsidin va alvat*) escaped punishment for many blood crimes (*jurm-i khun*) through the practice of intercession.[78]

A far more detailed account of crime and punishments, government failures, and proposed remedies was given in *Qanun-i Qazvini*, a work written in the aftermath of the execution of the reformist prime minister Amir Kabir in 1852.[79] Early in the work, Qazvini connected the government's monopoly on the legitimate use of violence to the rule of law: he argued that in every province (*vilayat*), there should be one legal court (*divankhanah*), one bastinado (for punishment), and one set of ordinances (*ahkam*) from the shah. No one had the sovereignty (*musallat*) to punish anyone else, not even their own slave, without "a ruling [*hukm*] from the Divankhanah established in each province."[80] Qazvini was troubled by the wanton use of punishments by individuals without legal authority: he complained that every province possessed at least fifty bastinadoes for headmen (*kadkhudas*), inspectors (*mubashirs*), notables and lords (*aʿyan va arbab*), and landowners (*malikin*).[81]

Qazvini argued that punishments were implemented inconsistently in Iran, thus signaling to would-be criminals that they had a strong chance of evading justice. He linked impunity in punishment to a loss of sovereignty while being careful to praise the shah for not tolerating two categories of criminals: the thief and the murderer, both of whom "would be executed" if the shah learned of them.[82] Despite this, murder and theft were rampant in Iran because of the ability of people in authority to protect criminals in their ranks. Using a distinctly ethnic set of categories, Qazvini claimed that thieves from among "the Turks, Kurds, and tribes [*ilat*]" would not engage in theft unless they had assurances from the head of the tribe (*sarkadah-i Il*). Even when murder and theft cases were proven by documentation at the Divankhanah, the guilty parties eluded punishment. Switching to the urban context, he claimed that the "city thief" (*duzd-i shahr*) was free to engage in their trade because of their partners among the *kadkhuda*, the *darughah*, or the governor's local agents and officials (*'ummal va awliya'*).[83] Thieves were so brazen because of the low likelihood of punishment; he speculated that only 1 percent or perhaps not even one in a thousand thieves were ever executed.[84] This reassured the criminals of their freedom so long as they had powerful officials on their side.[85] Inspired by the Russian example, Qazvini proposed sentencing thieves to life imprisonment and hard labor as an alternative to execution. More specifically, he argued for the establishment of a government workshop for prisoners to work in while they served a life imprisonment sentence (*habs-i abadi*), even if they deserved a death sentence (*vajib al-qatl*). This option was only available for criminals who did not pose a danger to others since the containment of harm, immorality, and the public good were, as with others writing in the advice literature genre, of paramount importance.[86]

While Qazvini recommended a more lenient approach to thieves, he supported the death sentence for three categories of crimes: the intentional murderer, the sodomite, and the person who pimps out his wife to a client (*harif*), without providing any further rationale.[87] Qazvini did, however, elaborate on the phenomenon of female and male prostitution, the reasons for its proliferation, and the need for clear government regulations to curtail it. He deplored the widespread existence of "adulterous women" (*zanha-yi zaniyah*) throughout Iran and wanted there to be a clear regulation (*qarar*) given about the punishment of this crime in accordance with the shari'ah. He claimed that being an adulterous woman had become "a permanent profession" (*kasb-i da'imi*)—a roundabout way of referring to prostitution—to such a degree that there were such women in every neighborhood in Tehran and other lands with the full awareness of the *kadkhuda*.[88] Such women were also supposedly in cahoots with the *kadkhuda*; the latter even took monthly payments (*ma-hanah*) from the women as part of their revenue (*madakhil*).[89] His solution to this situation was that a permanent guard should inform the government about any adulterous women and ruffians engaging in any type of moral corruption (*fasad*).[90]

Qazvini similarly proposed regulations for male prostitutes (*am-rad*), whom he considered to be worse than their female counterparts. *Amrad*s had made "illicit sex" ('*amal-i shani*') a permanent profession in Tehran and were even frequented by certain government officials. The officials' wives, seeing that their men were uninterested in them, decided to take on adulterous affairs, out of "spite or hatred" or "desire" or on the pretext that their husbands were having homosexual relations.[91] Qazvini went so far as to claim that if there had been such beautiful *am-rad*s at the time of the Prophet Muhammad, there would be a Quranic verse about them having to veil. He called on the shah to issue a regulation (*qarardad*) banning any man from shaving his beard, which if violated, would lead to imprisonment for several days until the facial hair reappeared, since appearing barefaced (*sadah*) in public was akin to nudity.[92]

Qazvini's most elaborate discussion of the private/public distinction and its relationship to hygiene, honor, chastity, and reputational information pertained to the Jews. He considered bad smells supposedly emanating from Jewish neighborhoods to the broader city a source of filth. Jewish women were seen as a threat to public chastity insofar as they did not veil themselves in front of men. He further accused Jewish male doctors of having seduced (*ighva*) Muslim women whose husbands were busy with *amrad*s or adulterous women.[93] Out of regard for reputational information that should remain secret, he argued that Muslim women should veil themselves in front of Jewish women because Jewish women would describe the attributes of Muslim women to their husbands, who would then have "bad thoughts" about Muslim women.[94] Finally, he argued that Jewish peddlers who went door-to-door and thus interacted with Muslim women in Tehran posed a threat to the chastity of Muslim women.[95]

Reformist Calls for Penal Codification

From the 1850s onward, reformists combined approaches to crime and punishment found in mirrors for princes with the criticisms of present conditions similar to those made by Navvab Tihrani and Qazvini. What made such reformist texts distinct, however, was the introduction of a rights-based discourse in discussing crime and punishment, a tendency toward the cultural translation of European penal concepts, and the articulation of a need for codification.

The most well-known Iranian reformist of the nineteenth century, Mirza Malkam Khan, wrote a treatise, *Kitabchah-i Ghaybi ya Daftar-i Tanzimat*, in 1858, which set out to culturally translate a Western notion of law (*qanun*) through both Islamic and advice literature concepts such as forbidding wrong and *siyasah*, in addition to setting out principles relevant to policing and penal law. He defined "government" (*hukumat*) as "the institution that in an independent nation is the source [*mansha*] of commanding and forbidding [*amr va nahy*]."[96] Law 29 of his treatise addressed the police (*zabtiyah*), which should be made up of five thousand individuals drawn from the army.[97] Policing officers had a mix of titles, which included existing ones such as *kalantar, darughah,* and *na'ib-i darughah* and new ones drawn from Ottoman nomenclature, such as chief of police (*amir-i zabtiyah*) and police officer (*zabit*).[98] He further laid out draft laws that protected the individual's inviolability while alluding to European discourses of rights: an individual could not be imprisoned, nor could their residence be forcibly entered without a legal ordinance.[99] One of the few punishments Malkam Khan included was a death sentence for a traitor to the government.[100] Again using very Ottoman terminology, he suggested that a "Reform Council" (Majlis-i Tanzimat) would draft five codes (*qanunnamahs*), one of which was a penal code (*jazanamah*).[101]

Of all the reformists writing about law, the Qajar statesman Mirza Yusuf Khan Mustashar al-Dawlah was the most deliberate in translating modern legal concepts into the language of Islamic jurisprudence in his 1870 treatise *Yak Kalimah*.[102] He set out the task of finding equivalents in Islamic jurisprudence for nineteen principles enshrined mainly in the 1789 *Declaration of the Rights of Man and of the Citizen* and subsequent French constitutions, of which only a subset dealt with criminal law.[103] Mustashar al-Dawlah argued that accounts of crimes should be publicly announced in newspapers as a form of public education. In the French code, such accounts were to be made known publicly (*tashhir va i'lan*) by being published in the official newspaper. Mustashar al-Dawlah saw this as being the equivalent of making the shari'ah known (*tabligh-i shar'i*).[104] He further equated defying injustice and forbidding wrong.[105] But unlike *fiqh* or advice texts, he viewed forbidding wrong as the equivalent of freedom of speech so long as it did not harm "public morality" (*akhlaq-i 'ammah*) or the law.[106]

Mustashar al-Dawlah selectively read *fiqh* punishments for various crimes to make them compatible with European notions of legality.[107] In his discussion of murder, he cited Quranic verses granting the right of *qisas* but neglected to mention compensation and forgiveness as alternative legal outcomes, perhaps to reframe murder as a public crime instead of a tort. He similarly redefined fornication (*zina*) as a violation of men's and women's "chastity and honor" (*'irz va namus*) that warranted one hundred lashes or stoning, depending on the context.[108] His somewhat ambiguous wording suggested that *zina* was rape, a reading that ignored consensual sex between unwed individuals or legal but nonconsensual sex between a male master and a female slave. Mustashar al-Dawlah also cited the Quranic verse regarding the amputation of hands for theft as necessary for protecting property (*mal*), while neglecting to mention that in classical *fiqh*, such a crime was considered a violation of God's rights and its punishment was not justified as a protection of property.[109]

Elsewhere, Mustashar al-Dawlah equated "individual liberty" (*hurriyat-i shakhsiyah*) with Islamic notions of privacy and due process. Individual liberty meant that "the body of every person is free, and no one has the power to slap or punch them, lie about them, or swear at them."[110] He saw this as linked to Islamic prohibitions on spying and entering the domicile uninvited.[111] He further defined individual liberty in negative terms; no one had the right to seize, imprison, fine, punish, or execute someone without a legal ruling.[112]

Mustashar al-Dawlah further justified a ban on torture and called for punishments commensurate in severity with the initial crime in

Islamic terms. He argued that government officials could not unlaw-
fully beat, torture, or swear at someone in order to extract a confession
or for other purposes.[113] Punishments such as lashings and beatings
should be banned because they were unworthy of pack animals, let alone
humans. He claimed that Islamic sources reflected the idea that a person should not be punished beyond what they deserve and that the
punishment should match the severity of the crime. He lamented that
Muslims had forgotten this aspect of shari'ah in punishments, while
contemporary Europeans applied it. Mustashar al-Dawlah gave the example of *hudud* punishments: if a governor extracted evidence through
spying or torture, then he would be "tearing the veils of honor" (*hatk-i
pardahha-yi namus*) of the person and violating their sanctity (*hurmat*).[114] He argued this caution against judicial torture and spying as
being the reason for the Prophetic hadith stating, "Avoid carrying out
hudud punishments if you can" (*idra'u al-hudud ma istata'tum*), although this was an unusual reading.[115]

The secular reformist Fath 'Ali Akhundzadah criticized Mustashar
al-Dawlah for painting too rosy a picture of the shari'ah and for forcing
it to be compatible with a modern European legal system.[116] On November 8, 1875, Akhundzadah wrote to Mustashar al-Dawlah both to praise
his call for the need for law in Iran and to criticize his attempt to reconcile the French constitution with the shari'ah. Akhundzadah chided
him, too, for believing that advice would ever work in Iran: "In Iran, does
anyone listen to advice [*nasihat*]?"[117] He argued that in Europe, such advice had failed, and the people had joined forces to overthrow their
government and compose a constitution.[118] Invocations of the public
good (*maslahah*) as advice would never bring about real change.[119] Instead, Iranians had to come together, kick out their oppressor, and then
write their own constitution.[120]

Akhundzadah argued that the shari'ah would never end despotism
since it was rooted in the inequality of women, non-Muslims, and slaves.
The Umayyads and the 'Abbasids had implemented the shari'ah, and yet
oppression and despotism continued unabated.[121] Akhundzadah argued
that the shari'ah and constitutionalism were incompatible on several
grounds. First, equality of rights in the constitutional sense did not exist in the shari'ah. If it did, on what basis were women imprisoned for

life in the Quranic *hijab* verse?[122] He also blamed gender segregation in the harem for encouraging rebels (*ashqiya*) to castrate young boys to be sold as eunuchs there.[123] Turning to non-Muslims, if a *zimmi* went before a Muslim judge and produced four reliable *zimmi* witnesses, their evidence would be insufficient because the judge required Muslim witnesses.[124] Since personal freedom was an element of the French constitution, then why, he asked, did the shari'ah allow for the buying and selling of male and female slaves while England had banned the practice worldwide?[125]

Akhundzadah also challenged the efficacy and justice of *hudud* penalties for illicit sex and theft. If the shari'ah genuinely guaranteed protection, freedom, and safety, why did it punish a fornicator with one hundred lashes?[126] The *fiqh* penalty of dismemberment for a thief who took a quarter of a *dinar* out of poverty struck him as equally discordant with these principles.[127] It would lead the thief either to recidivism or possibly to a death sentence.[128] By contrast, if their hand was not dismembered and they later repented, they would be able to engage in a productive form of trade.[129] Akhundzadah also objected to shari'ah-sanctioned execution. He argued that the verse used to justify killing polytheists in the Quran contradicted the principle of the "protection of life" found in the French constitution.[130] Akhundzadah argued, on the basis of unnamed English philosophers (possibly Jeremy Bentham), that the death penalty did not lead to greater safety, nor did it decrease the crime rate.[131] This explained why death sentences were rarely issued in contemporary Europe, while "in the East," if someone did not say their prayers or fast, that person could be given discretionary or *hadd* punishments, exposed to danger, or even executed.[132]

Despite such criticisms, others continued to synthesize penal ideas from advice literature, *fiqh*, and modern European law. In 1875, the Baha'i leader 'Abdu'l-Baha composed *Risalah-i Madaniyah* anonymously at the request of his father and Prophet-founder of the Baha'i Faith, Baha'u'llah.[133] The treatise was written as advice in response to early 1870s Qajar reforms, and 'Abdu'l-Baha hoped that it would lead Nasir al-Din Shah to establish "a foundation for justice" in a manner consistent with the Sasanian monarch Anushirvan.[134] Further echoing mirrors texts, he stated that statecraft, or political laws (*qavanin-i siyasiyah*),

entailed forbidding wrong.[135] Although making a case for moral education as crime prevention, 'Abdu'l-Baha critiqued the position that
"human nature" (*namus-i tabi'i*) was essentially good and that people
would not engage in "unseemly acts" (*a'mal-i qabihah*) in the absence
of "harsh punishment."[136] First, he said that children showed signs of
"overstepping and transgressing" boundaries from an early age, so they
needed "the discipline of a teacher" to help them distinguish right from
wrong.[137] Second, even if such good-natured people existed, they were
quite rare.[138]

'Abdu'l-Baha argued for individual freedom and protections
against arbitrary state violence. He emphasized the need for limits on
governors' "absolute political freedom" (*hurriyat-i mutlaqah-i siyasiyah*)
to seize property and act as they wished. In his discussion of criminal
matters, 'Abdu'l-Baha argued that there should be "a court of justice"
(*darbar-i ma'dilat*) and "councils [*majalis*] of justice before the shah's
throne" that supervised penal matters such as "the implementation of
qisas," execution, and imprisonment.[139] In fact, he made the implementation of *qisas* conditional on close investigation and the authorization
of justice councils, shari'ah court conviction, and the issuance of an imperial order (*farman-i padishahi*).[140] Only after proper investigations
have established the degree of "villainy and crime" and the immorality
of the act should the court implement a punishment.[141]

The Cultural Translation of Draft Penal Codes

Between the 1850s and the 1880s, three draft penal code translations were
produced by the statesman Mirza Ja'far Mushir al-Dawlah, an anonymous translator working at the Dar al-Tarjumah, and Mirza Malkam
Khan, respectively. What differentiated these draft penal codes from the
texts examined so far is that they included a statement of the nature of
the crime, the equivalent punishment, possible extenuating circumstances,
descriptions of criminal procedures, a format consisting of articles,
and a general absence of justification for each law. Mushir al-Dawlah
partially translated the 1851 (1267 H.) Ottoman Penal Code, titled *Kanun-
i Cedid*. The latter two draft penal codes, however, were translations and
adaptations: the 1881 Persian Penal Code (*Qanun-i Jaza*) was a relatively

faithful and full translation of the Ottoman 1858 Imperial Penal Code (*Ceza Kanunname Humayunu*), while the penal portions of Mirza Malkam Khan's 1883/84 *Law Book* (*Daftar-i Qanun*) included a partial translation of the French 1810 Napoleonic Code, which was the basis of the 1858 Ottoman Penal Code. The translators of these works employed numerous strategies to render these codes legible in the Qajar context. Curiously, the editors of all three of these texts were either unaware that these texts were translations or only gave vague indications of what the original text might have been.[142] All three translators did not mention that their texts were translations; instead, any references to specific capital cities (such as Istanbul) were changed to Tehran, and names of foreign institutions were indigenized. They probably did this deliberately so the draft codes could be adopted more readily as law.

Mushir al-Dawlah composed a short booklet (*kitabchah*), which included a partial translation of the Ottoman *Kanun-i Cedid*, sometime in 1858, when Nasir al-Din Shah was once again open to reform (figure 5).[143] The translation substituted Tehran for Istanbul throughout, indicating that it was intended for adoption. In the preface, Mushir al-Dawlah stated that one of the shah's responsibilities was to punish criminals and implement *qisas* according to shari'ah and law (*qanun*).[144] The code classified crimes according to familiar *fiqh* and mirrors categories: murder, theft or unlawful property appropriation, and crimes against honor (*hatk-i 'irz va namus*).[145] Mushir al-Dawlah's translation adopted some of the technical terms used in the Ottoman Penal Code for various categories of crimes: *qibahat*, meaning "infraction," was retained, but *jinayat* and *taqsir* were used to translate *cunha*, meaning "delict."[146]

Punishments drew on concepts from Islamic jurisprudence, advice literature, and penal codes. The 1851 Ottoman Penal Code and its translation adopted *fiqh* vocabulary of retaliation (*qisas*), compensation (*diyat*), fixed mandatory punishments (*hadd-i shar'i*), discretionary punishments (*ta'zir*), imprisonment, banishment (*nafy-i balad*), and lashes.[147] Consistent with advice literature, it made the sovereign's authority necessary for these punishments. Moving beyond the two genres, Mushir al-Dawlah's translation introduced execution and imprisonment for non-*fiqh* crimes, while also presenting new punishments such as

Figure 5: The Qajar statesman Mirza Ja'far Khan
Mushir al-Dawlah, translator of the 1851
Ottoman Penal Code into Persian.

(Source: *Ruznamah-i Dawlat-i 'Illiyah-i Iran*, n.476
[9 Rabi' al-Sani 1277 H./(October 24, 1860)])

being bound in chains and chain-gang labor, which were ultimately inspired by the Napoleonic Code. The latter two forms of punishment were used on rebels and people causing disorder against the government, who were to be "bound in chains" (*qayd-i zanjir-i muqayyad*) and imprisoned between one and five years, while imprisonment and chain-gang hard labor, which involved "being enchained and doing menial and abased labor" for one to five years, were due to a recidivist murderer who had been pardoned or had paid compensation to the heirs of the victim.[148]

The majority of the translation dealt with the procedural dimensions of criminal trials and the conditions for execution. This went to the heart of an understanding of jurisdiction that did not operate on the binary logic of *either* a shari'ah court *or* a central government court but on the logic of *both*. The first article of the draft code stated that no one could be executed, either "secretly or out in the open" (*sirran va 'ala-nan*), without a shari'ah ruling and the shah's *farman* after an investigation by the Ministry of Justice. Not intercession (*vasitah*), consideration of "class and profession," or even the heirs' acceptance of the blood price or forgiveness ('*afv*) would be considered if the shah issued a death sentence. Procedurally, a murderer, whether in Tehran or in the provinces, had to be taken to the Divankhanah-i 'Adliyah in Tehran, where a qualified *mujtahid* would examine them, and then they would be treated according to the conditions set out in "a penal code" (*qanun-i siyasat*).[149] For murders taking place outside Tehran, a shari'ah responsa (*fatva-yi shar'i*) along with a procès-verbal (*mazbatah*) of the local council (*majlis*) would be sent to the Divankhanah along with the accused murderer; the Divankhanah would then evaluate the evidence and seek the shah's ruling for execution, if applicable.[150] A government official, irrespective of rank, who dared execute someone solely on the basis of a *fatva* but before the shah issued a *farman* would themselves be subject to punishment.[151] This principle of the shah's *farman* being necessary before a death sentence—even one of *qisas*—could be carried out was one that would be reiterated in the *farman*s and codes of the Nasiri period.

Status distinctions were partially addressed in the draft code. In matters of *qisas*, murder was prohibited "whether the person was humble or noble" (*chih vazi' chih sharif*).[152] *Qisas* was equally applicable to both male and female intentional murderers. However, if a woman hired an assassin (*mu'in-i qatl*), then she would be placed in a "special women's prison" until she was reformed, a somewhat open-ended punishment reminiscent of the *fiqh* punishment for a female unbeliever.[153] Punishments that were less than *ta'zir* punishments were to "vary widely" according to the individuals' "station and nature" (*maqam va sha'n*). The 'ulama or sayyids worthy of respect would receive their *ta'zir* at the Majlis-i 'Adliyah. The middle ranks of society (*avasit-i nas*), such as tradespeople, were to be imprisoned or banished according to their degree of guilt. Finally, commoners (*ahad-i nas*) could be sentenced to imprisonment, banishment, and eighty lashes.[154] Punishments based on status-group distinctions later found expression in a number of official codes adopted by the Qajar government.

The full translation of the much longer and more elaborate 1858 Ottoman Penal Code in 1881 (Rajab 1298 H.) constitutes an even more significant and neglected facet of Iranian penal codification. The author was unknown and only referred to himself as the "anonymous servant" (*bandah-i gumnam*) who knew "Istanbul Turkish."[155] In all likelihood, the translator was Muhammad 'Arif Khan (or Big) Erzurumi, who worked at the Translation Bureau (Dar al-Tarjumah). Although there were four Ottoman Turkish translators at the bureau, Muhammad 'Arif Khan translated a number of other Ottoman legal and political texts into Persian, including the 1839 Ottoman Gülhane Imperial Rescript (Hatt-ı Şerif), the foundational text of the Ottoman Tanzimat.[156] In the preface to the Ottoman Penal Code, the translator recounted translating foreign political works and comparing them to the Islamic regulations (*qava'id-i Islamiyah*) with an eye toward seeing what was useful; he concluded that a penal code (*qanun-i jaza*) would be of public benefit (*fava'id-i 'umumi*).[157] The translator may have remained anonymous out of fear of antagonizing an opposition faction at the imperial court.

If the translator was indeed Muhammad 'Arif Khan, it is likely that I'timad al-Saltanah commissioned the translation. I'timad al-Saltanah feared that European-style law (*qanun*) would alter the shari'ah.[158] He may have considered a penal code from a neighboring Islamic country more palatable to Nasir al-Din Shah, who had grown increasingly suspicious of Malkam Khan and his fellow Westernizing reformers. I'timad al-Saltanah's rivalry with Conte di Monteforte, the founder and chief of the modern police force in Tehran, may have also been a factor in the timing and context of the translation. Conte di Monteforte had composed a Police Code in 1879 that the shah had authorized. Throughout I'timad al-Dawlah's diary, he lambasted Conte, described his police force as having "satanic attributes" (*pulis-i iblis sifat*), and lamented the harm his deeds had done to Islam and shari'ah.[159] Although the *Qanun-i Jaza* was a translation of the Ottoman Penal Code, the translator presented it as a penal code tailored to the Iranian context. It was beautifully illustrated on the front page with the lion and sun, the scales of justice, and a crown, and it had ornate borders on every page (figure 6). The translator probably presented it to the shah for approval as an official law in the hopes that it would counter Conte's influence at the court.

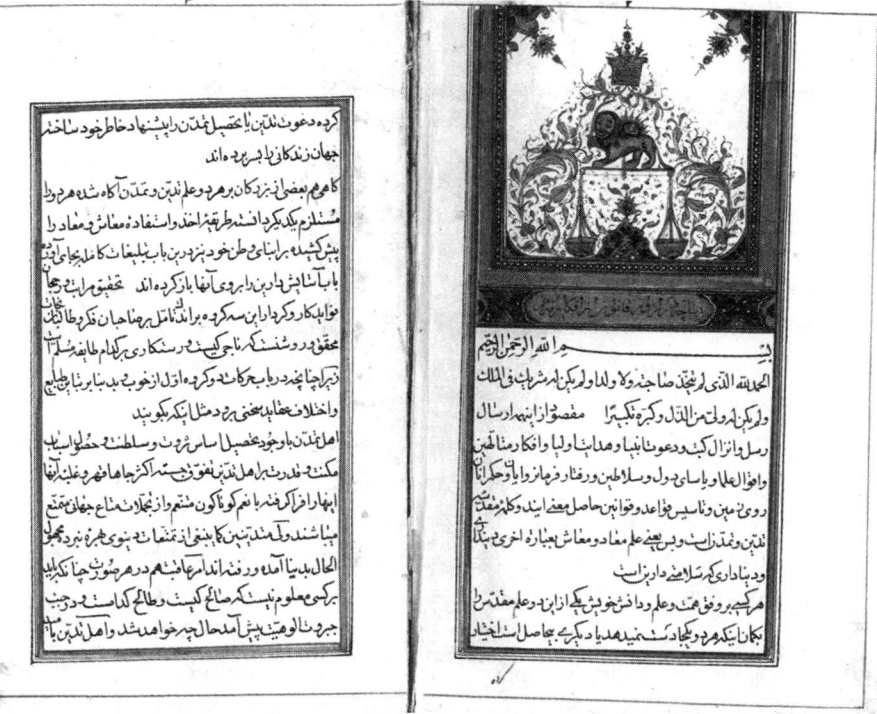

Figure 6: Front matter from the Persian translation
of the 1858 Ottoman Penal Code.

(Source: "Qanun-i Jaza," 1881, Majlis Library, no. 10-32094, folio 2)

The translator laid out their vision of penal law in the preface. He restated the idea found in early Islamic Greek philosophy that God made humans social by nature, and this entailed following a sovereign's command.[160] He similarly argued that legal ordinances required a hope for recompense and fear of punishment (*kayfar*) to operate and function smoothly.[161] Nasir al-Din Shah was praised as the Anushirvan of the age for his knowledge of both religious and worldly matters, proficiency in multiple languages, and gatherings meant to further these aspirations.[162] The translator viewed penal law as standing between the two poles of "religion and civilization" (*tadayyun va tamaddun*): while "the people of civilization" were concerned with establishing "wealth and dominion [*saltanat*]" and establishing power through "wrath and conquest," the "people of religion" turned away from worldly things and valorized poverty.[163] A third way provided a synthesis in which "the commands and prohibitions of civilization" (*avamir va navahi-i tamaddun*) and "government ordinances" (*ahkam-i 'urfiyah*) were well ordered and based on "principles and derivations" (*usul va furu'*) like religious knowledge.[164]

Shari'ah was also invoked as an equally valid and core component of law. The translator emphasized the principle of equity (*musavat*) and the importance and benefit of equality before the law found in the shari'ah.[165] Those who were bound by the *hudud* punishments were to be bound equally by penal laws (*qava'id-i siyasiyah*). The translator was careful to point out that *hudud*, *diyat*, and *qisas* cases would be turned over to a shari'ah court by a competent jurist, here meaning a jurist who was also in government service (as in the Ottoman Empire), for review.[166]

The *Qanun-i Jaza* introduced definitions of crime that were novel in the Iranian context for their clear distinctions and meanings, although certain adaptations were made not to offend the Shi'i 'ulama. For instance, while article 1 of the original Ottoman Code spoke of people in authority (*ulu al-amr*) being responsible for implementing discretionary (*ta'zir*) punishments under the shari'ah, the Persian translation called these "government discretionary punishments" (*ta'zirat-i 'urfi*) to make it clear that these were not Islamic *ta'zir* punishments. The Persian text further called for clear rules for shari'ah commandments and prohibitions pertaining to punishments to ensure that these did not exceed government discretionary punishments.[167] Article 2 categorized punishments according to a tripartite division that had its origins in the 1810 Napoleonic Code: crime (*jinayat*), infractions (*junhah*), and delicts (*qibahat*).[168]

Punishments were symmetrical and precise in relation to these three categories of crime. The three umbrella terms for punishments employed Persian terms that did not reflect either Ottoman usage in the respective codes: crime would receive "deterrent punishments" (*kayfar*) for the Ottoman *mujazat-i terhibiye*; infractions would receive "corrective punishments" (*mukafat*) for the Ottoman *mujazat-i tedibiye*; and delicts would receive "admonitory treatment" (*jaza*) for the Ottoman *muamele-yi takdiriye*.[169] Despite this, the specific punishments under each category remained the same and followed a descending order of severity: (1) "execution" (*qatl va i'dam*), (2) "temporary or permanent confinement in a fortress (*tab'id*)," (3) "temporary or permanent chain gang labor [*taqyid*]," (4) "permanent banishment" (*nafy-i abadi*); (5) "deprivation" (*hirman*; of rank and office), and (6) "permanent loss" (*isqat-i abadi*; of civil rights).[170] All of these punishments were to be accompanied by "public exposure" (*tashhir*), which in both Persian and Ottoman Turkish had resonances with the *fiqh* and government publicizing punishments. In article 3, *Qanun-i Jaza* defined *tashhir* as a convict standing with a board clearly stating their crime for two hours in a crowded public place where people would pass by. The crime would also be read and announced before the punishment's implementation. The Persian translation included *tashhir* for all six of the aforementioned punishments, while the Ottoman Penal Code reserved it only for chain-gang labor.[171] The remaining punishments for infractions and delicts were less elaborate. Article 4 laid out the punishments for infractions as being (1) imprisonment for more than one week, (2) "temporary exile," (3) "temporary dismissal" (*tard-i muvaqqat*; from office), and (4) "a fine" (*jaza-yi naqdi*).[172] Finally, article 5 stated that delicts would be punished by imprisonment for twenty-four hours to a week and a fine not exceeding twenty-five hundred dinars.[173]

Although Malkam Khan had called for a penal code in his *Daftar-i Tanzimat*, it was not until 1883/84 (1301 H.) that he produced a partial penal code within a larger set of proposed laws in his *Daftar-i Qanun*.[174] In this work, he defined government by playing with the dual meaning of *siyasat*: "Government in the realm of governance means *siyasat*. And *siyasat* means [issuing] a ruling and punishment [*hukm va tanbih*]. Without punishment, there is no ruling. And without a ruling, there is no punishment and no government. The first condition of a ruling is that the punishment for its violation is clear."[175] Malkam Khan described every ruling that did not include a clear "punishment for [its] violation" as "a counsel, a hope, or a manifest injustice."[176] He criticized official Iranian government newspapers for banning certain actions or providing regulations (*nazm*) without including punishments, since it was unjust to punish someone for violating a law without the government informing the public beforehand.[177] Like Qazvini, he criticized the fragmentation of juridical authority in Iran, since every leader would administer their own punishment (*tanbih*) on the basis of their own "whim and desire."[178] Instead, the government should use its monopoly on punishment to safeguard freedom, life, and property rights.[179] On the flip side, he appended a "Law for the Guarantee of Rights" (*qanun bar zimanat-i huquq*) to his treatise to ensure that the rights of subjects were protected in the legal system.[180]

Scholars have treated Malkam Khan's penal code as a purely original composition, when it was most likely a partial translation and adaptation from portions of French penal codes with occasional comparisons with Ottoman Turkish and Arabic equivalents.[181] Anticipating 'ulama objections, Malkam Khan stated that any regulation (*nazmi*) contradicting the shari'ah must be modified and that his code was meant to establish degrees of punishment that "no idiot could convincingly argue contradicted the shari'ah."[182] Malkam Khan defined a crime (*taqsir*) as "opposing a law," adding that "every crime, by law [*hukman*], will have a defined punishment [*siza-yi mu'ayyani*]." He proposed three degrees of crime in ascending order of seriousness: negligence (*takhalluf*), offense (*jurm*), and treachery (*khiyanat*), which appear to be his version of delicts, infractions, and crimes found in the Napoleonic Code. The three parallel punishments were chastisement (*ta'dib*), light punishment (*siyasat*), and harsh punishment (*ghazab*), which mirrored admonitory treatment, corrective punishments, and deterrent punishments mentioned in the *Qanun-i Jaza*.[183] These three punishments had detailed subpunishments as well. *Ta'dib* included confinement, a fine, and seizure of goods, while *siyasat* could involve imprisonment in a dungeon (*anbar*; literally, a storage house), negation of (civil) rights (*salb-i huquqi*), and a heavier fine (*tarjuman*). Finally, *ghazab*, the most serious of punishments, encompassed seven degrees of severity: execution, life in the penitentiary (*zajr-i mudami*), temporary penitentiary (*zajr-i muvaqqati*), prison (*zindan*), being bound (*zanjir*), banishment (*ikhraj-i balad*), and government disgrace (*iftizah-i dawlati*).[184]

Malkam Khan's penal code included a lengthy discussion of public exposure that paralleled *tashhir* in the *Qanun-i Jaza*. In his discussion of execution, for instance, Malkam Khan stated that the criminal condemned to execution would have his death sentence read aloud by an attendant of the Ministry of Justice before being beheaded at the execution site.[185] Next, the death sentence would be printed and distributed throughout the city to publicize the murder without resorting to parades. Public exposure was also a part of the penitentiary (*zajr*) sentence, which involved the criminal standing in the city square (*maydan-i shahr*) as an "exemplary lesson for the masses" (*'ibrat-i khalq*), with their name, crime, and punishment written on a board above their head.[186] This assumed a level of general literacy in publicizing the punishment, which in turn assumed that a modern education system was in place.

Malkam Khan also included productive labor as a punishment. Those who were given a life sentence in the penitentiary would have to engage in "the hardest of labors" while having a ball (*gululah*) chained to each foot.[187] Regular prison (*zindan*) meant that a criminal would be confined in a designated fortress, with visits allowed according to prison regulations.[188] Hard labor (*zanjir*), which lasted between five and ten years, involved labor at the chain house (*zanjirkhanah*). A criminal was entitled to a portion of the fruits of their labor, which would be apportioned according to "a special regulation."[189]

The other forms of punishment included banishment and government public humiliation, both of which were meant to be widely publicized events. Criminals would first face government humiliation before being banished from Iran for a period of five to ten years.[190] If the individual returned to Iran before that period, they would serve the remainder of their time in prison, which equated foreign banishment with domestic imprisonment.[191] The final punishment, government disgrace, entailed being removed from any government post, banned from wearing a government medal (*nishan*) or sword, barred from providing testimony, and prevented from acting as a guardian or serving as a teacher in a school. This, like all forms of *ghazab*s, was to be printed and distributed so as to become public knowledge.[192]

Malkam Khan's lesser forms of punishment, *siyasat* and *ta'dib*, were of shorter duration and intensity. At the most severe end of *siyasat*, the criminal engaged in dungeon labor as part of their imprisonment for six months to five years.[193] The next form of *siyasat* was "the temporary suspension of rights," followed by the *siyasat* fine (*tarjuman*) of two tumans.[194] Malkam Khan defined light chastisement (*ta'dib*) as confinement (*habs*) for one to five days in its most severe form, followed by seizure of goods for a person who had "illegally" (*takhalluf-i qanun*) appropriated property.[195]

In light of the evidence provided here, the centering of Malkam Khan in the history of Iranian penal codification, and of modern law more generally, requires serious revision. Mushir al-Dawlah's partial translation of the 1851 Ottoman Penal Code and an anonymous translation of the 1858 Ottoman Penal Code clearly predate and anticipate Malkam Khan's later efforts by introducing novel conceptions of how to define crime and punishment and situate penal codification in relation to the shari'ah and the sovereign's authority. Malkam Khan's *Daftar-i Qanun* came at the tail end of this process, even if he is credited with influencing Iranian constitutionalists in drafting a penal code after the 1906 Constitutional Revolution.[196]

Recasting Penal Law as Shari'ah

From the late 1870s onward, many authors avoided explicitly modeling their proposed legal reforms on European examples and instead used *fiqh* and advice literature terminology to repackage penal law as rooted in the shari'ah. This process was somewhat reminiscent of Muslim authors who presented ideas found in mirrors for princes as Islamic ones without any reference to pre-Islamic models.[197] Nasir al-Din Shah's increasing hostility toward European-style legal reform and his abandonment of earlier institutional experimentation probably explain this shift on the part of the reformers to present their ideas in a form more palatable to him. The works of Abu Talib Bihbahani and the anonymous author of *Ruh al-Islam* embodied these Islamizing efforts.

The little-known author Abu Talib Bihbahani composed *Minhaj al-'Ali* in 1877 (1294 H.) while residing in khedival Egypt. Despite having an awareness of French legal reforms via translations of texts into Arabic and Ottoman Turkish, he mocked blind Muslim imitation of the European ways and instead claimed that the shari'ah was superior to any other law. He even claimed that shari'ah was the foundation of all that was good in European law.[198] For him, the Quranic idea of consultation

(*shura*), Imam 'Ali's sayings, and wisdom literature were the foundation
of a well-ordered polity based on laws.[199] The shah's role in the absence
of prophets was to decrease "calamities, corruption, and murder" and
to act as a supreme arbiter in matters of the implementation of "shari'ah
law" (*qanun-i shari'at*) because of the conflicting opinions of the 'ulama
regarding shari'ah ordinances.[200]

Bihbahani focused significantly on the necessity of implementing
punishments. Justice entailed having "a punishment in response to a
crime." Iran could base its criminal ordinances on the shari'ah ordinances without modification.[201] Like Malkam Khan, Bihbahani stressed
the need to publicize punishments for crimes: he recommended drafting
a legal code in which the government "compiled all the various types of
crimes" and spelled out clear punishments for each on the basis of one's
religious affiliation (*millat*).[202] Bihbahani argued that punishments
must be commensurate with wrongdoing. The first volume of a legal
code would classify punishments for both generic and specific crimes,
including speech acts that led to moral corruption, such as swearing,
lying, and making false accusations.[203] Regarding theft in the bazaar,
he argued that the law required upholding public morality (*ihtisab*) in
the bazaar and the destruction of the evildoers.[204] Bihbahani stated
that people should not think that they could avoid *hudud* and other
punishments through bribes, trickery, or pardon.[205]

An anonymous reformist text, *Ruh al-Islam*, which dated from
1880 (21 Rabi' al-Avval 1297 H.) but was apparently started seventeen
years earlier, was notable for its claim that Islam was the foundation of
law (*qanun*) and that Islamic law was the best.[206] The author argued that
"the art of governance" (*siyasat-i mudun*) was meant to make life easier
and facilitate self-perfection.[207] Governance and sovereignty were instruments of the shari'ah, which was synonymous with the "universal public good" (*maslahat-i kulliyah*).[208] *Ruh al-Islam* presented European legal
principles as values embodied within the shari'ah.[209]

Ruh al-Islam charted a unique pattern in classifying laws by describing two forms of security (*itminan*)—of life and of property—and
six forms of freedom: of movement, tongue, pen, thought, commerce,
and assembly. Individuals were equal with regard to both rights and
punishments (*huquq va hudud*), since these were two sides of the same

coin.[210] Following religion meant that there was a reward for every trouble and service, while opposition to religion required restrictions and punishments. Similarly, for every "crime and infraction," there was a punishment that could take multiple forms.[211] Laws had to be enacted according to "the rule of equality [*musavat*]," irrespective of whether the person involved was a ruler (*amir*) or poor person (*faqir*), although differences in gender, religion, and slave status were ignored.[212] In a sense, equality before the law meant equality in facing punishments for its violation.[213]

Ruh al-Islam viewed the principle of bodily security as a demographic issue. This was why the Quran outlawed murder, since it would lead to a cycle of violence through vengeance, decrease the population, and cause societal breakdown.[214] *Qisas* was acceptable because it was intended to bring an end to this cycle of violence, much in the way that sacrifice brought an end to a crisis in many premodern societies.[215] Islamic texts justified execution for people causing "moral corruption on Earth" (*fasad fi al-'ard*) because it would lead to murder and a decrease in population, while jihad, which also entailed killing, was justified since it would destroy the causes of murder and moral corruption.[216] *Ruh al-Islam* argued that *hudud* penalties with a death sentence were also justifiable in demographic terms. Sodomy was forbidden because if it became widespread, undisciplined people would escape "the hardship of having a wife and children." This end to marriage would lead to a "cessation of reproduction."[217] Adultery involved a *hadd* punishment of execution by stoning (*rajam*) when the adulterers were married because it would lead to doubts about the parentage and the responsibilities owed to children. It was feared that this would lead to people withdrawing from their responsibilities and child-rearing duties, which in turn would lead children to perish. *Ruh al-Islam*, therefore, justified the people of the polis (*mardum-i shahr*) repelling adulterers through collective stoning.[218] By contrast, the second principle of protection, that of property, was tied to material progress.[219] The *hadd* punishment for theft, which was the cutting off of the hand, protected property.[220]

Ruh al-Islam discussed six types of freedom, all of which recast European legal ideals as core Islamic values. The first freedom, bodily autonomy (*ikhtiyar-i badan*), meant that everyone had a right to move wherever they wished and not to be hindered unless they were a hired laborer like a servant. Still, no one had the right to imprison or beat someone without legal authorization.[221] "Freedom of speech" (*ikhtiyar-i zaban*) was referred to as a form of commanding good and forbidding wrong: if someone saw another doing something illegal within their own status group, then they could either say something to them about it or report them to their leaders.[222] Freedom of the pen was a means of promoting "orderly law" by denouncing illegal actions in writing with the hope of deterring others.[223] Freedom of thought, on the other hand, meant that people were free to have their religion without oppression, consistent with the Quranic verse, "There is no compulsion in religion" (*la ikraha fi al-din*).[224] Freedom of assembly was cast in explicitly utilitarian terms: it was either to do beneficial things for the country or to repel evil.[225]

Taken together, these later authors presented many of the ideas of earlier reformers as expressions of the shari'ah. As in earlier advice literature, shari'ah and government punishments were cast as responsibilities of the sovereign. Unlike advice texts, however, these later works were at pains to justify freedom, equality, and foreknowledge of the law as the basis of punishment as fundamentally shari'ah principles without acknowledgment of European ideas.

A Fourteenth-Islamic-Century *Nasirian Qanun* and Legal Compendium

The reign of Nasir al-Din Shah coincided with the turn of the fourteenth century of the Islamic calendar in 1882 (1300 H.). The shah had largely abandoned European-style legal reforms associated with Mirza Malkam Khan. This became an occasion for two figures, the longtime minister of foreign affairs Mirza Sa'id Khan Ansari Mu'tamin al-Mulk and the Shi'i jurist Hajj Mullah 'Ali Shari'atmadar, to compose a legal code (*qanun*) and Shi'i legal compendium (*jami'*), respectively, to provide a standardized law for all of Iran. Ansari convinced Nasir al-Din Shah that a qanun in line with the shari'ah would bring about progress similar to that of the Safavids.[226] He then enlisted Shari'atmadar, who was residing in Mazandaran at the time, to be brought to Tehran for the task of composing "a Law of Islam" (*qanun-i Islam*).[227] This broader project, especially the legal compendium, had legal significance beyond codification. It promoted a vision of the shah's sovereignty and the shari'ah as being inextricably fused insofar as he was the king of Islam (*padishah-i Islam*). While it is tempting to read this effort in light of the Ottoman codification of elements of the shari'ah pertaining to civil law, known as the *Mecelle*, Ansari's and Shari'atmadar's works drew from previous Shi'i efforts to produce practical legal compendia.

The calendric significance of these twin texts probably drew on several precedents from Muslim societies, both of which had to do with Islamic millennial expectations of the eleventh Islamic century. The first connection may have been to a sovereign whose millennial status was connected to his establishing a law: the Ottoman Sultan Suleyman was known as "the Lawgiver" (*Kanuni*).[228] Second, Persian legal compendia emerged around the time of the Islamic millennium under the Safavids. After all, the life of Baha al-Din al-'Amili, the author of one such compendium, *Jami'-i 'Abbasi*, coincided with the year 1591 (1000 H.), and he himself was considered to have been an Islamic reviver (*mujaddid*).[229] Shi'i legal compendia were known as "jurisprudence for the shah" (*fiqh-i shahi*), although they were also intended as a practical manual (*risalah-i 'amaliyah*) for a broader readership.[230] Shari'atmadar considered the fourteenth Islamic century to be particularly unique since there were fourteen "Innocent Ones" (*Ma'sumin*) in Shi'ism, a reference to the Prophet, his daughter Fatima, and the twelve Imams.[231] Elsewhere, he expressed the hope that Nasir al-Din Shah, the "king of Islam," would "revive [*ihya*] the shari'ah ordinances of Muhammad," a turn of phrase that suggested that the monarch could play the role of a religious reviver.[232]

In 1882, Ansari completed his portion of the text known as *Qanun-i Nasiri*. Although it was mostly in the tradition of advice literature, he also laid out what the overall law would look like, presumably gesturing to Shari'atmadar's text. He described how the shah had ordered him to compose "a holy law" (*qanun-i muqaddas*) with the help of the 'ulama and jurists that would include "the divine rulings and commandments" in line with the shari'ah and based on both classical and recent compositions of the 'ulama. The text would be authorized by the 'ulama, signed by the shah, and not subject to change.[233] Repeatedly, Ansari referred to this text as a bound volume (*mujallad*) of the "holy Islamic law" (*qa-nun-i muqaddas-i Islami*).[234] He envisioned the book being implemented throughout Iran without opposition.[235]

Like earlier advice authors, Ansari argued that the government should implement *hudud* punishments in the absence of the Hidden Imam. Furthermore, "shari'ah punishments" that were due to "sinners and religious followers" should be implemented without any hesitation. Punishments simultaneously increased order (*nazm*) and decreased "troubles" for the government.[236] Arrestees still maintained certain rights: they should not be detained (*giriftar*) or taken away without knowledge of wrongdoing.[237]

In many ways, Ansari's text set the stage for the more substantive discussion found in Shari'atmadar's *Jami'-i Nasiri*. Ansari may have chosen Shari'atmadar to write this work because his father, Muhammad Ja'far Shari'atmadar, had written a legal compendium for Muhammad Shah, which was fittingly called *Jami'-i Muhammadi*, in 1840/41 (1256 H.). His father's text, however, dealt primarily with worship, commerce, gifts, inheritance, and loans but not criminal issues.[238] Shari'atmadar's text was much more comprehensive and included a wide-ranging discussion of the shah's role and relationship with the shari'ah in a way that made it a blended genre: it was simultaneously a Shi'i legal compendium, a mirror for princes, and an administrative manual.

Jami'-i Nasiri cannot be separated from the envisioned remodeled administrative and legal apparatus for which it was written. The book was designed to serve three purposes. First, Shari'atmadar intended the book to serve as an administrative manual (*dastur al-'amal*) for judges "far and wide," and for this reason, he employed "familiar language," meaning simple Persian, rather than the more arcane and "abandoned" prose of older texts. The book would also serve as a manual for a supreme judicial council, the Muhammadian Consultative Court (Mahkamah-i Shura-yi Muhammadi), which would complement the Nasirian Consultative Court (Mahkamah-i Shura-yi Nasiri). This implied a clearer jurisdictional division of labor for cases pertaining to the shari'ah and the government.[239] Second, the full title of the book, *The Abridged Nasirean Compendium* (*Jami'-i Nasiri-i Saghir*), implied that it was a precursor

to a lengthier *Comprehensive Book* (*Kitab-i Kabir*), presumably shorthand for *The Comprehensive Nasirean Compendium* (*Jami'-i Nasiri-i
Kabir*). This lengthier version of the text would include "rational, traditional, and customary [*'adiyah*]" legal dimensions that were otherwise
omitted in the abridged version.[240] Third, Shari'atmadar intended the
book to be a schema for the shah's perusal on how to set up "a court
based on shari'ah law" until such time that he could write the longer
version.[241]

Shari'atmadar's discussion of forbidding wrong and *hudud* punishments echoed positions more commonly found in advice literature, insofar as the shah had a role in both. Like Muhammad Baqir
Shafti, Shari'atmadar argued that forbidding wrong and *hudud* punishments were not in abeyance during the Twelfth Imam's occultation. Shari'atmadar differed by seeing this as the potential domain of
the sovereign so long as he was "a religious monarch" (*dindari padishahi*).
He viewed "the current imperial government" as capable of telling the
jurists to "do what is pleasing before God as you see fit," which meant
establishing a shari'ah court (*hukumat-i shar'iyyah*).[242] He stated that a
qualified jurist was capable of forbidding wrong and issuing rulings on
hudud cases, adding that failing to do so was a major sin.[243] He blamed
the real 'ulama, who do not claim leadership (*riyasat*) in religious matters,
for using the abeyance argument with respect to forbidding wrong as
an excuse (*'uzr*) for remaining silent while "wolves in sheep's clothing,"
a reference to pseudo-'ulama, sought leadership.[244] Shari'atmadar restated the classic Shi'i juridical formulation that only the Imam and his
deputy (*na'ib*) could rule on *hudud* cases but clarified that a well-qualified
jurist, as someone capable of making rulings, could in fact do the same.[245]
While the shari'ah judge's task was to make rulings through his guardianship (*vilayat*) on behalf of the lawgiver (*shari'*) (i.e., God), the shah's
task was to "implement God's punishments" (*ijra-yi siyasat Allah*).[246]
Shari'atmadar blamed the lack of implementation of *hudud* and *ta'zir*
punishments for contemporary disorder and hoped that the imperial
government would soon implement both and become an example (*sar-
mashq*).[247]

By most accounts, the shah was impressed with these two texts and
asked that the book be printed and implemented. In the meantime, how-

ever, Mirza Sa'id Ansari passed away. Of greater significance, opponents of this form of law, referred to by some people as "atheist freemasons" and by others as "traitors," banned its implementation. These were apparent references to Amin al-Sultan, who convinced the shah that the book yielded too much power to the people (*millat*) and reduced the shah's role to hunting and tax collection.[248] Later, when the shah had a change of heart and asked Shari'atmadar to continue work on the project, he refused, saying that the project had been that of Ansari, who was no longer alive.[249] Despite *Qanun-i Nasiri* and *Jami'-i Nasiri* nearly becoming law, which included a codified shari'ah with a significant penal component, they never saw the light of day. It would be nearly a hundred years later that Iran would produce a codification of shari'ah in the form of a penal code, but the legacy of these earlier efforts has largely been forgotten or ignored in telling the story of the Islamic Revolution.

Conclusion

By the closing years of Nasir al-Din Shah's reign, those who were writing on legal and political matters presented their reformist ideas as indigenous shari'ah and *qanun* because the shah viewed Western-style reform as a threat to his politico-juridical order. This Islamicization of the reformist genre was the outcome of a number of overlapping and contending intellectual currents, starting with mirrors for princes, followed by works critical of the fragmentation of juridical authority, and, by the 1850s, culminating in reformist literature that selectively appropriated European legal ideas. Across most of these works, the sovereign had the responsibility to forbid wrong and implement *hudud* punishments in the absence of the Shi'i Imam in order to uphold the shari'ah, which entailed the legitimate use of violence. The sovereign's authority to punish exclusively and legitimately, irrespective of his relative justice, was preferable to the alternative of anarchy and chaos. The sovereign's authority to punish crimes linked two understandings of the public. First, crimes that were manifest were within the domain of the sovereign and his officials. These crimes, in turn, had to be punished publicly and in an exemplary fashion. Second, the punishment served the public common good: the sovereign had to protect the generality of the population from harm by containing the ill effects of crimes through punishment. The flip side of the public nature of crime and its punishment was the protection of the individual, which was, in an important sense, private: it was about safeguarding the inviolability of the domicile from spying and violation; protecting the bodily integrity of the individual from injury, torture, and homicide; securing individual property from theft; and guarding the individual's reputation from slander, defamation, and other offensive speech acts. These latter duties were intended to temper the sovereign's wide discretionary powers. Advice and reformist literature was concerned with establishing guidelines for legality and due process. Laws had to be transparent; the population had to know what the laws were, what constituted a violation, and how violations would be punished. This implied a level of oversight and even review by the sovereign, especially over executions. Significantly, the sovereign's monopoly on the legitimate use of violence in such texts was very much in line with European conceptualizations of the state articulated by the likes of Thomas Hobbes, Max Weber, and Carl Schmitt.

Policing and Punishments through
*Farman*s, Codes, and Regulations

A well-timed punishment brings years of order. Without punishment . . .

affairs will not progress. Surely, without a wet stick, the *farman*

will not stick. This point is not lost on cows and donkeys.

—*Nasir al-Din Shah*

In contrast to Shi'i *fiqh* and advice and reform literature, imperial decrees (*farman*s), administrative manuals (*dastur al-'amal*s), codes (*qanun*), and regulations (*qavanin* or *qarardad*) were laws backed by sovereign violence. But even these laws were rarely systematically applied or referred to as rationales for court procedures, fines, and punishments in actual cases. Decrees, codes, and regulations should therefore not be confused with everyday practice.[1] Their historical value lies in understanding government definitions of crime and punishment, novel attempts at penal codification, techniques for crime prevention, procedural principles for criminal cases, and the envisioned jurisdictional division of labor among authorities.

Despite being consequential, *farman*s have rarely figured into discussions of Iranian legal histories. In Qajar sources, *farman*s were regularly referred to by the Arabic term *hukm*, the same term used for a judicial ruling made at a shari'ah court on the basis of God's ordinances (*ahkam*).[2] Often a jurist's ruling, particularly a death sentence, required the shah's *farman* confirming it, thus calling into question the idealized and often ahistorical presentation of shari'ah rulings having the force of law independent of government input in Muslim societies.[3] While No-buaki Kondo and Christoph Werner have suggested that the Qajar government merely executed the 'ulama's shari'ah rulings, this was not always true in criminal cases since the shah could (and often did) disagree with a *mujtahid*'s death sentence, as evidence from urban case studies will demonstrate.[4] The shah's *farman*s also authorized novel administrative manuals, modern police and penal codes, and sanctuary regulations. The *farman*, therefore, was a crucial mechanism for lawmaking that was not bound in the same way by a corpus of texts such as *fiqh* or by the restraints of custom. Legal regulations often emerged in a local context before being co-opted by the shah as administrative manuals that were sent out to the provinces for universal applicability, which suggests that the relationship between the central and provincial governments was far from unidirectional.[5] Qajar codes and regulations employed novel terms such as *qanun/qavanin*, *qarardad*, and *tanzimat* that simultaneously drew on past Persianate terminology and contemporary Ottoman legal and bureaucratic innovations known collectively as the Tanzimat.[6] The term *qanun* was well-known in earlier Persian texts and was sometimes employed in philosophical works or in Shi'i *fiqh* texts to mean principles, especially in the plural form *qavanin*. Authors regularly referred to *qanun-i shar'*, to mean shari'ah law or principle, in a range of legal texts in nineteenth-century Iran but did not necessarily mean by it codified shari'ah such as the Ottoman *mecelle*.[7] Neither the early Qajars nor their predecessors the Safavids, Zands, and Afshars seem to have developed a comprehensive Ottoman-style *kanunname*, which could have served as point of continuity with later codification efforts.[8]

In the legal texts surveyed here, several major themes emerge. First, policing was regularly justified through the Islamic principles of forbidding wrong and protecting public morality (*hisbah* and *ihtisab*) in a manner fully consistent with advice and reformist literature. Second, certain codes employed guarantorship, in which individuals were made responsible for the acts of people under their trust as a form of surveillance. This allowed the government to embed itself socially in light of limited surveillance capacity and policing manpower. Third, codes often mentioned the government's responsibility to carry out shari'ah punishments, such as *hudud* and *qisas*, and government-sanctioned punishments, such as *tanbih* or *siyasat*, which were based on more circumstantial evidence and sovereign discretionary authority. Local authority in gathering evidence and punishing was theoretically not absolute; the shah placed limits on governors' use of judicial torture and restricted executions, especially of a spectacular variety, by making it contingent on his assent. Instead, governors were limited to imprisonment and fines until further notice from the central government. *Farman*s and administrative manuals affirmed government commitment to non-Muslim rights and promised to punish Muslims who violated them through extortion, exploitation, sexual violation, harassment, and murder. These texts also regulated the use of sanctuaries by criminals, given the religious and cultural taboo of violently dragging them out of asylum zones. Throughout these *farman*s, codes, and regulations, the private/public distinction remained crucial, whether in the idea of one's bodily autonomy, integrity, and privacy being of paramount significance, the limits of the government in violating the sanctity of the domicile or sanctuary, the employment of police and guards to surveil public spaces and maintain order, or the use of guarantorship when the policing function of the government fell short.

Police and Penal Codes

Police and penal codes drew on three bodies of knowledge and practices: first, Islamic ideals of regulating public morality and punishing *hudud* crimes and murder; second, Iranian urban policing practices associated with *kadkhuda*s, *kalantar*s, and *darughah*s; and third, modern European forms of policing. In the Safavid era, numerous *farman*s tasked sayyids, judges, governors, *kalantar*s, *darughah*s, and others with the duty to forbid wrong. These *farman*s outlawed drinking alcohol, taverns, brothels, shaving beards, and entertainment music.[9] The Qajars did not generally produce similar *farman*s, although they prohibited public vice in other texts. Michael Cook has examined how forbidding wrong—a concept closely related to *hisbah*—persisted in the Qajar era in Shi'i *fiqh* and two reformist texts.[10] Both Willem Floor and Ann Lambton claim that the *muhtasib* lost their religious function and disappeared in the early nineteenth century.[11] Contrary to Floor's inaccurate portrayal of the *muhtasib* as exclusively a "secular" market police with no "religious" function, the regulations analyzed here demonstrate that their tasks involved policing the public consumption of alcohol, gambling, theft, and other forms of vice consistent with Islamic ethical concerns.[12] Even the claim about the *muhtasib* disappearing requires revisiting since the terms *ihtisab* and *muhtasib* were regularly used synonymously with police (*pulis*) well into the late nineteenth century. In fact, Nasiri-era regulations defined the police and/or *ihtisabiyah* as enacting the shari'ah. I argue in this chapter that codes and regulations were generally consistent with advice literature's insistence that the government had the duty to forbid wrong and to punish crimes according to the shari'ah and its discretionary powers.

Genealogies of Police, *Ihtisab*, and Forbidding Wrong

Two Qajar statesmen, I'timad al-Saltanah and 'Abdullah Mustawfi, provided useful accounts of urban policing and its connection to *ihtisab* and "forbidding wrong." Both men had firsthand knowledge of the inner workings of the Qajar government, especially I'timad al-Saltanah, who was the head of the Department of Public Morality (Idarah-i Ihtisab) between 1875 and 1878 (1292–95 H.). 'Abdullah Mustawfi was the grandson of Mustawfi al-Mamalik, a Qajar statesman who served as prime minister or acting prime minister under Nasir al-Din Shah on several occasions (1867–71, 1880–84, 1884–86).

    I'timad al-Saltanah considered *ihtisab* to be "from among the arts of the tree of law [*qanun*]." He elaborated on its Islamic genealogy by referring to medieval *hisbah* manuals, the works of al-Ghazali, chapters of jurisprudence dealing with forbidding wrong, and unflattering references in Persian poetry. The poet Khwajah, for instance, wrote, "the *muhtasib* broke the wine jar and I [broke] his head," a sentiment suggestive of the popular hatred of the *muhtasib* and his moralistic censure of alcohol consumption.[13] I'timad al-Saltanah also cited the well-known example of Shah Tahmasp's memoir (*tazkirah*), in which he had a dream of Sayyid Muhtasib al-Mulk taking his hand and repenting for all of the shah's "forbidden acts and sins" (*manahi va ma'asi*) at the foot of the shrine of Imam Riza in Mashhad. After this moment, the duty of *ihtisab* was put into place and eventually assimilated into the duties of the police (*zabtiyah*).[14]

I'timad al-Saltanah linked the formation of the Qajar-era police force to *ihtisab* and forbidding wrong. Acknowledging the origins of modern police in "Europe and America," he argued that the genesis of its Iranian equivalent was Nasir al-Din Shah's observations about the police in England in his travelogue.[15] When the shah returned from his second trip to Europe, he hired Conte di Monteforte, an Austro-Hungarian citizen of Sicilian heritage, to establish and run the police force.[16] Monteforte had the policemen wear distinctive clothing and carry special firearms in line with a European model. The police had an unmistakably public function: in Tehran, they were to patrol its workshops and shops with an eye to stopping theft and "protecting public order" (*hifz-i nizam-i 'amm*). Conveying this function, the head of the police department had the title Nazm al-Mulk.[17] I'timad al-Saltanah observed that the police, much like the *muhtasib*, were memorialized in verse:

> Oh libertines [*rindan*]! Beware and be weary of the police,
> You can't trick [*tadlis*] them, not even one bit.
> If Jupiter [*barjis*] makes one false rotation,
> It too shall die in the wooden fetters of the Conte di
>   Monteforte.[18]

This poem conveys the feared efficacy of the police, both with regard to surveillance and in being able to detain and punish any criminal. In response to this verse, however, came two popular ones, each mocking the police and their intrusive efforts at policing:

> Even if Satan joins hands with the police,
> [And even] if the secret reporter [*khufyah nivis*] enters
>   Mercury's orbit,

Not a hair of the libertines' pubes shall decrease,
Even if all of Paris became a depilatory.[19]

The second popular verse reads as follows:

Oh wine drinkers! Your days are numbered!
It is commanded that the police smell your mouths.
Take it from me and do a wine enema,
So that from now on they will smell only your farts.[20]

Both verses accuse the police of violating the privacy on which libertines relied to evade the authorities.

Echoing advice literature, I'timad al-Saltanah claimed that punishing criminals was the sole prerogative of the shah. He described Nasir al-Din Shah as "bound by shari'ah responsibilities" and charged with the protection of "divine ordinances."[21] He recounted how the shah addressed the 'ulama during his first visit to Europe, saying that "during the time of the occultation we have not shied away from implementing *hudud* punishments."[22]

'Abdullah Mustawfi's three-volume autobiography similarly connected the *muhtasib* and later urban police figures to the concept of forbidding wrong. He gave examples of early Muslim caliphs forbidding wrong by carrying out the duty during rounds in the bazaars. He related a story about 'Ali bin Abi Talib having a "judgment stand" (*dikkah al-qaza'i*), which was in the shop of a date seller in the center of Kufa.[23] By the end of the Umayyad period, the *muhtasib* emerged as someone who would roam around the bazaars to ensure that commercial products were of high standard and that those who violated public regulations were punished.[24]

According to Mustawfi, the *muhtasib*'s duties included preventing the drinking of wine, prostitution, and theft in the bazaar. He cited a striking anonymous poem critical of the *muhtasib*'s violence and hypocrisy: the *muhtasib* knows how to beat whores / Be happy, oh *muhtasib*, because your wife is a whore, [or be happy, you whore-beating *muhtasib*]" (*ruspi ra muhtasib danad zadan / shad bash ay ruspi zan[-i] muhtasib*).[25] Mustawfi speculated that it was this "lack of affection" toward *muhtasibs* that led *darughahs* to take over their functions in the Safavid era.[26] The *darughah* had a special stand (*takht*) that was in the four parts of the bazaar and similar to that of the *muhtasib*. The term *muhtasib* was subsequently used infrequently except by poets familiar with this classical figure. Mustawfi further claimed that under the Qajars, the *darughah* and the *kalantar* shared the mayoral duties (*shahrdari*) and the task of punishing crimes. Contradicting his claims, he mentioned that the title of Ihtisab al-Mulk was given to I'timad al-Saltanah, which suggests that the title continued to exist in modified form beyond the Safavid era.[27] Mustawfi's and I'timad al-Saltanah's two accounts clearly stress the equivalence between forbidding wrong/*ihtisab* and the urban policing of public vice, which was rooted in the sovereign's authority to punish.

The Military Code

The scholarship on Iranian legal history has ignored the Military Code (Qanun-i Nizamiyah), which was the first Qajar code dealing substantially with policing and punishment. This code and the process of codification should not be reduced to yet another facet of Qajar military modernization in the face of defeat by European powers on the battlefield.[28] Far more consequential were the early modern shifts in which military positions became urban policing ones: the positions of *biglarbigi* and *darughah*, for example, had their origins in Turco-Mongolian armies before taking on the meaning of mayor/police magistrate and chief of police, respectively.[29] A very similar dynamic was at play in the Ottoman Empire: the elite Janissary troops became urban policing figures over the course of the early modern period.[30]

Mirza Muhammad Khan Qajar Sipahsalar's lengthy 1865 Military Code was a formative text in the process of policing and penal codification.[31] Contrary to conventional wisdom about codification, it was not written during a high point of reform; instead, it was composed in the mid-1860s, when the reformist prime minister Amir Kabir (g. 1848–51) had long been executed and the reformist prime minister Mushir al-Dawlah (g. 1871–73) had yet to take office. Unlike most other codes, the Military Code was regularly referred to in accounts of criminal cases involving soldiers. It was the first official document of its kind that not only set out the responsibilities pertaining to public morality but also demarcated specific punishments for crimes. In discussing policing, it used the term *ihtisab* to discuss religious affairs and public behavior. The code included both government punishments (*tanbihat, siyasat*, and *mujazat*) and *hudud* punishments for convicted military officials. The code synthesized government and religious punishments by stating that all punishments to which soldiers were subject should be based on shari'ah and military law (*hukm-i shar' va qanun-i nizami*) (figure 7).[32]

The legal basis for codification was the shah's authority to issue *farman*s, which were sometimes referred to as rescripts (*dastkhatt*s). In

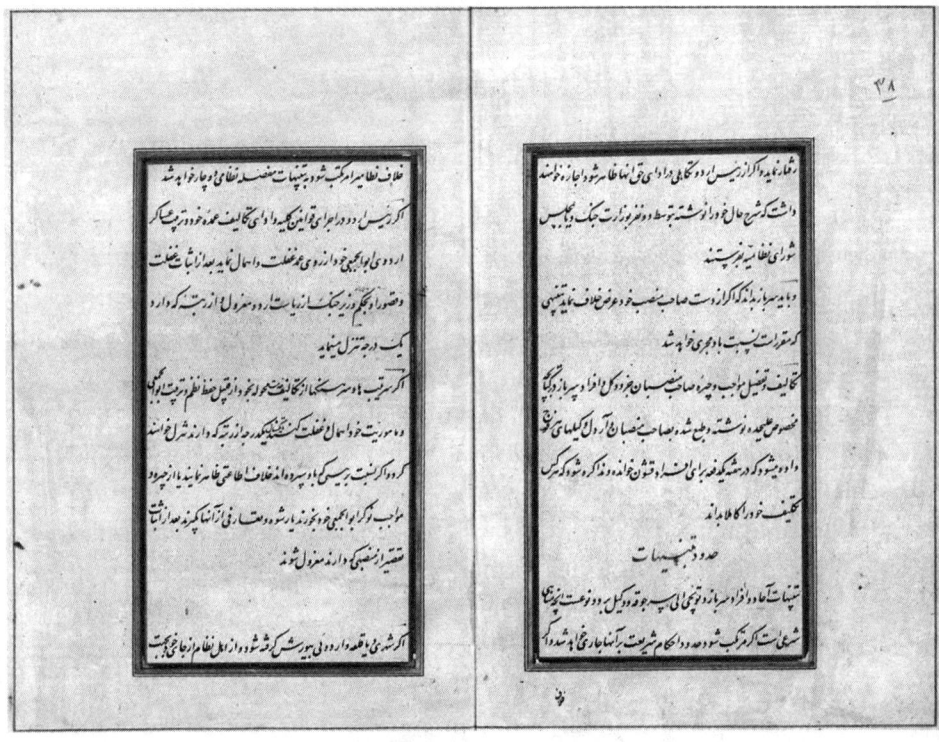

Figure 7: A page from the Military Code detailing punishments for soldiers, including for the contravention of the shari'ah.

(Source: Mirza Muhammad Khan Qajar Sipahsalar, "Kitabchah-i Qanun-i Nizamiyah," 1865, Majlis Library, no. IR 10-49188, folio 38)

Nasir al-Din Shah's *dastkhatt* preceding the Military Code, he stated that he had ordered Mirza Muhammad Khan Qajar Sipahsalar to compose the code in order to bring about order (*nazm*). The shah then commanded that this code be published (*chap zadah*) and distributed throughout Iran.[33] Institutionally, the Military Code envisioned a Military Council (Maslahatkhanah-i 'Askariyah) in both Tehran and Tabriz composed of both military and nonmilitary figures who would tend to military affairs and report to the Ministry of War. They were also responsible for issuing military commands and court rulings, suggesting both legislative and judicial functions.[34]

The code regulated public morality and crimes by invoking Islamic legal terminology. It defined illegal religious acts (*a'mal-i khalaf-i shar'*) as drinking, theft, gambling, and the broad category of "evil deeds and debauchery" (*shararat va harzigi*).[35] While drinking and theft fell under *hadd* punishments, gambling, evil deeds, and debauchery were activities that fell into the category of forbidding wrong. The Military Code made a distinction between *hudud* punishments, which were to be implemented on those who breached the shari'ah, and military punishments (*tanbihat-i nizami*), which were to be enacted for acts violating military law.[36] The head of the troops (*ra'is-i urdu*) was responsible for ensuring that shari'ah regulations (*qava'id*) were implemented.[37] He too had the task of ensuring the "public morality of the troops" (*ihtisab-i urdu*). He had to prevent "fighting and brawling" among his men, gambling, and drinking alcohol on military grounds. The code did not spell out the specific punishments for each of these crimes but stated that the offenders would be tried by a shari'ah judge (*hakim-i shar'*).[38] Similarly, generals (*sartips*) and colonels (*sarhangs*) had to ensure that no one in their "group division" (*fawj-i jam'i*) drank or gambled, or the offenders would be subject to both "*hudud* and prescribed [*tanbihat-i muqarrarah*] punishments."[39] That both *hudud* and prescribed punishments were to be applied in one case suggests a dual overlapping jurisdiction of both shari'ah and military courts.

The Military Code set out precise military punishments for various offenses such as neglecting duties, taking bribes, and theft. If a leader (*ra'is*) failed to enact military laws, he would drop one rank.[40] A military figure who took bribes or gifts would be deposed and imprisoned for a year.[41] A prison warden (*sar anbardar*) of the barracks (*qurkhanah*) or cannon barracks (*tupkhanah*) who stole, presumably from prisoners, would be enchained (*zanjir*) for a year and pay compensation.[42] Any military member who stole from his temporary civilian residences would be put in chains (*zanjir*) for a year, lashed one hundred times, and forced to return the stolen goods.[43] A soldier who caused financial loss or cheated someone was liable for the amount and would receive two hundred lashes. If this financial loss involved threats, then the penalty increased to three hundred lashes.[44]

The Military Code also included penalties for military officials who injured civilians, endangered public safety, or spied for an enemy. The shariʿah court would become involved in injury cases. If a military official acting as a guard or passing through a village injured an ordinary subject in the course of seizing food or drink from them, he would be subject to a shariʿah ruling. In addition to returning the goods or paying compensation, he would serve a three- to six-month prison sentence, depending on whether he took the goods through threats.[45] Here too, both shariʿah and military punishments applied simultaneously. Elsewhere in the code, it stated that if a soldier injured someone with non-life-threatening injuries, the soldier would be subject to a fixed mandatory punishment (*hudud-i shariʿah*).[46] The use of *hudud* to describe a punishment for an injury here is curious since, in *fiqh*, this type of punishment was considered *qisas*. Military officials also had a duty to protect public safety at their postings. If they deprived people of their freedom, then they would serve a ten-month prison sentence while also receiving an equivalent punishment for the bodily injuries caused.[47] Soldiers who, either alone or in concert, plundered (*yaghma*) houses and property or set fire to crops and storage houses would receive five hundred lashes and three months in prison and would be liable for the plundered goods.[48] Finally, military officials who tried to protect their own safety in the face of the enemy or who spied for the enemy would receive a "death sentence."[49] The Military Code was acutely aware of how Islamic notions of privacy and the sanctity of the domicile could be used to protect outlaw soldiers. The head of troops had the responsibility to stop tyranny and transgressions committed by his troops without "covering up" (*pardah pushi*) these transgressions.[50] It further punished those who hid (*pinhan*) deserters in their homes with a two-year prison sentence, which involved hard labor during the day and being enchained at night.[51] The code also employed guarantorship (*iltizam/zamin*) by making the *kadkhuda* or owner (*malik*) of a village the guarantor of conscripted soldiers in case of desertion.[52] Collective retribution and destruction of the domicile were other punitive tactics: deserters who failed to return to their troops would have their houses destroyed and their family members seized and detained.[53]

The Military Code also provided a window into the policing roles of soldiers and the punishments they would receive if they were derelict in their duties. Soldiers often served as guards (*qaravuls*) in urban centers throughout Iran. Their shifts were capped at two hours: if their commanding officer did not rotate them, then he would receive two hundred lashes. A soldier who was lax in his guard duties by sleeping, sitting on the floor, or placing his gun on the floor or against a wall would be punished with fifty lashes.[54] One hundred lashes were due to a soldier who did not attend to his guard duties.[55] If guards allowed people to pass into no-trespass zones, such as guard barracks or places of drill exercises, they received two hundred lashes.[56] Only one article mentioned the rights of a guard: if he was injured on duty, he was entitled to "shari'ah compensation [*diyah*]."[57]

The Military Code operationalized *hisbah* by making the head of a troop responsible for the public morality of his subordinates. It also envisioned a hybrid system of shari'ah and military punishments in which the former was left to the discretion of a shari'ah judge while the latter was fixed.

Mustawfi al-Mamalik's Administrative Manuals

Like the Military Code, Mirza Yusuf Khan Mustawfi al-Mamalik's two administrative manuals (*dastur al-'amals*) were composed after a period of reform, which in this case was the aftermath of the reformist prime minister Mirza Husayn Khan Mushir al-Dawlah's tenure (g. 1871–73). In his capacity as the shah's minister of interior affairs and the treasury, Mustawfi al-Mamalik composed these two texts, one in 1873 and the next in 1876, to provide provincial governors (*hukkam-i vilayat*) guidelines on policing and punishment. The shah fully endorsed these texts, which foreshadowed the emphasis on guarantorship, jurisdiction, and respect for the shari'ah found in later policing and penal codes.

Mustawfi al-Mamalik's first administrative manual, *Takalif-i Hukkam-i Vilayat*, dated November 24, 1873 (4 Shaval 1290 H.), was validated by Nasir al-Din Shah's *dastkhatt*, which stated, "This booklet was read in its entirety, and it is good and written correctly."[58] The shah warned that its contents should be implemented by governors; otherwise, they would be punished and deposed.[59] The text was referred to as both a *dastur al-'amal* and a law or code (*qanun*), suggesting the equation of the two concepts in official court circles.[60] It called for the formation of a council (*majlis*) in each administrative province and locality, composed of a member of the 'ulama, a military person, a famous merchant, and two or three *kadkhudas*, *kalantars*, or other well-known persons (*ma'arif*), who would meet to ensure that petitions and cases were investigated impartially.[61] Part of the council's task was to sort out jurisdiction: cases would be referred to either the governor's court (*hukumat-i 'urfiyah*) or the shari'ah court (*dar al-shar'*).[62] When the Ministry of Justice (Vizarat-i 'Adliyah-i A'zam) issued a ruling, the governor's duty would be to implement it without delay.[63]

The document laid out the underlying logic of sovereignty and the delegation of authority via guarantorship, which linked the shah to the governors, police magistrates, guards and policemen, neighborhood and village headmen, and other government officials. One of its articles stated that "the property, life, reputation, chastity ['*irz*], and honor [*namus*] of the servants of God who are inside and outside Iranian soil are under the protection of his imperial majesty."[64] The governor was responsible to the imperial government (*dawlat*) for maintaining public order at the local level.[65] Those who were beneath the governor had delegated "powers of coercion to maintain safety" (*qudrat-i istila-yi hifz-i amniyat*) in the city on behalf of the central government (*divan*) through the instruments of the *kalantar*, *kadkhuda*, *darughah*, *qarasuran*, and *qaravulan*. The governor was to take a "harsh guarantee" (*iltizam-i sakht*) from these figures to protect the streets and passageways, safeguard the people's "property and lives," and take liability for loss as a result of theft and evildoing.[66] In turn, governors had to report on and take responsibility for any stolen property, cases of disorder, murder, and evildoing.[67]

In May/June 1876 (Jumada al-Avval 1293 H.), Mustawfi al-Mamalik composed *Dastur al-'Amal-i Hukkam-i Vilayat*, which reiterated many of these themes with a slightly different emphasis. For shari'ah cases, he specified that rulings generally had to be issued in the presence of the plaintiff and the defendant, even in cases of *qisas* and injuries (*jinayat*).[68] Echoing the Ottoman imperial rescripts of the Tanzimat, he stated that the Ministry of Justice was to treat everyone equally.[69]

The Guard Barracks Code

In 1878 (1295 H.), the minister of foreign affairs and war, Mirza Husayn Khan Mushir al-Dawlah Sipahsalar drafted the Guard Barracks (*qaravulkhanah*) Code, which was officially adopted.[70] This code has likewise eluded scholars writing on the history of policing and codification in Iran. Printed in the official government newspaper *Ruznamah-i Iran*, it elaborated on the guards' duty to patrol the streets and address urban disorder, especially at night, which was associated with danger and vice. The organizational logic of the *qaravulkhanah* was distinctly tied to the barracks that dotted the urban landscape; each barrack was responsible for potentially illicit behavior within its radius. The guards investigated and often acted on the basis of circumstantial evidence. The code directed guards to make distinctions on the basis of respectability: individuals of civilian, military, or protected foreign status were treated according to separate protocols and procedures when engaging in potentially illicit acts. It also provided guidelines for the proper behavior of the guards and their punishments in cases of dereliction of duty, which, like the Military Code, included ample use of corporal punishment.

The code delineated the various types of guards, their duties, and their spatial boundaries. It defined a patrol as consisting of a head patrolman (*sargazmah*) and four or five patrolmen (*gazmah*) for a single neighborhood.[71] The *qaravul*, or guard, was expected to stand through the night until sunrise, since this was when stolen goods were typically transported.[72] The Guard Barracks Code stated that a barracks must include a commander (*sahib mansib*) carrying a sword, a scribe, two drummers, a reed flute player, and a trumpeter.[73] These three musical figures were to blow their horns and beat their drums to alert the guard barracks that help was needed.[74]

The guards' police jurisdiction was defined spatially in relation to the barracks and also by the publicness of the crime. They were responsible for catching drunks, thieves, and gamblers within fifty paces of their barracks but not beyond it and for writing an incident report (*ru-znamah*).[75] Much like medieval *hisbah* manuals, the code placed limits on the power of the guards to enter the domicile outside of an emergency situation. If an incident took place that required the assistance of the barracks, then a guard and a patrolman should go to the door of the house to investigate. They should not enter the house except once they had deduced (*istinbat*) that a theft or a murder was in progress. Only then could they, along with the head patrolman, enter the house to detain a thief or evildoer and bring them back to the barracks.[76] Unlike shari'ah forms of evidence, the code allowed for using deduction, a form of circumstantial evidence, as a basis for police action.

The code was only briefly concerned with punishments for corrupt guards but not regular detainees. A *qaravul* convicted of appropriating property and taking bribes from prisoners would receive three hundred lashes, while a convicted barracks commander would also drop one degree in rank (*darajah*).[77] Instead, regular detainees were dealt with differently depending on the type of crime they were suspected of and their status group. When drunks, evildoers, and other culprits were detained at night, they should be held until right before sunrise. Those who were apprehended during the day should be released one hour into the night.[78] Two soldiers were to accompany every single person who was apprehended, presumably to prevent their escape.[79] Criminals were to be referred to their local authorities after their detention period. In most cases, they were referred to Amirzadah Vajhullah Mirza, the apparent head of the Guard Barracks, who would then send the culprits to their respective neighborhoods, suggesting that their local *kadkhuda* was in charge of any further punishments.[80] Other detainees were referred to their respective authorities. For instance, if the *qaravuls* caught military officials who engaged in evildoing, they would hand them over to the head of the military (*ra'is-i nizam*) after having informed the head of the guard barracks.[81] Similarly, if the *qaravuls* caught a servant of a foreign embassy (*sifarat*) who was drunk or engaging in unruly behavior, they should take them to the embassy, leave them with the commander of the embassy barracks, take an incident report confirmation receipt, and write a report.[82] These provisions of the code indicate different procedures for individuals on the basis of their civilian, military, or protected foreign status, although no differentiation was made on the basis of slave status, gender, or religion, as commonly made in *fiqh* texts.

The code was primarily concerned with the surveillance of urban spaces at night. As Avner Wishnitzer has argued regarding the early modern Ottoman Empire context, night was a time associated with crime, illicit activities, and danger.[83] In the code, the blowing of the trumpet (*shaypur*) marked the beginning of the night, after which people required a lantern (*fanus*) and a special "night password" (*ism-i shab*) to walk around.[84] Those who were caught at night were treated differently based on their level of "respectability." If a "respectable" person had a lamp but did not know the night password, the *qaravul* would accompany them to their destination.[85] If, on the other hand, someone had a lamp and the night password but was drunk or engaging in "unruly behavior," then a soldier should follow them to their destination, investigate, record their movements, and paste a report to the guard barracks' gate.[86] A disreputable person without a lamp who was engaging in unruly behavior should be apprehended and taken back to the barracks.[87] When someone had the night password but their condition was unclear, irrespective of their respectability or their residence, they should be observed by one of the night guards to see if anything could be deduced. If they could not do so, then the guard should inform the next one when the suspect passed into their jurisdiction.[88]

The Police Codes

In the late 1870s, Nasir al-Din Shah commissioned the formation of a modern police force in Tehran. Conte di Monteforte composed the Police Code, which was authorized by Nasir al-Din Shah through an

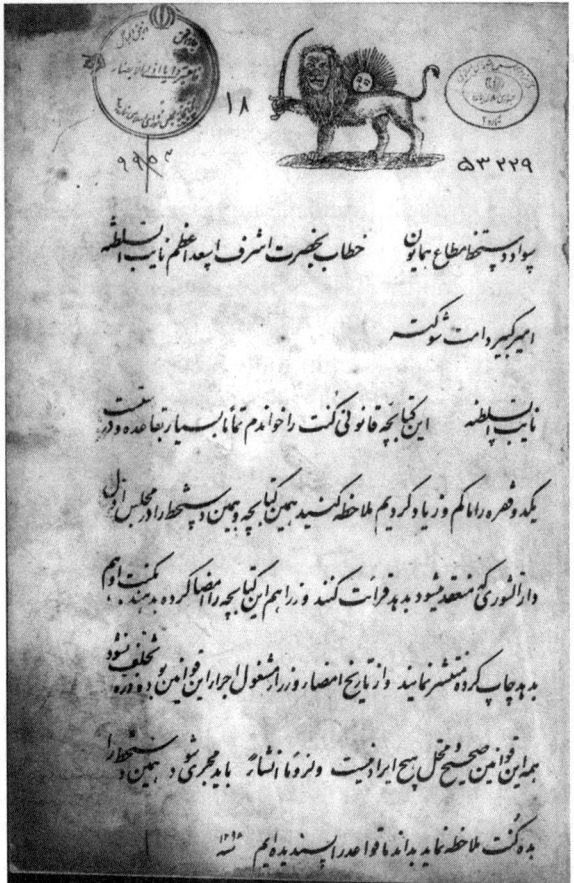

Figure 8: Nasir al-Din Shah's *farman* authorizing
Conte di Monteforte's Police Code.

(Source: Conte di Monteforte, "Kitabchah-i Qanun-i Jaza-yi
Kunt du Munt-i Furt," 1879, Majlis Library, no. 2–20359, 1)

imperial rescript in 1879 (1296 H.) (figure 8). The code made the link between the shah's decree and the legal authority of the police by stating,
"Whoever does not obey the code and regulation [*qanun va nazm*] of
the police has not obeyed the imperial ruling [*hukm*]."[89] An abridged
variation of the code, referred to here as the Summary Code, also appeared in the official newspaper *Ruznamah-i Iran* in 1879.[90] Given its
Tehran focus, the code explicitly defined the police's role in surveilling

public spaces for vice and violence, monitoring movements in and out of the city, and regulating commercial and guild relationships.

The Police Code could be read as yet another step along the path toward modernity, especially given the involvement of a European in its composition. Nobuaki Kondo considers the code to embody "outward respect for Islamic law along with discretionary measures in the police regulations." He mentions that the code "stipulated that murders must be judged in accordance with Islamic law" but included non-Islamic legal punishments such as "imprisonments and fixed fines" for other crimes. He concludes that "Monteforte had introduced modern elements into the details of the regulations which were supposedly in accordance with Islamic law."[91] In examining the establishment of protocols relevant to criminal law, Khaled Fahmy argues that the mere presence of a European should not be read automatically as evidence of "European modernity"; instead, he chooses to see these protocols in light of the way local jurists and thinkers incorporated and understood them.[92] The approach taken here mirrors that of Fahmy: the code should be understood as embodying continuities with previous mirrors for princes, such as the emphasis on justice and the equality of subjects before the sovereign, and *fiqh* concepts and terminology, such as invocations of the shari'ah, punishments of *hudud* violations, the protection of the rights of people (such as in cases of murder or injury), and the use of guarantorship.

The shah's prefatory *dastkhatt* to Kamran Mirza Na'ib al-Saltanah stated that he had read the "Conte's Code" and considered it to be based on "[proper] and correct principles," although he did remove one or two articles. The shah commanded that the code be read at the Consultative Assembly (Dar al-Shura) and that the ministers sign the code into law before having it published widely. He wished for the regulations to be implemented without delay.[93] The chief (*ra'is*) of police was granted discretionary powers to enact these regulations without having to present them to the shah, although he was obligated to take care of the people.[94] The people, in turn, had to show respect to one another and to the police.[95]

The Police Code employed the language of rights, law and order, public safety, and shari'ah. Employing the language of advice and reform literature, it tasked the police with the protection of the public ('ammah) and the public's rights (huquq). They had to prevent "disorder and injustice" in addition to property appropriation.[96] Among the limits placed on any government attendant or official, including the police, was that they did not have the right to beat or take money from a suspect.[97] Moving to more specifically Islamic terminology, the code intended its existence as a means of implementing "shari'ah ordinances and laws" and rooting out "moral corruption" (fasad).[98] The police, in turn, were bound by shari'ah ordinances and by "the specific principles of the sect," meaning Shi'ism.[99] The Summary Code provided further indication that the concept of forbidding wrong underwrote it: it asked the people of Tehran to be mindful not "to engage in acts forbidden [manhiyat] by the shari'ah."[100]

The main articles of the Police Code classified various crimes and provided specific punishments, although it did not spell out the judicial procedure for trials or court jurisdiction. Tehran's governor probably handled more serious crimes. The code included public crimes discussed in fiqh manuals, namely, those deserving hudud punishments, and public acts that created an obligation to forbid wrong. Specified punishments were usually noncorporeal, which included imprisonment and fines. In this respect, the punishments differed substantially from hudud punishments and from the lashing penalties of the Military Code. The Summary Code established the principle of equal rights in "the punishment of immoral acts [a'mal-i shani'ah]." It assured the subjects of Tehran that no one was exempt from "the implementation of necessary punishments."[101] The police were responsible for detaining a criminal and punishing them irrespective of their degree of guilt, with some exceptions. If the detainee was a member of the royal family, the case was to be referred to the shah himself. If the detainee was a member of the military, then the incident was to be reported to the "head of the military" (Ra'is-i Nizam) for punishment. The Police Code thus made status distinctions and adhered to jurisdictional boundaries in parallel ways to the Guard Barracks Code.[102]

Murder was the crime that was most explicitly linked to shari'ah procedures and principles. The preface to the code mentioned that qisas would be carried out in accordance with shari'ah rules. Although murder stood at the intersection of public order concerns of the government

and the private matter of tort, the Police Code upheld shariʿah procedures in murderer cases and recognized the role of the shariʿah court
in establishing legal facts and delivering judgments for intentional
homicide (*qatl-i ʿamd*), apparent intentional homicide (*qatl-i shibh ʿamd*),
and unintentional homicide (*qatl-i khata*).[103] The code oddly did not
explicitly mention that the murdered person's family had the option of
compensation or forgiveness. It did, however, mention two specific forms
of murder and its punishments: poisoning and hiring an assassin. The
first crime carried the same punishment due to a murderer, presumably
a death sentence. If there was a strong suspicion of such a crime, indicating only circumstantial evidence, then the person would be given life
imprisonment.[104] If there were other parties to this murder, such as a
pharmacist or a doctor, then they would be given one to five years in
prison.[105] A person who hired an assassin would be imprisoned one to
five years, depending on the evidence.[106]

While in Shiʿi jurisprudence, theft and banditry were *hadd* crimes,
the Police Code provided a different set of punishments for it. Banditry
(*qatiʿ-i tariq*) and theft earned a one- to fifteen-year prison sentence, depending on the degree of guilt.[107] This was a telling case in which a *fiqh*
penalty requiring corporal punishment was commuted to imprisonment
in much the same way as earlier draft code translations and adaptations.
Closely connected with theft and impersonation was the issue of coun-
terfeiting.[108] The punishment for this crime differed in its semicorporal
nature, which involved being bound in iron chains. If someone manu-
factured a fake imperial order (*dastkhatt*) or imperial seal, then they
would be imprisoned ten to twenty years, during which time their
hands would be bound in iron chains. The shah or the head of police
would be the only ones with the key to this criminal's prison cell.[109] The
penalty for someone minting counterfeit domestic or foreign coins was
similarly harsh: ten to twenty-five years in prison with hands bound
in iron chains.[110]

The Police Code extensively addressed criminal public speech acts,
such as disrespectful comments, defamation, false testimony, treasonous statements and texts, and blasphemy. Not respecting others, either
by word or by deed, constituted a crime. Echoing variations in sanctions
according to status group found in earlier codes, if someone disrespected

someone of a higher status or position of authority, the fine was greater (the greatest sanction being for those who offended the shah). Not showing respect (*ihtiram*) or violating someone's sanctity (*hatk-i hurmat*) both signified Islamic legal concepts. They both pointed to ideas intimately related to defamation, misinformation, ruining one's reputation, and violating one's privacy. Three of the articles of the Police Code dealt directly with treason, which was framed as offenses against the shah and/or the government. Article 1 stated that anyone who spoke against the shah or the royal family would serve a one- to five-year prison sentence.[111] Treason more generally was defined as causing trouble and stirring opposition to the government; a convicted person could face one to fifteen years in prison.[112] If someone had the "gall" (*jasarat*) to write a night letter (*shabnamah*) against the shah and paste it in the side streets, they would likewise face one to five years imprisonment.[113] The punishment for disrespect decreased depending on the social status of the offended party. If someone showed disrespect, in word or deed, to a minister (*vazir*), "an important person"—presumably a notable—foreign ambassadors, and people working in the Foreign Ministry, they would be imprisoned between four days and two years and pay a fine of five to one hundred tumans.[114] Those who showed disrespect to police officers or others who wore "official government clothing," either orally or by action (including by beating them), would be imprisoned between forty-eight hours and six months in prison and receive a fine of one to ten tumans.[115] Finally, a servant who, by word or deed, "violated the sanctity [*hurmat*]" of their master would receive between ten days and two months in prison and would be fined between five hundred qirans and two tumans.[116] While in the three aforementioned articles, the status group of the offender and/or the offended was included, article 23 generalized this principle without any reference to the persons involved, possibly because they were both of equal status. If someone disrespected another person either by word or through physical force, then they would receive between forty-eight hours and two months in prison and pay a fine of one to ten tumans.[117]

Illegal speech acts, which paralleled the *hadd* crime of making false accusations of *zina*, made their way into the code, although the terminology and punishments differed. If a person made a false accusation (*tuhmat*) against someone in written or oral form, they would receive one to five years in prison and pay a fine of five to one hundred tumans.[118] Publishing blasphemous or treasonous publications against the state and nation were grouped together as similar crimes. The punishment for someone publishing a book against the Shi'i creed, the government, or the nation (*millat*) was five months to a year in prison.[119] "Mocking one's own religion" orally was also something that warranted a punishment of forty-eight hours to six months in prison and a fine of five to one hundred tumans. The money from the fine was to be given to a *mujtahid* to spend on "religious expenses."[120]

Impersonation constituted a similar punishable form of falsehood. If someone tried to impersonate a government official in order to trick people into procuring ill-gotten gains, then this constituted a crime deserving between one and ten years in prison. Any of the ill-gotten gains would either have to be returned or seized in order to redistribute them to orphans, the poor, or charitable organizations.[121] Impersonation was also an issue when a man dressed as a woman to enter a house or when "ruffians and good-for-nothings" dressed as "learned people and mystics."[122]

The Police Code also addressed crimes of a sexual nature without reference to *hudud* punishments. Instead of employing the *fiqh* terminology of *zina* or *livat*, it used the catch-all phrase "immoral act" (*fi'l-i shani'*) to describe rape, sex outside of marriage, and adultery. Unlike *hudud* punishments, which involved lashes or execution for *zina*, the prescribed punishments involved imprisonment and fines. Article 13 stated that a person who had sex with a virgin girl (*dukhtar*) who had not reached "sexual maturity" (*rushd va bulugh*) would be imprisoned between five and fifteen years and be forced to pay for her livelihood until she reached puberty, at which time the parents could choose to marry her off to the man.[123] If a man deflowered "a mature female virgin" (*bakirah-i balighah*), he would serve one to five years in prison or be presented with the option of marrying her with the consent of the parents. Based on the "degree of the crime," he was liable to the parents for thirty to one thousand tumans, suggesting that this was a form of compensation for her dowry and property damage.[124] Such a principle was consistent with certain *fiqh* understandings of rape as property damage that warranted compensation to the violated female's guard-ian.[125] If a child was born of such an illicit sexual encounter and the man did not marry the woman, then he was liable to pay one to five qirans per day for daily expenses.[126] In the case of a man being convicted at the Police Administration (Idarah-i Nazmiyah) for having sex with a mar-ried woman, the person would serve between one and five years in prison and pay a fine of ten to one hundred tumans.[127] It was unclear, however, if this fine would be paid to the police or to the cuckolded husband. Most of the aforementioned sex crimes were discussed without reference to the space associated with its commission or the forms of evidence required for a conviction; it is perhaps for this reason that the terms zina and livat were studiously avoided, since these referred to public sex acts, while be-ing convicted of an "immoral act" indicated conviction based on cir-cumstantial evidence falling short of fiqh standards.

Both codes referred to sex crimes in reference to their public and private spatial contexts. The Summary Code banned lewdness (fahhashi) and disgraceful acts (fazzahi), whether during the day or night, "espe-cially outside of one's residence."[128] Someone convicted of having "forc-ibly [jabran] abducted a woman from a side street" would be imprisoned for forty-eight hours to a month and fined one to ten tumans.[129] A "man who dresses in women's clothing to enter houses," that is, a cross-dresser who violated gender-mixing norms possibly to embark on a sexual es-capade, would be imprisoned for a month to a year and fined five to ten tumans.[130] If a person did something "illegal" with a woman or child in a mosque, presumably of a sexual nature, they were to be imprisoned for a day to a month and fined one to five tumans in cash. This money would be offered to a mujtahid, who would place it in a "religious fund."[131] The crime in question violated the sanctity of a sacred public space, and therefore the punishment involved compensation to the religious insti-tution in a way that paralleled the increase in compensation in fiqh for committing injury or murder in the Masjid al-Haram in Mecca.[132] The Police Code addressed public decency by stating that "whoever ventures into the streets uncovered [ghayr-i mastur]" would be imprisoned be-tween twenty-four hours and one month.[133] Public harassment of women in side streets and bazaars was also a punishable crime akin to public defamation. Catcallers should refrain from disrespecting "the reputation and honor" (*nam va namus*) of women, nor should they "express desire or love for them" or use "unseemly words." The Summary Code mentioned "severe punishments" for the crime but left out the details.[134]

Both codes had regulations for drunk and disorderly behavior, the use of illegal substances, and gambling in public spaces. A person who became drunk in the side streets and in the bazaars and caused disorder as a result would be imprisoned for four days to a month and fined between five thousand qirans and five tumans.[135] Someone causing "a ruckus in the side street like an insane person" by screaming and being disorderly would be imprisoned for forty-eight hours to ten days and fined between one qiran and five tumans.[136] A person caught smoking opium would be imprisoned for six months to a year.[137] Those who played cards or engaged in other kinds of gambling in side streets would be imprisoned for forty-eight hours to a month, and their money would be seized as a fine.[138] Gambling houses (*qumarkhanah*) were banned outright, and gambling in coffeehouses was similarly prohibited.[139] If people engaged in horse racing in the side streets and bazaars (presumably for gambling purposes), they would be imprisoned for between forty-eight hours and a month, and the horses would be kept in the royal stables.[140]

Among the most striking features of the Police Code was its deft employment of guarantorship as urban surveillance. Unlike *fiqh* texts, which generally employed guarantorship for a specific set of circumstances, such as posting bail or transferring financial liability, the Police Code envisioned this technique as a means of regulating crime in urban spaces (especially coffeehouses, restaurants, and hammams), regulating social relations between servants and employers and between craftsmen and guild masters, and ensuring that people reported potentially harmful situations to the police. This technique extended the reach of the police by enlisting ordinary people to pursue their goals through mandatory reporting and monitoring of suspicious activities.

The Police Code singled out coffeehouses, restaurants, and hammams as potential criminal public spaces and made their proprietors liable for neglect. If a person fought or caused a fight in a coffeehouse (*qahvahkhanah*), a restaurant (*chilupazkhanah*), or other places, they would be imprisoned and fined.[141] If the owner of the shop (*dukkan*) was negligent, meaning that they did not inform the police right away and

thus prolonged the fighting, then they too would be fined and imprisoned, and their shop would be closed.[142] A person fighting and screaming (ʿarbadah) in the hammam would also be imprisoned. If the owner of
the hammam entered the fight, then they would be fined one to five tumans, and the hammam would be closed for ten days.[143] With respect to
potential theft, the hammam proprietor was made responsible for the
customers' belongings and their guarantor (mas'ul va zamin); a witness
had to be present when the belongings were placed into safe keeping. If a
thief stole any belongings or if the clothing of the customers disappeared,
the proprietor was liable. Failure to follow this rule would lead to imprisonment for between twenty-four hours and fifteen days.[144]

Servants had certain responsibilities to their masters, just as workers and craftsmen did to their guild masters. Servants and craftsmen
were considered to be guarantors of their master's property in their absence. If a servant left the house of their master without their permission or failed to protect the property within their place of work, then
they would face between forty-eight hours and one month of imprisonment and a fine of one qiran to three tumans.[145] Workers and laborers
(kargar va ʿamalah) had a similar responsibility to their guild master: if
they destroyed property entrusted to them, then they would be imprisoned between forty-eight hours and a month and be held liable for the
value of the items broken or ruined.[146] A craftsman who destroyed tex-
tiles given to them to be sewn or produced something other than what
their clientele specified would be imprisoned for twenty-four hours to
one month and be held liable for the item's value or its replacement.[147]

Ordinary subjects were also expected to act responsibly with their
own belongings and toward one another, in addition to reporting suspicious activities to the authorities. If someone neglected their belongings, the police were not the belongings' "guarantors," although they
promised to look for the stolen items.[148] This implied that police action
and surveillance were an expression of the guarantorship for the safety
and security of property and people: a responsibility that everyone shared
to some extent. If, for instance, someone found an unaccompanied child
in the street, they would have to bring them to the police station or face
a day's imprisonment and a fine of one to thirty tumans.[149] Neighborhood residents who saw a drunk or criminal were also obligated to in-

form the guards (*mustahfizin*) of the Public Safety Administration (Amniyat).[150] Ordinary subjects were thus responsible for reporting suspicious activity but should avoid taking the law into their own hands.

Related to guarantorship, the Police Code established a procedure for registering the movements of subjects in and out of the city. The goal was to identify strangers in the city in case they committed a crime. Unlike Ottoman Egypt, the Qajars did not explicitly combine registration with guarantorship.[151] But similar to Ottoman Istanbul and to earlier Iranian reformist proposals, the code mentioned a register that was meant to monitor migrants through an internal passport system to enhance security.[152] If someone wanted to take a trip outside of Iran or was returning from a trip, they had to inform the police administration so that their name would be recorded in a register (*daftar*) or face a day's imprisonment and a fine of one to five tumans.[153] The same conditions and penalties applied to someone leaving Tehran for more than four months, upon departure and arrival.[154] Even within the confines of the city, a person needed police permission to leave their home at night. They could request a police guard for such nighttime movements, or they could be required to have a police pass (*bilit*) so as not to be detained.[155] Visitors to the city were to present themselves to the local commander (*sahib mansib*) at the city gate, state their purpose in coming to Tehran and the duration of their stay, and present a statement with their name, background, and reputation, which would be recorded in the police register.[156] Labor migrants who came to Tehran but neither were residents of the city nor had prior work arrangements had forty-eight hours to leave the city. If they failed to do so, they would be cuffed and imprisoned as if they were a thief or drunkard.[157] Foreigners to the city who had come for previously arranged work or trade would have to present themselves at the Public Safety Administration (Da'irah-i Amniyat), where their name would be recorded in a special "register of foreigners and residents of the city."[158] As important conduits of information about temporary residents in the city, caravanserai owners were also obligated to report the names of their guests to the police or be imprisoned one to five days and fined one to ten tumans.[159]

The Police Code was simultaneously a partial penal code that defined what types of crimes fell under the jurisdiction of the police and also provided specific punishments for each crime, drawing on concepts found in *fiqh*, advice literature, reformist literature, and previous codes. The Police Code also employed guarantorship and registry to surveil the urban landscape in ways that synthesized ideas from advice and reform literature with everyday practice in novel ways.

Amin al-Sultan's Administrative Manual

In 1887/88 (1305 H.), Mirza 'Ali Asghar Khan Amin al-Sultan prepared an administrative manual intended for general use across Iran. The timing of the document coincided with Amin al-Sultan's efforts to establish new provincial guidelines in the aftermath of Zill al-Sultan losing his wide-ranging governorship over the provinces of Fars, Burujird, 'Iraq, Khuzistan, Luristan, Kimanshahan, and Kurdistan.[160] Amin al-Sultan's administrative manual divided provincial governments into five administrations, one of which was the Administration for Public Morality (Ihtisabiyah). In his schema, the Ihtisabiyah also encompassed policing, which was connected to the idea of forbidding wrong as a form of moral policing. It likewise deployed guarantorship for local government officials and those who protected criminals.

Amin al-Sultan provided an expansive definition of the Ihtisabiyah that connoted policing, hygiene and cleaning, and market regulation. Its specific policing functions included looking "after the order of the city, neighborhoods, houses, and shops," "barring fighting and conflict," and "forbidding [*nahy*] all shari'ah and government/customarily ['*urfi*] prohibited acts [*munkarat*]."[161] Amin al-Sultan was unambiguous in connecting the duties of the Ihtisabiyah to forbidding wrong, while his inclusion of '*urf* connoted both custom and local government executive regulations.[162] The head of this department was called Ihtisab Aqasi, and the individuals working for this department were to be known as *muhtasibs*, who would wear distinct clothing and medals.[163] Amin al-Sultan envisioned the professionalization of *hisbah* functions. He argued that salaries for members of the Ihtisabiyah would negate the need for a *farrashbashi* (head attendant) because this informal and nonsalaried station had been "the cause of harm and injury to the people."[164]

Amin al-Sultan also considered guarantorship necessary to ensure effective policing. He defined "the duty of [local] government
[*hukumat*]" as including the establishment of regulations for safety in
the streets and the province more generally, as well as in the city according to "law and regulations." The intent here was stopping theft
and mischief since these impeded prosperity and caused ruin.[165] To
this end, Amin al-Sultan deployed guarantorship for the *kalantar*,
*kadkhuda*s, and other urban officials (*ma'murin-i baladiyah*): if any
theft or evildoing occurred, they would immediately arrange for the
punishment of the thief and the return of the stolen goods. If a governor accepted any bribe, gift, or intercession from individuals on behalf of a thief or criminal, they too would be punished. If the governor
was convicted of such an act, they could face "up to execution as a
punishment."[166] A similar guarantee was to be taken from the mounted
police (*qarasuran*) in the city: if they were found guilty of committing
murder, injuries, and/or theft, then they would be sought from their
guarantors (*multazimin*), presumably their commanding officers. If the
guarantors were lax in turning over the guilty person, then they would
be punished in their place, even if that meant lex talionis (*qisas*).[167] This
degree of being held liable as a guarantor, which strictly speaking con-
travened the bounds of *fiqh*, essentially justified punishing the guarantor
in place of the criminal.

Amin al-Sultan's administrative manual emphasized the shari'ah
language of forbidding wrong, *qisas*, and *ihtisab* while also keeping the
conventional terminology of *kadkhuda* and *kalantar* for urban policing
figures in the provinces. This may have reflected a further turn away
from the approach of the Police Code for the provinces while preserving many of its features, including the use of guarantorship, regulating
police behavior according to a code, surveilling public spaces for vice
and violence, and ensuring the punishment of crimes.

The Limits of Judicial Torture and Torture as Punishment

Between the 1840s and the 1880s, the use of judicial torture was periodically banned in Iran through *farman*s and administrative manuals.
In Nasir al-Din Shah's *farman*s on the matter, he conveyed a prevailing

belief about the interdependence of law, order, and punishment. While he granted governors discretionary power to punish criminals on his behalf, he made this contingent on them providing due process and relinquishing cruel and excessive forms of punishment, torture, and arbitrary executions. Echoing advice and reformist texts, the shah banned the governors' use of torture and insisted on having the final say in executions in a series of *farmans* and *dastur al-'amals*. Governors were limited to imprisoning and bastinadoing criminals until a final determination regarding a death sentence was made by the shah, since he considered execution to be an expression of sovereign authority alone. Since these texts were meant to be implemented, they constitute a crucial and underexplored dimension of the lawmaking process as it pertains to crime and punishment, complementing contemporary police and penal codes.

The earliest ban on torture appears to date from the reign of Muhammad Shah (r. 1834–48). Writing on his behalf, Prime Minister Hajji Mirza Aqasi issued a document in March/April 1846 (Rabi' al-Sani 1262 H.) banning (*qadaghan*) the governors' use of torture (*zajr va shikanjah*) in gathering evidence for crimes, especially in theft, murder, and engaging in immoral acts. The document argued that judicial torture was against the shari'ah and "the necessities of justice and fairness." Instead, admissible evidence had to be made up of documents (*asnad*) from the "claimant and petitioner" (*mudda'i va 'arzchi*). Governors were to act according to the shari'ah responsum (*fatva*) of a trustworthy 'alim, and investigations had to be fair and free of harassment. Any governor failing to follow this command would themselves be subject to the shah's punishment.[168]

During the early Nasiri era, the English and Russian embassies requested that the ban on torture be reinstated. Prime Minister Amir Kabir, in responding to this request, included Nasir al-Din Shah's *farman* regarding the matter. What is significant about this exchange is that the shah did not want to appear as if he were kowtowing to European powers. The overall thrust of the *farmans*, thus, was that governors were justified in the use of torture during the exceptionally unstable period marking Nasir al-Din Shah's consolidation of power but that this was only a temporary measure. The *farman* addressed to the governors was significantly framed as a response to subjects' complaints rather than being prompted by outside pressure.

In a *farman* banning torture, dated February 11, 1850 (28 Rabi' al-Avval 1266 H.), which was included by Amir Kabir in a letter responding to English and Russian representatives, the emphasis was on the shah's justice and the exceptional circumstances of gubernatorial torture. The shah voiced his dissatisfaction with governors who tortured anyone since it contradicted his justice. He did, however, claim that ruffians and evildoers in provinces such as Fars, Arak, Yazd, and Khurasan were causing disorder and destruction and plundering the merchants' property. If governors tortured in such a context, it was to prevent their "boldness and temerity." He added that since now the country's affairs were in order, he would issue a *farman* to the governors banning torture.[169] The Russian and English representatives were thrilled with this response and reinforced the idea that such a *farman* was in line with the shah's justice and was done of his own accord without foreign interference or the need for a pact with a foreign government.[170]

On March 10, 1850 (25 Rabi' al-Sani 1266 H.), Nasir al-Din Shah issued the promised *farman* to the governors banning torture, and it was framed as a response to subjects' "complaints that had been read before the shah." The *farman* specifically addressed the use of judicial torture for crimes or to reveal hidden property. This ban differed slightly from the Muhammad Shah–era *farman* insofar as it listed torture as against not just the shari'ah but also chivalry (*muruvvat*) and imperial opinion (*ra'i*). Only after having someone had their guilt "proven and authenticated" would they receive a shari'ah or government punishment. If a governor violated this *farman* by torturing someone, they would be subject to an unspecified punishment.[171]

With the establishment of an official government newspaper, *Vaqayi'-i Ittifaqiyah*, under Amir Kabir, official *farmans* were not only sent to the governors for implementation but also circulated through print culture. The earliest printed newspaper *farman* banning torture was dated September 10, 1851 (14 Zi Qi'dah 1267 H.). It referred to torture as a tradition (*rasm*) that had been "common" among governors and commanders (*zubbat*) in the provinces during previous shahs' eras. But now the shah had banned and abandoned the practice out of his own "natural inclination," considered it an "immoral act" (*fi'l-i shani'*), and promised harsh consequences for governors and commanders who disobeyed these ordinances.[172] This *farman* is striking for its acknowledgment that torture had been customary under previous shahs and for seeing it as a practice subject to change according to the shah's discretion rather than claiming that it violated the principles of justice or the shari'ah.

Most *farman*s up to this point appeared to refer to judicial torture rather than torture as punishment. By the mid-1850s, there were increasing references to the latter form of torture, which was seen as arbitrary, exceeding the nature of the crime, and carried out without sufficient evidence of guilt. This time the official newspaper acknowledged that criticisms of torture emanated from European circles. In 1854, the Qajar government responded to criticisms that it lacked due process and that cruel punishments were employed in an arbitrary manner. It considered the claim that government officials punished "an accused person without evidence" according to their own "whim" as a "baseless accusation"; instead, severe punishment (*siyasat*) was only carried out after guilt was established. The shah reaffirmed his commitment to stopping "people's sanctity [*hurmat*] being violated" and avoiding "the pain of torture."[173] The lingering criticisms about arbitrary, cruel, and excessive punishments alongside torture set the stage for later reforms that sought to centralize decision-making for punishments exceeding the bastinado and temporary imprisonment.

It was not until the tenure of the reformist prime minister Mirza Husayn Khan Mushir al-Dawlah Sipahsalar in 1871 that the shah issued another *farman* and authorized an administrative manual on the topic. These texts both banned the use of torture and granted the shah final say in executions. The shah issued the *farman* in response to a specific situation in Azerbaijan before universalizing the principles embodied therein in the form of an administrative manual for provincial governors. The final version of the latter text was likewise published in the official newspaper, *Ruznamah-i Iran*.[174] I'timad al-Saltanah, who described this administrative manual as a "just law [*qanun*]," provided further context for its composition. He stated that in the past, governors and government officials would "cut off ears and noses" and inflict other punishments of their choosing without special permission from the government. The shah was therefore moved to change the situation by insisting on proof of guilt, whether based on shariʿah or custom/government rulings (ʿurfan), which would then have to be sent to the shah as a petition. The shah, in turn, would issue a ruling, which would have to be implemented.[175]

The administrative manual invoked a shariʿah justification for the ban on every type of torture by stating that torture was "outside of shariʿah law [qanun]." The manual decried the "common practices" of some governors who would carry out "limitless punishments" for the slightest infraction. It acknowledged a level of arbitrariness insofar as sometimes "real criminals" would be released "without punishment," while "innocent people" would be "subject to an array of tortures."[176]

Both texts offered solutions that strikingly resembled principles found in both the Ottoman and Mughal Empires by giving the sovereign sole authority to make death sentence determinations. For instance, the Persian translation of the 1851 Ottoman Penal Code stated that all death sentences were the prerogative of the shah (originally the Ottoman sultan), irrespective of the convict's status. Close to three centuries earlier, the Mughal emperor Akbar issued a farman in 1588 that stated that prisoners condemned to capital punishment were to be sent to the imperial court rather than dealt with by provincial officials.[177] The Qajar administrative manual stated that governors were expected to prove the guilt of suspects and obtain special imperial dispensation to carry out "lex talionis and execution" (qisas va siyasat). This was mandatory notwithstanding a criminal's social status (tabaqah) and the nature of their crime, which could be murder or "violating property and honor [namus]." Finally, the local government could at most imprison a suspect, report the matter to the Ministry of Justice (Vizarat-i ʿAdliyah), which would in turn petition the shah about it, and wait for a ruling about the appropriate punishments, which would then be implemented. The administrative manual expressed an awareness of a potential objection from the provinces: on the surface, this imperial decree appeared to reduce "the power and strength of the local government [hukumat]," but it promised that, if implemented correctly, it would only increase the local government's power. As usual, the administrative manual also promised necessary punishments for whoever violated these "firm commands."[178]

Mustawfi al-Mamalik's later administrative manual for the provinces reiterated many of the same principles. It specifically outlawed torture and extractive fines by governors while employing civilizational discourse: "Branding [dagh], torture, disfigurement [nasaq], and extractive fines [tarjuman] are barbaric acts that must be completely abandoned. The criminal must be imprisoned and sent to Tehran for punishment."[179] The parallels with India are once again quite striking; disfigurement there was also characterized as a barbaric act in the eighteenth century.[180] The Iranian semiofficial provincial press was also aware of contemporary Indian press charges of barbarism and disorder. The multilingual Indian newspaper *Mufarrih al-Qulub* ran a story in October 1872 claiming that Fars was in complete disorder, with bandits and troublemakers running rampant. The semiofficial Persian and Arabic provincial newspaper *Al-Muntabi'ah Fi al-Fars* refuted this by claiming that the governor of Fars, Zill al-Sultan, had restored order to the region. More poignantly, it used crime statistics published in the Indian newspaper to argue that there were more murders in Indian cities like Madras and Bombay and in European cities than there were in Fars province, which was supposedly very safe.[181]

Despite these general bans, the shah continually sent *farman*s to his governors, curtailing the use of excessive punishment in subsequent years. In a telegram sent by Prime Minister Mustawfi al-Mamalik to I'tizad al-Mulk on October 30, 1881 (6 Zi Hijjah 1298 H.), he mentioned that the shah had delivered a ruling in which governors were no longer to carry out "severe punishments such as dismemberment and wounds." The shah had ordered governors to desist from "implementing such rulings"; instead, they were only to use imprisonment and limited bastinado as punishments for criminals. If the criminal was guilty of "a severe crime," then they should be imprisoned until further notice.[182]

On June 6, 1885 (22 Sha'ban 1302 H.), the shah sent a telegraphic *farman* to Asif al-Dawlah, the governor of Khurasan, complaining about the "unusual punishment" carried out by Saham al-Dawlah, the governor of Bujnurd. Saham al-Dawlah had apparently punished individuals "by cutting off their beards and throwing them off roofs." The shah expressed "confusion and perplexity" that Saham al-Dawlah would do such things as a supposedly "rational, upright, and well-mannered person." The shah stated that "for years" such "illegal actions" had been "annulled and abandoned," a reference to his previous bans. He reiterated that the most a governor could do to a "guilty person" was "bastinado and imprison them." The shah asked Asif al-Dawlah to compel Saham al-Dawlah to summon the people that he had punished in this manner, apologize to them, and compensate them for his disgraceful actions. The shah further demanded that Asif al-Dawlah extract "strict guarantees" (*iltizamat-i sakht*) from the other governors in his province, promising not to engage in similar "uncustomary" and "immoral" punishments.[183]

Despite nearly half a century of the central government's efforts to limit the use of torture and gubernatorial punishments in excess of imprisonment and bastinado, provincial governors and their officials repeatedly employed torture to extract confessions and inflict punishments. The shah's *farman*s and administrative manuals were also meant to monopolize the imperial court's say in matters of life or death, even in *qisas* cases, in which heirs theoretically made this decision. The effort to curtail torture constituted a double move: first, to bring punishments in line with *fiqh* and mirrors for princes ideals; and second, to follow emerging international legal norms banning torture. Tellingly, none of the documents surveyed here stated that the shah could not employ torture. Sovereignty, after all, entailed not just lawful but also arbitrary violence.

Non-Muslim Rights and Protections in Imperial Decrees and Manuals

Assef Ashraf has convincingly argued that *farman*s were usually a response to local petitions, complaints, reports, and/or foreign consular intervention.[184] *Farman*s, and by extension, administrative manuals, were therefore not so much diktats but instead the product of a give-and-take process between subjects and the government. Non-Muslims in Iran availed themselves of this form of redress, since the shah's justice was theoretically universal. Qajar *farman*s and administrative-legal documents specified that local governments were responsible for punishing those who mistreated non-Muslims. While *farman*s and administrative manuals reflected the legal authority of the shah, they also invoked the shari'ah alongside *'urf* in justifying their content. In many of these documents, there was a concern with preserving the sanctity of non-Muslims, which meant preserving their lives, property, and honor.

The *farman*s of Fath 'Ali Shah and Muhammad Shah in the 1830s and 1840s reaffirmed Safavid-era principles of granting Armenians of New Julfa near Isfahan a measure of legal autonomy. Since the eighteenth century, Julfan Armenians had been allowed to apply their own laws, embodied in the eighteenth-century Astrakhan code, in civil, commercial, and even certain criminal matters.[185] The Qajars continued to allow this practice in their *farman*s and even tried to universalize it. In 1832 (1248 H.), Fath 'Ali Shah issued a *farman* to the governors of Isfahan and the surrounding areas, commanding them to show respect to the Armenian grand pope (Khalifah-i A'zam) of the Vank Church and to all Iranian Armenians. The shah ordered government officials to refer all cases (*da'avi*) between Armenians to the people and priesthood (*kashish*) of the Armenians.[186] On May 2, 1840 (29 Safar 1256 H.), Muhammad Shah issued a *farman* in Isfahan regarding the legal status of Iranian Armenian Christians. Invoking Safavid precedents, Muhammad Shah claimed that he was putting "into execution the regulations that the kings our predecessors Shah Abbas Shah Sefi and Shah Sultan Hussein ordained." He granted the Christians the ability to "follow the laws and precepts of their religion."[187] This relative autonomy was conditional on them "conforming . . . their conduct upon all occasions to the authority and laws of the realm."[188] Speaking more directly to issues of crime, Muhammad Shah discussed the public punishment of those who harassed Christian subjects by stating, "Every individual who interrupts the free exercise of their worship or molests them by ill treatment shall be liable to exemplary chastisement." The *farman* ended by stating that the local governors, *biglarbigi*s, and other important local officials would be notified of this edict and commanded to obey it.[189]

While these early *farman*s addressed Armenian Christians specifically, an early Nasiri-era *farman* recognized the rights of all non-

Muslims. On June 23, 1857 (1 Zi Qiʿdah 1273 H.), Nasir al-Din Shah issued a *farman* in the official newspaper *Vaqayiʿ-i Ittifaqiyah* that guaranteed the legal equality of non-Muslim subjects.[190] The timing of the *farman* suggests that it was probably less of a response to local events than to regional and international ones: the second Ottoman imperial rescript of the Tanzimat, the Reform Imperial Rescript (Islâhat Hatt-ı Hümâyûnu) of 1856, had just been issued, which went even further than its 1839 predecessor in guaranteeing equal rights to non-Muslim subjects, especially in administering justice.[191] Like the Ottoman Tanzimat imperial rescripts, the shah's *farman* should not merely be understood as the result of European influence and pressure.[192] What was particularly striking about Nasir al-Din Shah's *farman* was that it invoked the notion of "equality" (*musavat*), which was commonly employed in advice texts discussing the equality of all subjects before the sovereign. The text stated that in Iran, "every sect and religion [*milal va mazahib*] enjoys equality, and there should not be a difference in bringing about that which ensures the safety and repose of all of the imperial subjects, whether they be Muslim Shiʿis or Jewish, Christian, Zoroastrian, or other religions and sects." The *farman* also referred to the shariʿah, especially the *zimmi* pact, alongside customary forms of authority: it asked subjects to "behave toward them [non-Muslims] in accordance with the laws taken as a pact [*muʿahid*] in the shariʿah and custom/executive authority [*ʿurf*] and follow good lines of conduct and not act against the law or violate one another's sanctity [*hurmat*]."[193]

The same 1857 *farman* explicitly stated that transgressions against non-Muslims would result in harsh punishments. It reiterated that "the ruffians, riffraff, and Muslim children [*atfal-i muslimin*] of Tehran and the other regions" should refrain from "harassing and acting against the sanctity of all religions and sects."[194] Using a similar logic to guarantorship, the *farman* asked the kin (*ʿaqilah*) and parents of such people to stop their children from engaging in illegal acts.[195] Failing that, the *farman* warned that the governor, steward (*pishkar*), *kalantar*, and *kadkhuda*s of Tehran and the provinces "would punish and chastise the ruffians, riffraff, and kin of children to such a degree that they would never bother and harass imperial subjects ever again." Nasir al-Din Shah's threat of punishment bordered on collective reprisals similar to the tactics used for deserters in the Military Code. The *farman* ended by stressing the need to act lawfully and with the utmost humanity (*insaniyat*) toward all in order to encourage trade and prosperity, a possible nod to Mirza Malkam Khan's ideas.[196]

Despite this *farman*'s universal scope, non-Muslim populations continued to face inequitable situations, prompting them to send petitions to the central government. In the province of Azerbaijan, the complaints of Christian Armenians from Urumiyah and Salmas were compiled in the form of a report by the minister of foreign affairs, Mirza Sa'id Khan Ansari.[197] The petition was possibly written in the early to mid-1860s, given that the administrative manual prepared in response to it was composed in 1864. While the report covered a wide range of complaints, crime and exploitation were prominent themes. The Armenians complained about how twenty-four women in the past several years had been violently kidnapped and taken to the house of local leaders.[198] The local headman (*aqa*) was accused of sexual transgressions against Christian daughters, children, and wives. Even if girls escaped from their kidnappers and returned home, their sexual honor (*abiru*) would be irreparably damaged.[199] Ruffians were seen as equally violent and exploitative toward Christian women. The complaint mentioned how ruffians kidnapped Christian girls, either "because of their beauty" or in order to gain "power and wealth," presumably by selling or ransoming them. These ruffians would compel the girls to convert to Islam and, failing that, forcibly drag them to the 'ulama, at whose court they would marry them. The Armenian petitioners requested that this practice be banned.[200] Women were exploited in other ways as well. When Christian men left for Russia, presumably for work, their wives would be taken for labor purposes.[201] In cases of conflict between two Christians, the local headman would take the opportunity to extract approximately ten tumans from the two sides. If they refused to pay, he would punish them with the bastinado.[202]

In response to this report, the shah had an administrative manual prepared for the governor of Urumiyah on April 12, 1864 (Zi Qi'dah 1280 H.).[203] In 1871/72, the 'ulama and local leaders (*umara*) signed a version of the text, thus endorsing its contents.[204] The administrative manual, which was also referred to as a "regulation" (*qarardad*), took the form of a numbered code.[205] The first and second articles laid out the right of the Christians to present their petitions and complaints and to be treated with respect: those who refused to grant them their rights, especially from among the government officials, would be subject to punishment. The third article suggested the logic of the second: Christians were not to ask foreign governments to mediate (*tavasut*) on their behalf with the government; instead, they should petition the Iranian government directly.[206] Throughout the Qajar era, the government wanted non-Muslims to avoid using foreign consulates as a mediator or protector; by channeling all complaints to the government directly, it hoped to avoid European involvement in the local legal process.[207]

The administrative manual likewise addressed sexual violations, apostasy in cases of genuine conversion, and extortion by people in positions of authority. It stated that if ruffians acted illegally and treacherously toward Christians or kidnapped their girls and wives, they would be subject to a government reckoning and severe punishment.[208] If an Armenian converted to Islam, then they would have to be registered (*sabt*) with full name and details in an imperial register (*daftar-i 'alijah*), apparently to ensure that the conversion was sincere and not made under duress.[209] Once the person's conversion was authenticated, however, they would receive a *hadd* punishment if they reverted to Christianity.[210] Significantly, only in the case of apostasy from Islam did the manual refer to a *hadd* punishment; otherwise, punishments were referred to as *tanbih* or *siyasat*. Finally, the manual addressed the issue of conflicts between two Christian subjects by "strongly forbidding" (*qadaghan-i akid*) the landlords (*mallaks*), *aqas*, and *zabits* from using conflicts between subjects as an excuse to extract money from the parties.[211]

As Nasir al-Din Shah traveled abroad, there were further attempts at ensuring the rights of non-Muslims. In the undated *Qanun-i Hukumat-i Iran*, possibly composed in the 1870s, the Ministry of Foreign Affairs was tasked with ensuring the safety of Jews and Armenians from harassment. The ministry was responsible for monitoring cases of non-Muslims being detained, "administering justice" (*ihqaq-i huquq*), and blocking all manner of "morally corrupt" (*mafasid*) behavior toward them.[212] During Nasir al-Din Shah's travels in Europe, he again addressed the issue of equality between Muslims and non-Muslims. In 1873, Malkam Khan wrote on behalf of the shah to the Anglo-Jewish Association, arguing that the shah did not want distinctions based on "classes" (meaning status groups, including religious ones) and that he was a proponent of religious freedom.[213] Mustawfi al-Mamalik's 1873 administrative manual discussed the status of non-Muslims, both domestic and foreign, by stating that different religious communities were under the shah's protection (*himayat*).[214]

In an editorial piece published in the Isfahan newspaper *Farhang* in the mid-1880s, the editors claimed that the legal position of non-Muslims was quite favorable in Iran when compared to the poor treatment of non-Christians in European countries. Claiming that such prejudice did not exist in Iran, it cited the fact that non-Muslims could use the Divankhanah-i 'Adliyah or the shari'ah court (*mahzar*) for their cases and conflicts. The piece then argued that foreign missionaries had introduced sectarian divisions in the country by trying to force their own laws. *Farhang* stated that Islamic law and justice did not prevent non-Muslims from progressing and being free, except for new groups (*tava'if*) such as Babis, whose rights could not be guaranteed by the shari'ah (*mashru'iyat*). It compared the status of Babis to that of socialists in Europe, suggesting that they were political enemies.[215] Taken together, the Qajar approach to non-Muslim communities in official documents was for the government to present itself as their guardians, recognize some form of equal protection, and guarantee a minimal standard of safety.

Sanctuary Regulations and the Cessation of Punishments

*Farman*s, administrative manuals, and codes assumed that the government was responsible for surveilling public crimes, established set punishments, limited the use of torture and execution, and protected non-Muslims against extortion and arbitrary violence. But the practice of taking refuge at sanctuaries seriously limited the government's ability to capture and punish criminals, since violence was forbidden within such spaces. Sanctuaries operated as a liminal space: on one level, they were "private" like the home and enjoyed many of the same protections from violation and invasion; on another level, they were profoundly "public," visible spaces open to all who sought their shelter. Although sanctuaries functioned as spatialized arenas of redress and places of political protest, their common use by people accused of crimes became particularly problematic for a government that was trying to uphold a notion of equal application of the law across all territories under its domination.

The precise origin of criminals taking asylum at sanctuaries is difficult to discern since this was a widespread practice in Zoroastrian, Jewish, Christian (especially Catholic), and Islamic societies.[216] Beyond mainstream religions, anthropologists have also often noted similar sanctuary practices in settled agrarian villages and among nomadic peoples.[217] The justification for sanctuary in Islam rests at the intersection of a series of practices, such as safeguarding someone and granting them protection (*himayah, aman, ijarah*), intercession (*shafa'at, tavasut*), and the sanctity of the holy precincts (*haram*), the archetype of which is Mecca and, to a lesser extent, Medina.[218] The sanctuary was a space in which carrying out punishments was suspended. Generally, violence was prohibited in the sanctuary, not only toward humans but even toward animals and plants. Violence constituted a polluting force that was taboo in a sacred space. Sanctuaries were, therefore, exceptional legal spaces that created an uneven legal geography.

What constituted a sanctuary in nineteenth-century Iran varied greatly. The most common and inviolable sanctuaries were shrines, particularly those of Imams or Imamzadahs, mosques, and, to a lesser extent, the homes of religious notables. Other sanctuaries were tied to the charismatic authority of the shah: palaces, royal stables, and even telegraph offices, which were entrusted to royal princes and fed the royal court sensitive information from the provinces. As Iran joined modern international diplomacy, consulates and embassies likewise served as sanctuaries because of the principle of extraterritoriality.[219]

Government efforts at applying the law consistently across space invariably paralleled attempts to either abolish or regulate the use of sanctuaries by criminals. The famous Italian eighteenth-century penal theorist Cesare Beccaria captured the thrust of these efforts well when he stated,

> Within a country's borders there should be no place which is outside the law. Its power should follow every citizen like a shadow. Impunity and asylum differ only in degree, and since the certainty of punishment makes more of an impression than its harshness, asylums invite men to commit crimes more than punishments deter them from them. To increase the number of asylums is to create so many little sovereign states, because where the law does not run, there new laws can be framed opposed to the common ones and there can arise a spirit opposed to that of the whole body of society.[220]

For similar reasons, Amir Kabir sought to abolish the practice of *bast* in cities like Tehran and Tabriz, with varying success.[221] He similarly protested European diplomatic protection of people pursued by Iranian authorities as a violation of local sovereignty.[222] While the reasons for Amir Kabir's eventual downfall are complex and multifaceted, an immediate trigger was his supposed violation of the sanctuary. In the Qajar court chronicle's account of his final year in office, Amir Kabir boasted, "It was I who destroyed the rebels of the court and left no place as a sanctuary and refuge [*malja va panah*] [for them] in [all of] Iran."[223] Upon hearing this, Nasir al-Din Shah became upset and launched into a tirade, telling him that removing all sanctuaries in Iran was "the greatest treachery" he had done "to both religion and government."[224]

Nasir al-Din Shah defended the use of sanctuaries as a spatialized form of redress for the wronged. At the religious level, the shah considered Amir Kabir to have held the ʿulama, who were the trustees of the Prophet, and their refugees in contempt by violating the right of sanctuary. He further stated that "from the earliest of times," people were aware of the "custom of sanctuary," in which they could go to a safe haven until government trustees could address their issue with justice.[225] In cases in which the shah had undertaken a voyage and there was no "threshold of an Imam or house of a hero" where "fearful people" could take refuge, then competent ministers and wise men of the court decided that the shah's stables would function as sanctuaries. The shah spelled out why royal stables were sanctuaries: it was to avoid fearful people from going to a foreign land, perhaps a veiled reference to the contemporary context of people seeking sanctuary at foreign legations and embassies or fleeing Iran altogether. From the sanctuary, the person could "wait to find an intercessor." Similarly, he gave the example of someone who had committed a sin at a military camp who could safely take refuge at the royal stables if he feared for his life, alluding to greater misfortune that could occur if they were denied: "it is not unlikely that a man no longer fearing death will undertake a bold endeavor and cause great injury such that reason is incapable of understanding it." The shah counseled Amir Kabir to take heed of this "wisdom of great men."[226] After this heated exchange, the head dragoman of the Russian legation suggested that Amir Kabir take sanctuary "under the dome of an Imamzadah or at a noble threshold" until such time as the shah calmed down and forgave him, but Amir Kabir responded that he had so alienated everyone that "today no one has the power to intercede on [his] behalf, . . . nor could he go to anyone for intercession."[227] Shortly thereafter, Amir Kabir was assassinated in Fin, close to Kashan, ironically having dismantled the very institution that may have protected him from the shah's wrath.[228]

Despite the pretext on which the shah removed Amir Kabir from office, he was subsequently concerned with preventing criminal asylum in sanctuaries. In 1852, he issued a *farman* in which only the Shah 'Abd al-'Azim Shrine near Tehran and the Ma'sumah Shrine in Qum were recognized as sanctuaries for "the oppressed and afflicted." The *farman* excluded evildoers (*ashrar*), troublemakers (*mufsidin*), criminals (*muqassirin*), and murderers from taking refuge. The only legitimate refugees were those "seeking justice" (*mazalim*); the central government would investigate their grievances and ensure justice was done.[229] More elaborate bans on criminal asylum emanated from the provinces before being adopted countrywide. In 1854, Mu'ayyad al-Dawlah, the governor of Shiraz, banned the use of city shrines for illegitimate asylum. Using guarantorship, he first made shrine servants promise to block "thieves, murderers, troublemakers, and corrupt government officials" from entering their shrines. His argument for the ban expressed a spatial logic in which justice was to apply uniformly: "The sanctuary [*bast*] was intended for a wronged person who was unable to find someone to deliver justice to them. Now, praise be to God, justice and equity [may be found] everywhere as it pertains to the rights of the wronged ones, so there is no need for people to take refuge in the holy precincts or elsewhere."[230] His argument mirrors those made in early modern Europe for dismantling criminal asylum in sanctuaries on the grounds that equality before the law, universal rights, and due process ensured justice and thus rendered sanctuaries redundant.[231] Four years later, in 1858, the administrative manual of the Ministry of Justice (Divankhanah-i ʿAdliyah) reiterated these limits on sanctuary practices. It stated that *bast* was banned in Tehran and in other lands, with the exception of special places listed in a previous *farman*, a possible reference to the shah's 1852 *farman*.[232]

Despite the previous efforts of the governor of Shiraz to curb the use of sanctuary by criminals, the practice continued unabated for nearly seven years. In April/May 1861 (Shaval 1277 H.), Asadullah, a government official in the service of Muʾayyad al-Dawlah, produced a report based on a gathering of certain notables, ʿulama, and relevant parties, who produced a series of regulations for the use of sanctuaries in Shiraz.[233] In September of the same year, the report was reproduced almost verbatim for the reading public. Muʾayyad al-Dawlah turned this into a regulation (*qarardad*). The shah not only approved it but made it a part of the administrative manual for other provinces. The shah obtained the endorsement of certain ʿulama, notables (*aʿazim*), and other "affected parties" in the form of a signed guarantor document. The agreement consisted of four main articles, two of which were directly relevant to crime. The third clause stated that murderers and thieves should "absolutely" be barred from the sanctuary. If they were given such entrance, it was the responsibility of the shrine guardian to detain them and turn them over to authorities to face a "ruling in line with the shariʿah" and "punishment commensurate with their actions." This marked a unique shift by making shrine guardians responsible for policing and imprisoning suspected criminals. The fourth article placed a further restriction: in order to avoid the ballooning of sanctuary spaces, it limited the sanctuary's borders to the Shah Chiragh Shrine, the Sayyid Mir Muhammad Shrine, and the Masjid-i Naw Mosque, while excluding the madrasahs, shops, and bazaars in its environs.[234]

By 1863, the government issued another regulation specifically for the Shah 'Abd al-'Azim Shrine, since there was a growing concern about a decrease in the "order provided by shari'ah rules." The drafting of this document included a consultative body (*majlis-i shura*) and two members of the local 'ulama, one of whom stated that this document would "strengthen God's commandments" and ensure "the implementation of *hudud* punishments." The text of the document said that three categories of criminals—murderers, thieves, and violators of "chastity and honor" (*'ismat va namus*)—should be barred from the sanctuary and not be protected. If they entered the sanctuary, the shrine guardian should hold them there as prisoners, without molesting or torturing them, for a period of three months. In the case of murderers, a shari'ah trial would determine whether the heirs of the murdered were entitled to *qisas* or compensation. In cases of theft or rape, there should similarly be a determination as to whether the *hudud* punishments applied. If the suspects proved their innocence through appropriate legal documentation, they were to be released immediately.[235] This version of the ban was almost exclusively framed in relation to shari'ah crimes and the necessity of carrying out *hudud* and *qisas* as part of God's commandments, in marked contrast to similar earlier documents. The timing of this shift roughly coincided with the drafting of the Military Code and the administrative manual for the Armenians of Azerbaijan, both of which tended to draw more firmly on shari'ah terminology of *hudud* and *qisas* and avoided explicitly reformist language common in the 1850s and 1870s.

In a slightly different version of a similar *farman* dating from 1865/66 (1282 H.), criminals and especially murderers were referred to by the terms "oppressor" (*zalim*) and "traitor" (*kha'in*). The *farman* stated that the heirs to the murdered would have to prove their case at the court of the 'ulama. If successful, the heirs would have the right to drag the murderer out of the sanctuary to carry out *qisas* on them.[236] If the murdered individual had no heirs, then the murderer could be convicted as a traitor and punished accordingly, meaning that the government would act as the heir's surrogate and punish the murderer because they con-stituted a threat to public security.[237] The *farman* claimed that shari'ah judges viewed the implementation of a shari'ah ruling as taking precedence over respect (*ihtiramat*) for those who had committed a crime against either the people or the government in asylum. The *farman* claimed that previous inauspicious sovereigns had dragged people out of the shrine with violence, but during Nasir al-Din Shah's reign, the governor of Tehran would have six attendants and cavalry guard the shrine and block the criminals from escaping, in addition to having their property and house seized and their families detained until such time as they came out. Otherwise, they could stay there until they died.[238]

In both of Mustawfi al-Mamalik's administrative manuals, dated 1873 and 1876, the issue of sanctuary was framed alongside the principle of equality before the law. It stated that asylum had caused disorder because thieves, evildoers, and murderers had abused it. Thus, the prac-tice was banned (*mawquf*), and governors were to avoid allowing sanc-tuaries to be invested with such authority that murderers and criminals could not be pursued there. Echoing the idea of the law applying to everyone, the text stated that "God's ordinance" was "the due of every-one who deserved it."[239]

Conclusion

Official government documents on policing, punishments, protecting non-Muslims from crimes, and sanctuary regulations drew from the conceptual vocabulary of *fiqh*, advice literature, and reformist texts. These official documents were concerned with policing public vice, at times through an invocation of Islamic notions of *hisbah*, Iranian and Turco-Mongolian functions of urban military-police officials, and mod-ern policing reforms. These documents often made private/public dis-tinctions in considering lewdness, drunkenness, gambling, and the like in the streets and other public spaces as crimes worthy of surveillance, detention, and punishment, while sins hidden from plain sight were be-yond their scope. Guarantorship amplified the surveillance capacity of government officials since it also made ordinary subjects responsible for the property, safety, and criminal acts of others. Government-sanctioned punishments generally moved away from corporal punishment and spectacles of punishment toward imprisonment, fines, hard labor, and, for the most egregious crimes, swift executions. Governors were also banned from using judicial torture and excessive punishments. Implicit in many official laws was the assumption that circumstantial evidence was admissible; unlike *fiqh*, which set the evidentiary bar for conviction quite high, codes tended to speak of degrees of guilt and implied probabilities rather than certainties, which perhaps explains why individuals were often found guilty of crimes for which there were few or no witnesses.

Since Qajar shahs viewed themselves as the protectors of recognized non-Muslim populations, *farmans* and administrative manuals, often written in response to petitions, charted out the limits of extortion, depredation, and humiliation directed toward them. By the middle of the nineteenth century, the Ministry of Foreign Affairs increasingly became responsible for legal matters affecting *zimmi* populations as opposed to local governors, signaling an attempted jurisdictional shift in authority. While new laws were meant to apply uniformly throughout Iran, asylum practices were a major barrier to this objective. The sanctuary's unique spatial configuration within prevailing understandings of public and private, especially in urban contexts, made it difficult for the authorities to violently remove criminals from the sanctuary, since it was both inviolable like a private domicile and also a public space. The Qajar approach to dismantling the criminal use of sanctuary was to limit its borders, reduce the number of spaces considered to be genuine sanctuaries, and instruct shrine guardians to prevent criminals from entering or leaving the shrine until the proper authorities arrived, although these efforts faced challenges in practice as well.

Violence, Lawmaking, and Law Maintenance in Isfahan, "The Abode of Sovereignty"

ccording to David Graeber, "in its minimal sense, sovereignty is simply the recognition of the right to exercise violence with impunity."[1] In Qajar Iran, individuals who engaged in violence outside of the sovereign's will sometimes declared war on the sovereign and made a competing claim to sovereignty, which involved spectacular displays of violence. Speaking of this phenomenon, Walter Benjamin argues that the lawmaking violence of the "great criminal . . . confronts the law with the threat of declaring a new law."[2] Sovereignty in the making mirrored an emerging state: extortion rackets paralleled taxation, while torture and murder paralleled legal interrogations and executions insofar as these actions relied on either violence or the threat of violence.[3] In early- to mid-nineteenth-century Isfahan, settled tribesmen, ruffians (*lutis*), the 'ulama, and urban notables made competing claims to sovereignty through such violence.

This chapter begins by considering shari'ah rulings made in homicide cases heard at the court of the Shi'i jurist Muhammad Baqir Shafti. Shafti's rulings imagined God as the ultimate sovereign, the 'ulama as the shari'ah's interpreters, and the victims' heirs as the decision-makers in life and death, with little to no reference to government authorities. It then examines what Benjamin describes as "lawmaking" sovereignty through the use of violence in three separate instances illustrating the intimate connection between juridical sovereignty and violent punishments in Isfahan: the Hashim Khan Bakhtiyari incident of 1824–25, the crisis of succession after the death of Fath 'Ali Shah in 1834, and, finally, the disorder of 1839, which led to Muhammad Shah's march on and occupation of the city.[4] Next, the chapter shifts emphasis to law-maintaining violence in the aftermath of challenges to authority. Persian primary sources allow us to understand how local governments maintained legal authority both through violence (as per Benjamin's definition) and through nonviolent means (such as adjudication, arbitration, and reconciliation) during the reigns of two governors of the 1840s and 1850s, Manuchihr Khan Mu'tamid al-Dawlah and Chiragh 'Ali Zanganah.[5] They both began their respective governorships by similarly entering Isfahan during a period of relative disorder before reestablishing Qajar authority through the capture, banishment, and punishment of oppositional figures and the destruction of spaces associated with them. Both closely monitored conflicts, crimes, and disputes in the city and developed alternative nonviolent techniques for conflict resolution that often involved the 'ulama and even ordinary subjects in community policing. By foregrounding space in studying the operation of law in Qajar Isfahan, I argue in this chapter that the lines between arbitrary violence and punishment, the licit and illicit, and the legal and extralegal shifted according to novel socio-spatial configurations in a manner that has deeper implications for the writing of urban legal histories of the Middle East more broadly.

A Jurist's Rulings on Homicide Cases

The prominent early nineteenth-century jurist Muhammad Baqir Shafti issued several rulings on homicide cases at his shari'ah court in Isfahan. While we know of jurists issuing similar rulings from chronicles and government reports, Shafti was unique in keeping records of some of these rulings over the course of the 1810s and 1820s in his collection of responsa (*fatavi*) titled *Question and Answer (Su'al va Javab)*.[6] Portions of this book were published in 1831 (1247 H.), which perhaps constitutes the first printed "practical manual for believers" (*risalah-i 'amaliyah*) in Iran, although it excluded the rulings on homicide cases.[7] The longer manuscript version of his responsa included cases in which Shafti provided either guidance or issued a death sentence (*hukm-i qatl*) for homicide cases.[8] Unlike most works of Shi'i jurisprudence, these texts provide a much-needed glimpse into how *fiqh* theory and practice came together in actual cases, the ritual dimensions necessary for *qisas*, the decision-making authority of the heirs of the murdered individual, and the limited role envisioned for the government.

Shafti ruled on two cases that did not entail a death sentence. In an undated case, Shafti ruled Karbala'i 'Ali's murder of Karbala'i Rahim to be an accidental homicide (*qatl-i khata*). His ruling was based on eyewitness testimony in addition to other circumstantial evidence (*qara'in*). He set compensation (*diyah*) at 10,000 dirhams, the equivalent of 328 tumans and 1,250 dinars, which would be paid by the agnate clan (*'aqilah*), the male members of the murderer's family (brothers, nephews, uncles, and cousins). The rest of the document discusses how the *diyah* should be apportioned.[9] In another document, dated June 3, 1816 (6 Rajab 1231 H.), Shafti ruled the incident to be manslaughter (*qatl-i laws*).[10] Hasan, the son of Yusuf Kupa'i, died as a result of injuries inflicted on him by Muhammad Khan. Before he died, several people witnessed him saying repeatedly that Muhammad Khan had injured him. A large group also witnessed Muhammad Khan confessing to having injured Hasan. These individuals wrote their testimonies, sent them to Shafti, and awaited his ruling. In his response, Shafti ruled that "the justness of written testimony" (*'adalat-i shahadat*) was not proven (*sabit*) since it was not given in his presence, although it established "strong suspicion" (*mazinnah-i qavi*) that Muhammad Khan was the murderer. He then laid out the next steps: in order to prove a manslaughter case, an oath procedure (*qasamah*) would have to be initiated, after which the family of the slain man could choose to carry out *qisas*.[11]

The remaining three cases included Shafti's death sentences. In the first case, Shafti began with the following Quranic quotation that granted heirs the authority to choose *qisas*: "And whoever is killed wrongfully,

We have given his heir the authority."[12] 'Ali Mardan, the son of Hasan Mardashti, confessed (i'tiraf) that on the fifth of Ramazan, he set out for Shiraz from his village of Mi'yan. Between that village and the village of Qumshah, he encountered Mahdi Sa'idabadi, at which point, he stated in his confession, "In summary, insolence overcame me, and I took his pony and struck him with a club. He fell back on his head, and blood started pouring out. I opened his belt or underwear string and bound his hands with them. I threw him in that place." After listing the children of the murdered man, Shafti laid out the conditions for the payment of the diyah, which must be the equivalent of ten thousand dirhams. If the heirs chose qisas, then they had to ritually wash (ghusl) the murderer three times. Then the man was to be wrapped in a shroud before being struck with a single sword blow to the neck. After the heirs reattached the head to the body, they would recite the prayer for the dead and then bury the corpse. The paternal uncles of the murdered man had to deputize one person to carry out the execution. Shafti added that since it was "a hot season" (fasl-i hararat-i hava), they should avoid executing him in the middle of the day; instead, it should be carried out at the beginning or end of the day.[13]

The second case leading to a death sentence occurred on February 10, 1821 (7 Jumada al-Avval 1236 H.), when a group of people, including 'Ali Riza, killed Mullah Hasan (figure 9). 'Ali Riza was convicted through an oath procedure that was initiated by Mullah Hasan's brother and two sisters in the presence of Shafti. Shafti ruled that should the heirs choose qisas, they were to be assisted by Isfahan's biglarbigi to ensure that no one would prevent it from being carried out. Shafti laid out the ritual requirements of ritually washing the murderer with water mixed with lotus leaves (sidrah), camphor (kafur), and then pure water, wrapping him in a burial shroud, striking him with a single blow to the neck, reattaching his head to his body, wrapping him once more in a burial shroud, reciting the ritual prayer for him, and finally, burying him. The heir could deputize someone to carry out the execution, but this person would have "to express their intention to be a deputy during the execution." Since it was "a cold season" (fasl-i burudat), qisas would have to take place during the middle of the day, when the weather was warm.

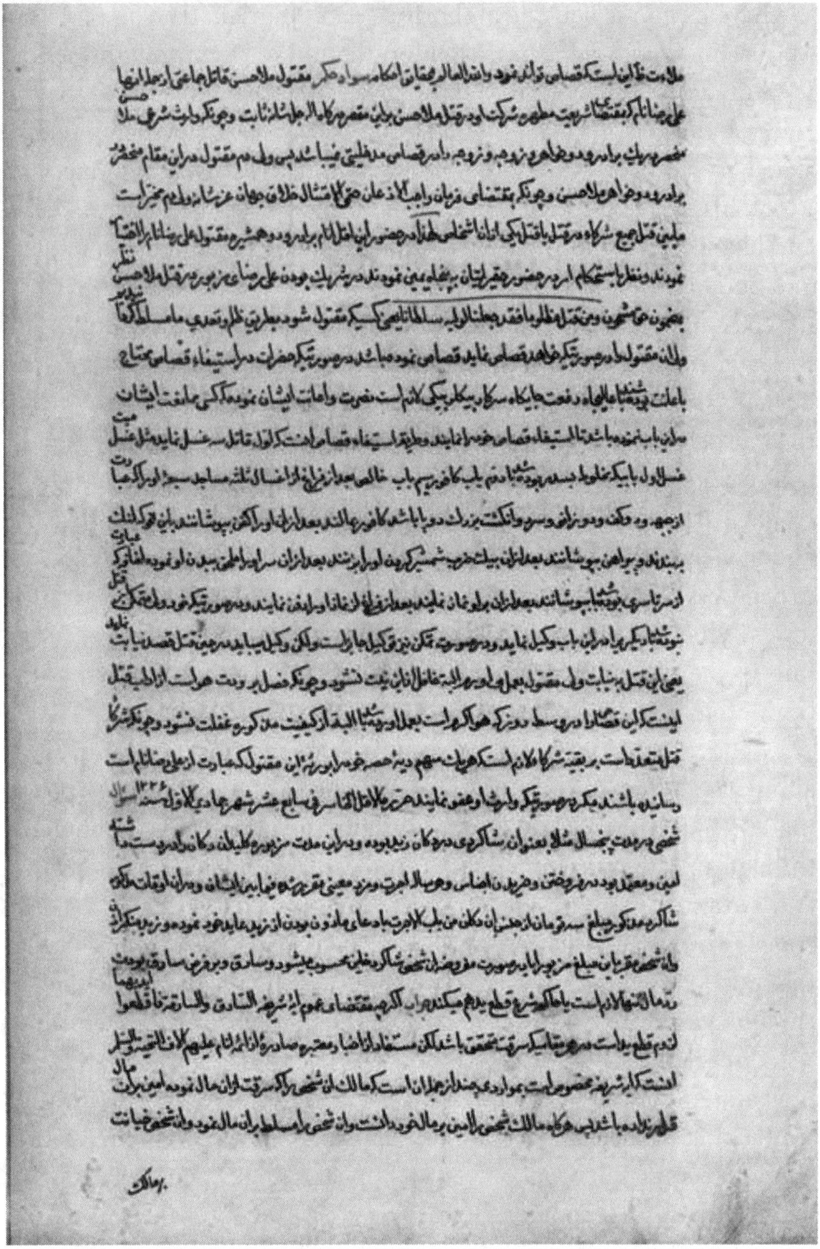

Figure 9: Muhammad Baqir Shafti's death sentence
(*hukm-i qatl*) issued in a murder case.

(Source: Muhammad Baqir Shafti, "Su'al va Javab," ms., n.d.,
Majlis Library, no. 11-01179, folio 360)

The other members involved in the homicide would have to pay their share of the *diyah* to the heirs of 'Ali Riza unless the heirs chose to forgive (*'afv*) them.[14]

In a third document, dated January 20, 1824 (18 Jumada al-Avval 1239 H.), Shafti ruled on another homicide case that required an oath procedure. Sadiq and Kazim, the sons of Aqa Ja'far Burujani from Naghnah, set out for their homes; upon hearing about this, Hajji Ahmad and Mirza 'Abdullah took up arms (*aslahah*) and followed them, whereupon they became embroiled in a fight, leading to Hajji Ahmad's death. There was ample eyewitness testimony (*shahadat-i shuhud*), including by two *'alim*s, Akhund Mullah Sadiq and Mullah Karim, to the murder. Weighing the evidence, Shafti was convinced (*qati' shudam*) that the murderer was none other than one of these two people, but it was not clear which one, which meant that only manslaughter had been proven. Therefore, the mother of the murdered man and his two brothers, Mirza Mahdi and Mirza 'Abdullah, successfully completed the oath procedure. Since the heirs of Hajji Ahmad were three young children and the mother of the murdered man insisted on *qisas*, Shafti transferred "the right of retribution" from those three children to the mother. He asked that "the *biglarbigi* and other authorities and notables who are believers must help the aforementioned [woman]," possibly in carrying out the execution should she choose not to do so herself. The text then repeated the ritual procedure for the murderer's ritual washing, execution by a sharp sword, and burial. It added further details about the prayer for the dead: the father of Kazim could grant someone permission to recite the prayer for the dead if it was congregational. Since it was "the cold season," it was preferable that the execution take place in the middle of the day. The text concluded by excluding Kazim from any right to compensation for the injuries he sustained during the fighting since he and Sadiq had set out to injure the two other men, who acted in self-defense.[15]

Several key features stand out about these homicide cases. First, Shafti's rulings were consistent with the idea of a high evidentiary bar being required for proving intentional homicide, which involved confession or strong circumstantial evidence leading to an oath procedure. Second, the rulings illuminate the ritual dimension of the execution: since the executed murderer would have had their sin expiated, they were due full burial and prayer rites, which were scripted in precise detail. Third, Shafti subscribed to the idea that *qisas* could only involve beheading by the single strike of a sword rather than the opinion that it should replicate the manner of the initial crime. Finally, Shafti only occasionally mentioned local government officials such as the *biglarbigi* as aids to the heirs, meaning that they would block anyone from preventing *qisas* or provide an executioner. In Shafti's worldview, God was sovereign in establishing the shari'ah; the 'ulama were collectively deputized to interpret it authoritatively in cases such as *qisas*; the heirs had the authority to choose retaliation, compensation, or forgiveness; and the government had little or no role to play.

A Tribesman Turned Urban Sovereign

Between 1823 and 1825, Hajji Hashim Khan, a settled Shirani Lur tribesman of the Lunban neighborhood of Isfahan, made a daring claim to sovereignty not only through violence and extortion rackets but also through the creation of his own judicial court.[16] Surrounded by a group of Lurs, Bakhtiyaris, and ruffians, Hashim Khan used the cover of night to raid the houses of the rich with the intention of extorting money from them, often through torture. If he failed to obtain the sought-after wealth, he would have them killed.[17] His retinue targeted craftsmen and merchants, who had their goods seized "without any legal documentation [*hujjati va sanadi*]."[18] In addition to stealing property, he and his men sexually assaulted people, thus violating their sanctity (*hurmat*).[19] In killing a sayyid, a descendant of the Prophet Muhammad, he violated a general taboo on shedding their blood.[20] According to one account, a common person from the Lunban neighborhood could stab a respectable member of Isfahani society in front of many witnesses with impunity, indicative of how Hashim Khan's exceptional status extended to his neighbors.[21]

Hashim Khan took measures to legitimize these seemingly illegal acts. He created a court of justice (*divankhanah*) and punishment grounds (*farrashkhanah*) without the permission of government officials. He and his men would round up "both innocent and guilty people" from the "streets and bazaars by [any] excuse" before bringing them to his court. Qajar sources claimed that the purpose of this court was to illegally "appropriate their property."[22] A well-known popular poem collected and translated by a European folklorist claimed that the Khan displayed his ostentatious collection of pricey possessions to demonstrate his authority. These items included a "golden veil," a "golden candlestick," a "lamp set with precious stones," a "famous shirt," "costly dresses," a "silvery brazier," "diamond snuffers," and seventy to eighty "spare-horses." The poem admonished him for his foolishness in wishing "for the war with the Kajjars" and described him as "mad-brained" and a "madcap" for "meddl[ing] with the shah."[23]

Hashim Khan extended his raids to the nearby Armenian town of Julfa. By so doing, he chose an easy target for the extraction of wealth, insofar as Julfan Armenians enjoyed a level of economic wealth but a relative absence of political power. He was partly drawn to the Armenian district because of the ready availability of alcohol in its taverns, where he would spend quite a bit of time engaging in leisure, often accompanied by musicians and a Jewish dancing boy.[24] In targeting the Armenian district, Hashim Khan was aided and abetted by an Armenian woman, Parinaz, with whom he was in love and who appears to have been the proprietor of his favorite tavern. She provided him with names of Armenians to target, including an old man named Sulayman who objected to the drinking parties.[25] On November 9, 1824, Hashim Khan entered an Armenian convent in Julfa along with a few of his men and ordered several of his musicians to perform (figure 10). Several Armenian monks of the convent tried in vain to convince him not to have music played in this sacred place. Hashim Khan had one of the monks stripped, tied to a tree, tortured, and eventually killed by one of his henchmen. Although the nominal governor of Isfahan, 'Abdullah Khan Amin al-Dawlah, came to Julfa to learn more about the episode, nothing was ever done. Hashim Khan and his men raided several homes in Julfa before returning to Isfahan without sanction.[26]

How was Hashim Khan able to act with such impunity? Part of the reason was his familial bond with the governor; his sister was married to Amin al-Dawlah. The governor was unwilling or unable to stop Hashim Khan. Eventually, Fath 'Ali Shah was made aware of the situation in Isfahan through petitions and letters intended to reestablish the

Figure 10: The Vank Cathedral in New Julfa.
(Source: Flandin and Coste, *Voyage en perse*, vol. 8, pl. 42)

Qajar legal regime. According to one account, Amin al-Dawlah himself complained to the shah about his brother-in-law's behavior.[27] According to another, it was the mother of a sayyid, whose son had been unjustly hanged by Hashim Khan, who petitioned the 'ulama to intercede on her behalf with the shah in order to avenge her son's murder.[28] A third source claimed that a notable woman robbed by Hashim Khan also petitioned Tehran about her situation the day after the theft.[29]

In response, Fath 'Ali Shah marched on Isfahan with his troops shortly after Nawruz in 1825 to reassert his authority. Hashim Khan and his men greeted the shah and offered him gifts, believing they would be exempt from royal punishment.[30] The shah instead detained Hashim Khan, had two hundred of his supporters killed, and leveled his neighborhood of Lunban. He then personally presided over the upstart's punishment. Hashim Khan seems to have believed that the shah's anger with him had to do with an earlier episode in which Hashim Khan was at a gathering with several imperial servants, one of whom was sitting on a chair in imitation of a king. When Hashim Khan entered the gathering, he asked an imperial servant to rise and proceeded to take his place on the chair before reciting the following poem: "The world does not remain without a sovereign / When one leaves another takes his place" (*jahan ra namandah ast bi kadkhuda'i / yaki raft digar biyayad bih ja'i*). When Fath 'Ali Shah was questioning an enchained Hashim Khan during his trial, he repeated this poem and swore at him. Hashim Khan taunted him in response: "Why are you swearing? Command that they tear me to pieces!"[31] Before he was executed, an unnamed prayer leader (*pishnamaz*), possibly the Friday prayer leader (Imam Jum'ah) Aqa Mir Muhammad Mahdi Kalbasi, tried in vain to intercede on behalf of Hashim Khan to spare him from being executed.[32]

The shah seized all of Hashim Khan's property and made efforts to return stolen property to its rightful owners. The shah then had Hashim Khan's beard shaved with a dull razor, an act meant to symbolically remove the visible marker of his honor and manhood, and blinded, an act disqualifying him from claiming sovereign status, before having him executed.[33] A vivid missionary report largely agrees with the Persian and Armenian sources but adds further details of the spectacle of punishment:

> Almost his first act was to cause the arrest of Hajee Hashim, who was brought into his presence bound in fetters. The King, after having previously investigated the matter, and found Hajee guilty of the most savage crimes, ordered him to be exposed on the rack, and the severest torture inflicted upon him. He accordingly suffered the utmost rigour of the law, his beard was shaved without water, and with a blunt razor his nose was slit open, and a black cord passed through it, he was placed on an ass, holding the tail, and carried through all the bazaars, amidst the ridicule of the spectators; he underwent the severe punishment of the bastinado on the main road Ghaysery, his eyes were plucked out, his ears cut off, his body branded with red hot iron, and he was compelled to eat his own ordure.[34]

Two features of this punishment are quite striking: first, Hajji Hashim was tortured and maimed publicly, both in the bazaar and on the main road, in a similar manner to what Hashim Khan did to his victims; second, he was made to eat his own feces, a punishment that matches the popular Persian expression for having made a "grave mistake" (*guh khuri*). The shah further had his uncles and the elder Lurs and Bakhtiaris around him imprisoned.[35] As for Amin al-Dawlah, he was chastised (*ta'dib*) for having been too lax toward his brother-in-law by being removed from office.[36] The shah also forced the former governor to pay a hefty sum of thirty thousand tumans to the treasury.[37] In his place, the shah appointed the Qajar prince Sultan Muhammad Mirza, who was given the title of Sayf al-Dawlah, as governor of Isfahan.

The case of Hashim Khan fits a familiar pattern of sovereignty: a man from a tribal background settled in an urban area and began to engage in arbitrary acts of violence and extractive extortion rackets. Although he was ultimately unsuccessful in his bid for power, the Hashim Khan episode illustrates the process of urban juridical sovereignty in the making through the establishment of an alternative court of justice, a taxation system, and a novel spatio-legal order.

A *Luti* Sovereign and Dual Local Sovereignty

Fath 'Ali Shah came to Isfahan once more, just prior to his death, because of frequent plundering in and around the city and the appropriation of taxes by the prince-governor, Sayf al-Dawlah. Arriving in Isfahan in late September 1834, Fath 'Ali Shah melted down the precious metals contained in the personal ornamental goods in the governor's possession in order to have coins minted for the central treasury.[38] By the next month, the shah had passed away, which triggered a crisis of succession. In Isfahan, a number of social actors, including local urban notables, *lutis*, and the 'ulama, filled the power vacuum by making multiple claims to sovereignty.

In 1834, a *luti* named Ramazan and his companions embarked on extortion rackets, raids, and arbitrary violence similar to that of Hashim Khan.[39] He also targeted the Armenians of Julfa for his "lawless violence" and extortion.[40] But unlike comparable events in Isfahan and elsewhere involving *lutis*, Ramazan claimed sovereignty rather than playing an ancillary or complementary role to an urban notable. His associates dubbed him Ramazan Shah, and he even had "gold and silver coins . . . struck in his name."[41] Beyond legitimizing his sovereignty, minting coins may have been an extension of his extortion rackets and general raiding. In David Graeber's study of debt, he notes that the genesis of the minting of coins by the state seems to have occurred in the midst of looting, violence, and theft since soldiers (in this case, other *lutis*) preferred to be paid in cash rather than in IOUs.[42] Ramazan Shah appears to have been from the Chimlan region near Isfahan: "After a while, Ramazan Chimlani, the leader of the ruffians of Isfahan, would threaten, terrify, and plunder the dwellers of the city before declaring himself shah. And later, like shahs, he would issue orders to this and that person and powerful subjects; like a military ruler, he would take whatever he wanted and spend it on the ruffians."[43] While details are slim about Ramazan Shah's biography, it is telling that he met his end at the hands of a rival *luti*, possibly from a competing neighborhood and as a result of a turf war.[44]

The succession crisis also led Shafti to assert his authority in local affairs beyond his shari'ah court.[45] According to his biographer Mirza Muhammad Tunakabuni, Shafti carried out seventy executions himself as part of his commanding good and forbidding wrong.[46] Both his theory and practice of shari'ah might explain his general aloofness from Fath 'Ali Shah and Muhammad Shah when they visited Isfahan and his willingness to collaborate closely with *lutis* to challenge the dynasty's authority in periods of crisis.[47]

Shafti encouraged *lutis* to carry out violent extortion schemes. The *lutis* used a great mosque as "one of their chief storehouses of the spoil," suggesting the tacit consent of the 'ulama.[48] According to a Russian diplomat, the *lutis* were able to commit "outrages in open day with impunity, because they were protected by the clergy."[49] Shafti employed a distinctly spatial technique in challenging the Qajars: he regularly granted asylum (*bast*) to *lutis* "who wished to avoid the law" in his Bidabad neighborhood.[50] By making the neighborhood a sanctuary, he spatialized his charismatic authority and created a network of violent agents acting with impunity parallel to those associated with the Lunban neighborhood a decade earlier.

Alongside this *luti*-ʿulama alliance, the former governor Amin al-Dawlah and the ruling prince-governor, Sayf al-Dawlah, came to a power-sharing agreement. Amin al-Dawlah made a pact with the governor in which he would retain juridical power by tending to the day-to-day affairs of governance in exchange for Sayf al-Dawlah's symbolic legitimacy as a Qajar.[51] Amin al-Dawlah further insisted on the spatial segregation of the nominal governor at the palace, akin to the way sacred kings were often spatially confined to their palaces while a close confidant, often from the bureaucratic class, was charged with the task of direct governance.[52] The former governor's sovereignty partly rested on the support of Bakhtiyaris and Lurs residing in the Lunban neighborhood, an apparent holdover from his connection to Hajji Hashim Khan's supporters and kinsmen. Amin al-Dawlah's first act after the pact was juridical and intended to restore order: with the help of Muhammad Baqir Shafti and Aqa Mir Muhammad Mahdi (Kalbasi) Imam Jumʿah, he rounded up several *lutis* and had them publicly punished in the Naqsh-i Jahan Square before Sayf al-Dawlah.[53] Amin al-Dawlah lent his support to the governor of Fars, Husayn ʿAli Mirza Farmanfarma, who made a claim to the Qajar crown.[54] He counseled Farmanfarma in a letter to him to stop "spending his time in the citadel in Shiraz" and "minting coins and having sermons read in his own name" if he wanted to become the shah, implying that he should mobilize for war and march on Tehran.[55] His advice fell on deaf ears, as Muhammad Shah took Fath ʿAli Shah's place on the Qajar throne, and Farmanfarma was brought to Tehran to be blinded.[56]

The 1834 episode shared key features with Hashim Khan's earlier claim to sovereignty: the *lutis* played a central role in violence, extortion rackets targeted merchants and other economically productive segments of societies (including the Armenians), and juridical acts were indicative of sovereign claims. Unlike the earlier episode, however, there were multiple simultaneous claims to sovereignty: Amin al-Dawlah and Sayf al-Dawlah had their dual-sovereign pact, the *luti* Ramazan Shah emerged as a unique plebian sovereign, and Shafti granted asylum to his *luti* supporters to bolster his juridical claim to sovereignty.

Muhammad Shah's March on Isfahan

By the mid-1830s, the *luti*-'ulama nexus had challenged Qajar juridical authority once more, leading to Muhammad Shah's march on Isfahan in 1839. In 1836, Khusraw Khan was appointed governor to bring an end to the bloodshed. He rounded up ruffians and had them punished. When the Imam Jum'ah tried to intercede for a ruffian at the governor's court, the latter refused. This conflict over jurisdiction sparked a major conflict, which culminated in the Imam Jum'ah leading an uprising consisting of elements from the city and its surrounding rural areas in late 1838. Khusraw Khan and his largely Armenian troops were badly besieged and forced to take shelter in the Sa'adatabad Palace south of the Zayandah Rud. While the hostilities eventually died down, perhaps because the Imam Jum'ah feared a general massacre of Armenians in Julfa, Khusraw Khan stepped down as governor and complained to the shah about the uprising.[57] Fazl 'Ali Khan replaced him as governor, but ironically, he faced an uprising by his predecessor at the instigation of the 'ulama, which led him to be deposed shortly thereafter.[58] The reaction of the state was swift and decisive in a manner that paralleled Fath 'Ali Shah's military mobilization and occupation of Isfahan: Muhammad Shah himself tended to the trial and punishment of the most violent *lutis*, with the goal of reestablishing Qajar sovereignty.

In the run-up to Muhammad Shah's occupation of the city, the *lutis* regularly raided homes and acted violently toward merchants and ordinary people. They attacked the bazaar and forced the merchants to pay a "tax" to them. If the merchants resisted, their houses would be raided, their properties stolen, and their women and children seized.[59] The *lutis* then engaged in "disgraceful actions" (*fazihat*) with the merchants' women and children. If the victims sought justice or discussed the crimes, they would be killed the next night. In broad daylight, the *lutis* also brazenly stole from, murdered, and raided ordinary subjects, which included the "weak and the poor," without "being held accountable."[60]

The 'ulama were more involved in *luti* violence and extortion rackets than they had been in 1834.[61] The event was said to have "shaken the foundation of the government," and the 'ulama were blamed for using their wealth to bring the *lutis* under their banner.[62] Shafti, with the supposed backing of roughly thirty thousand *lutis* in Isfahan, allowed them to engage "in all manner of theft and treachery."[63] One chronicle claimed that the 'ulama and the notables (*ashraf*) had "appoint[ed] the riffraff and ruffians as governors of the city," in a manner reminiscent of Charles Tilly's insight into the structural homologies between criminal organizations and states in the making.[64] The local 'ulama apparently viewed the *lutis* as more palatable allies than the Qajars, especially since Muhammad Shah was known for his Sufi tendencies.[65] The court chronicler Sipihr described how "the ruffians would take the weapon with which they killed Muslims and wash it in the pool of the mosques and would take pride in this."[66] While the 'ulama were major players in this event, later sources also blamed a scion of the Safavid dynasty and Amin al-Dawlah for the uprising, although contemporary evidence for this is patchy.[67]

In response, Muhammad Shah marched on Isfahan on February 29, 1840 (25 Zi al-Hijjah, 1255 H).[68] The shah reasserted his sovereignty through two interconnected legal acts: the mass arrest of *lutis* and the establishment of a temporary Divankhanah from which to try and punish those who were found guilty of crimes. Initially, the *lutis* blocked the royal troops, composed of roughly four thousand soldiers, from entering the city. The Imam Jum'ah eventually ordered that the troops be let in by the Northern Gate of the city; the troops, like the Ottoman Janissaries, marched to the beat of drums, trumpets, and panpipes, meant to invoke terror.[69] Muhammad Shah appointed Nasrullah Khan Kishikchibashi to capture the evildoers and establish a Divankhanah, where thousands of people were able to tell their stories, especially women who had harrowing tales of sexual assault.[70]

After being tried, convicted *lutis* were subjected to spectacles of violence. Some eyewitnesses recounted that the locks of their hair were cut, their nails and teeth were broken, some had their bodies buried halfway into the soil, and still others had their heads buried in the sand. Bestialization was a feature of these punishments. One leading *luti* had his nose and tongue cut off and his teeth put around his neck. He was paraded around like a donkey and tortured for three days. Women insisted on personally cutting off the hands and heads of those who had sexually assaulted them. Before being executed, the *lutis* were interrogated about the whereabouts of their stolen goods. If they failed to answer, pieces of wood would be placed under their nails, their teeth would be pulled out and hammered into their heads, and they would be paraded around like pack animals with a bag of flour around their necks until they starved. The headless corpses of the executed were arranged visibly in the city as a deterrent lesson.[71] Although the exact number of people executed, exiled, and punished is difficult to establish with certainty, some accounts put the number executed as high as three hundred, while others mention as few as seventy. The remaining *lutis* were exiled to Ardabil and Tehran.[72] Muhammad Shah also destroyed the *lutis'* houses, pursuing a spatial strategy of removing not only prominent *lutis* but also the reminders of their existence.[73]

The prominent *mujtahids* involved in the episode were spared corporal punishment because of the taboo against acting violently toward sacred religious figures. One *mujtahid*, presumably the Imam Jum'ah, who was accused of trying to "establish a government apparatus," was banished to Karbala.[74] In order to further curtail the *mujtahid*'s authority, the shah ordered that eleven of his *lutis*, including a sayyid, be killed so that the "name of the *mujtahid* and his followers would be destroyed."[75] The other major *mujtahid*, Shafti, escaped any form of punishment, although Manuchihr Khan, the future governor of Isfahan, removed the *lutis* who had taken asylum in Shafti's Bidabad neighborhood before sending them to Tehran to be executed.[76] By violating the sanctity of the *bast* and having the *lutis* executed, Manuchihr Khan sent a message that Qajar sovereignty trumped that of even the most powerful of local *mujtahids*, thus setting the stage for the future prime minister Amir Kabir's repeated violation of the *bast* in penal matters. The 1839–40 episode shared certain similarities with previous uprisings, such as the shah's march on Isfahan, the setting up of a court of justice, and the public punishment of opponents to Qajar sovereignty. It differed insofar as its leaders were members of the 'ulama rather than a settled tribesman, a *luti*, and/or former or contemporary governors.

Manuchihr Khan's Spatio-Legal Techniques

The tenure of Manuchihr Khan marked a new era in the juridical history of Isfahan.[77] The governor rigorously monitored and policed neighborhoods to prevent the outbreak of large-scale violence. He was initially tasked with mobilizing government troops against Muhammad Taqi Khan Chahar Lang, who had been challenging Qajar authority in nearby Khuzistan.[78] In Isfahan, he also set up his own court of justice, consisting of government and religious figures.[79]

The primary sources, including government reports and manuals, for the governorship of Manuchihr Khan differ from those of earlier governors, insofar as they provide a granular picture of the everyday aspects of law and policing. His governorship did not witness sovereigns in the making claiming legal authority, which indicates the efficacy of his techniques. While Manuchihr Khan reined in the *lutis* out of a concern with challenges to Qajar authority, he also turned to honing techniques for maintaining order by effectively employing the *darughah* and *kadkhudas* for surveillance, *mujtahids* for cases involving the shari'ah, and even neighborhood subjects for community policing and dispute resolution. Manuchihr Khan left a detailed textual record of mundane neighborhood events as part and parcel of his techniques for monitoring urban spaces and preventing conflicts.

Much like Amin al-Dawlah, Manuchihr Khan made a small fortune from his landholdings and productive irrigation projects in and around the city.[80] Unlike Sayf al-Dawlah, Manuchihr Khan was not a Qajar by lineage, and unlike Amin al-Dawlah, he was not a member of a bureaucratic family. Instead, as a eunuch, Manuchihr Khan came from inside the trusted palace circles whose connection to the Qajars dated to the reign of the dynasty's founder, Agha Muhammad Khan.[81] A poem found in a later local chronicle memorialized his wealth and manliness while mocking his status as a eunuch: "We are endowed with testicles [*khayah*] matching his wealth / suddenly a cry arose, 'the eunuch is truly a man.'"[82] He was credited not only with establishing peace and prosperity in the city but also with promoting economic productivity by expanding irrigation and agricultural works.[83]

In the early years of Manuchihr Khan's reign, he was primarily concerned with the swift and definitive punishment of *lutis* to make an example of those who would challenge Qajar sovereignty. The French traveler Eugène Flandin penned a vivid account of the governor's court proceedings and approach toward punishment. It began with two *lutis* attacking Flandin and his retinue while attempting to steal their horses. Despite being injured, they were able to detain the two culprits and drag them to the Russian legation. From there, the Russian ambassador formally complained to Manuchihr Khan. The governor summoned the victims to his court under armed escort to ensure their safety as they marched through the city's streets.[84]

Consistent with Qajar practice, Manuchihr Khan's residence doubled as a court. In the courtyard of the building, four soldiers waited to implement the punishment. Once everyone was in the presence of the governor, he asked Flandin and his companions to narrate their accounts of the episode. Occasionally, he would interject by saying, "Those bastards!" By the end of the proceedings, he asked Flandin what would be a fitting punishment, a request consistent with the way victims were often afforded the chance to enact retribution or have a role in determining the punishment for their assailants. When Flandin suggested the bastinado as a punishment, Manuchihr Khan suggested that beheading both *lutis* would be more appropriate.[85] When Flandin expressed fears that harsh punishments would make the Europeans a target for reprisals, the governor revealed his own logic for punishing the *lutis* publicly: "These ruffians, these bastards, should become a deterrent lesson to others. Please allow me to cut off their heads. At least command that I cut off their noses or ears."[86] Flandin, however, insisted that the bastinado would suffice. Manuchihr Khan reluctantly concurred, and the two men were punished by soldiers who set upon them with lashes.

Manuchihr Khan played a similar role as a judge in another case involving a fatal altercation between two Armenian Christians. In the Julfa Square (Maydan-i Julfa), Asaduvazadu from Faridan fought with another villager, named Hayraput, over whether some wheat that had been kept in the former's trust should be distributed among Armenian villagers, with the understanding that this wheat would be replaced after the harvest. Since the region had suffered a famine the year before, Hayraput was greatly upset by Asaduvazadu's refusal to do so, because the merchant who owned the wheat had arrived. He injured Asaduvazadu's head with a mace, which the latter answered by stabbing Hayraput with a barbecue skewer. After seventeen days, Hayraput died. Although the heirs of Hayraput could have brought the case before Armenian notables and clergy, they petitioned the governor instead and demanded *qisas*. Manuchihr Khan agreed to have Asaduvazadu executed for his crime but commanded that the man be brought to Julfa Square, the site of the original crime, in the hope that the matter could be resolved without bloodshed through the mediation of Armenian notables. Before such a resolution could take place, one of the male heirs insisted on a speedy execution, which was carried out by the governor's executioner, much to the chagrin of many Armenians, who preferred a peaceful resolution.[87] The heirs' decision to bring the case before the governor instead of the Armenian notables was a deft navigation of local jurisdiction meant to secure a desired legal outcome.

Beyond these Armenian and European accounts of Manuchihr Khan's rulings, we do not have many further accounts of his court proceedings and punishments. His reign did, however, witness an increasing concern with producing sample legal documents, indicative of a new textually focused approach to the law in which the production of documents was meant to decrease legal ambiguity. An administrator in his circle, Muhammad bin Sabz 'Ali Isfahani, composed *A Brief Exposition on Writing* (*Vajizat al-Tahrir*), a manual intended for administrators on how to write both government and shari'ah legal documents.[88] The collection included sample texts on how to compose death sentences, contracts, settlement documents (*musalahahnamah*), and manumission documents.

While *Vajizat al-Tahrir* addressed the formal aspects of the juridical order, a series of detailed reports reflect the everyday practices of policing and dispute resolution in Isfahan under Manuchihr Khan. Titled *The Events of the Sultanic Abode of Isfahan* (*Vaqayi'-i Dar al-Saltanah-i Isfahan*) and spanning several months between 1840 and 1841, these reports were presumably prepared by the city's *darughah* for the benefit of the governor or shah. Organized by date and neighborhood, the reports appear to be the earliest of their kind and precursors of later police reports; the pages are filled with brief accounts of parties, gatherings, visits and receptions, military drills, domestic disputes, and crimes (figure 11). Unlike earlier local and European sources that focused on extraordinary cases of violence and political uprisings, these reports provide details about ordinary Isfahanis, their daily conflicts, and the methods used for their resolution.

The Events concentrated predominantly on crime and punishment in Isfahan. The darughah and occasionally the kadkhuda carried out these punishments based on their discretionary powers. The reports are usually unclear as to the exact nature of the punishment, although minor infractions were probably punished by bastinado, while more serious crimes involved imprisonment, banishment, and death. The oft-repeated formulaic phrase "that it may serve as a lesson to others" (ta 'ibrat-i digaran shavad) in connection with punishments echoed past practices of deterrent spectacles carried out in Isfahan. The Events also illustrated the close relationship between the 'ulama and government officials, since certain cases were referred to the shari'ah court. The emphasis was often less on prosecution and punishment and more on reconciliation and social harmony, especially when the darughah and even ordinary subjects brought conflicting parties to an amicable settlement.

Local officials employed a number of strategies for the socio-spatial containment of the lutis in light of their prominent role in previous uprisings. In August 1840, a group of kadkhudas and their retinues went to detain the famous luti Aqa Mahdi Big at his house. When he was not there, they went to the house of a certain 'Ali Khan. Although he was not there either, the neighbors began screaming that someone was on 'Ali Khan's roof, but the suspect escaped.[89] Three days later, however, the authorities detained 'Ali Naqi Khan, one of the famous luti's servants, in the Taymur neighborhood.[90] In another case, the government had detained a group of six lutis who were about to be banished from Isfahan to Tehran, but a brawl erupted among them in the Sayyid Ahmadiyan neighborhood. During the course of the brawl, several of them escaped, which led officials to pursue them.[91]

Figure 11: A diamond-shaped neighborhood
government report including accounts of crime.
(Source: "Vaqayi'-yi Dar al-Saltanah-i Isfahan I," ms., 1840
[1256 H.], Malik Library, no. 2256133)

The *luti*s were quite adept at employing a range of strategies to continue with their activities, including recruiting new members, creating new spaces of operation, and even reaching out to local diplomats. Local authorities were concerned about ordinary subjects from craftsman backgrounds becoming "mixed up" with the *luti*s and being recruited to their ranks. The reports mention 'Ali Banna (the builder) from the Darb-i Jadid neighborhood and Husayn Sangtarash (the stone cutter) from the Shahshahan neighborhood, who were both "mixed up with the *luti*s."[92] *Luti*s were able to challenge government authority by carving out their own distinctive spaces in the city. For instance, a group of "ruffians and toughs" ripped up parts of the city wall and created a hangout for themselves from which they would harass passersby and cause disorder.[93] The *luti*s were savvy enough to use the extraordinary powers of diplomats in their favor. For instance, the *luti* Ramazan from Shiraz tried to convince the minister plenipotentiary (Vazir Mukhtar) of an unspecified consulate to intercede on his behalf in an undisclosed business matter. The Vazir Mukhtar refused and later asked his people to bar the *luti*s from contacting him.[94]

Although governors and their officials regularly used violence, banishment, and imprisonment toward *luti*s, they often displayed striking flexibility in their approach toward other social segments, through lighter punishments or reconciliation. Disputes were also resolved by the intervention of local residents and with minimal government intervention. Because of the granular detail of *The Events*, it brings to light the role of women in cases of violence and conflicts, sometimes as victims and other times as protagonists; women used a range of techniques to make themselves heard by the authorities.

Domestic disputes between husbands and wives often led to violence: women sometimes inflicted self-harm through opium ingestion or sought justice directly outside the home. In both situations, women made their domestic disputes publicly legible by forcing local officials or 'ulama to become involved. When a certain Husayn fought with his wife in the Talvaskan neighborhood, she ingested opium and needed a medical examination. The *darughah* intervened in the case and decided to punish Husayn so it would "serve as a lesson to others."[95] Similarly, after Aqa Jan fought with his wife in the Shamsabad neighborhood, she ingested opium. The wife was examined and found to be healthy, so the husband was not punished. Instead, she decided to reconcile with her husband.[96] In another case, the wife of Karam 'Ali Khan of the Nima-var neighborhood left her home without a trace after a fight with her husband. She had sought asylum at the house of the Imam Jum'ah, seeking justice. Later, the parties involved decided that the Imam Jum'ah should bring about reconciliation.[97]

When women within the neighborhood fought among themselves, officials held their husbands responsible for the public disturbance. In a striking case from the Khwaju neighborhood, two women started fighting with each other. It was rumored that one of them was pregnant and suffered a miscarriage as a result of the fight, but further investigation by a midwife proved this to be false. In response to the public disturbance, the neighborhood kadkhuda "made the husbands of both women guarantee [iltizam]" that they would bar their wives from leaving the home to fight.[98] Instead of punishing the women, the kadkhuda shifted moral responsibility for maintaining peace to their husbands through guarantorship, in which husbands were assumed to be guardians and caretakers of their wives.[99]

Property disputes were another form of familial conflict that was brought to the attention of the authorities. In the Shahshahan neighborhood, a group of siblings exchanged words over an inherited shop. A reconciliation was brought about, and the affair passed amicably.[100] In another property dispute, Hasan and Muhammad 'Ali fought over a house. The darughah chastised (ta'dib) the two sides.[101]

Conflicts also regularly erupted in the bazaar involving ordinary subjects, which could end in punishments, settlements, and/or reconciliation. In the Chaharsuq neighborhood, a baker was fighting with another man. The darughah intervened and punished both sides.[102] When two forage vendors ('allaf) started fighting in the same neighborhood, the darughah punished them both but also brought about reconciliation.[103] In a fight involving a soldier who served as a watchman in the Darb-i Jadid neighborhood and a melon vendor (kharbuzahfurush), the people of the neighborhood intervened to bring about reconciliation. In the course of their intervention, they ordered that the melon seller pay compensation to the soldier. When the governor Manuchihr Khan

Mu'tamid al-Dawlah heard of this, he deemed the settlement unfair. He therefore delegated a government agent (*farrash*) to return the compensation to the melon seller, who was very grateful for the governor's ruling.[104] Among the more colorful episodes was one involving Muhammad Rahim Khan, who went to the door of a public bath in the Mirabad neighborhood and requested that the bath attendant (*dallak*) "shave [his] face." The bath attendant refused, since doing so was tantamount to being complicit in making the man look like a beardless youth (*amrad*).[105] The two men then exchanged words and blows. Meanwhile, the *darughah* was informed of the situation, but by the time one of his men arrived, several people had already brought about a reconciliation.[106]

As indicated in this last case, ordinary subjects engaged in community policing when violence broke out among people in the neighborhood and often reconciled the parties before the authorities arrived. Residents often fulfilled a legal function akin to officials and religious authorities when issues could be resolved amicably. The neighborhood thus constituted an entity capable of ensuring basic security measures without outside recourse. In the Pa-yi Qal'ah neighborhood, a sayyid fought with a servant of Hajji Mirza Muhammad 'Ali Mudarris. The "people of the neighborhood" (*ahl-i mahallah*) intervened, reconciled the two parties, and ensured that the matter was resolved "amicably."[107] In the Chaharsuq-i Shiraziha neighborhood, two sons of different linen merchants (*bazzaz*) started fighting, before the people of the neighborhood reconciled them.[108] Similarly, in the Bab al-'Asr neighborhood, Sabz 'Ali Big and Lutf 'Ali came to blows; several neighborhood residents reconciled the two and sent them to their respective homes.[109] In the case of two men, Aqa Mahmud and Sayyid Salman, who were fighting over a debt, it was the "people of the neighborhood and several sayyids" who brought about reconciliation.[110] When the son of the deceased Mirza Khan Navvab fought with 'Ali the weaver (*nassaj*), several people from the neighborhood "reconciled [*musalahah va ashti*] them so that enmity would not arise again."[111]

The 'ulama similarly played the role of mediators and reconcilers alongside issuing shari'ah rulings. In the Bab al-Sharaf neighborhood, Javad and Rabi fought with each other. The *mujtahid* Hajji Muhammad Ibrahim Furutani summoned them both to his presence and reconciled them with the goal that they would act "kindly" (*mihrabani*) toward each other.[112] In the Bab al-Sharaf neighborhood, Hajji Ramazan and Muhammad 'Ali Nassaj were fighting over a house. The *darughah* summoned them both to his presence, before forwarding their case to the shari'ah court for a lawsuit (*murafa'ah*), presumably because they would have to furnish property deeds endorsed by the 'ulama.[113] In the Chaharsuq neighborhood, Ghulam Riza accused his wife of sexual impropriety. They went to the house of Mullah 'Abdullah for their lawsuit. Mullah 'Abdullah found evidence that the accusation was false, so he ruled that Ghulam Riza be punished for acting against the shari'ah.[114] Given the high standard of evidence needed to prove adultery and the seriousness of making false accusations of it, Mullah 'Abdullah's decision was broadly consistent with Islamic jurisprudence.

Manuchihr Khan's governorship marked a shift in approach to law and order, one that aimed to deepen the Qajar urban legal regime in ways that would prevent local sovereigns in the making from appearing. After initially embodying the law through displays of violence, the governor emphasized the government's role as a neutral and honest legal actor among conflicting parties. A tight network of *kadkhuda*s and the *darughah* monitored and policed urban spaces closely and intervened when conflicts arose among ordinary Isfahanis. Meanwhile, the 'ulama issued shari'ah rulings and encouraged reconciliations. Finally, ordinary residents proactively engaged in community policing and conflict resolution.

The Rustam Big Murder Case

Just prior to the coronation of Nasir al-Din Shah, Mirza Gurgin Khan, a trusted official of Manuchihr Khan, briefly served as governor, starting in September 1847. By June of the following year, Mirza Nabi Khan had become the titular governor, with Mirza 'Abd al-Husayn serving as his minister (*vazir*) and de facto governor. The murder of Rustam Big, the Muslim *darughah* of Julfa, by an Armenian was the most significant legal episode of this period.[115]

The murder revolved around an Armenian prostitute, Shushan Simunian Muradyanitas. The *darughah* Rustam Big of Julfa, who was a

Kirmanshahi Lur with a criminal past, and Garapat Havanisian, an Armenian butcher popularly known as "the mustachioed," vied for her affection. In fact, Rustam Big forbade Garapat from seeing Shushan, something that the lovelorn Garapat would not accept. On the night of April 28, 1848, Garapat held a party at his house along with several of his friends. Later, they sat on a bridge, played *sihtar*, listened to the nightingales, and drank some wine. When three shadowy figures appeared, both sides asked each other to identify themselves. Upon hearing Rustam Big announce his name, Garapat leapt to his feet, grabbed his gun, and shot the man dead. Garapat and his friends quickly fled the scene and hid from the authorities.[116]

In the aftermath, Rustam Big's wife petitioned the acting governor, Mirza 'Abd al-Husayn. Meanwhile, a group of three thousand Lurs from Lunban, Land, Sichan, Qinan, and elsewhere marched on New Julfa, armed with swords and shovels, and threatened to carry out a massacre of Armenians. They suspected that Garapat and his friends had taken refuge at the Vank Church, although this was not the case. Mirza 'Abd al-Husayn was forced to come to New Julfa with armed government retainers to prevent large-scale violence and looting.[117] On April 30, government officials detained Garapat and brought him to the acting governor. When Rustam Big's wife saw Garapat shortly thereafter, she carried out vengeance by ripping off his mustache with her bare hands and burning the remaining hairs with the flame of her lamp.[118] This act of ripping or burning facial hair was a form of humiliation often employed in Qajar-era punishments.

Although the case was initially referred to the acting governor, it was subsequently referred to the Imam Jum'ah, Mir Muhammad Mahdi, which indicates jurisdictional collaboration in certain criminal cases. The Imam Jum'ah heard various testimony about the crime, including Garapat's confession to being the sole murderer of Rustam Big. Garapat claimed to have acted out of fear for his life and a desire to be with Shushan. The Imam Jum'ah took into consideration that Rustam Big had young children in determining that a blood price was preferable to retribution. He commissioned an assessment of the value of Garapat's belongings and had it transferred to Rustam Big's heirs, although many Armenians in New Julfa feared arbitrary retribution by Lurs supporting

Rustam Big's wife. Both the acting governor and the Imam Jum'ah tried to allay these fears by ensuring, through letters and proclamations, that no harm would come to them. Although Garapat was also imprisoned for his crime, he later escaped incarceration, fled to Tabriz, and entered Russian government service.[119]

The Rustam Big case highlights the enduring spatial tensions between Lurs residing in Lunban and Armenians in New Julfa, in which certain underprivileged urban Muslim populations carried out, or attempted to carry out, acts of violence and plunder against Armenians as a result of a criminal case to compensate for their overall material deprivation. That a case involving an Armenian and a Muslim was tried by a Shi'i *mujtahid*, albeit one who was sympathetic to the Armenian community on the whole and who sought to avoid retribution, is telling of the legal mechanisms in place for interreligious conflicts.

The Governorship of Khan-i Khanan and the Dueling Ministers

After the death of Muhammad Shah in 1848, the country plunged into a familiar pattern of contested authority. As with the death of Fath 'Ali Shah, Isfahan once again became the site of urban violence. Nasir al-Din Shah appointed his uncle, Sulayman Khan Khan-i Khanan, as governor of the city and Mirza 'Abd al-Vahhab Gulistanah Mustawfi as his minister (*vazir*). Another man from the scribal class, by the name of Mirza 'Abd al-Husayn Sarrishtahdar, had sought the same ministerial post. Khan-i Khanan became increasingly partial toward 'Abd al-Husayn, who displayed a greater degree of humility before him than 'Abd al-Vahhab did. But because 'Abd al-Vahhab had been appointed by decree (*manshur*) of the shah, he felt entitled to the position.[120]

The affair transformed from a dispute over a ministerial appointment to an all-encompassing urban conflict, although the sources differ about the social makeup of the conflicting sides. According to a court chronicler, both sides of the dispute were composed of "guildsmen, craftsmen, and bazaar elements."[121] Another account confirms that the city was divided evenly in its loyalties but adds that the majority of the people from the agricultural districts (*bulukat*), Lur population, and ruffians were with Mirza 'Abd al-Husayn.[122] The more rural makeup of Mirza 'Abd al-Husayn's supporters indicates that tax collection may have partly been at issue. An Armenian account noted that the conflict also spilled into New Julfa, leading to *luti* raids and the murder of two Armenians with impunity. Although Armenians petitioned the sympathetic Imam Jum'ah about the crimes committed, he was unable to provide immediate assistance, despite promises to set up a court to hear their cases.[123] That Mirza 'Abd al-Husayn was from the Shamsabad neighborhood while 'Abd al-Vahhab was from the Shahshahan neighborhood suggests a further spatial inflection of the conflict.[124]

'Abd al-Vahhab's petitions to Tehran alerted the central government to growing local violence.[125] The government tasked Chiragh 'Ali Zanganah, a trusted confidant of Amir Kabir, to reinforce the authority of 'Abd al-Vahhab, the initial appointment of the shah, and to bring Mirza 'Abd al-Husayn back with him to Tehran.[126] Chiragh 'Ali essentially entered a war zone in which the bazaars had been closed, with the exception of a few greengrocers. As a first step, he assured the traders and other bazaar elements that it was safe to reopen their shops.[127] He also met with the governor and the Imam Jum'ah to deliver government communications addressed to them. In the course of these meetings, he realized that both the governor and the Imam Jum'ah were partial toward 'Abd al-Husayn. Chiragh 'Ali now faced a dilemma: if he took Mirza 'Abd al-Husayn back to Tehran with him and left Mirza 'Abd al-Vahhab in place, this would be against the wishes of local officials. He also feared that such a move would lead to further bloodshed and tumult, given the dominance of Lurs and ruffians aligned with Mirza 'Abd al-Husayn, whom only government troops could put down.[128]

Chiragh 'Ali decided to use his discretionary powers to reverse the central government's position by resolving to take Mirza 'Abd al-Vahhab back with him to Tehran instead. He conspired with Khan-i Khanan to have the entire population of the city and its environs attend a large gathering in front of the Chihil Sutun Palace. Before a large crowd, Chiragh 'Ali announced the supposed contents of the government decree— namely, that it was Mirza 'Abd al-Vahhab who would be brought back to Tehran and Mirza 'Abd al-Husayn who would remain in Isfahan. Then the governor commanded that everyone go home, adding that anyone who disobeyed would be killed. Subsequently, order was restored to the city.[129] In the meantime, 'Abd al-Vahhab had taken refuge at the residence of the Imam Jum'ah, who was not sympathetic toward him and issued an ultimatum: "If you do not go by your own volition, Chiragh 'Ali will remove you by force of law [*hukman*]."[130] By doing so, the Imam Jum'ah recognized Chiragh 'Ali's imperially sanctioned authority to break the privilege of asylum. 'Abd al-Vahhab accepted this and agreed to be taken to Tehran.[131]

When Chiragh 'Ali returned to Tehran and informed the central government of what he had done and why, he was praised for his acumen and quick thinking, since ensuring peace was a top priority at such a volatile early stage in the shah's reign.[132] Prime Minister Amir Kabir was even upset with the shah's choice of his uncle as governor and, in a remarkably frank letter, blamed Khan-i Khanan's incompetence for the general disorder in Isfahan, noting that thousands of people were mobilized against him in the city.[133] Shortly thereafter, the shah's uncle was recalled from his post.

Ghulam Husayn Sipahdar and the "Navvab Revolt"

In light of the political disorder, Nasir al-Din Shah replaced Khan-i Khanan with Ghulam Husayn Khan Sipahdar, who, in turn, appointed Muhammad Husayn Khan Khalaj as his assistant governor (*na'ib al-hukumah*) in the summer of 1849.[134] Early on, Sipahdar maintained social peace by cultivating a positive relationship with the leading 'ulama of the city and embarking on a more effective tax-collection process through his assistant governor.[135] However, a group attached to Khalaj appeared to "engage in illegal appropriations in gathering taxes" without the consent of the governor.[136] A slightly different account by Farajullah Munshi described these government agents as "mosquitos on honey" when it came to their tax collection; when they feared losing their illegal taxation scheme, they conspired to kill Khalaj.[137] Opposition in the "surrounding areas" of the city to excessive taxation threatened the fragile social peace.[138] Spatially, the nexus of the opposition revolved primarily around an alliance between two neighborhoods: Bidabad, which had historically been connected with Muhammad Baqir Shafti and his sons, and Shamsabad, which was associated with the recently deposed Isfahani minister Mirza 'Abd al-Husayn Vazir. Other neighborhoods aligned with the opposition included 'Abbasabad and Chaharsuq (previously known as Lunban). Given that three of these neighborhoods—Bidabad, Shamsabad, and Lunban—had figured prominently in previous episodes of violence, their alliance and mobilization against the governor were particularly potent.

The spark for the violence came from a direct confrontation between soldiers and local Isfahanis over the moral violation of a woman and insults hurled at the Imam Jum'ah. After the Friday prayers at the Imam Juma'ah mosque, one of his followers and a soldier started exchanging words and fighting.[139] One chronicler described the altercation as being "without reason."[140] But Riza Quli Khan Hidayat attributed the brawl to a soldier harassing a woman who was leaving Friday prayers. When she informed others of the incident, the supporters of the Imam Jum'ah came to her defense.[141] A general brawl ensued between a group of soldiers and followers of the Imam Jum'ah. The Imam Jum'ah himself came out of the mosque because of the tumult and tried to calm everyone down. In response, the soldiers disrespected him. The Imam Jum'ah then went to the house of the governor and petitioned against the soldiers. Sipahdar agreed to have the soldiers punished in the morning.[142]

What happened next demonstrates how a crowd composed of ordinary subjects felt authorized to take the law into their own hands. Before the agreed-on punishments could take place, a large crowd composed of "craftsmen, guildsmen, and bazaaris" assembled in the Masjid-i Jum'ah.[143] They started chanting slogans against the soldiers and in defense of the Imam Jum'ah.[144] When Sipahdar caught wind of the mobilization, he sent Khalaj to calm the situation and possibly apologize for the actions of the soldier, but he was met with hostility. Before he could speak, Ahmad Mirza Navvab Safavi, backed by a crowd, directly attacked Khalaj and had him thrown into the pool of the mosque. The Imam Jum'ah, who did not appear to have been involved in instigating or promoting the attack, sent for a surgeon to operate on him, but to no avail; Khalaj died shortly thereafter.[145] In the aftermath of this incident, two hundred *luti*s tried but failed to assassinate the governor. They then went to the grocery shops close to the Naqsh-i Ja-han Square, where they raided and looted the fruits and melons before taking refuge at the house of the *'alim* Zayn al-'Abidin.[146]

A formidable network of individuals joined forces to unseat Sipah-dar from the government. The main person behind the murder was Ahmad Mirza Navvab Safavi, a scion of the Safavid dynasty. He formed an alliance with Mirza 'Abd al-Husayn, the former *vazir*, and an urban notable by the name of Ibrahim Khan.[147] This group sought the support of members of the 'ulama. They turned to the two sons of Shafti, Aqa Sayyid Asadullah and Zayn al-'Abidin, the latter of whom granted them sanctuary at his residence during the ensuing violence.[148] 'Abd al-Husayn convinced the leadership of local *lutis* to join their cause by offering them a number of incentives: he gathered them around and offered them "rice from Linjan [a productive agricultural district situated to the north of Isfahan], a share of government taxes, a certificate of tax exemption, and a thousand other things." Among the prominent *lutis* who joined the cause were Rahim Baqir Sihdihi, Hashim Nuhchiri, Husayn Nikabadi Zayn al-'Abidin (aka Husayn Nanva), Muhammad (aka 'Ali Bujar), and Hajji Muhsin. Each of these individuals was provided with a gift (*in'am*) and a station (*nasibi*), suggesting that there were more immediate ma-terial and social incentives provided to the *lutis* by the leadership of the movement.[149]

In response, Sipahdar formed an alliance with many of the city's leading 'ulama to gain Islamic legal justification for his intended vio-lent crackdown. He invited Aqa Sayyid Asadullah, the Imam Jum'ah, and Aqa Muhammad Mahdi (the son of Hajji Ibrahim Kalbasi) to his house to discuss the situation. Sipahdar denounced the opposition as consisting of ignorant people (*juhhal*) who hated the shah. In a stern warning about the possibility of innocents being killed, he told the group, "I fear that once the fire rises, the wet and the dry will burn together." The group of 'ulama responded, "So long as we live, we cannot be thank-ful enough for the bounties of the king of Islam [*padishah-i Islam*]. We recognize these ruffians [*ashrar*] as rebels [*muharib*] whose execution is legally incumbent [*vajib al-qatl*]." The use of the category of *muharib* here is significant: it was one of the *hadd* categories in Islamic jurispru-dence that could warrant a death sentence, especially if the rebels had been involved in murder.[150] They then proceeded to compose and seal a document that endorsed "the legality of spilling their blood" (*ibahat-i dam-i ishan*) for the Sipahdar, meaning that if he did so, he was not liable for retaliation or compensation. When Asadullah returned home, he forbade his brother Zayn al-'Abidin from protecting the ruffians at his residence, but Zayn al-'Abidin refused.[151] Upset with the situation, Asadullah eventually left the city for 'Atabat, the twin Shi'i shrine cities in Iraq.[152] Sipahdar also recruited a British official, K. E. Abbott, to speak with the Imam Jum'ah about the situation: "At the Governor's request, I had an interview with this High Functionary, and, by exposure to him of the possible consequences of the conduct attributed to him, I obtained his promise to support the Authority of the Shah's Governor, and to go hand in hand with him in restoring order."[153] The Imam Jum'ah consistently acted in support of Sipahdar in subsequent events.

On November 30, 1849 (15 Muharram 1266 H.), the *lutis* attacked government positions at the Burj-i Jahannama building, which was met with cannon fire. The ensuing street battles set the pattern for future engagements between the rebel forces and the government.[154] At this stage, a number of individuals associated with the occult sciences began to make predictions and prognostications that were meant to legitimize the actions and sovereign claims of Ahmad Mirza: "evil prognosticators [*shanahbin*], geomancers [*rammal*], witches [*jadugaran*], and rice-and-fork-seeking *darvish*s wrote rulings [*hukm*] that within three years, Ahmad Mirza would sit on the throne and Mirza 'Abd al-Husayn would be the steward [*pishkar*] of Iran."[155] On December 3, 1849 (18 Muharram 1266 H.), government troops rolled through the streets of the 'Abbasabad neighborhood with cannons and many gunners on their way to Shamsabad.[156] In Shamsabad, they raided and looted the house of Mirza 'Abd al-Husayn, an act that galvanized popular sentiment against Sipahdar.[157] At this point, Zayn al-'Abidin provided his own legal justification for violence in retaliation for this raid by appealing to Islamic legal norms about the inviolability of the domicile: "Those who enter the house of someone without permission must be killed [*vajib al-qatl*], and their repulsion [*daf'*] is imperative according to the shari'ah."[158] In retaliation for the raid, a group of supporters left the neighborhood of Bidabad to defend the residence of Mirza 'Abd al-Husayn in Shamsabad; in the ensuing engagement, they killed several soldiers and an important military figure while taking others as prisoners to a mosque near the house of Zayn al-'Abidin.[159] Sipahdar asked the shah for a large troop mobilization, which constituted a significant escalation of the situation.[160]

On December 30, government troops and the opposition fought in the Shamsabad and Chaharsuq neighborhoods. The government troops marched on Qasr-i Shamsabad, where the opposition had built fortifications (*sangar*). They eventually conquered the palace and publicly punished a leading *luti* at the Farrashkhanah by having him blown out of a cannon.[161] On January 3, 1850 (19 Safar 1266 H.), the fortieth night commemorating the martyrdom of the Shi'i Imam ('Arba'in), Sipahdar commanded his troops to observe a cease-fire for a day and night in recognition of this holy date. But Ahmad Mirza used the cease-fire as an opportunity to launch a surprise attack, resulting in the deaths of numerous soldiers. In support of the governor, the Imam Jum'ah took the pulpit to condemn the followers of these ruffians as denying the bounties of the shah and as having destroyed the city. In response to this, Mirza 'Abd al-Husayn put a green flag on the roof of the Muhammad Baqir Shafti mosque and declared a jihad; this attracted throngs of people from the "city and agricultural districts" in his support.[162] The declaration of jihad signaled another legal justification for violence against the governor and a claim that his right to rule had been religiously compromised.[163]

As the violence dragged on, the government troops clearly had the upper hand, which stoked fears that Bidabad would be destroyed.[164] Ahmad Mirza and Mirza 'Abd al-Husayn turned to Aqa Muhammad Mahdi Kalbasi for help by using another significant legal mechanism: intercession. At first, Kalbasi sternly rebuked them and made clear that interceding on their behalf would be difficult: "You left no space for intercession [*shafa'at*] with Sipahdar, and now you have thought to pollute me by this deceit. I will not take part in this." He later changed his mind and interceded on their behalf with Sipahdar. Sipahdar accepted this intercession by granting the group safe passage out of the city, with the goal of decreasing bloodshed.[165] The two men were followed by a large group consisting of their 'ulama, sayyid, and ruffian supporters who went to Tehran seeking "the administration of justice" (*davari*) according to the "just law" (*qanun-i 'adl*) executed by the central government trustees in Tehran.[166] This suggests, in principle at least, that they recognized the shah's jurisdiction and authority in adjudicating between them and Sipahdar about who was in the right while simultaneously making a claim to local sovereignty. One opposition figure, Mirza Murtaza, asked forgiveness from the governor with a Quran and sword in hand.[167] Many of the *lutis* who had taken asylum were rounded up and captured. The Imam Jum'ah was a willing participant in violating the sanctuary; he delivered an opponent named Muhammad 'Ali Khan, who had taken asylum at the Masjid-i Jum'ah by disguising himself in the turban of the Shaykh al-Islam.[168]

The two leaders of the uprising, far from receiving the justice they sought, were both killed. Ahmad Mirza reached Qum, where he was killed by a relative of Muhammad Husayn Khan Khalaj as *qisas*.[169] Mirza 'Abd al-Husayn lived in Qasr-i Kashan and later Kashan before being kicked out by the local governor. He came back to the environs of Isfahan in the village of Dih-i Naw, but his host informed Sipahdar that 'Abd al-Husayn was back, leading to his capture. The governor had him imprisoned and wrote to Tehran about his fate. After some time, Sipahdar received an imperial execution order for 'Abd al-Husayn, which he carried out by strangulation.[170] As for the sayyids, seminarians, and ruffians who had supported the uprising, government troops tracked them down, had their belongings looted, and brought them back to Isfahan in chains. Sipahdar gave each of the ruffians their "due" (*kayfar*) according to the degree of their "guilt" (*gunah*).[171] Among them were a number of prostitutes (*ajanidha*), who were apparently thankful to be released, including one who was the "point of adoration" (*qiblah*) of Mirza 'Abd al-Husayn.[172] Despite the restoration of order, the central government decided that Sipahdar should be deposed.[173] This appears to have been in response to a petition asking for Sipahdar to be summoned (*ihzar*) to Tehran in light of the bad blood between him and many of the city's notables and 'ulama.[174]

The anti-Sipahdar network was particularly potent in its leadership because it brought together three forms of leadership and authority that were embodied in its main protagonists: bureaucratic competency, an

alternative royal lineage, and religious authority. Seen from a legal perspective, several features stand out. The declaration of a jihad against
the local governor was the ultimate claim to a loss of juridico-political
legitimacy and to the breakdown of the circle of justice. As with other
significant violent episodes in Isfahan, space played a crucial role. The
opposition was able to mobilize and challenge state authority from a
sanctuary, first the Masjid-i Jum'ah and later the residence of Zayn al-
'Abidin in Bidabad. The eventual cessation of hostilities also involved a
containment of the danger represented by the opposition through banishment: it was agreed on that the leaders of the movement would leave
the city and be granted a measure of amnesty, at least outside Isfahan.
This agreement was reached by way of a prominent 'alim's intercession.
The episode ended with the opposition intending to travel to Tehran in
order to bring its case before the shah, who was recognized as having
ultimate jurisdiction in the conflict between them and the governor.

Cleaning Up Crime under Chiragh 'Ali Zanganah

By the late 1840s, there were several outbreaks of violence in and around
Isfahan similar to those of the 1820s and 1830s. In the early 1850s, Amir
Kabir introduced and implemented a series of countrywide reforms that
were intent on strengthening the power of the central government
through its military and administration.[175] To this end, Amir Kabir once
again sent Chiragh 'Ali Zanganah as the new governor after the recall
of Sipahdar to Tehran, to restore law and order to the city.[176]

Out of this mission, Chiragh 'Ali penned a short but detailed account of his early time as governor in Isfahan starting in September 1851
(1267 H.). This diary, titled *The Events of Isfahan* (*Vaqayi'-i Isfahan*), differed from the government reports prepared for Mu'tamid al-Dawlah
insofar as Chiragh 'Ali centered himself in the narrative. The account
focused on Chiragh 'Ali's successful pacification of unruly urban and
nonurban elements and his approach to crime and punishment. Part of
this approach built on that of Mu'tamid al-Dawlah: he recounted sending monthly government reports (*ruznamah-i dawlati*) to Tehran that
were probably of a similar detailed nature.[177] The reason for writing his
diary is unclear, although it may have been written for Amir Kabir's and

Nasir al-Din Shah's benefit to demonstrate that he had faithfully carried out his duties. Alternatively, he may have intended it as a historical model for other new governors who were taking up their posts in a tumultuous time. Given that Sipihr's account of his governorship summarizes the main details of Chiragh 'Ali's diary, the court may have solicited the text for the purpose of writing court history.[178] Chiragh 'Ali's techniques for dealing with the breakdown of the law usually involved playing various factions against one another and granting immunity to elements willing to cooperate with him. He often leveled spaces associated with rebels, especially forts, to prevent future rebellion. Furthermore, he continued the state practice of using spectacular violence to punish convicted criminals.

Chiragh 'Ali entered Isfahan on September 20, 1851 (24 Zi Qi'dah 1267 H.), and immediately began undoing the negative legacy of extortionate taxes of the previous era. He blamed the prior "chaos and disorder" on the previous assistant governor, Muhammad Husayn Khan Khalaj, and the previous minister, Hasan Tafrishi.[179] Chiragh 'Ali brought an end to the practice of collecting taxes by force through the bastinado; instead, he engaged local ordinary subjects and eventually collected the taxes that had been in arrears since the governorship of Khan-i Khanan.[180]

Next, he turned to capturing and punishing ordinary lutis and ruffians who had been among the ranks of the opposition to Sipahdar. He had them punished publicly according to the principle of proportionality: "I captured all of them, and in the Naqsh-i Jahan Square of Isfahan, I punished them according to the evilness of their actions. I had those individuals who were not deserving of execution [qabil-i siyasat nabudand] sent in fetters and chains to the Imperial Punishment Grounds [farrashkhanah-i mubarakah] in Tehran and imprisoned. Most of them died in a dungeon [anbar] as they deserved."[181] The men's punishment in the most visible city square, Naqsh-i Jahan Square, was an act meant to restore Qajar sovereignty (figure 12). Chiragh 'Ali was at pains to stress that the punishments fit the crime: the most serious offenders were killed, while lesser offenders were chained, exiled, and imprisoned. This was a rhetorical departure from Manuchihr Khan's emphasis on harsh punishments exceeding the seriousness of the crime as necessary for deterrence but consistent with how Sipahdar handled criminals.

Figure 12: Naqsh-i Jahan Square, with a depiction
of corporal punishment in the far left corner.

(Source: Eugène Flandin, "Meidan-i-Chah ou Place Royale, Ispahan,"
Victoria and Albert Museum, South Kensington, https://collections.vam.ac.uk/
item/O143763/meidan-i-chah-ou-place-watercolour-flandin-eugène-napoléon/)

Chiragh ʿAli's mix of negotiation and violence informed his approach to the *lutis*' nonurban equivalent: bandits (*yaghis*). Two prominent bandits operated outside the city proper, and both had created
spatial and strategic advantages for themselves through forts.[182] Past governors had struggled to bring their juridical authority to bear on the
bandits, given these advantages. Chiragh ʿAli first set his sights on Karim
Arujani, a bandit who had been raiding and stealing since the governorship of Sayf al-Dawlah.[183] Previous troop mobilizations had failed and
led to many casualties.[184] Chiragh ʿAli took a different approach: he cut
a deal with Arujani and eventually had him captured. He then destroyed
Arujani's fort, so other bandits could not make use of it. Those from
among Arujani's retinue who were not killed were exiled to Tehran.[185]
Chiragh ʿAli then turned his sights to ʿAli Mirza Khan Faridani, another
bandit who was active in Isfahan's environs, after two subjects petitioned
(*tazallum*) against him.[186] Chiragh ʿAli requested a full account of the
bandit's misdeeds from the two subjects before composing a petition on

their behalf for Amir Kabir. In response, Amir Kabir authorized Chiragh 'Ali to mobilize troops against Faridani.[187] Before making a show of force, Chiragh 'Ali met with the bandit to convince him to avoid bloodshed through negotiation.[188] He offered the bandit safe passage in exchange for Faridani tearing down the fort and the surrounding towers, to which he agreed.[189] Chiragh 'Ali's insistence on the destruction of the forts belonging to both bandits points to his spatial understanding of Qajar sovereignty: these spaces were both a source of potential danger since they could be used by future bandits and a polluted symbol of rebellion that needed to be cleansed by annihilation.

Alongside *luti*s and bandits, Chiragh 'Ali was gravely concerned with punishing Babis. The picture that emerges by reading government sources alongside sources sympathetic to the Babi movement is jurisdictional cooperation between the governor and the 'ulama in heresy trials.[190] In the closing months of 1851, a young Babi seminarian, Shaykh Isma'il, in the aftermath of the execution of the founder of the Babi movement, Sayyid 'Ali Muhammad the Bab, and a general milieu of messianic expectation, proclaimed himself to be the return of the Prophet Muhammad. He had gathered around him a group of male and female followers in Isfahan. After some time, he commanded his right-hand man, Aqa Muhammad Qasim the cloak weaver (*'abaduz*), whom he designated as the "return of Imam 'Ali," to announce, "The Prophet Muhammad has appeared!" (*ala ala qad zahara Muhammad*) in the bazaar.[191] While Shi'i jurists considered the secret belief in such an idea a sin, its public proclamation constituted a manifest crime deserving of punishment. The *mujtahids* sent a message to Chiragh 'Ali stating that "a group of the misguided Babi faction are residing in a certain place and conspiring to cause trouble [*ashubi*] tomorrow morning."[192] In response to their letter, Chiragh 'Ali commanded the city's *darughah* and *kadkhudas* to surround the house and detain the suspected Babis.[193]

The ensuing interrogations and trials demonstrate the symbiotic legal relationship between the governor and the 'ulama. The Babis were brought before the governor at the government building (Dar al-Hukumah), where they were tortured during their interrogation. Chiragh 'Ali concluded that each of the men "claimed the station of an Imam and had declared twelve Imams for themselves."[194] Through the use of judicial torture and the interrogation of the three initial suspects, a list of one hundred Babis was compiled. This was significant because, had the men first been brought to a shari'ah court, confessions elicited by torture would be considered inadmissible. Those of the hundred men who were only nominally Babis paid "a certain amount in cash" and repented (*tawbah*), while those who refused to do so were turned over to Hajji Mirza Hasan Mujtahid for further investigation. Since in crimes of apostasy, doubt and insanity were means of avoiding a death sentence, the *mujtahid* appears to have offered the Babis a choice to repent (thus causing doubt) and/or claim insanity. Shaykh Isma'il, who had begun to fear for his life, repented: Hajji Mirza Hasan Mujtahid "ruled that he was insane" (*hukm bar jununash dadah*) and commanded that he be incarcerated at his father's house for an undisclosed amount of time.[195] Hajji Mirza Hasan Mujtahid issued a death sentence, which was endorsed by other *mujtahid*s in Isfahan, for the remaining Babis who refused to revert to Islam.[196] As an early indication of the principle of judicial review by the shah for death sentences, Chiragh 'Ali sent the city's *mujtahids*' death sentence to the shah, who confirmed via mail (*chapar*) that the "rulings of the 'ulama" should be implemented. Like the *luti*s, the Babis were brought to the Naqsh-i Jahan Square for execution, although another source claims that they were instead paraded around the bazaar, where they were assaulted by a crowd of people and ripped apart by daggers (*khanjar bar khanjar*).[197] Chiragh 'Ali barred their corpses from being buried in a Muslim cemetery, as did local Armenians and Jews from their cemeteries; the corpses were subsequently devoured by "dogs and other beasts."[198] The justification for this execution also had clear contagionist elements: the two men were convicted of "causing corruption in religion" (*fasad dar din andakhtand*), which warranted a "shari'ah execution."[199]

Chiragh 'Ali's willingness to cooperate with the 'ulama on this matter may have been a bid to cement an alliance with them against a new common enemy. His stance differed from Manuchihr Khan's generally cordial relationship with the Bab and signaled a move toward further collaboration with the Shi'i Usuli jurists, who promoted a more active role for the 'ulama in worldly affairs.[200] The general agreement between the government and 'ulama on the Babi question set the stage for similar legal proceedings, punishments, and executions throughout the nineteenth century.

A similarly revealing and well-documented case involved a homicide in the village of Mahyar near Isfahan in July 1852. The case was unique insofar as it was attested to in three near-contemporary sources: Chiragh 'Ali Zanganah's firsthand account, the court chronicle *Nasikh al-Tavarikh*, and the government newspaper *Vaqayi'-i Ittifaqiyah*. These sources provide a detailed picture of the homicide, the investigative procedure, the basis of a shari'ah ruling for *qisas*, and the public execution that followed. As in the case of the Babis, the 'ulama cooperated with the acting governor in the proceedings, which ended in a spectacular public execution.

Zayn al-'Abidin, the village headman (*kadkhuda*) of Mahyar, feared that Mashhadi 'Ali, a subject from the same village, was intent on taking over his position. He therefore arranged for Mashhadi 'Ali to be killed by strangulation upon entering his house. With the aid of his maternal nephew and son, Zayn al-'Abidin dragged the corpse through the desert, had the body chopped into pieces, and buried it in an underground oven.[201] Mashhadi 'Ali's worried family members brought the matter to Isfahan's authorities for further investigation, especially in light of the enmity between Zayn al-'Abidin and Mashhadi 'Ali. Chiragh 'Ali sent a bailiff (*muhassil*) to the village in order to summon both sides for an investigation. In the course of interrogations in Isfahan, the brother and maternal nephew of the *kadkhuda* confessed that they murdered Mashhadi 'Ali but claimed to be unaware of what happened to the body after doing so. Chiragh 'Ali sent both sides to the shari'ah court (*dar al-shar'*). Before a ruling could be given, two falconers found the body of Mashhadi 'Ali when vultures dropped his hands from their beaks, leading the falconers to the murdered man's remains.[202]

Sources differ on how the *kadkhuda* was convicted at the shari'ah court. According to Chiragh 'Ali, the *kadkhuda* confessed to the crime in light of the aforementioned evidence. The shari'ah court then issued a death sentence on the basis of this confession.[203] The official government newspaper, however, reported that the death sentence was said to have been issued on the basis of a *qasamah* procedure that was consistent with "shari'ah law" (*qanun-i shari'at*).[204] Both sources agree that he was sentenced to *qisas* and that an offer of compensation was made. In the newspaper account, a group of the *kadkhuda*'s supporters offered up to one thousand tumans to the heirs of the deceased to forgo retribution.[205] Chiragh 'Ali's account indicates that the dual jurisdiction of the case entailed a dual form of compensation as well: one to the heirs and another to the governor. In his version, the *kadkhuda* was a man of means who offered one thousand tumans to the governor and five hundred tumans to the murdered man's heirs to "change the death sentence to life [imprisonment]" (*az qatl bih abad muqarrar*). He even increased this offer to two thousand tumans for the family members of the deceased, but the latter refused and insisted on retribution.[206]

The female heirs remarkably carried out retribution with their own hands, but sources disagree as to why. In the government newspaper version of events, the heirs offered thirty tumans to the executioner to carry out the retaliation, but he refused.[207] It is possible that the *kadkhuda* or his supporters paid off the executioner in the hopes of pressuring the heirs, who were mainly women, to accept compensation. In the end, Chiragh 'Ali had the *kadkhuda* brought to the Naqsh-i Jahan Square and handed him off to Mashhadi 'Ali's family. The two women of the family, Mashhadi 'Ali's wife and daughter, carried out the execution themselves since the boys were too squeamish about doing so: "[they] went forward and first threw the rope on his neck and gave the head of the rope to the daughter and choked him with the utmost fearlessness."[208] The wife then cut the *kadkhuda* to pieces with an instrument of war (*harbah*). The manner of *qisas* redramatized the initial crime in precise detail: strangulation followed by hacking the corpse to pieces. After this, the wife and daughter threw his body in the square and left. Chiragh 'Ali's narration of what happened next provides insights into the function of having the corpse of a murderer displayed in a public square: "Whoever saw the corpse of that cruel one [*zalim*] was in wonder and would curse that faithless one. And when they would see the wife and children of the aforementioned *kadkhuda*, they would look at them and say, 'This is imperial justice; it carries out *qisas* like this for your husband.'"[209] According to Chiragh 'Ali, the public display of a murderer's corpse conveyed imperial justice, despite the fact that the shah was not mentioned in any of the existing accounts of the execution and that it was based on a shari'ah ruling. Much like the previous Babi case, Chiragh 'Ali cooperated closely with the 'ulama in holding hearings at both the governor's court and the shari'ah court, issuing a death sentence, and ensuring public punishment at the city's main square.

Conclusion

In Qajar Iran, sovereignty was the point at which law and violence were indistinguishable and where the lines between punishment and taxation on the one hand and murder, extortion, and theft on the other virtually disappeared. An emerging sovereign, therefore, made a juridico-political claim through the practice of arbitrary violence, which defined the contours of the licit and illicit. How did this play out spatially? For one, a sovereign claimant with strong neighborhood networks sought to extend his sovereignty over the city through violence. Those who were associated with a would-be sovereign's neighborhood, Lunban or Bidabad, enjoyed legal impunity. Writ large, sovereignty within a country entailed extending this logic beyond the confines of a smaller geographic unit, such as a city, through conquest and war.

Hajji Hashim Khan's bid for power illustrates the endurance of tribesmen (albeit settled) as urban claimants to sovereignty because of their capacity for violence. Similarly, *lutis* were capable of transforming their potential for violence into support for an urban notable's claim to authority or, in the rare case of the *luti* Ramazan Shah, a direct claim to sovereignty. Prominent members of the 'ulama, such as Muhammad Baqir Shafti, claimed the authority to mete out punishments and executions directly and without reference to local and imperial government authorities. Shafti's authority took on a spatial form through the expansive sanctuary rights associated with his neighborhood of Bidabad—an authority that granted *lutis* engaging in arbitrary violence a safe space from which to escape state punishment. The central paradox of *bast* as a legal space was that it was simultaneously a space in which state violence was suspended and a space that enabled *luti* extralegal violence. At crucial moments, the Qajar shahs came to Isfahan to reassert their authority through spectacular acts of violence in the form of punishments. They convened temporary courts of justice, where they tried and punished criminals and would-be sovereigns.

Manuchihr Khan, who was appointed the governor of Isfahan in the aftermath of Muhammad Shah's reassertion of authority in the city, restored order in the city on behalf of the Qajars through his many public punishments, especially of renown *lutis*. He next established a system of monitoring conflicts in the city, as expressed in *The Events*, in which we hear of regular domestic conflicts, conflicts between neighbors, and property disputes. Nonstate actors also played a significant role in the juridical life of the city: the city's 'ulama acted as mediators and judges in shari'ah cases, while ordinary subjects mediated between and reconciled conflicting parties without recourse to government officials. This form of legality involved the government functioning less as a guarantor of order through spectacular violence and more as an entity monitoring and addressing conflicts in their early stages and encouraging a peaceful resolution through mediation and reconciliation. But violence did not disappear altogether, since it still underwrote the law; instead, the government deployed spatial techniques of control over urban spaces.

The death of Muhammad Shah in 1848 once again led to challenges to the local authority in Isfahan. People opposed to the governorship of Khan-i Khanan and the imperial ministerial appointment effectively mobilized ruffians, tribal networks, and neighborhood toughs, leading to Chiragh 'Ali Zanganah's decision to appoint the oppositional figure as minister to preserve social peace. The next episode of violence brought together people claiming the dynastic legitimacy of the Safavid lineage, the legitimacy of religious authority, and the bureaucratic competency of a former minister to violently challenge the local governor by appealing to religious justifications for killing, including jihad. Unlike previous episodes, where the would-be sovereigns were killed immediately, this ended with certain leaders traveling to Tehran in hopes of the shah adjudicating between them and the governor, which was tantamount to recognizing the shah's legitimacy. From this point onward, rather than lawmaking being the focus of popular mobilizations, law-preserving violence became the norm, although what law required preservation and who had the right to interpret it at the local level were open questions.

Chiragh ‘Ali Zanganah’s governorship paralleled that of Manuchihr Khan’s: the former restored order through the use of spectacular punishment of *lutis* and the crushing of bandit resistance at the city’s margins, followed by an emphasis on hearing court cases. Zanganah often relied on Isfahan’s *mujtahids* for collaboration in murder and heresy cases. He also ensured that regular reports were prepared to monitor city events that may have been pertinent to crime prevention. The spatial dimensions of Chiragh ‘Ali’s approach to rule are quite striking: he destroyed geographic sanctuaries for bandits, such as forts and towers, and he made regular use of public punishments as a means of projecting authority.

Policing Vice in Shiraz

Sex, Alcohol, and Music

I n September 1899, the Zoroastrian philanthropist Khusraw Khan had a mausoleum made of iron and wood for Shiraz's famous fourteenth-century poet Hafiz. Knowing that such an homage to a poet renowned for his verses on wine, entertainment music, and a libertine lifestyle might upset the city's 'ulama, he gave generous "gifts" to the city's *mujtahid*s, including the prayer leader of the Vakil Mosque, Sayyid 'Ali Akbar Falasiri, in exchange for their assurances not to block the mausoleum's erection. When the structure was nearing completion, Falasiri and his followers went to the burial site, destroyed the structure, and stripped its materials for people to take away. In the ensuing days, the government did nothing to punish Falasiri. Muzaffar al-Din Shah did, however, order that the mausoleum be rebuilt, this time on the government's dime.[1] Flying into a rage, Falasiri mounted the pulpit at the Vakil Mosque and screamed, "If the shah rebuilds it a thousand times, I will destroy it!"[2]

Hafiz's verse embodied a worldview antithetical to that of Falasiri. Playing on the theme of private sin and public crime, the Shirazi poet gave advice on how to evade the moral censure of the orthodox:

> Though wine brings joy and the rose's scent wafts on the
> breeze,

Do not consume wine to sound of a harp for the *muhtasib*
    is severe.

If you obtain a wine flask and a companion,
Drink with sense, for we live in tumultuous times.

Hide the wine cup in your cloak's sleeve,
For blood flows in this age like wine from the flask's spout.[3]

Hafiz admonishes his readers to be discrete because vice committed
behind closed doors was not subject to the strictures of public regulations.

In Shiraz, crimes related to sex, alcohol, and music entailed polic-
ing public activities considered to be particularly morally transgressive.[4]
Historically, the figure of the *muhtasib*, or "the inspector of public
places," had the authority to "command good and forbid wrong."[5] As
Kristen Stilt has demonstrated in her study of the *muhtasib* in Mamluk
Egypt, this authority was rooted in both Islamic jurisprudence and the
political authority of the state to implement discretionary punishments.[6]
According to several imperial decrees from the Safavid period (1501–
1722), the *darughah* was directly charged with the task of forbidding
wrong, a fact that calls into question oversimplistic characterizations of
this figure as a "secular" police officer.[7] By the mid-nineteenth century
in Shiraz, many of the *muhtasib*'s functions, such as market inspection
and patrolling the streets for public drunkenness, prostitution, and other
forms of vice, were taken over by the *kalantar/biglarbigi*, the *darughah*,
and the *kadkhuda*.[8]

In the latter decades of the nineteenth century, certain *mujtahid*s,
like Falasiri and his followers, had articulated a religious justification for
policing and punishing vice without reliance on government authority.[9]
Although there is a long-running debate in Imami *fiqh* literature about
whether anyone was qualified to forbid wrong with violence in the absence of the Hidden Imam, Falasiri and his followers did precisely that.[10]
These followers, who included seminarians, sayyids, and ruffians (*alvat*
or *ashrar*), repeatedly detained and punished prostitutes; destroyed alcohol pitchers or distilleries run by Jews; raided parties where alcohol,
prostitution, and/or music may have been involved; and broke musical

instruments. Those who were found guilty of such crimes were sometimes subject to *hudud* punishments, while in other cases, they were punished according to the government's discretionary powers. What is striking about the punishments for such moral crimes is their very public nature: "ignominious parading" (*tashhir*) through the city's streets and bazaars was a favored means of publicizing the individual's transgressions, as was the shaving the hair of one's head, beatings, and banishment.[11] Public moral crimes often became contested jurisdictional battlegrounds between government and religious authorities over who could police and punish offenders. Criminal cases involving people suspected of illicit sexual activities, producing and consuming alcohol, and playing and listening to music both in public and behind closed doors shed light on the contours of the boundaries between public and private in defining crime.

Sex Crimes

Sex crimes involved illicit sexual relations outside marriage (temporary or otherwise), which could include consensual affairs, sexual assault, and rape. Within Islamic jurisprudence, *zina* constituted a *hadd* crime but one for which the evidentiary bar was very high, insofar as there had to be either a confession or four male witnesses to sexual penetration with consistent testimonies.[12] This would suggest, as Intisar Rabb has argued, that *zina* was a public sex act that was "punishable only when [it was] so public as to meet the most stringent of standards of proof, thereby infringing on the public values that the *ḥudūd* prohibitions aimed to protect."[13] In practice, family members who became aware of adulterous affairs often took matters into their own hands by punishing the offending parties without notifying government or religious authorities. The most common form of sex crime involved prostitutes, both male and female, whose mere presence in public constituted a moral danger for those who wanted to rid the city of their "corrupting" influence.[14] The category of beardless youths (*amrads*) in a criminal context often referred to a male prostitute whose suspected crime was engaging in anal sex (*livat*), which was a punishable act in *fiqh*. In cases involving abduction and/or rape, the focus was on the transgressor and their actions, although the social status of the victims and perpetrators affected legal outcomes.[15] Despite the Islamic legal terminology of *zina*, *livat*, and *ghasb* (for sexual assault), Qajar-era sources often employed an alternative ethico-legal terminology to describe rape and sexual assault, which was usually some variation of an "immoral act" (*fi'l-i shani'*, *'amal-i shani'*), "shameless act" (*bi sayrati*), "act contravening the shari'ah" (*'amal-i khalaf-i shar'*), and "unchaste act" (*bi 'ismati*), as the basis of punishment.[16] This alternative terminology reflects conviction on the basis of a lesser burden of proof than the high standard demanded by *fiqh*, one that compensated for the lack of direct "manifest" evidence for the suspected crime.

ADULTERY

In Shiraz, the punishment of adulterous women took on a uniquely spatial dimension. According to several nineteenth-century accounts, women convicted of adultery were historically thrown down the Chah-i 'Ali Bandar, a well constructed of solid limestone situated outside the city gates, close to the grave of the poet Sa'di and connected to the Bandar Fort (Qal'ah-i Bandar).[17] Charles Wills, an English physician residing in Iran between 1866 and 1881, recounted a Shirazi interlocutor's detailed account of a ritualistic punishment of an adulterous woman:

> The woman was paraded through the town bareheaded, with her hair cut off, on an ass, her face being to the tail. She was preceded by the lutis or buffoons of the town singing and dancing, while the Jewish musicians were forced to play upon their instruments and join in the procession. All the rabble of the town of course thronged around the wretched woman. The ass was led by the executioner, and it was not till nearly dusk that the place of punishment was reached. The victim had been mercifully drugged with opium, and was probably unaware of her fate; she was ordered to recite the Mussulman profession of faith; this she was of course unable to do. Her hands were bound behind her, a priest recited the profession of faith in her name, and the executioner, saying "Be-ro!"

("Get thee gone!") by a touch of his foot launched her into eternity. Such executions are getting less common in Persia than formerly.[18]

This account is remarkable for several reasons. First, the woman was paraded bald and without a head covering, signifying her lack of chastity. This was unusual because Shi'i jurisprudence banned such a punishment for fornicating women but prescribed it for men in certain instances.[19] Second, the parade had a carnivalesque dimension to it: Jewish musicians were forced to play music, while *lutis*, here meaning performers, sang and danced. Even a *mujtahid* ("priest") participated in the ritual theater by reciting the profession of faith in the condemned woman's name. Finally, the spectacle's audience included the city's "rabble," possibly because they enjoyed such spectacles but also because they were prone to contravening the law. The government's "spectacle of the scaffold," according to Michel Foucault, thus conveyed the state's ultimate sovereignty over the bodies of its subjects to such an audience.[20]

Some adultery cases appear to have been dealt with informally. Wills claimed that most affairs were "hushed up" and dealt with by the families. In the absence of an amicable resolution, the husband's family would often take matters into their own hands by "fling[ing] the woman from a roof or into a well, or administer[ing] a dose of poison." Wills mentioned the case of Abdul Hamid, a gold lace maker in Shiraz, whose cousin and wife regularly committed adultery. The man's mother, who was considered "the guardian of her son's honour," informed her son of the affairs; he then notified his brothers-in-law. They all resolved to punish her collectively. One of the brothers-in-law brought a "corrosive sublimate" to poison her. Then "the woman's own mother, her mother-in-law, her brothers, and her husband compelled her to swallow a fatal dose of the drug," thus bringing an end to the issue without the involvement of any external authorities.[21] This extrajudicial punishment took place without the authorities becoming involved or punishing the family for doing so. The main concern was to restore family honor once the affair had become public.

Adultery cases within Shiraz's Jewish community often included similarly harsh intended sanctions but required the assent of Shiraz's government authorities in order to be carried out. In a case reported in the *Jewish Chronicle* on April 10, 1896, the rabbi of Shiraz had convicted a Jewish man of adultery and pronounced a death sentence, presumably on the basis of laws found in Deuteronomy and Leviticus.[22] The rabbi went to the governor of Shiraz to carry out the death sentence, but the governor refused for unknown reasons. Meanwhile, the woman in the adulterous affair had left Shiraz, presumably because she either was banished or voluntarily left to escape the "social death" of continuing to live in the city.[23]

PROSTITUTION

Unlike adulterers, whose crimes were often difficult to trace or prove, prostitutes were a common object of moral policing in both private and public spaces by both government officials and certain *mujtahids*. *Mujtahids* and their followers regularly raided private parties on the suspicion that sexual norms were being violated; by doing so, others accused them of violating Islamic privacy norms. Such raids contested the government's authority in purging the city of prostitution, whose mere presence raised concerns about moral pollution.[24] Punishments for prostitutes reflected this contested authority, as evidenced by the religious and government terminology used to describe it.

Governors, *biglarbigis/kalantars*, and *kadkhudas* periodically punished prostitutes, both to bolster their credibility as moral authorities and to extract exorbitant fines. In the summer of 1877, the governor Farhad Mirza Mu'tamad al-Dawlah found three women guilty of prostitution. He issued a ruling in the government garden before a "public crowd" (*dar mala'-yi 'amm*) that their hair was to be shaved off and that they be were to be paraded around the bazaar without a hijab by the executioner (*mir ghazab*). Despite precedents for such punishments of sex criminals, the city's population reacted unfavorably; people in the bazaar were upset and intended to "cause a disturbance," saying, "What kind of action is this that is occurring in a Muslim land in punishing [*tanbih*] women?" Before this punishment could be carried out, Qavam al-Mulk, the *kalantar*, prevented it from happening.[25] The source of popular opposition was that the punishment compromised the chastity of the spectators, who would be forced to see a woman in a form of naked exposure. This case paralleled one in eighteenth-century Damascus, in which an Ottoman governor demanded that all women, aside from those connected to his and his lieutenant's households, remove their veils in public in order for his officials to identify prostitutes, who would then be banished from the city. Similar to the Iranian case, these intrusions by the governor's men caused "public outrage."[26] In the spring of 1887, a prostitute *amrad*, who had already been punished by the local government in Shiraz, was again engaging in "evil deeds and disorder" among the city's shop owners. The government ruled that he should be beaten with a stick and have the locks of his hair shaved off in a manner similar to what was prescribed for female prostitutes and adulterers.[27] The *amrad* was then banished (*nafy va ikhraj*) from the city, a common punishment for prostitutes in the Ottoman Empire as well.[28]

Shiraz's *biglarbigi* regularly detained prostitutes in the course of his policing duties. In two curious cases, the prostitutes cross-dressed to facilitate commingling with the opposite sex in public and as part of a sexual fantasy. Samad Aqa, the Shirvani merchant and Russian subject, had Mihri Bihbahani, a famous prostitute, dress up as a man.[29] Together, they went to the public garden Bagh-i Rashk-i Bihisht. While returning to the city on horseback, the *biglarbigi* recognized the woman and imprisoned her, since this was a flagrant violation of norms governing the mingling of the sexes in public.[30] The boundaries between public and private were more blurred in another case of cross-dressing in 1900. As'ad al-Saltanah, the son of the deceased Qashqa'i Ilkhan, had a prostitute over to his house, where he asked her to dress up in his mother's clothing and dance for him in an almost oedipal role-playing fantasy. His sister was not amused by the performance and informed the *biglarbigi*, who was a relative, thereby making her brother's sexual tryst public knowledge. This was somewhat unusual since such illicit behavior was typically kept secret because it would compromise her family's honor.[31] This concern for family honor may explain why the *biglarbigi* did not punish As'ad al-Saltanah; instead, he had the prostitute arrested and punished. In the ensuing days, the *biglarbigi* used this occasion to have the city's *kadkhuda*s round up the city's prostitutes, bring them to his house, and punish them. These punishments included fines (*tarjuman*) adding up to three to four hundred tumans, illustrating how fines were used as an alternative to harsher sanctions.[32]

Leading 'ulama in Shiraz and their followers challenged the government's ability to carry out the moral policing of prostitution, often taking matters into their own hands by independently carrying out *hudud* punishments. Their justification for policing vice appears to have been that forbidding wrong could be done by ordinary Muslims without government sanction, a position that was strikingly similar to that of al-Ghazali.[33] In September 1894, Sayyid 'Ali Akbar Falasiri was informed of the presence of several prostitutes in the Maydan-i Shah neighborhood (figure 13). He mobilized two to three hundred seminarians and ruffians (*awbash*) to raid the house where they had gathered. Strictly speaking, such a raid of a private residence violated Islamic norms of privacy, according to many jurists, although some made an exception if the informant was reliable and a serious crime such as murder was imminent.[34] The prostitutes, who caught wind of the raid, ran away. The crowd gathered to assault the neighborhood *kadkhuda* for having failed to prevent such parties, but he too fled. When the government sent attendants to the house to expel the seminarians, they were beaten up instead. Meanwhile, Falasiri and another *mujtahid*, Aqa Mirza Muhammad 'Ali, ruled that the *kadkhuda* should leave the city or face a death sentence (*hukm-i qatl*). The *kadkhuda* intended to comply with the banishment, and the government was unable to prevent it.[35] The two *mujtahid*s apparently condemned the *kadkhuda* for having failed to forbid wrong, even though the vice had occurred privately. Since knowledge of it had become public, however, they may have argued that privacy protections no longer applied.

Three years later, Falasiri carried out a *hadd* punishment directly on a prostitute. When a soldier and a prostitute were caught together outside the Sa'di Gate (*darvazah*), a common site of illicit activities in Shiraz, they were brought to Falasiri instead of the government. He did not punish the soldier; instead, he implemented a *hadd* punishment on the woman by having her beaten. Later, he kept the same prostitute as his temporary wife (*sighah*), thus rendering sexual relations with her licit.[36] Given that she received a *hadd* punishment, either she confessed or four male witnesses provided consistent testimony to the sex act.

Figure 13: Sayyid 'Ali Akbar Falasiri.
(Source: Sa'idi Sirjani, *Vaqayi'*, verso 584)

Alternatively, Falasiri took liberties with the strict *fiqh* standards of evidence in making the judgment.

When Europeans became involved in prostitution, this only amplified the perceived failure of the government to police prostitution. In April 1902, a written announcement was posted in several places, including the door of the residence of the *karguzar*, the official in charge of foreign subjects and non-Muslims in Iran, stating that "the wife ['ayal] of a Russian subject" was "residing in the house of a Christian merchant called Malkam," where she was "engaging in unseemly and immoral acts," meaning prostitution. The text continued by warning, "If she is banished from the city, then this is very good. Otherwise, there are sixty of us who promise to invade the house of the aforementioned person, forcibly remove the woman, and harass all of them."[37] The logic of the threat was clear: violating the sanctity of the home through home invasion was permissible once it had become well-known (and thus "public") as a place of vice. The anonymous authors (possibly Falasiri or his followers) proposed that the woman be exiled, a distinctly spatial solution to the moral contagion of illicit sex acts.[38]

The Russian consul became embroiled in another prostitution case that fueled fears of a backlash against Europeans. The consul left his house dressed in Arab clothing to disguise his identity and went to the house of one of his servants in the Darb-i Shahzadah neighborhood, where they were entertained by a musician and several dancing prostitutes. As news of the consul's attendance at this party in disguise spread throughout the city that night, he decided it would be prudent to visit the ruins of Persepolis outside the city until the uproar died down. Meanwhile, neighborhood residents wanted to raid the house and capture its attendants, but the authorities prevented them from doing so.[39] When the prostitutes left the house the next day, they were detained and thrown into prison. The government even wanted to punish the prostitutes by throwing them down a well, presumably Chah-i 'Ali Bandar, but decided against it upon further consideration.[40] In this case, the neighbors rather than the government or religious authorities policed morality in private residences, indicating that they saw it as a communal prerogative.[41]

TRICKERY, ABDUCTION, AND RAPE

Sex crimes also encompassed trickery, abduction, and rape, which all involved force and coercion. Tricking women into compromising situations was a gateway to sexual procurement. In October 1860, an elderly maidservant (*kanizah*) tricked the wife of a merchant into attending a party with unrelated men. The maidservant convinced the merchant, who was described as "unfamiliar with the wiles of women" (*az makr-i zanan ghafil*), to allow his wife to attend since her presence would honor the gathering (*mihmani*). The next day, the two women, along with a younger maidservant, went to the party. As soon as the merchant's wife entered the home, she saw four unrelated (*ajnabi*) men there who were sitting down and partying. She refused to unveil completely; instead, she removed her outer veil garment (*chadur*), sat in the middle of the room, and showed the men hospitality. After smoking from a water pipe (*ghalyan*), she requested the ewer (*aftabah*) to relieve herself in the courtyard; she used this as an excuse to escape from the house along with her younger maidservant. She reached a baker's shop and reported the event. The baker summoned her husband to pick her up. In the meantime, the elderly servant and her houseguests escaped.[42] The report suggests that had she not managed to escape, she (and her younger maidservant) may have been raped or coerced into a life of prostitution after having their reputation compromised by mingling with unrelated men.

An undated government report appears to provide a resolution to this case. It recounted an incident in which a woman went to the house of another woman, where ten to fifteen people hindered (*zajr*) the guest from leaving. The *farrashbashi* of the city caught the female pimp (*jakish*), shaved off her tresses (*gis*), put her in a bridle, placed her on a pack animal, and paraded her around the bazaar so that others "would hold themselves accountable" (*hisab-i khud ra bidanand*).[43] The spectacle of punishment had elements of bestialization (the bridle, the pack animal) and public shaming (shaving hair and the parade) that were so central to Qajar-era *tashhir* punishments.

The forced abduction of women and *amrad*s for sexual purposes was another common sex crime. The abductors were typically punished, in contrast to those who frequented prostitutes. Since many of the abductors were soldiers and military officers, they were often subject to the Military Code (*qanun-i 'askari*).[44] Not all cases ended with the perpetrator being caught, as in the case of a drunk man who violated the sanctity of a home. In 1899, a drunk man entered a house in which six or seven men and women were sleeping in the courtyard (*hayat*) of the house. The man kidnapped a ten- to twelve-year-old girl, who was the occupant's daughter, from her bed. While he was carrying the girl off in the streets, she started screaming and yelling, which woke the home's residents and made them aware of her absence. They left the house to find the girl, and they found her just as the drunk man was about to rape her. The man released the girl and ran away toward the Bagh-i Mushiri as he escaped into the night. The account leaves it unclear if he was ever caught or punished.[45]

Ordinary subjects involved in abduction with the intent to rape were usually subject to state punishments. In the summer of 1867, Muhammad Ibrahim, a servant of Hajji Masqati, tried to "abduct a woman by force [zur]." The government issued a *siyasat* punishment for the man.[46] In 1890, several ruffians abducted an *amrad* child and took him to their house. The father of the boy petitioned the government about the situation. Government officials then tried to detain the ruffians, but two of them managed to take sanctuary at the Shah Chiragh Shrine. The *biglarbigi*, Sa'id al-Saltanah, encircled the shrine without the ruffians being informed. When they tried to escape from the shrine, they were detained and thrown into the government prison until they could receive a *siyasat* punishment.[47] It took close to three years for this punishment to be delivered, which involved the three men being beaten with sticks. One of them had both ears cut off, and the other two men had one ear cut off. The government also intended to banish them from the city as further punishment.[48]

Frequently, commanding officers rather than the governor would deal with soldiers who were involved in abduction. Several soldiers from the Kamarah and Bazachlu troops touched a woman's breasts in a bazaar and intended to abduct her. Qavam al-Mulk's men stopped the abduction from taking place, but the soldiers swore at them and fought back. The bazaaris rushed to her defense as well. Navvab Mustafa Vala summoned the soldiers in question and gave them "full military punishments" (*tanbih-i nizami-i kamil*), meaning those found in the Military Code.[49] In a similar case in 1899, Nasir Lashkar, the accountant (*mustawfi*) of Nizam al-Mulk, took Musharraf, a beardless youth in the Zarand troops, to his home between noon and "three hours after sunset." The two started drinking alcohol together. Nasir Lashkar slipped something into his drink to facilitate raping him. Musharraf realized what was happening and started yelling and screaming. The guards (*qaravuls*) of the neighborhood, who were also from the Zarand troops, realized what was happening and wanted to raid the house with their fellow soldiers. Baha al-Sultan, the commander (*sahib mansib*) of the

Zarand troops, managed to turn them back. In the morning, he reported the situation to Nizam al-Mulk. Nizam al-Mulk summoned Nasir Lashkar and was very upset with him. He did not appear to deliver any corporal punishment, perhaps given the offender's relatively high social status as an accountant from the scribal class; instead, he ruled that he should leave Shiraz altogether.[50] The following year, several soldiers from the Makhsus troops abducted a boy and intended to rape him outside the city. The boy started yelling and screaming. Several men arrived, wrested the boy away from the soldiers, and took the soldiers to the city. Qavam al-Mulk punished the soldiers directly instead of turning them over to a military official. In the aftermath of this incident, the Makhsus troops were relieved of their duties and forced to set up tents outside Shiraz because of their continuous rowdy behavior.[51]

Rape was the most violent sex crime but did not always receive harsh punishments; instead, the social status of the people involved and patron protection affected legal outcomes. In spring 1900, a Kashani Jewish man raped a Jewish girl who was ten or twelve years old at his residence. When other Jews learned of this, they gathered together and, remarkably, took refuge at the Masjid-i Naw, apparently to pressure the authorities to imprison the rapist. The *biglarbigi* responded by detaining and imprisoning the rapist. The Jews who had taken refuge presented their understanding of Jewish law to the authorities: "According to our religious community's custom [*rasm-i millat-i ma*], this person must be harshly punished [*siyasat*] and banished."[52] Such a punishment was vigorously contested by Mullah Aqa, a famous Jewish musician, who protected the Kashani Jewish man because his son was a famous dancing boy in his troupe. The city's Jewish musicians, headed by Mullah Aqa, took refuge at another mosque to protest the rapist's detention. Meanwhile, the *biglarbigi* held the man in prison and made substantial revenue (*madkhul-i khubi*) from mediating between the two sides.[53] The case demonstrates how non-Muslims would pursue their legal objectives differently: one side sought punishment according to Jewish custom and asked the government for enforcement, while the other side sought to protect the accused and contest the case. Remarkably, both Jewish parties sought refuge at mosques, which was rare except for cases in which Jews converted and then took sanctuary in times of upheaval.[54]

In cases where individuals were from significantly different status groups, punishments were more common. In spring 1901, a fifteen-year-old Black slave of the son of Mustafa Quli Khan Abu al-Vardi, sodomized (*lavat*) a fourteen-year-old boy. The family of the boy petitioned the governor's *farrashbashi* about the case and framed it as rape, since to confess to consensual anal penetration would be a crime in itself. The *farrashbashi* had the Black slave beaten thoroughly, had his ears cut off, and had him paraded around the bazaar in a bridle (*mahar*).[55] Unsatisfied with the punishment, the family of the boy petitioned the governor, Shu'a' al-Saltanah. He ruled that disfigurement (*nasaq*) of the ears was insufficiently severe; instead, he ruled that the slave's four fingers should be cut off and his master should pay a fine of fifty tumans. The victim's status as a free subject and the perpetrator's slave status probably affected the legal outcome to the latter's detriment.[56] In a similar case from May 1900, a ten- to twelve-year-old apprentice baker took the son of his master, who was fourteen years old, from the Darb-i Dukkan to his home. He raped him on the way there. The boy was detained and taken to the *biglarbigi*, but the report did not indicate any further punishment.[57] Although sayyids were sometimes protected from facing punishments because of their lineage and connection to the 'ulama, there were exceptions when they were unprotected outsiders from a lower social strata. A sayyid from Isfahan came to Shiraz in 1903, where he raped a five- to six-year-old child. The provincial government seized him, cut off his ear, and put him in a bridle before parading him around the bazaar. Then he was escorted by several cavalrymen beyond the borders of Fars province.[58]

The privacy and physical inviolability of a large standalone residence were often the prerogative of the rich. The lower strata of society usually resided in multifamily dwellings, where the culturally desirable practice of gender segregation, particularly among unrelated people, was nearly impossible.[59] In September 1899, a hat maker (*kulahduz*) lived in a unit of a multifamily residence where a woman and her ten- to fifteen-year-old daughter also resided. One night, he came to their room and began raping the virgin daughter in her sleep. She awoke yelling and screaming, which alerted the other residents to what was happening. The next day, the people of the neighborhood raided the hat maker's home, where they found him dead. The cause of death was unclear; one account claimed that he had committed suicide by opium ingestion, while another claimed that the residents of the house had beaten him to death.[60] In either case, it appears that the government did not pursue further investigation, which, if the second account is true, means that they tacitly condoned the rough justice of the residents.

Far from falling into one discrete jurisdiction, moral policing spanned the government's policing figures, the 'ulama, sayyids and seminarians, and even ordinary subjects. Most sex criminals were subjected to a scripted and highly ritualized public punishment, one that paraded the offender around town in an abased condition, such as in a bridle, partially disfigured, or on a pack animal, to reenact the shame of their offense. Although the 'ulama handled adultery and prostitution cases, they were conspicuously absent in tending to rape cases, which may suggest that it was not considered a type of crime handled at a shari'ah court. Finally, the social status of the offender and the accused were often key determinants of legal outcomes.

Alcohol Production, Consumption, and Unruly Behavior

Similar to concerns over illicit sex, authorities and residents in Shiraz were preoccupied with the policing and punishment of alcohol production and consumption. Alcohol was associated with Shiraz's small Jewish population, since Jewish distillers had replaced Armenians as the main producers of alcohol in Shiraz over the course of the nineteenth century.[61] Theoretically, alcohol production was meant for internal non-Muslim consumption or export to other cities, but in practice, many local Muslims consumed alcohol. This led Jewish distillers to become the object of scrutiny by upholders of religious morals and sometimes by governors. In Shi'i jurisprudence, the manifest consumption of alcohol constituted a *hadd* offense. Jews repeatedly had their alcohol pitchers destroyed, their wine spilled, and their distilleries raided on the pretext that their alcohol production was both against the shari'ah and a cause of disorder in the city. As part of local authorities' policing duties, they closely monitored those who drank openly or became drunk and disorderly. What was more complicated legally, however, was the private consumption of alcohol, since this sometimes blurred the lines between public and private. Using forbidding wrong as a justification, *mujtahid*s and their followers raided private parties on the suspicion that alcohol was being consumed. By doing so, they transgressed, in the eyes of many people, the Islamic principle of the home's inviolability. More significantly, they also challenged local and imperial state officials' claims to a monopoly on the legitimate use of violence.

Muslim merchants engaged in the moral policing of Zoroastrian merchants consuming alcohol openly in their shared caravanserai; the ensuing controversy led to the local governor and the Ministry of Foreign Affairs, which was in charge of non-Muslim affairs, becoming involved. In 1867, when Zoroastrian merchants began "drinking alcohol publicly" (*sharb-i ashkara*) in a caravanserai, a fight broke out between Muslim and Zoroastrian merchants, the former accusing the latter of not drinking discretely. The Zoroastrian merchants reported their version of the events to Mirza Muhammad 'Ali Khan, the secretary of foreign affairs, who presented the matter to the governor, Hisam al-Saltanah. The government report suggests that the Zoroastrians presented Muhammad 'Ali Khan with a large gift to emphasize their mistreatment and lack of fault. Hisam al-Saltanah found the Muslim merchants to be at fault, had them beaten with sticks, and took a thirty-tuman fine (*jarimah*) from them. In response, the Muslim merchants took asylum at a local sanctuary, claiming, "Why should Muslim sayyids be disgraced [*muftazah*] by being beaten with sticks without cause or reason for [the sake of] four Zoroastrian in Islamic lands?" In response to their petition, the local agent of the minister of foreign affairs, Mirza Abu al-Hasan Khan Mushir al-Mulk, agreed that the initial incident had been misrepresented to the governor, which led the latter to summon the two sides for a resolution. Initially, Muslim merchants negotiated to buy the Zoroastrian caravanserai chambers so that they would not have to share the space, which the governor tentatively accepted.[62] But in the end, the governor took a three-hundred-tuman gift from the Zoroastrian merchants to allow them to stay in their chambers, while a three-hundred-tuman fine was forcibly taken from the Muslim merchants so that they would not dare speak to their Zoroastrian neighbors anymore.[63]

More so than Zoroastrians, Jews were heavily involved in alcohol production.[64] The issue of Jews producing and distributing alcohol within Shiraz repeatedly became a lightning rod of contention between the government and certain *mujtahids* over the jurisdiction of monitoring and punishing violations of prohibitions on alcohol consumption. At the heart of such jurisdictional conflict was the issue of who had the duty to forbid wrong with violence.

The issue of authority came to the fore in the summer of 1881 when a Jewish man was carrying a pitcher of liquor (*'araq*) to the house of a Muslim. Sayyid 'Ali Akbar Falasiri carried out summary justice on this Jewish individual when he encountered him on a side street: he broke the man's pitcher and cut off his locks (*zulfha*). The cutting of hair as a punishment for Jews functioned as a shaming mechanism, a means of further visually differentiating Jews from Muslims, and a form of emasculation.[65] This punishment did not, however, go uncontested. At night, the Jews taped a broadsheet (*kaghaz*) to the *mujtahid*'s house, stating, "Why do you forbid us from selling wine? Ban your own mullahs who buy our alcohol. If you want to do such things in the future, we will kill you." Laced with several unmentioned curse words, this message sent Falasiri into a rage. The next day, he mounted the pulpit at the Masjid-i Vakil, from which he read the broadsheet and asserted that at the appointed time, "we must kill [the Jews]." He promised to do so after the month of Ramazan had passed, since killing was forbidden during the holy month, and put a shroud around his neck. Hajji Amir, the Amir-i Divankhanah (head of the central government judiciary) in Shiraz, went to speak to Falasiri in the aftermath of his sermon: "What kind of ruling is this that you have made? Is the killing of Jews in your hands? This is a government issue [*in kar-i dawlati ast*]. Do you want to throw Fars and the country of Iran into disarray?" Hajji Amir's response indicates that the Qajar government viewed violence in the form of punishments toward subjects as its prerogative and not that of the 'ulama. In response, Falasiri was momentarily silent but then spelled out the logic of his threat: "Selling wine and playing music [*mutribi*] must stop. They [the Jews] must shave their locks and not wear elegant clothes [*libas-i fakhir*]. If they do not do so, I will do what I must do."[66] This exchange demonstrates that for Falasiri, the *mujtahids* had direct jurisdiction over punishing infractions of shariʻah, in a manner consistent with the theories of Muhammad Baqir Shafti.[67] In the aftermath of Falasiri's sermon, Jews closed the doors of their homes and refused to engage in commerce out of fear of the city's ruffians. Most Jewish musicians shaved their locks to preempt any possible punishments. Some Jews even hid their belongings in their basements or the homes of sympathetic Muslims.[68] For unexplained reasons, Falasiri abandoned his call to kill the Jews and claimed to have forgiven them, possibly because of a handsome gift given in exchange for his "forgiveness."[69]

The following year, the minister of foreign affairs contacted the governor, Sahib Divan, stating that he had received several reports that Falasiri continued to harass Jews. He further complained that Falasiri was not paying attention (*i'tina*) to the governors or the local government and demanded to know why he was causing such disorder (*mufsidah*). He further ordered the governor to stop Falasiri's behavior and inform everyone that "oppression against the Jews is not allowed" (*tazallumat-i yahud ja'iz nist*).[70] Sahib Divan, annoyed by the Jewish petitions against him, accused them of being nosey (*fuzuli*) and assured the minister of foreign affairs that he was taking care of them personally. He believed the root of the problem was that the Jews were selling alcohol to the local population from their distillery. He acknowledged that Falasiri occasionally terrified (*vahshat*) them with his words but promised to "block and banish him" if he moved from words to action.[71]

In fall 1894, a group of Jews purchased a "property in ruins" in the environs of the Bagh-i Hukumati on which they had built a distillery. Falasiri, who passed by this property with forty seminarians, heard that this property had previously been the site of a mosque. Seeing this as a defilement of sacred land, he immediately ruled that all the Jews' pitchers of wine and liquor there should be broken; the seminarians then raided the distillery. The Jewish distillers petitioned the local government about the incident, but the government hesitated to confront Falasiri directly. Instead, the government told the Jews to petition the shah directly without its mediation since they paid taxes to the central government and Falasiri had destroyed their means of producing revenue.[72]

In the meantime, the local government mobilized and armed its soldiers in case Falasiri caused an uprising. In response, Falasiri barricaded the roof of his house in case government troops tried to capture him. At night, throngs of people from all neighborhoods gathered at Falasiri's house armed with weapons, saying they would execute whatever order he gave with their property and life. The government stationed soldiers at the government residence in case Falasiri ordered his ruffians to attack. On the morning of the second day of this standoff, the shah responded to the Jewish petition with the command, "Banish Hajji Sayyid ʿAli Akbar [Falasiri]." The local government took the telegram to the officer of the royal household (*pishkhidmat*), who was charged with informing Falasiri of its contents. After reading the telegram, Falasiri responded as follows: "Go and tell the government that I will not leave my house and family, nor [will I] exit the city. Either kill me so that I will leave this world a martyr, or if you want to force me out of the city, I will kill [them] with every ounce of my life and strength, and if I die, I will be counted among the martyrs."[73] He then proceeded to bad-mouth the shah, the government, and Mustashar al-Mulk, before saying, "I will not prevent the [implementation of the] commandments and prohibitions [*avamir and navahi*] that God and the Prophet have commanded, nor will I forsake it irrespective of what might befall me."[74] The reference to "commandments and prohibitions" was an unambiguous invocation of the Islamic principle of forbidding wrong, which Falasiri took to mean that he, as a *mujtahid*, had direct jurisdiction over moral violations such as illegal alcohol production on sacred ground. His challenge led to the assertion of imperial juridical authority when local authorities feared becoming involved.

Falasiri was not the only one, however, to make rulings against alcohol; the local government occasionally issued bans on alcohol production in response to drunken and disorderly conduct. Such bans served both to demonstrate that a local governor was tough on crime and to preempt extrajudicial violence by the likes of Falasiri. In 1903, several servants of provincial government officials went to the garden of Mirza Mahmud Khan, the bank translator, where they became drunk, engaged in disorderly conduct, and injured one another. The provincial governor summoned them and had them beaten with sticks the next morning. He also summoned Mirza Mahmud Khan to ask him why he had "built a coffeehouse" in his garden where people could "engage in

disorderly conduct [*harzigi*]." The governor's officials were ready to bastinado Mirza Mahmud Khan, but he pleaded with them; instead, the
officials closed down his coffeehouse and stationed a guard there to
prevent further disorder. Next, the Jewish distiller (*shirahchi*) who sup-
plied the alcohol was summoned. He was ordered not to sell alcohol, and
the colonel (*sarhang*) of the Cossacks, 'Ali Pasha Khan, was tasked with
breaking any wine and "alcohol containers" in the Jewish neighborhood.
The Jews started pleading with them, "We obey your order not to sell alcohol. Why are you breaking our instruments [*asbab*]? This will cause
[financial] loss." The provincial government responded, "Now that you
fear loss, you will be punished with sticks." 'Ali Pasha Khan and the
Cossacks then raided the Jewish neighborhood, causing much disorder
and close to one thousand tumans in damages to the distillers. The government extracted a harsh guarantor document (*iltizam*) in which the
distillers promised not to make alcohol anymore, not to sell it to anyone, and not to drink it themselves. The government then dialed back
these terms by allowing the distillers to make alcohol for export to Tehran or Bushihr, although they had to promise not to sell it to Muslims
in the city. If any alcohol was sold to Muslims, then the house of the
seller would be destroyed in retribution.[75]

The governor again took a harsh stance toward Jewish distillers
half a year later when they were caught selling alcohol to drunk revelers
in the city. Several servants of the oil chief (*ra'is-i naft*) came to Shiraz,
where they drank heavily and roamed around the streets in a drunken
state. These men were caught and brought to the governor, 'Ala al-
Dawlah. He had them beaten with sticks and asked them who had sold
them the liquor, to which they responded, "The Jews." The governor was
surprised since he had strictly banned them from selling alcohol to Muslims. He therefore summoned Fath al-Iyalah, the deputy (*na'ib*) of the
Jewish neighborhood, as well as the distillers themselves.[76] 'Ala al-Dawlah
was very upset and had the deputy beaten with sticks for having allowed
the Jews to sell alcohol, although the Jewish distillers appear to have been
spared.[77]

Government and religious officials also regularly punished Muslim consumers of alcohol without also punishing Jewish suppliers. In
October 1884, eight muleteers (*qatirchis*) went to a distiller in the Jewish

neighborhood, where they consumed large amounts of alcohol and fought with several Jews over a pitcher of liquor. The Jews informed their deputy, Husayn 'Ali, who arrived at the scene, silenced the muleteers, and kicked them out, but not before being injured by them. The muleteers also injured several bystanders, including a servant of the English government's consular agent, Haydar 'Ali Khan Navvab. The family of the injured servant petitioned the Sahib Divan, who had the muleteers imprisoned for a few days before being bastinadoed and then released.[78]

In one case, religious officials punished drunken and unruly individuals directly before handing them over to the government for further punishment. In May 1887, a man passed the door of the *mujtahid* Hajji Shaykh Muhammad Husayn Mahallati in a drunken state. The people of the neighborhood took the man to Shaykh Muhammad Husayn, who had the man beaten according to "the shari'ah *hadd* punishment." The *mujtahid* then had the man sent to the local government prison (*habs-i hukumati*).[79] This was a rare case in which a *mujtahid* employed a *hadd* punishment for public drunkenness, although it is notable that he also had the offenders sent to the government prison in recognition of the overlapping jurisdiction between the 'ulama and the government in criminal matters.

Other cases pertaining to suspected alcohol consumption by Muslims were much more contentious, since several 'ulama and their seminarians violated the Islamic sanctity of the domicile and the prohibition on spying in the course of policing vice.[80] In the summer of 1890, two 'ulama, Mirza Muhammad Husayn Mujtahid and Hajji Shaykh 'Ali Pishnamaz, heard sounds coming from the house of Mirza Aqa, which they assumed to be signs of a drinking party. They then dispatched a group of seminarians, who, instead of knocking on the door and making their presence known (as prescribed in the Quran), entered the residence from "the door and the wall," where they found nothing but a few broken bottles of sour grape juice (*ab-i ghurah*) and lemonade. Despite this, they started to drag everyone out of the residence. In response, these individuals, along with the people of the neighborhood (*ahl-i mahallah*), beat up the seminarians. In the morning, the offended party collectively requested that the government punish the seminarians for their actions. The government investigated the matter and decided that it was against the shari'ah for the seminarians to enter the house "without notice," drag out the respected men, and pass such judgment. It decided not to expel the seminarians but made them promise to desist from such actions in the future.[81] Intriguingly, the government invoked a shari'ah justification for its ruling since the seminarians had violated Islamic privacy norms, although they were not punished.

In the spring of 1883, two women were publicly drunk and approaching Shiraz from the direction of the Bagh-i Naw. Several men with "bad intentions" approached them between the Sa'di and Isfahan gates of Shiraz. People from both gates rushed to the women's assistance, which led to an altercation. Before a brawl could break out, kadkhudas and the attendants of the biglarbigi arrived to separate the two sides. They took the two drunk women to the house of Qavam al-Mulk, where it was discovered that they were the wives of seminarians studying under the Imam Jum'ah. It was unclear if they were punished or if they were referred to the Imam Jum'ah.[82]

In early 1887, two soldiers and a prostitute went to the Bagh-i Takht in "a completely drunken state." There the biglarbigi's attendants tried to separate the prostitute from the soldiers, but the soldiers beat them up. They relied on help from villagers from Dih Buzurg to subdue the soldiers, beat them up, and take the prostitute to the house of the biglarbigi. The soldiers then regrouped to take the prostitute back from the house of the biglarbigi. When they reached the Sa'di Gate, they fought with government attendants, leading to more injuries. Since the governor, Sahib Divan, was in the Dilgusha Garden, the biglarbigi went directly there to report the issue to him. Sahib Divan mounted a horse and returned to the house immediately. He calmed down the soldiers, but the next day, he summoned the general (sartip) of the troops and had the guilty individuals punished.[83]

During the month of Ramazan, a traveling mendicant (darvish) found himself on the receiving end of the local community's ire for flagrantly contravening the shari'ah. The darvish had been "drinking intoxicants" out in the open (zahiran) in his residential chamber. His neighbors reported this to Falasiri, who sent his followers to drag him out of the room and blacken his face, a tashhir punishment that drew inspiration from apocalyptic Islamic imagery about the fate of sinners on the Day of Judgment.[84] Once in the presence of Falasiri, he was struck by many lashes before being banished. The case remarkably did not involve the government: the neighbors monitored and reported it, while Falasiri and his followers punished him. The anonymous composer of the report was well aware of the implications: "These types of actions by the sayyid [Falasiri] are somewhat opposed to the wishes of the government [*hukumat*]. The sayyid is by nature desirous of leadership [*riyasat*] and strives to carry out governmental commandments and prohibitions [*avamir va navahi-i mulki*]. To some degree he has progressed in this." The reporter viewed Falasiri's actions as overstepping his bounds by taking over government functions such as punishing the *darvish*.[85]

As these cases illustrate, the policing of alcohol-related crimes involved not only local government officials but also certain *mujtahid*s, their followers, and even ordinary neighbors. At times, such policing was done in tandem, but it often involved more jurisdictional conflict than cooperation. Seminarians and others who raided private homes did so by invoking the principle of forbidding wrong, which was in sharp tension with Islamic privacy norms.

Entertainment Music

Unlike fornication and alcohol consumption, listening to and playing music did not constitute a *hadd* offense. But music was seen as a gateway vice since it often occurred alongside other vices. Islamic jurists viewed entertainment music as dangerous for its emotional effects, which could lead one to consume alcohol or engage in illicit sex.[86] *Mujtahid*s and their followers patrolled neighborhoods for sonic evidence of parties where all three vices might occur. Jewish musicians were under intense pressure and scrutiny as figures deeply enmeshed in Shiraz's vibrant leisure scene (figure 14). They were regularly hired by the city's elites, both foreign and local, for private parties. Despite musicians performing behind closed doors, sound often spilled out into the streets, thus prompting raids in which musical instruments were destroyed and musicians and attendees were beaten up.[87]

Figure 14: Shirazi Jewish musicians.
(Source: Sa'idi Sirjani, *Vaqayi'*, verso 588)

While most entertainment music cases involved Jews, an early recorded case involved an Armenian tied to the local English consulate
who had his house raided by a local Shirazi Islamic scholar (*akhund*)
and his servants in 1867. The translator of the English reporter (*balyuz*)
was invited to the house of one of the local Armenians, where wine,
music, and song were plentiful. The Armenian lived next door to Mirza
Mahdi Ardistani, an *akhund* who objected to the music. He and two of
his servants entered the Armenian's house, proceeded to swear at the attendants, and broke the musical instruments. He then commanded the
night guard to seize anyone who came out of the house. The aggrieved
translator initially petitioned the governor, Hisam al-Saltanah. During
the governor's investigation, Mirza Mahdi boasted that he commanded
fifty thousand Muslims and continued to hurl insults at the English resident and others. The governor responded to the petitioner that "punishing [*muvakhazah*] the 'ulama" was not in his power, since if he were
to do so, he would be branded an unbeliever (*kafir*) and the city would

"be in an uproar." Next, the local English minister plenipotentiary (Vazir Mukhtar) petitioned the minister of foreign affairs that one of his subjects felt that his life was unsafe in Shiraz and suggested that surely the imperial government had the power to summon the *akhund* to Tehran for questioning. The minister of foreign affairs instead asked the governor to write Mirza Mahdi and convince him to show "kindness and empathy" to the translator through the deputy (*vakil*) of the English consulate, but the English minister was insistent on his approach. Although the shah also feared the 'ulama's reaction, Mirza Mahdi was eventually exiled to Karbala.[88] Given the taboo on punishing the 'ulama, banishment was one of the few penal instruments available to the shah in such cases.

Falasiri and his followers targeted Jewish entertainment musicians and performers for similar reasons. In the month of Ramazan in 1889, the famous Jewish musician Mullah Aqa had a party at his home during which he and other Jewish musicians played entertainment music (*tarab*). According to the report, this dinner-party spread was "fully in line with their religious law [*qanun-i mazhabi*]"; since it was behind closed doors and not in violation of Jewish law, it did not contravene Islamic law. But a group of Muslims caught wind of the party and prevented the Jews from their leisure (*'aysh*). Falasiri was informed of this event the next night and commanded a group of Muslims to gather and kill the Jews, presumably because the party took place during Ramazan. The *biglarbigi* Qavam al-Mulk, however, made a pact (*ta'ahud*) that he would punish and chastise the Jews on the condition that Falasiri not act on his pronouncements. Despite the oath, the *biglarbigi* apparently failed to punish the Jews, which set the stage for subsequent incidents.[89]

In June 1889, four Jewish musicians (*mutrib*s) performed at someone's house at night. Falasiri sent a group to raid the party and destroy all the musical instruments. The crowd detained the four men and had them taken to Falasiri's home, where they were detained until the morning. Falasiri then had the four men "thoroughly punished" and had their locks shaved off.[90] Jewish musicians subsequently did not attend parties out of fear of Falasiri and preferred to disperse in villages and agricultural districts.[91] According to another, very similar account of events a year later, Falasiri had Jewish musicians brought to him and imprisoned. In the morning, he had a *hadd* punishment carried out on them and had their locks cut off.[92] In response, the government sent someone to inform him that carrying out such actions independently was wrong, to which he replied that he would sacrifice himself in the path of the shari'ah.[93] The exchange illustrated once again the contested issue of criminal jurisdiction in the city. Since Qajar shahs portrayed themselves as protectors of *zimmi* populations, Falasiri's actions gained attention in Tehran by July. The Ministry of Foreign Affairs sent a telegram to the governor, Mu'tamid al-Dawlah, stating, "Who is this Sayyid 'Ali Akbar who is bothering the Jews this much? Why are you, the governor, not preventing this?" The central government feared an uprising, so a meeting was organized by the governor in the Bagh-i 'Afif, which included several mullahs and Falasiri, to avert possible violence. Meanwhile, the Jews feared going out into the side streets and bazaars and passing by his house.[94]

Several years later, however, Falasiri continued to raid private parties. In 1892, Falasiri sent several seminarians and a sayyid to a residence where several Jewish musicians were performing. They caught the musicians and brought them to the *mujtahid*, who punished them extensively with lashes and shaved their locks. Upon learning of this, the *biglarbigi* summoned the neighborhood's day guard (*pakar*) and had him bastinadoed and imprisoned for not informing him of the incident. This upset the city's *kadkhudas* and *pakars*, who protested the *biglarbigi*'s punishment by taking refuge at the Masjid-i Naw, stating, "We will not perform our policing duties [*kadkhuda'i*]."[95] The *biglarbigi*'s decision to punish his underlings instead of taking on Falasiri points to his fear that the latter posed a threat to local government sovereignty and his tacit normalization of the raids on private residences.

The *biglarbigi* continued to hesitate in confronting Falasiri in a case involving a Jewish musician and his dancing boy. Mullah Aqa was a famous Shirazi Jewish musician who employed a fourteen- to fifteen-year-old Jewish dancing boy. A shoe weaver (*urusiduz*) invited the two to his house on several occasions, but they refused. One night, the shoe weaver spent quite a bit of money on a party and invited ten to twenty guests. Mullah Aqa attended but did not bring the dancing boy with him, which annoyed the shoe weaver. Later, the shoe weaver started harassing Mullah Aqa and the dancing boy while they were at another residence. When the two were on their way home late at night, the shoe weaver gathered fifteen men armed with clubs to attack them and abduct the dancing boy. Mullah Aqa managed to fend them off temporarily, but he suffered two injuries, one on his forehead and one on his head. The crowd managed to abduct the dancing boy. That same evening, Mullah Aqa informed the *biglarbigi*, who dispatched his head attendant and several agents to investigate. Their investigations went nowhere, but the next day, the dancing boy turned up at Falasiri's house. Falasiri's son intended to shave the boy's locks, but Mullah Aqa offered Falasiri's son a gift in exchange for the boy. Meanwhile, the *biglarbigi* planned to punish the crowd that had abducted the boy, but they responded that they were merely carrying out Falasiri's son's ruling (*hukm*). The *biglarbigi* once again was too timid to confront Falasiri's network and let the matter slide.[96] In the interim, Falasiri was personally involved in a raid on a private residence when, one night, he was on his way to the Mushir al-Mulk Mosque to pray. He heard the sound of music, so he and his followers raided the house, beat up the Jewish musicians, and forced them to scatter. The crowd also roughed up the residents of the house and took some of their belongings.[97]

Mullah Aqa often found himself caught between competing, powerful elites insisting on his attendance at their parties. One night, he had an appointment (*maw'id*) at the house of Baha al-Sultan, the commander of the Zarand troops, but on his way there, he was intercepted by the agents of Intizam al-Sultan, the head attendant of Nizam al-Mulk, who informed him that his services were wanted by legal order (*hukman*) at the house of the Russian subject Samad Aqa Tajir Shirvani. Mullah Aqa ignored this order and proceeded to the house of Baha al-Sultan. The next night, Intizam al-Sultan had Mullah Aqa summoned. Upon entering the gate, the head attendant had his agents catch Mullah Aqa, beat him with sticks, and strip him of his belongings, which amounted to twenty to thirty tumans. They then wanted to imprison him. To buy his freedom, Mullah Aqa had to pay fifty tumans in cash to the head attendant and ten tumans to his assistant and other attendants to secure his release. The local government heard about this and asked the head attendant about what had transpired. He lied about the situa-

tion and claimed that Mullah Aqa "had an altercation with the government agents and said very bad things about the government and
government officials," which led him to act in this manner. He added
that he had not taken "more than thirty tumans from him" in total.[98]
However, Baha al-Sultan corrected the record. The government then
awarded Mullah Aqa a shawl as an official robe of honor (khal'at-i rasm).
The head attendant was then ordered to give back whatever he had taken
from Mullah Aqa, but he refused to do so.[99]

In 1903, the governor, 'Ala al-Dawlah, changed tactics with the Jewish musicians: he attempted to have them work as spies and prepare
reports about their parties. The musicians, however, refused to do and,
out of fear for the governor, refused to work. The majority of musicians
and their troupes were leaving for Bushihr and Baghdad, as the situation became increasingly difficult for them.[100] This order demonstrates
how events had come full circle: the local government, which had objected to raids on private residences in the past, had now resorted to trying to co-opt Jewish musicians as spies.

Conclusion

To conclude, three forms of vice—illicit sex, alcohol, and music—were
at the center of concerns regarding public morality in nineteenth-century
Shiraz. Since many of the city's alcohol producers and musicians were
Jews, the policing of vice often took on intercommunal dimensions. Who
had jurisdiction to police vice revealed underlying tensions between government and religious authorities, with government officials viewing it
as their sole prerogative, since for them, political sovereignty rested
on "the *monopoly of the legitimate use of force* within a given territory," forbidding wrong, and upholding public morality.[101] On the other
hand, Shi'i *mujtahids* viewed themselves collectively as deputies of
the Hidden Imam of Twelver Shi'ism with the delegated authority to
forbid wrong and implement *hudud* punishments. Given that both forbidding wrong and *hudud* punishments implied that the vice in question was somehow public, this raised the question of the extent to which
the sanctity of privacy trumped the possible intrusion of government
or religious authorities into private spaces. Repeated raids by certain

*mujtahid*s and their followers on private parties, despite Islamic values upholding the inviolability of the home, and the condemnation of those raids, either by government officials or the affected parties themselves, suggest a contested legal terrain through which a variety of actors defined the contours of public and private.

Murder in Shiraz

Retribution, Punishment, and Compensation

I
n nineteenth-century Shiraz, the question of who had the authority to try murder cases revealed a complex jurisdictional terrain involving local, imperial, and religious authorities. At the heart of
the matter was sovereignty over life and death. The execution of
murderers often entailed public spectacles in which the logic of equivalences prevailed: the execution ritually reenacted the crime, by using the
same instruments of murder, inflicting the same injuries leading up to
the execution, or choosing the same or a nearby spot for execution. The
government intended for public executions to restore public order and
deter would-be murderers.[1] Murderers treated most harshly included
ruffians and outlaws who also engaged in theft, banditry, and terroriz-
ing the population. They rarely appeared at shari'ah courts; instead, the
government punished them directly by way of exemplary public executions (*siyasat*). People convicted of murder according to shari'ah
principles had their fate placed in the hands of the heirs (*varasah*) of the
murdered individual: they could choose retribution (*qisas*), compensation (*diyah* or *diyat*), or forgiveness without compensation. Often, the
local governor executed ordinary murderers without a shari'ah ruling
or the involvement of heirs on the basis of their discretionary authority.
Sometimes governors had to wait for an imperial decree to execute murderers in light of Nasir al-Din Shah's efforts to have the final say in this

form of punishment. Executions were often avoided because of insufficient evidence, doubt, intercession by powerful notables and members
of the 'ulama, taking asylum (*bast*) to bide time for a favorable ruling,
and offering government officials gifts in exchange for leniency.

Sex crimes occasionally led to extrajudicial honor killings but
were usually heard before the governor and/or the shari'ah court. In
nineteenth-century Shiraz, mothers played an exceptional role as executioners in murder cases, despite this role typically being played by
male kinsmen. The women in question sometimes refused to hire the
local executioner and opted to avenge their murdered children with
their own hands. In murder cases more broadly, the marginal social
status of the victims and the accused affected legal outcomes: women,
individuals of modest socioeconomic status, non-Muslims, African
slaves, prostitutes, and *amrads* were regularly subject to differential
treatment. While this differential treatment could partly be explained
by principles found in Islamic jurisprudence, such as in the case of slaves
and non-Muslims, the reasons for the other categories of marginality
had more to do with the absence of heirs to pursue justice and the priv-
ileged socioeconomic status of the murderer or their families. When
people involved in murder were of foreign citizenship, jurisdictional issues became even more complex, even if all the people involved were of
the same religion, since foreign consulates sought to resolve the issue
through a negotiated settlement.

Crimes of Passion, Illicit Sex, and Murder-Rape

Individuals often murdered family members whom they suspected of engaging in illicit sex out of a sense of honor instead of turning them over
to the authorities.[2] It will be recalled that certain Shi'i jurists, such as
Muhammad Baqir Shafti, justified the patriarch executing wives, slaves,
and sons if they were caught in flagrante delicto in the domicile.[3] Despite this defense, local Shiraz authorities sometimes punished murderers in such cases.

In early 1883, two sons killed their mother and her presumed lover
in the Kaziri agricultural district (*buluk*). According to one account, one
son shot his mother's presumed lover. His mother fled and hid, but the

same son found and killed her. When a report was sent to Tehran government officials, they ordered local Shiraz authorities to find him and carry out *qisas*. The guilty son was taken to the Canon Square (*maydan-i tupkhanah*) and beheaded.[4] According to a second account, the two sons both killed their mother's presumed lover and beat their mother to within an inch of her life. They were both caught, but only the brother held responsible for the murder was punished "according to shari'ah punishments [*mujazat*]," meaning *qisas*.[5] Curiously, the heirs of the murdered man were conspicuously absent, suggesting that he did not have any; instead, the central government or the local government acted as the heirs of the murdered individual. Since the sons murdered their mother, they could not act as her heirs because they would benefit from compensation for their own crime. In late June 1890, the government dealt more leniently with a similar crime of passion. In the village of Rahmatabad, a young man suspected (*istishham*) that his sister was unchaste and killed her. Government officials (*karguzars*) beat him and threw him in prison, but he was apparently not subsequently executed. The difference in treatment between this and the aforementioned case may have been because the former involved a murder outside the family while the latter involved killing someone within it.[6]

Family honor was central to a crime of honor involving a Qazvini soldier who murdered a local notable, Mirza 'Abbas Sarrishtahdar, in 1861. Several years earlier, a Qazvini man who had impregnated a woman after they had illicit sex (*muvasilati*) died shortly thereafter. Sarrishtahdar took the woman and child under his protection, the former becoming his servant. The Qazvini man's brother, who was a soldier, showed up at his house one day, started arguing with him, and stabbed Sarrishtahdar to death. Neighbors and passersby apprehended the soldier. The heirs of Sarrishtahdar petitioned the governor, Mu'ayyad al-Dawlah. Since the man was a soldier, he was punished according to both the shari'ah ruling and the Military Code (*qanun-i 'askar*), which the newspaper describes as his "just deserts."[7]

In murder-rape cases, the rapist often murdered the victim to ensure their silence. In January 1856, a five- or six-year-old female orphan was found dead in one of the city's ruins (*kharabah*). A group discovered her body and reported it to the governor. Mirza 'Ali Khan Biglarbigi, the *biglarbigi* of Shiraz, and the *kadkhuda*s investigated but failed to turn anything up. In the meantime, a Black slave (*ghulam-i siyah*) narrated to a group of people that three months earlier he had taken a girl matching the orphan's description to a ruin, where he drank alcohol and, in his drunken state, had sex (*mubashirat*) with her until she died. He left her there and ran away. Those who heard the story reported it to the *kadkhuda* of their neighborhood, leading to the slave's arrest. The governor subsequently interrogated the suspect, and he confessed. Following the logic of equivalences, the governor had him taken to the same ruin where the crime occurred, thus producing a symmetry between the crime and the punishment: there he was executed (*siyasat nimudah*) "in accordance with his unseemly [*na-shayistah*] acts."[8] The governor appears to have acted as the orphan's heir since she had no known family. The use of the term *siyasat* instead of *qisas* for the execution suggests that it was carried out on the basis of the governor's discretionary authority rather than a formal shari'ah trial.[9]

In a similar murder-rape, a man from the village of Dih Maydani went to the door of a coppersmith's shop in Shiraz to buy a copper tray in late 1897. The villager asked for the shop owner's fourteen-year-old son's help in carrying home the tray. Several days passed without any sign of the man or the boy. Later, the boy's body was found choked to death in an underground irrigation canal (*qanat*) outside the Shadi Allah Gate. When the villager was caught, he confessed to having engaged in "an act against the shari'ah" (*'amali khalaf-i shar'*), meaning rape. The boy had threatened to tell his father, leading to the villager killing him for fear of the "hardship" this would cause. He later threw the corpse down a *qanat*. The authorities sent a telegram to the governor, 'Abd al-Husayn Mirza Farmanfarma, asking for a ruling for this confessed murderer, although it is unclear what decision was made.[10] Given the confession, it is likely that he was either executed or made to pay compensation.

In a similar case, an Islamic teacher (*akhund*) murdered his student to keep his rape secret in November 1861. Islamic jurisprudence generally encourages preventing an older man and a younger boy from meeting in a "morally hazardous private sphere" (*khalvat*), such as an empty room or house, where illicit sexual acts could take place.[11] In precisely such circumstances, Mirza Mahdi Nayrizi, a children's teacher (*mu'allim-i atfal*), raped the unnamed son of the deceased man, Mirza Husayn Khan Kashani. When the child reported the incident to his paternal uncle (*amu*), 'Abdullah Khan, Mirza Mahdi was kicked out of the house. Mirza Mahdi sought revenge by poisoning the child with some sweets (*nuqli*), leading to his death the following day. The family of the child deduced that the death was related to the sweets, but when they tried to find the teacher, they learned that he had taken sanctuary (*bast*) at the Shah Chiragh Shrine, which only strengthened their suspicions. The family petitioned the governor, Mu'ayyad al-Dawlah, who brought Mirza Mahdi out of the sanctuary for an interrogation.

During this interrogation, Mirza Mahdi confessed to visiting his student's house and to giving him sweets. Meanwhile, another person gave testimony (*guvahi*) that Mirza Mahdi had told him that the child in question would die on the ninth day of the month and that his mother would mourn for him. During the trial, a sayyid came with a handkerchief (*dastmali*) that Mirza Mahdi had entrusted to him, which included sweets and some pills (*qurs*). Several of these sweets were given to Mirza Mahdi, who was kept overnight but did not show signs of illness. The next day, Mirza Mahdi was brought out in "a distraught state" (*halat-i parishani*), possibly because of the pills, a guilty conscience, and/or torture. It was confirmed that he had confessed to the murder, presumably at a shari'ah court, and he was entrusted to the boy's uncle, 'Abdullah Khan, who used a sword to carry out retaliation. Unlike most other *qisas* cases, the execution scene was illustrated by Sani' al-Mulk, the official government newspaper's editor, and published in the *Ruznamah-i Dawlat-i 'Illiyah-i Iran* newspaper (figure 15). This illustration provides a rare example of the realistic visual idiom of Qajar-era punishments.[12]

These cases demonstrate a tendency toward punishing murders involving a sexual or family honor component, with rare exceptions. Murder-rapes often ended in *qisas*, which implies that shari'ah trials must have taken place. Governors played a central role in such cases, indicative of a symbiotic relationship with shari'ah courts in *qisas* cases and an independent role when *siyasat* punishments were delivered.

Figure 15: A lithograph depicting the execution of an
Islamic schoolteacher (*akhund*) convicted of raping and murdering
his male student, carried out at the hands of the boy's uncle.

(Source: *Ruznamah-i Dawlat-i 'Illiyah-i Iran*, n.504
[10 Jumada al-Avval 1278 H. / (November 13, 1861)])

Women Carrying Out *Qisas*

When heirs opted for *qisas*, a male family member usually carried it out,
or they hired the city's executioner (*mir ghazab*). In the early to mid-
1850s, however, three elderly mothers remarkably opted to carry out
qisas directly, either because they did not have an adult male kinsman
or because they were unable to afford hiring an executioner. As in similar cases in Isfahan, women participated in legal retribution not just as
decision-makers but also as physical executioners (figure 16). This unprecedented role of women in *qisas* was apparently not justified in Islamic
jurisprudence, nor did it seem to have continued beyond the 1850s.

Figure 16: A lithograph depicting a woman executing a man.
(Source: *Mukhtarnamah* 1261 H. / [1845], reproduced in Marzolph, *Narrative*, 72)

In two cases from 1854–55, mothers of murdered men carried out *qisas* in a public spectacle. Although the governor presided over the trials and issued *qisas* orders, a *mujtahid* was either present at the same trial to issue such a ruling or issued one at his court. In December 1854, a Kurrani man murdered someone from Badisyah, leading his heirs to petition the Shiraz governor, Mu'ayyad al-Dawlah. The governor sent a bailiff (*muhassil*) to detain the murderer and bring him to Shiraz for investigation. The governor ruled that the murderer be handed over to the murdered man's shariʻah heir (*varis-i sharʻi*), who happened to be his elderly mother. She dragged the murderer by chain (*zanjir*) to the city square (*maydan*), where she laid him to the ground, picked up a stone, and smashed his head and brains in with it "as *qisas* for her son's blood."[13] This *qisas* simultaneously operated as an exemplary public deterrent since it took place in the city square.

In March 1855, a Kuvari man killed another man of the same background. Muʻayyad al-Dawlah had the murderer detained and brought to his presence along with his family and the sole heir of the murdered man, his elderly mother. The murderer's family tried in vain to convince the old woman to take compensation. They even offered a gift (*pishkish*) to the governor in addition to the *diyat*, signifying that murder was an offense against both the victim and a sovereign authority, but the governor ruled that the elderly woman was entitled to *qisas*. She too carried out the execution herself in a gruesome fashion by slitting the man's throat with a knife, drinking his blood, and using it as rouge for her cheeks and hands before leaving the corpse.[14]

Finally, a mother carried out *qisas* on her son-in-law for murdering her daughter in July 1855. In a village just outside of Shiraz, a group of men sat and joked around with one another. One turned to the other and said, "Your wife is loose in morals [*karash musavvab nist*], and she takes a companion [*rafiq*] for herself." The offended man stood up, returned to his house, and, in a fit of rage, seized his wife violently. She pleaded and begged, saying, "These words are false and were said in jest." The husband rejected this explanation and proceeded to torture her to death. The murdered woman's elderly mother petitioned the Divankhanah in Shiraz, thus invoking the central government's jurisdiction rather than the governor's. Muhammad Hashim Khan Divanbigi, the head of the Divankhanah, summoned the murderer and further investigated. The husband confessed to killing his wife, but he "pretended to be insane," knowing that this was grounds for evading a death sentence. The governor, Muʻayyad al-Dawlah, carried out a second investigation that proved the villager's full culpability.[15] He ordered that the man's mother-in-law had the right to carry out *qisas*, which she insisted on doing so that "it could mend [her] heart [*tashfiyah-i qalb*]." She had the man bound and entrusted to her; then she had him lie down before cutting off his head "like a lamb." She "drank some of his blood," said a prayer while facing him, and then "went on her way."[16] The case illustrates the overlapping jurisdiction of the Divankhanah and the governor, who carried out multiple investigations to determine guilt and assess the suspect's mental state before issuing a ruling. Once again, *mujtahids* were oddly absent from the account, although they were a part of investigatory councils of either the Divankhanah or the governor.

In 1850s Shiraz, women remarkably carried out executions, indicating that they participated in a form of legal sovereignty typically reserved for men in *qisas*. This unique role of women as direct executioners of male murderers seems to have disappeared after the 1850s in Shiraz and Isfahan, possibly because, as the government increasingly adopted measures to centralize and streamline decision-making over executions in Tehran, female heirs no longer engaged in this particular form of popular justice.

Social Status, Homicide, and Legal Outcomes

The social status imbalance between victims and the accused often affected legal outcomes. Social outcasts, deviants, or otherwise-marginal figures were subject to harsher punishments when found guilty of murder. Meanwhile, those who killed someone from a marginal background often faced lesser sanctions. The following cases look at four categories of marginality—prostitutes, beardless youth (*amrads*), Jews, and Black slaves—to explore how marginality affected legal outcomes in homicide cases. Shi'i jurisprudence made distinctions in *qisas* punishments and *diyat* payments depending on whether the victim was a slave or a non-Muslim. Prostitutes and beardless youth also faced differential treatment, not because of legal doctrine but because of the government's reticence to investigate and punish murderers of people who were at once marginal and lacked heirs demanding justice.

In the summer of 1877, the corpse of a prostitute was found in a ruin close to the wall of the city's fortress (*qal'ah*). People who stumbled across the body reported it to the local government: an investigation ensued. The prostitute's female neighbor testified at the governor's court that two soldiers from the Khassah troops killed the woman. The governor ordered the entire troop to his presence so the woman could identify the murderers, but she said they were not there, apparently because they had purposely not appeared. The government eventually dropped the entire matter despite the lead.[17] The murder victim's marginal status and lack of family members probably factored into the government dropping its investigation. It is also possible that the Khassah troops' commander protected the men, although this was a punishable offense under the Military Code.[18]

In late 1888, a secretary (*munshi*) of the governor, Sultan Uvays Mirza Ihtisham al-Dawlah, attended a party at the house of a Shirazi prostitute. He laid his hands on her throat and choked her to death, although the report stated that it was unclear if this was done with harmful intent or "in jest." The homicide was reported to the *biglarbigi*, who withheld news of it from Ihtisham al-Dawlah for fear that this would dishonor (*badnami*) government officials. Ihtisham al-Dawlah learned of the homicide several days later and beat his secretary with a stick; he also chided the *biglarbigi* for not issuing a report (*ruznamah*).[19] Aside from these minor measures, the governor did not further investigate or punish his secretary for the homicide, indicating that the local government avoided punishing one of its own to the full extent of the law out of concern for its reputation.

In contrast, local authorities vigorously investigated prostitutes when they were murder suspects. In May 1900, a one-eyed prostitute befriended—meaning she took on as a client—a soldier from the Zarand troops while secretly befriending others as well. One day, her initial soldier companion (*rafiq*) saw her having sex with another soldier. Heartbroken, he committed suicide by ingesting opium. Several days later, the second soldier was having a meal at the prostitute's residence. He suddenly died upon returning home. The authorities suspected her of poisoning the man, so they apprehended her and placed her in Qavam al-Mulk's prison. There were no further reports on whether she was found guilty or punished.[20]

Like prostitutes, *amrad*s were similarly identified primarily by their involvement in sex work.[21] Unlike female prostitutes, *amrad*s' family members pursued justice with the authorities in murder cases. The presence of *amrad* families suggests less of a social stigma for their sex work than for that of their female counterparts. In 1888, several people started drinking in the Sardizak neighborhood with an *amrad* in their midst. One of the men killed the *amrad* in a drunken state before throwing his corpse in the Sardizak mosque. The *amrad*'s father, who was a drover (*chubdar*) responsible for bringing sheep from around Fars to Shiraz's slaughterhouse, along with a large crowd, took the *amrad*'s corpse to the government fortress (Arg-i Hukumati). The government summoned Aqa Jan, the *farrashbashi* of the *biglarbigi*, to track down the murderer. For three days, the *farrashbashi* and other attendants searched for the murderer until they found one of the murder suspects in the house of his brother (*hamshirahzadah*), the Qashqa'i Ilbigi Mirza Sayyid Riza Mirza'i Darab Khan, along with the two other suspects. The three men were rounded up and thrown into the local government prison. The parents of the murdered boy suspected that one of the three men had murdered their son; the government concurred and initially intended to execute one of the three men. Meanwhile, several elders wished "to bring an end to the blood feud" (*khunbast kunand*) by brokering a settlement.[22] Given the doubt over the identity of the boy's murderer, a shari'ah conviction for intentional homicide with the option of *qisas* appeared unlikely.[23] The family of the murdered *amrad* demanded and was granted a hefty fine (*tarjuman*) of one thousand tumans from Darab Khan's kinsmen to end the blood feud.[24] Meanwhile, the government refused to rule for *qisas* given the ambiguity over the murderer's identity.[25] The *amrad*'s mother, who appears to have been the main decision-maker, agreed to forgo *qisas* if one of the two suspects, who was without a high station (*ism va rasm nadasht*), agreed to leave the city for thirty years.[26] She took some money from the other suspect, the son of an accountant (*mustawfi*), who was released.[27] This case demonstrates how doubt in homicide cases paved the way for a settlement, even in the case of a marginal victim whose parents were willing to pursue the case.

When the *amrad* was the murderer, the legal outcome was indeterminate based on the available evidence. An *amrad* fought back against a rapist, who eventually died from his wounds. The unnamed *amrad* went to a representative of the central government (*divan*) and confessed:

"I am the murderer. I did this action so that they would kill me and so that I would not be dishonored [*ta giriftar-i nang nabasham*]."[28] The *amrad* expected to be executed for the murder, despite defending himself against a rapist, but justified the crime as a restoration of his honor. The report does not mention whether he was ultimately executed for his actions.

Black slaves' marginalized social status also affected legal outcomes in murder cases. In Islamic jurisprudence, a free Muslim could never be executed as *qisas* for having murdered a slave, but their heirs were still entitled to *diyat*.[29] However, the heirs of Black slaves often faced difficulties in securing compensation because of their legal status. In early 1884, the son of Hajji Aqa Jan, the *farrashbashi* of the *biglarbigi*, tried to enter his father's house in a drunken state. The *farrashbashi* sent his Black slave to catch his drunk son. In the process, the son injured and killed the Black slave before being caught by the chain master (*zanjirban*), who was also injured. The issue was petitioned to the governor, Sahib Divan, but he delayed issuing a ruling because of his close association with the *farrashbashi*.[30] Shortly thereafter, Sahib Divan had the son of the *farrashbashi* thrown into the government prison. The *farrashbashi* then brought a generous "gift" of five hundred tumans to the governor so that his son would not be transferred to the much-harsher dungeon (*anbar*). The gift was accepted, and the son was instead imprisoned in the house of Na'ib Husayn. In the meantime, it was decided that if the chain master of the *biglarbigi* died, then the boy would be "executed in his place," but if not, then an arrangement would be made for the Black slave's heir.[31] When the chain master did not die of his wounds, compensation for the slave's murder remained outstanding.[32]

The *farrashbashi* delivered another large gift (*pishkish*) to Sahib Divan while the issue of compensation for the slave's heir remained unresolved. The sole heir, his sister (*hamshirah*), then traveled from Shiraz to Isfahan to petition Zill al-Sultan, the governor of Fars province, saying, "The son of Hajji Aqa Jan, the *farrashbashi* of Qavam al-Mulk, has killed my brother and trampled [*pamal*] on his blood." Zill al-Sultan sent a "special bailiff" (*muhassil-i makhus*) to address this issue and others in Shiraz. The bailiff decided that the *farrashbashi* must take back his gifts. He also took an undisclosed amount of money from the *farrash-*

bashi as compensation for the "blood of the Black slave."[33] While formal steps were taken to imprison the murderer in this case, the issue was initially resolved through payments to the governor for preferential treatment and forgoing justice for the slave's heir. Despite this, the slave's sister sought recourse by invoking the jurisdiction of the provincial governor to ensure monetary compensation.

Convicted Muslim murderers of Jews were similarly not subject to retaliation. In some cases, Jews hesitated to seek compensation or even report the murder for fear of popular anti-Jewish mobilizations. Even imprisoning a suspected Muslim murderer of a Jew could lead to serious opposition from certain *mujtahid*s. Most recorded instances of Jewish homicide were left unresolved or ended with a financial settlement, although in at least one case the possibility of *qisas* was raised, which was contrary to Shi'i jurisprudence.[34]

In April 1853, a Jewish individual and Aqa Husayn Kirmanshahani, a Muslim resident of Shiraz, were engaging in commercial "trade and transactions" at the latter's house. Aqa Husayn, who had a gun by his side, pointed the gun at the Jewish man in jest. The loaded gun went off, leading to the Jewish man's death. The issue was reported to the Shiraz agents (*karguzaran*), who caught and imprisoned Aqa Husayn. The people involved agreed to do whatever the 'ulama ruled according to the shari'ah, which might involve *qisas* or "compensation for the blood of a Jew" (*diyah-i khun-i yahudi*).[35] Although the report did not provide further details, given that the homicide appears to have been accidental and that the slain man was Jewish, compensation to the victim's heirs would be the most likely resolution at a shari'ah court.[36] The fact that the case was referred to the 'ulama rather than the central government was quite striking since typically non-Muslim affairs were dealt with by the Ministry of Foreign Affairs. Similarly, *qisas* being raised as a possible legal outcome was unusual since most jurists ruled out this option even in cases of an intentional Muslim homicide of a Jew.[37]

When ruffians murdered Jews, the latter's heirs sometimes feared reprisals and intimidation while also not having faith in the local government to deliver justice. In the early months of 1877, two *luti*s were drunk and strolling around the Jewish neighborhood in the middle of the day. They went to the homes of several Jews and tried to forcibly take wine from them. The local Jews prevented them from doing so, which led to several injuries on the Jewish side. The Jews informed the governor about this, and he, in turn, dispatched his men to apprehend the *lutis* for punishment. At night, those same two *lutis* went to a Jewish home to complain about being reported to the authorities. This time the *lutis* injured the throat of the owner of the house, an old man, and started brawling with a Jewish crowd. The Jewish crowd started screaming and shouting. The governor heard about the tumult. He sent the *farrashbashi* and several attendants to investigate the loud noises emanating from the Jewish quarter. The *farrashbashi*, having understood the issue, reassured the Jews and promised further investigation in the morning. The next morning, the governor ordered that the group of Jews who were screaming at night be detained for causing a disturbance, which included roughly fifty Jews knocking on the door of the government building ('Imarat-i Hukumat) with sticks, and that they be fined 150 tumans. An injured Jewish person subsequently died fifteen hours after the initial altercation, and the *luti* murderer went into hiding. The slain man's heirs did not bother petitioning the local government about the murder for fear of reprisals.[38]

Even when the local government detained a Muslim murderer of a Jew, it hesitated in punishing them because of certain 'ulama's objections and fears of anti-Jewish mobilizations. In a case dating from 1889, a Zarqani man fought with a Jew over two tumans of debt. He kicked the Jewish man in the stomach, which led to the Jewish man's death three days later. Qavam al-Mulk was informed of the matter. He sent for the Zarqani man and had him imprisoned. Having heard of this, the *mujtahid* Sayyid 'Ali Akbar Falasiri sent a message to Qavam al-Mulk, saying, "Why is a Muslim being imprisoned for [the murder of] a Jew?" This led to a harsh exchange of words between the two men. Falasiri's objection was not to the payment of compensation but to the imprisonment. At issue was jurisdiction: Should it be dealt with according to the shari'ah, or did the government's authority apply? The Zarqani man was eventually released when another Zarqani acted as his guarantor (*zamin*) in case the government needed to summon him. Falasiri still did not relent, and he even threatened to harass the city's Jews. Shortly thereafter, the government summoned the Zarqani murderer for punishment, but the Jewish heirs forgave him and did not seek compensation. Once again, Jewish heirs did not insist on justice for fear of collective retribution. As in other instances, this case became an opportunity for Falasiri to challenge local government authority in legal matters.

When people from marginal backgrounds were victims of homicide, their murders were often only halfheartedly investigated. At times, the government avoided prosecuting the murderer altogether, especially if the murderer was a government official or if they enjoyed the protection of a military superior. When Jewish subjects demanded justice, they often feared reprisals, from the city's *lutis*, the 'ulama, or some combination thereof. Slaves or Jews could still receive a measure of justice from the provincial governor or the *karguzar*, meaning that they had to invoke the jurisdiction of an alternative legal authority. The degree to which heirs of marginalized victims of homicide pursued justice also affected legal outcomes.

Siyasat as *'Ibrat* for Outlaws

The local government in Shiraz regularly executed outlaws in a ritualistic and spectacular manner, which was meant to act as a deterrent lesson (*'ibrat*) to the broader population. These outlaws were usually bandits or *lutis* who had repeatedly pillaged and murdered people. Contrary to Wael Hallaq's claim that in Muslim societies, states did not seek to display sovereignty over the bodies of subjects through punishments for murder, the historical evidence from nineteenth-century Iran tells a very different story.[39] The punishment for outlaws was almost always referred to as *siyasat* and differed significantly from straightforward *qisas* execution: unlike the latter, the emphasis was not on a logic of equivalences, nor did the heirs partake in deciding or carrying out the execution. Instead, these executions were closer to what Foucault has called the "spectacle of the scaffold," or spectacular displays of excess violence in punishing crimes as a means for the government to articulate sovereignty over the bodies of its subjects.[40] Local governors typically decided on such executions, sometimes in consultation with the shah, suggesting that the tort dimension of *qisas* was absent. Instead, the local governor or the shah considered the outlaws' crimes to be a threat to public order and safety, which advice literature and administrative manuals clearly stated the sovereign was responsible for safeguarding. Government executions often took on distinct spatial dimensions, with the Qassabkhanah Gate being the preferred site of such spectacles.

The practice of publicly burying people alive in small towers and living tombs in Shiraz dates back to at least the governorship of Manuchihr Khan in the early to mid-nineteenth century. These punishments probably reflected everyday government practices meant to communicate awe for the sovereign's violent capacity. In the course of putting down unruly elements from among the Mamasani Bakhtiyaris of Fars, Manuchihr Khan built a tower, named Mamasani or Mu'tamid, in the Dasht-i Shiraz neighborhood, where each prisoner had a sealed room with a window through which people could watch them starve and die of thirst.[41]

Similar punishments occurred at or just outside the Qassabkhanah Gate in the southeast section of Shiraz throughout the latter half of the nineteenth century. The Fars governor, Farhad Mirza Mu'tamid al-Mulk, had numerous ruffians strung up on the Qassabkhanah Gate in 1877.[42] The Iranian world traveler Hajj Sayyah, who entered Shiraz on August 3, 1877 (23 Rajab 1294 H.), described being taken outside the same gate and witnessing seventeen small tower-like structures made of plaster, each of which held individuals who were "buried alive" (*zindah bih gur*) after having been accused of theft and other crimes. Although he felt disgust at the sight, he noted that others in Shiraz were more ambivalent about the governor's spectacles; on the one hand, they complained about the spilling of blood, but on the other hand, they praised his annihilation of bandits to ensure safety on the roads.[43] The English scholar Edward Granville Browne largely corroborates Hajj Sayyah's account on the basis of what others told him and what he saw himself. A local Black slave relayed to him that the governor, Farhad Mirza, "had bricked up alive a multitude of less notable outlaws by the side of the highways that had witnessed their depredation."[44] The spectacle was therefore intended for other outlaws who might think of doing the same. Browne described these structures as "a double series of pillars of mortar" of ten or twelve in total, "which had formed the living tomb of an outlaw."[45]

Other governors consulted the shah before executing *lutis* for their crimes. In December 1852, a group of *lutis* and wine drinkers committed an undisclosed crime against Hajji Muhammad Hashim Khan Divanbigi. The governor, Nusrat al-Dawlah, ordered the *biglarbigi* and *kadkhudas* of the neighborhoods to detain them. Three of them were caught and punished (*tanbih va siyasat shudand*), but the most famous of the group, Riza, ran away to the Tupkhanah-i Mubarakah, presumably to take asylum, and intended to run away to another location from there. Before he could do so, Riza was caught and brought to the governor, who ordered that Riza be "imprisoned for life" (*habs-i abadi*). He also reported the matter to the shah, because Riza was guilty of theft, "shedding blood" (*safk-i dima*), and other evil acts. The shah overturned the life imprisonment ruling and instead ordered that the criminal be given his "just deserts" in Shiraz, meaning an execution. After three months of imprisonment, Nusrat al-Dawlah had Riza executed, much to the delight of the people of Shiraz, among whom were many of his victims.[46]

The punishment of outlaws and notorious *lutis* demonstrates that the punishment of murder, usually in combination with other crimes such as highway robbery, theft, drinking, and/or rebellion, was not treated as a shari'ah court case since it compromised public safety. Their fate was therefore almost exclusively decided by governors and/or shahs, who meted out *siyasat* punishment rather than *qisas* with the goal of building confidence in the government's authority to contain the polluting danger of unbridled violence. Burying someone alive in a tower was an especially powerful metaphor of containing the danger of the outlaw in mortar walls.

The Murder of a *Darvish* Drug Dealer

On Wednesday, August 20, 1884 (28 Shaval 1301 H.), two Quran reciters and a few others at the Dar al-Salb Cemetery found a single shoe and a trail of blood leading to a nearby well. Alerted to this, Hajji Aqa Jan Farrashbashi arrived at the well, whose surrounding area was drenched in blood; a bucket dipped into it brought up water with a reddish hue. On the basis of these indications, a water engineer (*muqanni*) went down the well and retrieved a dead man's body. His body was badly mutilated; not only had he been beheaded, but his lips and nose had been cut off. A petition regarding the case was presented to Muhammad Riza Qavam al-Mulk, who in turn appointed the *farrashbashi* and twenty *farrash*s to track down the murderer. After a full day of searching Shiraz and the graveyard, they finally stumbled across a lead: a witness had seen two men, 'Abd al-Husayn and Sayyid Mirza 'Ali, with the murdered man, who was a Tabrizi traveling *darvish* known as Mir Aqa, at a coffeehouse close to the graveyard the previous day. They had been together until the early evening, when they left the coffeehouse and headed back toward the city.[47]

The *farrashbashi* had sufficient evidence for a heinous murder to justify violating the sanctum of the domicile: he raided the house of 'Abd al-Husayn to capture him. Through this raid, he obtained circumstantial evidence of the crime, including a bloodied knife and clothing.[48] 'Abd al-Husayn was interrogated about the *darvish*'s murder, but he denied any involvement. Next, the *farrashbashi* subjected the man to judicial torture, despite repeated *farman*s banning the practice and shari'ah prohibitions on the practice. He had 'Abd al-Husayn beaten with sticks and branded (*dagh*) for three days, but this failed to garner a confession. 'Abd al-Husayn's accomplice, Sayyid Mirza 'Ali, faced a similar fate for three days. Although the latter could withstand being beaten by a stick, when the rod was put in the flame to brand him, he buckled. The sayyid stated, "Do not brand me and also promise that you will not kill me so that I will tell you the truth of what happened." In front of his friend, Sayyid Mirza 'Ali narrated what had happened, after receiving his assurances:

> On the night of Tuesday, we two people, along with the murdered [*darvish*], were in the coffeehouse of the Dar al-Salb Cemetery until two hours into the night; then we returned to the city. In the cemetery, 'Abd al-Husayn had bread, kabab, and cannabis oil [*rawghan-i bangi*] with him. He mixed the cannabis with the kabab and gave some bread and kabab to the murdered person, who ate it and passed out. First, he hit him two or three times, thus rendering him lifeless; [then]

he told me to take his two feet, which I did. He cut off his head, his nose, and two lips. [He then] stripped him and threw him in a well.[49]

After this testimony in the presence of Qavam al-Mulk, the two men accused each other of lying. 'Abd al-Husayn claimed that he was the one who held the man's two feet while Sayyid 'Ali cut off his head.[50] But the question of motive remained unclear until the sayyid volunteered the motive for the crime. 'Abd al-Husayn, who was an opium roller (*taryak-mali*) by profession, had stolen opium from the house of a merchant and hired the *darvish* to sell it. The *darvish* had sold thirty tumans of opium but refused to give 'Abd al-Husayn his share of the profit: in fact, he threatened to "reveal 'Abd al-Husayn's theft."[51]

In the meantime, the governor, Sahib Divan, reentered Shiraz after having traveled to the city's environs for some time. The two men both presented their cases before him and made claims against each other. Without "hesitation," the governor ruled according to the "oath" (*qa-sami*) of Mirza 'Ali Sayyid, which identified 'Abd al-Husayn as the murderer.[52] The executioner reenacted the manner of the crime in his punishment: he started by striking 'Abd al-Husayn several times, before cutting off his nose and lips and finally beheading him. Ironically, cutting off the nose and lips was a punitive form of mutilation known as the *maslah*, which was otherwise considered excessive in Islamic jurisprudence.[53] The Sahib Divan, in reporting on this case, stated that he had ordered 'Abd al-Husayn to be injured just as the Tabrizi sayyid had been injured and killed; after being mutilated, he received *qisas*.[54] Mirza 'Ali Sayyid was somewhat more fortunate, possibly because he was a descendant of the Prophet: he had his right hand cut off and was released.[55]

As with other similar cases in which heirs were absent, the government acted as the plaintiff in what was referred to as a *qisas* case. What complicates this picture, however, is that the shari'ah rules of evidence were not followed, since judicial torture was used as the basis of the execution. Otherwise, the principles of equivalency found in many *qisas* punishments were used: the murderer was executed in a similar manner to his victim, even if this meant violating the sanctity of the face.

Intention, Doubt, Intercession, and Protection

Many homicide cases ended in a financial settlement (*sulh*) and/or for-giveness because of the lack of clarity regarding the murderer's intent, doubts surrounding the details of the events, ambiguity regarding the identity of the individual delivering the fatal blow, economic concerns for the parties involved, the intercession of powerful notables, and the use of sanctuary to gain protection from the authorities. When defini-tive proof of murder was lacking, payment amounts reflected the prob-ability of guilt.

Those who killed others unintentionally sometimes tried to settle out of court since the government could still carry out discretionary punishments and/or fines over and above shari'ah liability. In Shiraz, a farmer (*dihqan*) was passing by a grocery shop in December 1852 when his load caused some displayed shop goods to topple over. In a fit of anger, the grocer kicked the farmer in the side of his body, leading to his immediate death. Fearing harsh punishment (*siyasat*) by the gover-nor, he implored the heirs of the farmer to forgo petitioning the governor, presumably by securing a settlement (*musalahah*) document at a shari'ah court.[56]

In 1882, a murderer from an 'ulama background did not face *qisas* when he accidentally killed a woman while drunk. Hasan Fasa'i, the son of the Mullabashi of Fasa, attended a party, became drunk, and started brawling with another guest. He then pulled out a gun. A female neigh-bor tried to stop the fight but ended up being shot accidentally. The *da-rughah* caught Hasan Fasa'i and turned him over to the government, which had him imprisoned. Two days later, the woman died from her bullet wounds. After Hasan Fasa'i's trial (*muhakamah*), he was to be banished from the city.[57] Since the homicide was accidental, he was not subject to *qisas*, although the source does not mention anything about him paying compensation either. Given his 'ulama social status, he was spared corporal punishment but was still banished for his crime.

When homicide was not proven by shari'ah rules of evidence, a settlement was a preferred option, especially if the killer was the sole breadwinner. In 1882–83, a grocer fought with a blind pigeon-flier (*ka-butarbaz*). In the course of their fight, the grocer punched the pigeon-flier, who subsequently died. Since the heirs were content to forgo retaliation, Sahib Divan, the *biglarbigi*, and other notables agreed to pay the heirs a cash settlement. The settlement was facilitated by the fact that intentional homicide "was not proven [*sabit*]," possibly because a fist was not considered an instrument of intentional homicide according to the criteria of *fiqh*.[58] The grocer was also the sole provider for his old mother and numerous younger siblings, which mitigated more punitive measures.[59] Another account of this case provided slightly different details. In this version, it was two pigeon-fliers (*kabutarbaz*) who fought over a pigeon, and one killed the other with a rock rather than a punch. The murderer was imprisoned, but the Sahib Divan did not want to see him executed. Instead, he facilitated a "blood price" (*khun baha*) to be given. Since the murderer did not have much in the way of financial means, the Sahib Divan gave seventy tumans from his and his family's money to the heirs.[60] The Sahib Divan's contemporary personal account of the case in a telegraphic cable sheds further light on the possible confusion regarding the murder instrument. He claimed that the two eighteen-year-old boys had fought over a pigeon when one youth threw a rock at the other, which led to the other boy responding with a fatal punch to the head. The killer was obtained and took the shari'ah court, but since there were no witnesses except two women, meaning that this fell short of the evidentiary bar for shari'ah conviction, "it could not be proven." As a result, the Imam Jum'ah gave one hundred tumans for a suspension of blood claim, along with the "humble house" that each of them had. Sahib Divan also gave fifty tumans, and Qavam al-Mulk and others gave fifty tumans to end this matter, since he did not see it fit that "for one pigeon, two people be killed."[61]

Despite enjoying certain discretionary authority, the Sahib Divan occasionally demanded a shari'ah conviction from heirs before carrying out *qisas*. In August 1887, a tobacco seller and several other people were drinking alcohol outside Shiraz's Isfahan Gate. They encountered several *farrash*s, with whom they started fighting. In the ensuing brawl, a villager from Dih Buzurg passing by was badly injured by the tobacco seller. The *farrash*s eventually detained the tobacco seller and took him to prison. When the villager died two days later, his fellow villagers took his corpse to the Darb-i Bagh and demanded justice from the Sahib

Divan by petitioning him to "carry out *qisas* on the murderer." His response suggested that there was a level of doubt regarding the murderer's identity and that therefore the case fell short of shari'ah standards of evidence: "There were several people. Prove it, obtain a ruling [*hukm bigirid*], and bring it [to me] so that *qisas* [can] occur."[62] Although his own *farrash*s were involved in apprehending the tobacco seller, the governor wanted witnesses to be produced at a shari'ah court as the basis for *qisas*.

Doubt in murder cases could lead litigants to invoke the overlapping jurisdictions of local *mujtahid*s, the governor, and the shah, in pursuit of favorable outcomes. One night in March 1899, Mirza Mahdi, the secretary of Nasir al-Mulk, held a party with guests from Shiraz and the nearby village of Fasa. At the end of the night, he became very drunk and started shooting at his guests with his gun as they were leaving. The guests ducked for cover. A neighbor, Shahzadah Aqa, who was the son of a prominent 'alim, Sadr-i Shirazi, and a Qajar prince (*shahzadah*) from his mother's side, came to the gate of the alley to see what was happening. Mirza Mahdi shot and killed Shahzadah Aqa. The government *farrash*s detained Mirza Mahdi the same night and threw him in prison. Initially, the princes, 'ulama, and other city residents gathered in the house of the slain man and intended to see that the killer was given his just deserts, meaning *qisas*. In the absence of the governor, however, a ruling could not be made.[63]

Very quickly, the scribal class, made up of accountants (*mustawfi*s) and scribes (*mirza*s), gathered in the Masjid-i Naw, presumably to make a show of protest, claiming that Mirza Mahdi had not committed intentional homicide. The majority of Shiraz's 'ulama, despite their initial condemnation of Mirza Mahdi, came together to issue a legal responsum (*fatva*) stating that Mirza Mahdi should not be executed because it was not "an intentional homicide" (*qatl-i 'amdi*); instead, "it had been by accident [*khata*]." On the other hand, the city's princes, including Shaykh al-Ra'is, who was both a prince and a member of the 'ulama, supported Mirza Mahdi's execution. The prime minister also became involved via a telegram to the Shiraz government, saying that after Mirza Mahdi was "confirmed" to be the murderer, then lex talionis (*qisas-i shar'i*) should be carried out.[64] In subsequent weeks, the government tried to carry out *qisas* on Mirza Mahdi, but the 'ulama prevented it. The central government ordered that Mirza Mahdi be sent to Tehran so that after "proving" the case against him, *qisas* could be carried out. The local government dispatched cavalry and foot soldiers to deliver Mirza Mahdi to Tehran.[65]

Mirza Mahdi managed to escape and hide in various places in Tehran and Isfahan. Roughly six months later, he returned to Shiraz, where he stayed with the prince Shahzadah Jamal al-Din Mirza, who granted him refuge (*panah*). The prince summoned the mother and family of the murdered Aqa Shahzadah to his house, with the goal of a settlement. He asked them, "What would you do if you saw Mirza Mahdi, the one who has your blood [of your relative] on his hands?" They responded that they would carry out *qisas* on him. Jamal al-Din Mirza dramatically stated, "He is with me. Murder one of my children in his place since he has taken refuge with me." The family declined this offer since it violated the principle of punishing the guilty party and not the innocents connected to them.[66] The prince then consoled the mother of the slain prince and her family; he convinced them "to forgo retribution." They prepared a written document stating "that they would no longer pursue him" and agreed that Mirza Mahdi would take "his wife and family" to one of Nasir al-Mulk's properties outside Shiraz for an undisclosed amount of time.[67] The prince probably offered financial compensation as well. This case demonstrates how the involvement of multiple jurisdictions alongside the use of asylum facilitated a negotiated settlement in a homicide case where there was a degree of doubt, despite the central and local governments' willingness to push for *qisas*.

Non-Iranians, Murder, and Foreign Jurisdiction in Shiraz

Unlike most homicide cases, subjects from different foreign nations who murdered one another in Iran posed a particular legal challenge because of the multiple legal jurisdictions involved.[68] The case of two Russian subjects who murdered an Ottoman subject reveals the complex mechanisms for bringing a resolution to claims against the murderer. While treaties between Iran and foreign governments included provisions for what to do in murder cases involving two foreign subjects of the same country in Iran or one Iranian and one foreign subject, the issue of how to resolve a murder case involving subjects from two different countries was unclear. An 1874 (1291 H.) treaty between Iran and the Ottoman Empire, which was still in effect during the murder in question, provided some indication of what should be done when there were "lawsuits and conflicts" (da'avi va munaza'at) between subjects of different foreign countries in one another's country: it was to be resolved according to an agreement reflecting past practices.[69] As Robert Crews has argued in the case of Russian subjects in Iran, one should be cautious about uncritically using treaties, even very unequal ones granting many privileges to foreigners, such as in the case of Russians in Iran, as a credible source for legal practice, since local governments had significant authority.[70] Since this case involved Muslims on both sides and was an intentional homicide, qisas was an option. The intervention of foreign consulates, however, led to a negotiated settlement.

In the early months of 1901, Fattah, an Ottoman hide merchant, who resided in the Hajji Aqa Jan Caravanserai, was invited to the home of two Russian Shirvani merchant brothers, Sattar and Muhsin, who also worked there. After dinner, the two brothers took Fattah to his merchant room and noticed his hides and other belongings. Sattar threw Fattah to the ground, took out his silk handkerchief, and put it on his mouth. With the help of Muhsin, Sattar choked Fattah to death before burying him beneath the grounds of their residence. The next day, Sattar and Muhsin dug up the body, smashed the bones of Fattah's hands and feet, stuffed him in a sewn-up bag, and put him in a chest under some small belongings. Sattar sent his wife out of the house with the chest to make it look like she was doing some "spring cleaning." They took the chest to the Qurkhanah-i Qadim in the Qassabkhanah Gate area, where they threw it down a well.[71]

Sattar and Muhsin then took Fattah's key and brought it to their caravanserai. They told Fattah's apprentice, "Fattah gave us this key and said I am a guest somewhere tonight. Prepare some dinner, and I will come at night." At night, Sattar and Muhsin came into his room, ate

dinner, and proceeded to take whatever valuables they found, including Ottoman liras, *qirani*, notes, and deeds, to their house. The value of
their stolen loot was fifteen hundred tumans. Meanwhile, Fattah's apprentice became suspicious: he told his father that Fattah had still not
returned after two days. They tracked down Muhsin and Sattar, who denied having any news of Fattah's whereabouts. They then informed the
biglarbigi, who then summoned Sattar and Muhsin. After two or three
days, the government's investigatory council (*majlis-i tahqiqat*) determined that they were the killers. The *biglarbigi* summoned the wife of
Sattar and threatened to brand (*dagh*) her to reveal (*buruz*) what happened. Under the threat of torture, she recounted the entire story and
revealed the location of the body. A *muqanni* was called in to recover
the corpse from the well. The *biglarbigi* had the body buried and arrested Sattar, his wife, and Muhsin. Since the case involved foreign
subjects, he sent telegrams to the prime minister and the governor,
Shu'a' al-Saltanah, asking about the next steps.[72]

　　Close to a year later, the case had not been resolved. Sattar remained in prison. The Russian consulate in Isfahan wrote to Samad
Aqa, a fellow Russian subject, to secretly arrange for a "cessation of
the blood feud" without the involvement of the local Iranian *karguzar*
and others. Samad Aqa sent for the Ottoman Shahbandar (consul) and
the imperial appointee (*mu'in-i humayun*) to obtain a meeting. They
also summoned an Ottoman consular representative (*vakil*) and the son
of Fattah, but these two remained in another room. Samad Aqa managed to get the representative very drunk in the hope of extracting a
signed document to put an end to the claim. And although the representative became drunk, they were unable to extract a concession from
him before he was taken home due to excessive drunkenness.[73] Despite
the Russian consulate's best efforts, the Shirazi *karguzar* ultimately became involved as a mediator. The two sides were brought to the house of
the *karguzar*, who in the presence of 'Abbas Tajirbashi, a Russian subject, and the Ottoman consular *vakil*, heard a financial claim (*iddi'a'-yi
maliyah*) for the blood of Fattah. In the end, they opted for a settlement
(*musalahah*) in the amount of twelve hundred tumans that was to be
awarded to the son of Fattah and the *vakil*. The payment of this amount

was a condition for Sattar to be released; however, the government, the *karguzar*, and others had to receive "payment" before "the case was closed," since the murder was as much an injury to local government authority as it was against the heirs of the murdered.[74]

This case points to the complexities of murder cases involving subjects from two different foreign countries in Iran. Although the authorities obtained a confession under the threat of torture, this did not automatically lead to the heir being granted retaliation or compensation, possibly because the confession was made under duress. The Russian consulate pushed for a financial settlement without Iranian government involvement, possibly to avoid further expenses. Finally, the fact that the case ended in a settlement instead of retaliation points to the difficulty of executing a foreign subject for murder.

Conclusion

Murder cases reveal the jurisdictional negotiations involved between various legal authorities. In Shi'i jurisprudence, heirs had the option of executing people convicted of intentional homicide or accepting compensation or settlement. Despite this framework, governors and shahs regularly executed murderers on the basis of their own discretion. Legal outcomes did not follow a predictable pattern based on any legal texts; instead, they were the product of numerous factors including the status group (including religion, occupation, and social rank) and gender of the parties involved, the degree to which notables and/or 'ulama interceded on behalf of the affected parties, the specific proclivity of a given governor toward making an example of murderers, and the degree of doubt regarding the intentionality or circumstances of the homicide. Both *hadd* crimes and murder required a high burden of evidence in Islamic jurisprudence. This meant that a murder conviction, short of a confession, often required the act to have taken place in public view of witnesses. Since few murders fit this criterion, governors dealt with such hard cases on the basis of circumstantial evidence and confessions elicited by torture. Such judicial torture involved a movement from the private to the public: suspects were forced to divulge the secret of their actions. Punishment for murder, whether carried out by heirs or government executioners, almost always took place in public as a deterrent and an act restoring public order. In *qisas* cases, the execution often re-enacted the crime or was a simple beheading, while in *siyasat* executions, the spectacle dimension embodied excess befitting the gravity of the crime: the murderer could be subject to mutilation or be buried alive in mounds at the Qassabkhanah Gate for subjects to view.

Seeking Refuge in the Shrine City of Qum, "The Abode of Faith"

Out of all of Iran's cities, Qum has the curious distinction of being the favored resting place of shahs between the seventeenth and nineteenth centuries. Early in the reign of Fath 'Ali Shah, he cultivated a self-image as a Shi'i patron of shrine cities, by funding shrine renovations not only in Najaf and Karbala but also in Mashhad and especially in Qum. By choosing the shrine of Fatimah Ma'sumah in Qum as the site of his own resting place before his death, he further solidified the association between the shrine, the city, and the Qajar dynasty. Strikingly, Qum was paradoxically a magnet for criminals and outcasts who took sanctuary in the major shrine. Studying crime in Qum is therefore a useful way to understand the relationship between jurisdiction and sovereignty in the 1860s–1890s.

This chapter begins by examining Qum's simultaneous association with sacredness and crime. It then turns to the governorship of Adib al-Mulk, a man intent on "cleaning up" crime in the 1860s through a number of hands-on reforms that involved the close monitoring of urban spaces and the establishment of guarantorships for individuals "prone" to criminal behavior. The governor further sought to circumscribe the boundaries of the sprawling sanctuary (*bast*) zone, neutralize the authority of the powerful head shrine guardian (*mutavallibashi*), and put an end to the criminal activities of shrine servants (*khuddam*).

The chapter then considers the effects of famine on the daily operation of law in the early 1870s, during which time people turned to extralegal "rough justice" and the violation of bodily privacy in cannibalism cases. Between the mid-1870s and the 1890s, the governor I'tizad al-Dawlah and his successors faced the persistent challenges associated with *bast* zones under the authority of the *mutavallibashi* in criminal matters, especially in hotly contested murder cases. Finally, the chapter ends by considering the crime of Baha'i apostasy as indicative of how the boundaries between the private sin of heretical ideas and the public crime of manifest apostasy were constantly being questioned. In response to the charges and legal proceedings, Baha'is navigated local, imperial, and even Shi'i courts in seeking a measure of legal protection against local harassment and to undue death or life imprisonment sentences.

Holiness and Vice in the Sanctuary Zone

In 712, Qum's association with Shi'ism began with those who were escaping Umayyad persecution and seeking refuge there. But the city's ultimate prominence as a shrine city derived from it being the city in which Fatimah bint Musa Kazim Ma'sumah (d. 816), the sister of Imam Riza, was interred. According to Shi'i tradition, she and her family members were attacked in the nearby town of Savah in the early ninth century. After having been poisoned, she asked to be transferred to Qum, where she later died. The shrine erected over her resting place, known as the Ma'sumah Shrine, developed into a major pilgrimage site.[1] In the early nineteenth century, Fath 'Ali Shah repaired and improved the shrine and its courtyard, bestowed lavish gifts on the shrine, and furnished the Shi'i jurist Mirza Abu al-Qasim Qummi (d.1815/16) with funds to revive teaching circles and distribute among the city's impoverished sayyids. The shah's intention in cultivating a close relationship with Mirza Qummi appears to have been a means of promoting Qum over Najaf as a major center of Shi'i learning and pilgrimage and thereby of decreasing the influence of Shi'i 'ulama beyond Qajar lands. He also chose to be buried in Qum, thus raising the city's profile and reinforcing its connection to the Qajar dynasty.[2]

Unlike the two other prominent shrines in Qajar Iran, the Shah 'Abd al-'Azim Shrine close to Tehran and the shrine of Imam Riza in Mashhad, Qum's shrine was devoted to a woman and drew throngs of female pilgrims. The Shi'i faithful believed that Fatima Ma'sumah had powerful intercessory powers, much like the Catholic belief in those of the Virgin Mary.[3] Women often went to Qum with very specific intentions: to transform their husbands' lack of attention into love or, conversely, to turn their own lack of affection for their husbands into genuine love, to seek forgiveness for unfaithfulness, or to ask for help in becoming pregnant.[4] This close connection with the feminine might explain why women sometimes held political power over the city. For example, the daughter of Nasir al-Din Shah, Fakhr al-Muluk, held the reins of power in the city.[5] Similarly, Anis al-Dawlah, the wife of a governor of Qum, was described as the de facto governor of the city.[6] Beyond this, prominent women like Mahd-i 'Ulya, the mother of Nasir al-Din Shah, used her pilgrimage to the Ma'sumah Shrine as a way of asserting her "queen motherhood" early in his reign and during conflicts with Prime Minister Amir Kabir.[7] Although Qum's shrine was considered less sacred than the Imam Riza Shrine in Mashhad, it lay in closer proximity to other major Iranian urban centers, such as the capital city Tehran, Isfahan, Hamadan, and Yazd, thus making pilgrimage to Qum less arduous and costly than to Mashhad, Najaf, Karbala, and Mecca and Medina.

From at least the seventeenth century onward, Qum was a sanctuary for criminals.[8] One observer compared the extraordinary protections afforded to asylum seekers in Qum to the concept of habeas corpus, insofar as they operated as a check on arbitrary government authority.[9] Some trace the origins of the practice to the ancient Jewish custom of having cities of refuge.[10] Looking to more contemporary equivalents, a European traveler drew parallels between Qum's sanctuary practices and the Alsatia neighborhood of London and the precincts of Holyrood in Edinburgh, which had similar asylum functions.[11]

Qum's high concentration of criminals made it notorious for illicit activities.[12] John Ushher pinpointed the economic power of the sanctuary's gatekeepers as being rooted in the fact that they "possess[ed] the privilege of sheltering from justice or oppression any criminal or victim,"

Figure 17: Photograph of ʻulama, shrine servants, and *farrash*s outside the
Maʻsumah Shrine in Qum, taken by ʻAbdullah Qajar in 1313 H. / 1895.
(Source: Qaraguzlu, *Qum-i Qadim*, 133)

which "yield[ed] in consequence a considerable revenue to the holy
guardians of the sacred places who form a large portion of the population of the city." He continued by stating that the shrine guardians and
their servants did "pretty much as they [chose] under the protection of
[the shrine's] sacred character" and that they formed "a body which both
on account of its numbers and the great influence which it possesses over
the populace, it would be very dangerous to interfere with."[13] Shrine
guardians and their servants wielded great economic power, partly
because of the generous "donations" of their temporary guests (figure 17).

Adib al-Mulk, Policing, and Spatial Regulation

The tenure of the Qum governor ʻAbd al-ʻAli Adib al-Mulk in the 1860s
witnessed a novel assembly of techniques to monitor vice, curtail the
criminal use of sanctuaries, and employ guarantorship for people in

authority over criminals.[14] Adib al-Mulk entered Qum on November 25, 1862 (3 Jumada al-Sani 1279 H.), tasked by Nasir al-Din Shah with restoring order to the city in the aftermath of local instability.[15] His firsthand account paints a bleak picture of official appointments being farmed out to unsavory characters, rampant extortion rackets, prostitution rings, and conflicts around ritual occasions. Like his near contemporary Chiragh 'Ali Zanganah in Isfahan, Adib al-Mulk outlined his multipronged strategy to address crime, which included tackling the social, economic, and ecological sources of conflict; making redress at the governor's court free and accessible; and introducing novel spatial techniques for policing. Most significantly, Adib al-Mulk sharply delineated the sanctuary zone associated with the Ma'sumah Shrine, curtailed the privileges of the head shrine guardian and his servants, and insisted on punishing criminal refugees at the shrine instead of granting them indefinite immunity.

ADDRESSING SOURCES OF CONFLICT

Adib al-Mulk identified several key reasons for conflict, extortion, and crime in Qum and formulated his policies accordingly. His measures were meant to ensure equitable and fair access to food and water and to prevent highly charged Muharram processions from spiraling into violence.

Adib al-Mulk's policies addressed market regulation, which was part of the category of *hisbah*. He identified fair access to food in the city as a top priority since it was "a need for everyone from the high to the low, from the rich to the poor, and . . . from the settled to the passersby."[16] He therefore ensured that the weights used in the bazaar were accurate by issuing a public pronouncement threatening to treat those who tampered with them as thieves, meaning that they would receive a punishment of "dismemberment of the hand [*buridan-i dast*], a fine, and being beaten five times with a stick."[17] He also wanted to guarantee high-quality and plentiful bread in the bazaar, so he had his inspectors (*mubashirs*) visit the bakeries and other grocery shops to buy bread and other foodstuffs. Since shopkeepers continued to tamper with weights, he had agents conduct spot inspections two to three times a week and send spies to the shops; consequently, tradesmen adjusted their behavior.[18] Adib al-Mulk sought to keep the price of staple goods, such as bread, meat, and other foodstuffs, as low as possible by compelling bazaaris to do so. For prices that could not be reduced, he extracted a guarantee (*iltizam*) that their prices would remain the same until Ramazan, at which time the prices would be reduced.[19]

Another of Adib al-Mulk's priorities was access to water. He did not view water scarcity as rooted solely in Qum's arid climate; instead, he pointed to human agency in creating artificial scarcity through neglect and extortion rackets.[20] Shortages of ice, which was an excellent source of freshwater in the summer months, meant that pilgrims had to consume bitter and salty water from the "water of the bathhouse."[21] If pilgrims wanted to drink freshwater, they would have to pay the exorbitant sum of twenty tumans.[22] This was because the "icehouse owners" (*sahiban-i yakhchal*) had not made proper provisions for ice during the winter and spring seasons, and previous governors had failed to organize them.[23] Consequently, Adib al-Mulk obtained a guarantor document from the icehouse owners to carry out their duties.[24] He also prevented water shortages by having *qanat*s cleaned and repaired regularly.[25]

Beyond neglect, Adib al-Mulk identified extortion rackets, involving both previous governors and water masters (*mirab*s), as the main reason for water shortages.[26] In theory, the *mirab*'s function was to guarantee fair water shares to ordinary subjects since it was considered a public good. In practice, Qum's *mirab* often sold water to the rich and let the poor suffer. *Mirab*s presented governors with substantial "gifts" (*ta'aruf*) to carry out their extortion rackets, which in turn led to much water being "wasted and appropriated," to the point of depriving the general population of it.[27] Adib al-Mulk believed that this alliance of past governors, the *mirab*, and his followers resulted in a lack of water for ordinary people's farms and gardens, "except those watered by the river." People petitioned against government inspectors (*mubashirin-i divani*) for "selling water and not assisting helpless people."[28] Since the *mirab* and his gang would sell water for twenty tumans per day, Qummis, including young children and their mothers, would suffer from thirst. In the year prior to Adib al-Mulk's arrival, the *mirab* and his gang extorted an extra 150 tumans for the use of river water on top of the money extorted from selling water illegally from the Nasiri Qanat, which was intended to be free and for public use.[29]

Adib al-Mulk's solution to the problem of water extortion involved spatial surveillance. He had two elders from orchards and farming areas and a trusted government representative appoint two people to stand by the *mirab* as he carried out his duties. Both sides were to pay these two appointees, whose sole task was to ensure that the *mirab* did not sell water and that a portion of the Nasiri Qanat's water was allocated to farms and orchards servicing the needs of the neighborhoods.[30] The governor appointed his trusted servant, Muhammad Taqi Big Arbab, as a separate *mirab* whose task was to deliver water to the neighborhoods on a weekly basis at the Darvazah Gate. *Kadkhuda*s would pick up the water and deliver it to the houses in their quarters. Adib al-Mulk also secured guarantees from the *kadkhuda*s that if anyone from their neighborhood complained of unfair water allotment, then the *kadkhuda* would be subject to harsh punishment.[31] The result of these policies was that water from the Nasiri Qanat was not wasted, people received their fair share of water, and there was a plentiful harvest.[32]

Adib al-Mulk also had to contend with violence during Ashura mourning processions. He treated such violence, a common occurrence in Qajar-era processions, as a question of logistics and organization. He noted that "in previous years, there would be a widespread conflict between chest-beaters," resulting in injuries and even death. While his predecessors had banned such groups from gathering altogether, Adib al-Mulk allowed for the reconstitution of such gatherings and processions, but he enforced a strict order (*nazm*) for the procession such that no violence occurred.[33]

LEGAL REDRESS, GUARANTORSHIP, AND POLICING

Over the course of Adib al-Mulk's tenure, he removed court fees, ended the practice of intercession in legal cases, and reconstituted urban policing through the *kadkhuda* system and interlocking guarantorships. These were key components of centralizing authority vis-à-vis the local 'ulama and other actors who had carved out pockets of jurisdiction against the local government.

Shortly after having entered Qum, Adib al-Mulk met with local notables, 'ulama, prominent sayyids, the *mutavallibashi*, and Qajar princes to assess the city's problems. He also listened to ordinary people's conversations about local affairs.[34] The governor compared the task of ordering the city to a game of chess; his objective was to checkmate his opponents.[35] He insisted on inscribing government control over urban spaces through the composition of daily reports (*ruznamahs*) by *kadkhudas*. Adib al-Mulk also relied on another textual expression of juridical authority: the signing of guarantor documents (*iltizamnamahs* or *zimanatnamahs*) by people in a position of authority capable of preventing conflicts, crimes, and extortion rackets.

Adib al-Mulk viewed fragmented urban authority as a hindrance to delivering justice consistently and uniformly. He perceptively noted that there were multiple sectors of society that enjoyed something akin to government judicial authority: "Everyone from among the 'ulama, the nobles [*a'yan*], the notables [*ashraf*], the powerful [*mu'azzizin*], and perhaps anyone who had some sort of authority [*miknah*], possessed a type of government [or jurisdiction] [*naw'-i hukumati dasht*] over those who were around him and in his circle. He had a form of leadership and authority [*riyasat va siyasat*] in leading those under him such that every time that the governor of the subdistrict [*vilayat*] wanted to summon a suspect, he would not do so for fear of the person's protector."[36] This fragmented nature of local authority meant that the governor lacked the necessary sovereignty to command the people's respect. The result was that "punishments and rulings were delayed" (*hudud va ahkam mu'attal*) and "the judgment of governors was meaningless and nonsensical."[37] Adib al-Mulk specifically blamed the 'ulama for being "out to establish a position for themselves."[38]

Adib al-Mulk's first order of business was to ensure that his judicial court was equitable, immune to outside influence, and free of prohibitive fees. He commanded a town crier (*jarchi*) to announce that petitions would be heard every day of the week, with the exception of Mondays and Fridays, for anyone who had been wronged.[39] The government would investigate legal issues without regard to social status, and intercession (*visatat va shifa'at*) would not affect due process or sway the ruling.[40] The measure had the desired effect: "The people saw that intercession and taking bribes were forbidden and [that the government] investigated and tended [*risidigi*] to [legal] matters."[41] The 'ulama eventually fell into line by refraining from intercession. Adib al-Mulk also made court cases heard before the government court (*divankhanah*) free of charge, banned bribes, and made the presence of both the accuser and the accused mandatory.[42] Ordinary people therefore stopped frequenting the house of mullahs for court cases and instead used the Divankhanah. The governor required both sides to provide supporting documentation (*asnad*) at court and had cases recorded in a book (*kitabchah*) for future reference. The government would then issue a "clear ruling" (*hukm-i qat'i*) that both sides would have to stamp in the aforementioned book.[43]

Since a significant portion of Qum's population consisted of travelers, pilgrims, and outsiders, the government feared the city's penetration by undesirable social elements. Adib al-Mulk feared moral contagion insofar as these social elements could corrupt and wreak havoc in the city. He therefore sought to make the settled inhabitants of the city legible by way of a census, which recorded a permanent population of 22,473 people and 3,968 households.[44] The government used these figures to determine who should and should not be in the city. In addition to wayward pilgrims, Adib al-Mulk was concerned with seminarians who came to Qum for criminal exploits. He, therefore, extracted a guarantee from the servants of the madrasah only to accept "trustworthy people" as "seminarians [*tullab*] of religious knowledge." Madrasah servants were asked to deny outsiders (*khariji*) into their ranks, presumably because their moral pedigree would be difficult to assess in the absence of people who could vouch for them.[45] Since the city gates were the entrance and exit points of Qum, Adib al-Mulk wanted these spaces to be closely monitored to ensure the moral integrity of those who entered.[46] Adib al-Mulk established a permit system (*qarar-i balid*) in which everyone who entered or exited the city (with the exception of farmers and others who needed to work in the city daily) had an exit permit (*balid-i kharij*). He also had the commander (*dahbashi*) of the cavalry and the imperial soldiers (*ghulams*) of the mounted police monitor the outskirts of Qum and report on who was entering and exiting the city.[47]

Adib al-Mulk's most consequential reform was the reconstitution of effective *darughah* and *kalantar* policing.[48] He accused past governors of "renting out" (*ijarahdari*) the *darughah*'s position, which created ripe conditions for extortion rackets and bribery to recover the cost of gaining the rank.[49] Adib al-Mulk instead obtained a guarantee from the *darughah* to maintain the order of various neighborhoods, bazaars, and caravanserais. Prior to his arrival, the *kadkhuda* system had been neglected to such a degree that neighborhoods were left without them. He met with city notables and elders in order for them to appoint a *kadkhuda* for their respective neighborhoods. The appointed *kadkhuda* would be "contractually obligated" by a guarantor document to ensure order in their neighborhood and to provide "a daily written report" (*ruznamah-i vaqayi'-i ittifaqiyah*) to the governor.[50] The elders and notables initially expressed doubts that this would work since it was unprecedented, but after three days, they sat together and divided the city into four neighborhoods and appointed four people as *kadkhuda*s. Adib al-Mulk made the *kadkhuda*'s guarantor document state that if they acted against its stipulations or their administrative manual (*dastur al-'amal*), their guarantors (meaning the elders and notables) would be punished.[51]

The *kadkhuda*s monitored neighborhoods and prevented manifest crimes. They were to stop "ruffians and evildoers" (*juhhal va ashrar*) from gathering, detain those who were drunk in the streets, and ambush those who took prostitutes to their house as soon as they exited (in other words, in a manner that respected the domicile's inviolability). They were also tasked with detaining female and male (*amrad*) prostitutes who entered someone's home. At night, they had to monitor the neighborhood to prevent theft. When neighborhood disputes required further investigation, they were obliged to bring contesting parties to the government building (Dar al-Hukumah) without any connivance or bribery.[52]

Since the *kadkhuda* enjoyed discretionary power, the *mutavallibashi* of the Ma'sumah Shrine, Hajj Mirza Sayyid Husayn Fayz Asar, resisted such an appointment for his Astanah neighborhood. After a long and protracted negotiation with the *mutavallibashi*, Adib al-Mulk secured a *kadkhuda* by the name of Hajji Hashim for this neighborhood and composed a guarantor document outlining his duties and rights.[53] Hajji Hashim turned out to be diligent in his duties; he delivered his reports daily, which included accounts of criminals (*muqassirs*) and asylum seekers at the shrine. Hajji Hashim's duties included detaining people drinking wine, engaging in prostitution, sleeping with an *amrad*, stealing, fighting, and engaging in unseemly acts in the houses of the shrine servants (*khuddam*). If someone took asylum at the shrine, he had to investigate to determine who they were and why they had done so. After his investigation, he would compose a report. Hajji Hashim visited the governor twice daily (every morning and evening) to deliver his reports.[54]

Hajji Hashim's diligence led to conflict with the *mutavallibashi* since Hajji Hashim was technically under his authority as well. The *mutavallibashi* was upset with Hajji Hashim for informing the governor about a criminal case involving a sayyid hosting a prostitute at his home since the *mutavallibashi* expected the *kadkhuda* to keep the sayyid's secret. Since the *mutavallibashi* stopped acting "kindly" toward him, the *kadkhuda* asked the governor to write the shrine guardian a letter instructing him to do so once again. Instead, Adib al-Mulk told him that he was now a "government servant" (*nawkar-i divan*) and not the servant of the *mutavallibashi*, so it did not matter how the latter behaved.[55] He promised to request "government wages and a livelihood" for Hajji Hashim from the central government so that he could live comfortably enough to carry out his duties.[56]

SHRINE ASYLUM AND CRIME

Despite these measures, the greatest barrier to consistent policing and penal measures emanated from the Ma'sumah Shrine (figure 18). The shrine's sacred status attracted all manner of criminal activities, vice, and extortion rackets. At the heart of this paradox was the unique spatial status of the shrine in relation to the practice of taking asylum (*bast*): the very sacredness of the shrine space enabled some people to act criminally with impunity.

Shrine servants used the shrine's unique spatial status for prostitution rings, drunken parties, theft (especially of pilgrims), and disor-

Figure 18: A photograph taken by Abu al-Qasim Nuri in 1319 H. / 1901
of the Ma'sumah Shrine in Qum, where criminals often sought asylum.

(Source: Qaraguzlu, *Qum-i Qadim*, 150)

derly conduct. Adib al-Mulk cited an Imami hadith in support of his
negative assessment of the shrine servants: "The evil of mankind are
[from among] the servants of our graves."[57] He described the shrine servants' drunken parties in the following unflattering terms: "Three or
four hours into the night, they gather together at the top of the cemetery and at the head of Muslims' graves where they drink wine and play
tanbur [a lute instrument], gamble, and engage in all sorts of disorder
[*harzigi*] and evil with female and male prostitutes [*ajanadah va ama-
radah*]."[58] The main spatial nexus for their criminal activities were their
residences, which were located in the shrine's vicinity and therefore
considered within the *bast* zone. Shrine servants tricked pilgrims into
residing with them before robbing them or "extending their hands" to
their women and children. They also housed murderers, wine imbib-
ers, thieves, immoral people, and appropriators of government funds.

Whenever a governor tried to bring these people to account, this re-sulted in an uprising against the government.[59]

Shrine servants facilitated prostitution rings at their homes for male pilgrims who were away from their wives. Male and female pros-titutes were allowed to carry out their trade as the shrine servants' "pro-tected people" (ma'man) and "protected residents" (mustajir), which generated tremendous revenues (madakhil) for the shrine servants.[60] In a later period, Qum government officials would similarly maintain their own brothels and allocate two hundred tumans of government taxes for their upkeep. When certain 'ulama heard of this, they objected but were assured that the women would have temporary marriage contracts prepared by a member of the 'ulama to make such unions shari'ah compliant. The jurist Hajji Sayyid Javad later learned that this government-supported brothel did not involve the 'ulama, so he mobi-lized his supporters against it, suggesting that the main conflict was over who should be paid for prostitution/temporary marriages.[61]

Adib al-Mulk explained why reforming seven-hundred-year old bast practices in Qum was particularly challenging. He cited a proverb stating that the eyes of Qummis (and in fact all Iranians) were fixated on two domes (gunbads): the golden dome of the Shrine of Fatimah and the green "dome" on the head of the mutavallibashi, who combined the ranks of sayyid, leadership (riyasat), and shrine guardianship (tuliyat). This image was apt because it captured the significance of the dome as a physical space of refuge and as a metaphor for the social network around its guardian, who benefited from its exceptional spatial status. Adib al-Mulk realized that changing bast practices could be done through neither the "command of religion and the sect" (amr-i din va millat) nor the principle of "the well-being of the government" (masla-hat-i dawlat). Instead, he pointed out that the bast zone had ballooned far beyond the initial shrine area to encompass houses in the side streets adjacent to the shrine sanctuary (haram) and at the head of the ceme-tery, which collectively constituted half of the city. He considered bast's intention to be for the public common good (maslahat), but instead the shrine servants' homes had become dens of "the most corrupt corrupt-ers."[62] Adib al-Mulk, therefore, set out to reform (islah) the neighborhood around the shrine and its adjacent areas, since all other reforms hinged on greater control over this space.[63]

Adib al-Mulk embarked on a heated debate with the *mutavalli-bashi*, Fayz Asar, about the nature and intention behind *bast*, since, without the consent and cooperation of the *mutavallibashi*, the governor would be incapable of actualizing his desired reforms.[64] The exchange between the two men revealed the various vested material interests behind the tradition of *bast* and its religious justifications.[65] It also showed how, despite being a government official, Adib al-Mulk redefined the meaning of *bast* by invoking the shari'ah while attempting to circumscribe its spatial boundaries in a manner consistent with earlier and contemporary efforts promoted by Nasir al-Din Shah.

In Adib al-Mulk's letter to Fayz Asar, he articulated his understanding of criminal liability, in which people in authority were responsible for their subordinates. Therefore, Fayz Asar was responsible for the shrine servants' actions because he was "the leader of the group" (*shaykh al-ta'ifah*) and thus capable of bringing them to account, punishing them, and banishing them from the shrine grounds. Adib al-Mulk admonished Fayz Asar to act as "the guarantor of all of his officials" and asked him to stamp a guarantor document to this effect.[66] He also wanted some of the shrine servants to be stripped of their positions, detained and sent to Tehran, or summoned to seek forgiveness for their criminal acts. Adib al-Mulk was troubled by the fact that the number of servants was unclear, and so he asked Fayz Asar to compile a list of their names so that the government would know whether their numbers were "ten, fifty, or a hundred people."[67] This, he hoped, would deter them from acting against the public interest and make them subject to shari'ah punishments.

Fayz Asar responded to Adib al-Mulk in a meeting by highlighting the economic reasons why the shrine servants would not sign a guarantor document, the inability of past governments to control activities in their residences, and the inviolability of the *bast* principle in Islam. He claimed that the shrine servants, who numbered roughly seven hundred with two to three thousand dependents, would lose their power, status, and livelihood from criminals operating in their homes if they signed a guarantor document.[68] The *mutavallibashi* further pointed out that no government official had ever enjoyed "sovereignty" (*tasallut*) over their houses, nor had they succeeded in expelling thieves or prostitutes from their doors. Since not even the powerful former prime minister Amir Kabir was capable of undoing *bast* practices, why would Adib al-Mulk be any different? He reasoned that the *bast* tradition traced back to the origins of Islamic history and had a seven-hundred-year history in Qum, so it could not be easily violated.[69]

Adib al-Mulk countered with religious reasoning as well, which was rooted both in the shah's *farmans* and Islamic jurisprudence. First, he argued that *bast* was reserved only for the "wronged" (*mazlumin*) and not for the "troublemaker, fornicator, ruffian, and evildoer," language that echoed the shah's *farmans*.[70] Second, he claimed that criminals should be subject to God's rulings (*hukm-i khuda*), meaning the shari'ah. Shrine servants should therefore expel criminals from the sanctuary by cutting off their water and food supplies so government officials could capture them and punish them according to retribution (*qisas*) in cases of murder and other laws depending on the circumstances.[71] He asked the *mutavallibashi* rhetorically why he, as a believer in shari'ah, would allow the houses of the shrine servants, which were located next to the *haram* of the descendant of the Prophet Muhammad, to become distilleries (*shirahkhanah*), brothels (*jindahkhanah*), and dens of thievery (*duzdgah*). This constituted the ultimate disrespect to the "sanctity [*hurmat*] of the shari'ah."[72] Adib al-Mulk differentiated himself from Amir Kabir by pointing out that the latter had tried to ban the *bast* through force and without the shah's consent, while he had secured guarantor documents from many people and acted on behalf of the shah's authority through an imperial decree (*hukm-i padishahi*).[73] The governor even threatened to petition Nasir al-Din Shah, saying that everyone stamped the guarantor documents except the shrine servants because the *mutavallibashi* refused to do so. He then reminded Fayz Asar that all shrine guardians were mere representatives of the shah, who was the ultimate guardian of all of the country's endowments (*awqaf*); therefore, he could strip them all of their position at any moment.[74]

Fayz Asar apologetically accepted Adib al-Mulk's terms in the face of this threat. He promised to gather the shrine servants in his home and have them stamp the guarantor document.[75] Despite these assurances, the efforts of the local *kadkhuda* Hajji Hashim in curbing crime were limited because the shrine's *bast* area extended to houses and streets connected to the cemetery and other places beyond it, which allowed for continuing disorder (*fitnah*) by ruffians. The governor therefore announced that the houses of the shrine servants and 'ulama were no longer *bast* zones; only the Ma'sumah Shrine's buildings were to retain that status. This announcement pleased certain 'ulama, innocent figures (*abrar*), tradesmen, merchants, and foreigners, although it upset the *mutavallibashi*, trouble-seeking shrine servants who were also *lutis*, and fornicators (*fajjar*).[76] Fayz Asar was particularly upset because he had agreed to act as the guarantor of the shrine servants, but Adib al-Mulk responded that he took this action to preserve the "sanctity and strength" (*hurmat va taqviyat*) of the shrine space.[77] Adib al-Mulk's measure included a definition of the *bast* zone in the following terms: "From the entrance under the chain of the hospital [Dar al-Shifa] until the end of the shrine [*haram-i muhtaram*] and the women's courtyard [*sahn-i zananah*]. In other words, the *bast* means the Dar al-Shifa, the Madrasah, the imperial building ['*imarat-i sultani*], the holy courtyard [*sahan-i mubarak*], the pure resting place [*rawzah-i mutaharrah*], and the women's courtyard."[78] This definition excluded other commonly used *bast* zones, such as the shrine guardians' residences and the head of the graveyard, since sultans or governors had only intended these *bast* zones for temporary use. In all of Iran, Adib al-Mulk claimed there were only three genuine *bast* zones: the Ma'sumah Shrine in Qum, the Imam Riza Shrine in Mashhad, and the Shah 'Abd al-'Azim Shrine near Tehran.[79] In response, the *mutavallibashi* acquiesced reluctantly and let out a deep sigh.[80]

CASES OF *BAST*, DISPUTE RESOLUTION, AND CRIME

Adib al-Mulk recounted specific cases of crime and punishment that highlighted the connection between his legal reforms and everyday practice. Pilgrims, and "strangers to the city" more generally, were often at the center of these crimes, including many pertaining to prostitution. Given the thriving economy of pilgrimage, temporary marriages, and sex crimes, there was a close relationship between vice and sanctity.

Adib al-Mulk provided accounts of how he physically cordoned off the residences where criminals took refuge in the precincts of the shrine, which in a sense was emblematic of the containment of moral pollution. When someone took refuge in such residences, "their [own] residence would be sealed [*muhr*]," and if the safehouse was in the "precincts of the shrine," then their family and kin outside the sanctuary area would be detained and held liable. These family members would only secure their freedom upon bringing their relative out of *bast*, a practice consistent with guarantorship.[81] The governor had thieves captured and forced them to return their stolen goods to the victims. He then punished them with the dismemberment of one of their hands.[82]

At his court, Adib al-Mulk ignored the bankruptcy declarations (*iflasnamah*s) issued by mullahs on behalf of people trying to "appropriate the money of strangers."[83] For instance, a high-profile mullah tried to intercede for one such person to prove the authenticity of his bankruptcy. The governor ignored the intercession and ordered that the person be detained.[84] In another case involving strangers, Sadiq, an apprentice copper maker from Tehran, stole from his master (*ustad*) and sold his goods at a lower price in Qum. The *darughah* became aware that Sadiq did not own these goods and brought him to the governor for further investigation. Sadiq confessed to his crimes and received "comprehensive punishment" (*tanbih-i kamil*), while the master craftsman was notified that he would have his stolen copper goods returned to him.[85] Strangers were often accused of theft as well. Hajji Jasbi accused a man of having stolen twenty-eight tumans from him. The accused man, who was from Isfahan and was traveling to Qazvin, had fifty tumans in cash with him. The suspected thief was imprisoned while the officials wrote to Isfahan. Meanwhile, trustworthy merchants and the 'ulama from Qazvin vouched for the Isfahani man, stating that he was not a thief. As a result, Hajji Jasbi had to return the money to the accused man, since it appeared to be a case of mistaken identity.[86]

Adib al-Mulk involved the major 'ulama of the city in a murder case. A group of Khurasani pilgrims had killed a fellow female pilgrim. The suspected female murderer was obtained after four hours. The 'ulama forbade the murderer from being killed, on the grounds that both "the murderer and the murdered woman had children" and because the execution of a female murderer was not permissible (*ja'iz*) according to the shari'ah until half of the blood price was given, especially since both were from outside (*kharij*) the city. Because these people were outsiders, the 'ulama believed that punishing them would not result in greater order; instead, they seized the money of both women and surrendered it to a trustworthy person in the presence of a leading *mujtahid*, Hajji Mullah Muhammad Sadiq.[87]

Many sex crimes occurred in Qum, ranging from sexual harassment and illicit sexual relations to prostitution. A female pilgrim who went to the house of a sayyid asked for water for her ablutions during 'Ashura. He invited her to take the water from the women in the private quarter (*andarun*). As soon as she entered, the sayyid closed the door and started to grope her with the intention of raping her (*ba u zina kunad*). The woman screamed, causing the neighbors to intervene and extricate her from the situation. Adib al-Mulk used this as an example of why *bast* was contrary to justice.[88] In another case, the *kadkhuda* of the Ma'sumah Shrine neighborhood detained a sayyid shrine servant and his brother for associating with an unrelated woman. Since these servants were from among the "great and powerful shrine servants," the *mutavallibashi* forgave them and "requested that they not be disgraced [*pardah dari*]," meaning that their private sins not be made public.[89]

Prostitutes, who were typically strangers to the city, carried out their affairs in shrine servants' residences. In one instance, two female prostitutes set up operations in a shrine servant's house. The *kadkhuda* learned of this and detained the two women. Since they repented at the residence of Mullah Muhammad Sadiq, they were allowed to leave the city.[90] Repentance coupled with voluntary banishment constituted expiation of sin and the physical removal of moral contagion from the community, respectively. This case stands out as an intriguing reversal of Ibrahim Gulistan's iconic 1967 short story "Safar-i 'Ismat," wherein a prostitute visits the Imam Riza Shrine to repent for her sins, only to be persuaded by a sayyid to continue her trade under the religiously sanctioned institution of temporary marriage (*sighah*).[91]

In contrast, a prostitute from Tehran named Malik Tarkah was far from repentant. In the late 1860s, Nasir al-Din Shah issued an imperial decree instructing Tehran's *biglarbigi*, 'Ala al-Dawlah, to banish Malik

Tarkah—whom he referred to by the Persian expletive "burnt father" (*pi-dar sukhtah*)—from the city, while ensuring that she did not leave from one city gate only to return by another.[92] After her banishment from Tehran, Malik Tarkah took up clandestine residence in Qum at the house of the shrine servant, Sayyid Talib. The city's ruffians would secretly visit the residence, thus making use of the domicile's inviolability. When the *kadkhuda* Hajji Hashim saw a *luti* frequent this residence, he deduced that illegal activities were transpiring there. He visited the residence, saw the woman, and detained her. It was ruled that the *kadkhuda* would take ten tumans for himself and that the woman and her pimp (*qurumsaq*) shrine servant would be banished from the city gates. When the *kadkhuda* went to collect the ten tumans, she came up short, so Sayyid Talib gave her four tumans to make up the difference. In a ritualized parade, Hajji Hashim put the woman on a donkey and banished her from a city gate. As she left the city, she turned to the crowd and said, "There is not a single man to be found in [all of] Qum who could keep me in this land, and so I have to leave this place in a state of utmost abjectness and poverty." After Malik Tarkah left, the lovelorn Sayyid Talib followed her to Tehran, promising her a silk clothing set.[93]

In Tehran, Malik Tarkah faced the wrath of the shah, who had banished her earlier. Despite the efforts of an unnamed correspondent to have her exiled to Kerman under armed guard to live out a life sentence of imprisonment, which they described as a fate "worse than death," Nasir al-Din Shah insisted in a subsequent *farman* that she should be executed: "Malik Tarkah is definitively [*yaqinan*] sentenced to death [*vajib al-qatl ast*]. She must not remain alive. She is a pimp [*qavvadah*] and must be killed. Seize all of her property like a dog" (figure 19).[94] The shah's reference to her as a pimp indicates that he considered pimping deserving of a death sentence rather than banishment and life imprisonment. Shi'i jurisprudence prescribed a death sentence for a male pimp convicted for a fourth or fifth time (particularly if he was unrepentant), which may have informed the shah's ruling.[95] It is unclear if and how Malik Tarkah was executed on the basis of this *farman*, but she does not appear in subsequent archival sources.

Adib al-Mulk stands out as a governor who projected authority by embedding government within social relations. He addressed the

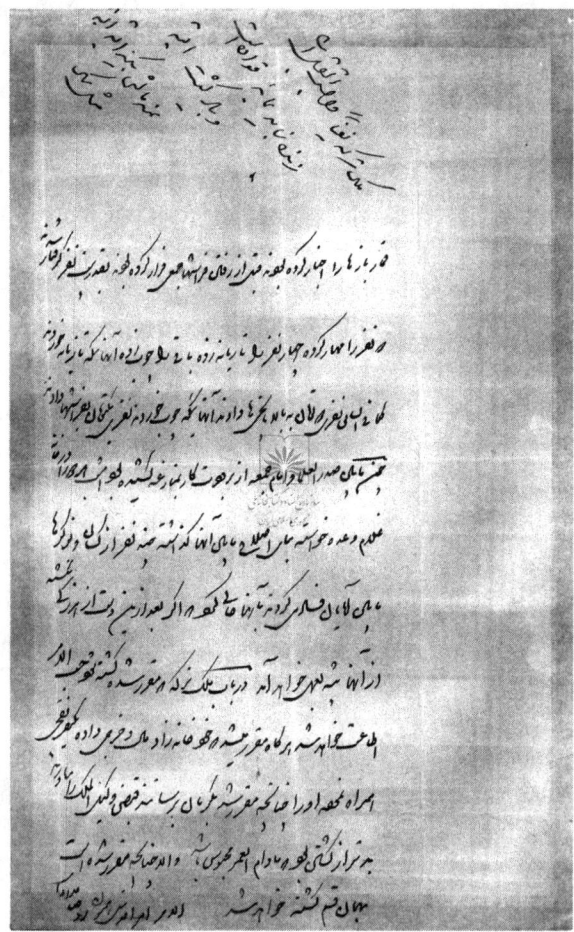

Figure 19: Nasir al-Din Shah's death sentence for the
female prostitute and pimp Malik Tarkah.
(Source: "Guzarish-i Dastgiri," n.d., SAKM 296/1676)

causes of conflict through provisioning, planning, and greater government monitoring of key resources. Through guarantorships, he created mechanisms for monitoring urban crime, especially through the
reconstituted *kadkhuda* system and regular reporting. By curtailing
the boundaries of the *bast* zone and banning its use by criminals, he
aimed for a more spatially uniform application of the law across the
city. Finally, the governor used the familiar mix of banishment, parades,

dismemberment, and collective retribution to assert his legal authority and communicate that justice would be done.

Law in a Time of Famine

While Adib al-Mulk confronted ecological conflicts over water, 'Abbas Quli Khan, the governor of Qum in the early 1870s, faced the ecology of famine.[96] The main reasons for the famine appear to have been drought, extreme cold weather, and the resultant breakdown of watermills.[97] Famine had the potential to accentuate social conflicts and crime, increase suspicions leading to the violation of bodily privacy norms, and lead to extraordinary and extralegal forms of community punishment. The shrine guardian 'Ali Akbar Fayz's extraordinary firsthand account constitutes a compelling vector through which to examine everyday theft, murder, and cannibalism against the backdrop of famine in Qum.[98] Outsiders were typically suspected of cannibalism and therefore subject to spot questioning and inspections for carrying illegal substances (in this case, body parts), which would ordinarily be deemed a violation of bodily privacy/sanctity (*hurmat*).[99] Since the famine in Qum constituted a state of emergency, people often used extralegal mechanisms of redress, a form of "rough justice," without waiting for shari'ah or government rulings.

In Islamic jurisprudence, cannibalism was generally prohibited on the grounds that the human body was inviolable and sacred.[100] Those who allowed for it out of necessity (Arabic: *darurah*; Persian: *zarurat*), meaning starvation, were in a small minority and only allowed homicidal cannibalism to save one's own life if the person in question was already sentenced to death, an infidel waging war, or an apostate.[101] Zoltan Szombathy's study of cannibalism discusses a famine in 1201 (597 H.) in Egypt during which people killed others, often defenseless children, with the purpose of consuming them. Those who were convicted of this form of homicidal cannibalism appear to have been universally sentenced to death, despite claiming to have done so out of necessity.[102] There are many telling parallels between this and the famine in Qum, insofar as it led to two simultaneous crises in bodily sanctity: the first had to do with the consumption of human flesh, and the second had to do with the policing of suspected cannibals' bodies.

Fayz's narrative was based on government and 'ulama eyewitness accounts of crimes and court cases. Governors and other government officials, such as Navvab Hisam al-Saltanah and Navvab Amirzadah Abu al-Fath Mirza, heard and tried criminal cases. *Mujtahids* such as Hajji Mullah Muhammad Sadiq and Hajji Sayyid Javad also tried cases at their shari'ah courts.[103] He also learned of instances of spot questioning and inspections and punishments from the head attendant, Muhammad Riza Farrashbashi, who carried them out. In cases where Fayz heard the account from lesser-known figures, he justified the authenticity of the source by adopting an almost hadith-like narrative structure by stating, for example, "a trustworthy sayyid narrated" (*sayyidi mu'tabari hikayat kard*).[104] Fayz's cases generally involved murderers who confessed to their crimes. He usually also mentioned their punishments, although when he did not, the accused had confessed to murder, so they probably either faced a death sentence or had to pay compensation.

Given the devastating effect of drought on raising livestock, butchers in the bazaar resorted to selling dog meat as lamb.[105] The punishments for this crime varied from admonishment and beatings to ignominious parading and even execution. The governor 'Abbas Quli Khan's response took the form of market regulation (*hisbah*) to ensure that there was no cheating in the bazaar. When a butcher was "selling dog meat as lamb" in his shop, the people caught on and reported it to the governor. After summoning the butcher and inspecting the dog meat, the governor ruled that the butcher's "ears be cut off and for him to be put in a bridle [*mahar*] and paraded around so that it could be a lesson for others ['*ibrat-i digaran*]."[106] This punishment was intended to restore confidence in the integrity of meats in the bazaar. Similarly, when a man stole a "pack of dogs" and started selling their meat, the governor had the man beaten and then chastised (*ta'dib*) him, perhaps because it was a first-time offense.[107] Another butcher who sold dog meat and was presumably a repeat offender was not so fortunate: Navvab Husam al-Saltanah had this butcher killed.[108]

The vast majority of legal cases during the famine involved theft, murder, and cannibalism due to scarcity. Those who were implicated included strangers to the city, women, children, and beggars. While government and shari'ah courts heard many cases of murder and cannibalism directly, ordinary people occasionally meted out rough justice since they found the offense to be so outrageous.

In the context of food scarcity, many people turned to theft, which ended in violence. The wife of Hajji Hasan Kulahduz, who resided in Khiyaban-i Pa'in, went out one day to buy some bread, leaving her fourteen-year-old daughter in the house alone. Upon her return, she found her daughter dead in the outdoor fountain (*hawz*). Her valuables had also been stolen. Ten days later, the thief was apprehended and brought before the court of Mullah Muhammad Sadiq. He subsequently confessed to his crime. He had initially come to the house to beg but saw the girl alone in the house. When she told him that there was no bread for him, he asked to drink from the house's fountain. The girl allowed him to enter; he then asked the girl if he could eat a fish or two from the fountain, but she replied that there were no fish in there. He lied and told her that there was a big fish, which she, out of curiosity, came to see. He threw her in the fountain and drowned her before stealing all of the house's valuables.[109] Although no punishment was reported, given the confession at the shari'ah court, he was probably either executed or made to pay compensation. A female thief from Karamjakaniyah came to steal from the house of Navvab Amirzadah Abu al-Fath Mirza. Navvab Amirzadah dealt with her directly by having her caught and detained (*zajr*) and chastised her. Navvab Amirzadah swore at her and blamed her for stealing, killing, and eating people's children. In her defense, she claimed that she had only eaten three children. Her fate was similarly unclear.[110]

In the midst of the famine, ordinary people conducted their own spot questioning and inspections of suspicious characters, especially strangers to the city. Strangers, as René Girard has argued, serve as convenient scapegoats in the midst of social crises.[111] In one case, people stopped a man from Farahan who was begging for bread. They found the hands and feet of children in his pockets and the load he carried on his back. The people referred the case to the governor, 'Abbas Quli Khan, who, in turn, referred the man to a shariʻah judge. During the course of the investigation, the man confessed to having killed five children, including a female sayyid whom he had picked up on the pretext of feeding her. She had begged him not to kill her, but he did and then proceeded to roast and eat her outside the city at the Gulkhan Hammam. After his conviction, a group of people decided to carry out the execution order themselves, possibly because she had no heirs. They may have also felt that the community had been harmed by such a heinous act that only they, collectively, could serve justice. In a ritual spectacle, they dragged the man to the center of the city by the neck, where they stoned (*sangsar*) him.[112]

Rough justice against cannibals could also involve stoning. Ordinary subjects randomly inspected a man from Khavah who had come to Qum with his two wives. Although the man attempted to stop the inspection, a crowd gathered and opened up his load, where they found children's body parts. The man confessed to having been desperate to eat something when he entered the city, so he abducted two children from the icehouse of the Friday Prayer Mosque (Masjid-i Jamiʻ). He then choked one child to death and beheaded the other before consuming them. Soon thereafter, the mother and father of one of the children arrived. The crowd intended to take the man to the court of Hajji Sayyid Javad, but along the way, they started throwing stones at the man. They beat him and his two wives to death. Their corpses became food for the animals in the city square (*maydan*), meaning that they were denied proper burial.[113] On another occasion, the head attendant, Muhammad Rizaʼi Farrashbashi, was walking along Hawz-i Qahvah street when he was approached by a young beggar. The head attendant saw that the beggar had a load, so he had a servant search it, which turned up body parts. As an immediate punishment, the man was beaten, and the body parts were taken away for burial, although his ultimate fate was unclear.[114] The official government newspaper reported that a group of suspicious individuals were hanging around outside Maʻsumah Shrine gate; they were found to be in possession of two small children's toes. One of them was brought to the governor's building and roughed up. He confessed to killing and eating five children. The shah ordered that the man be executed in the people's presence.[115]

Military officials on the outskirts of Qum carried out similar spot questioning and inspections. At the residence of the governor, the imperial slave soldier (*ghulam*) of Mustafa Quli Khan Sartip came to discuss the case of a man who had the body parts of a woman in his load while traveling on the road between Qum and Yazd. The *farrashbashi* summoned the man and interrogated him for an hour, during which he confessed to his crime: he had been traveling with his sister to Kashan when they met a corpulent Yazdi prostitute who was traveling from Tehran to Yazd. After they became fellow travelers, the man killed her because he coveted her many belongings and then consumed her ample flesh for sustenance. The cavalry detained him at the Pasangan caravanserai and seized his belongings.[116]

Women also engaged in cannibalism during the famine. Muhammad Taqi Arbab's sister-in-law left her house and fell victim to a female cannibalism ring. This group of women enticed others by claiming there were edible vegetables in a garden. Once they lured people in, the gang of women killed and ate them.[117] A man who had been searching for his lost cow stumbled across billows of smoke close to a tower. He went toward the smoke, where he found three women grilling and eating a woman whom they had just murdered. The man took the women to the shari'ah court (*mahzar*) of Mullah Muhammad Sadiq, where one of them confessed. She claimed that initially the women were searching for straw to consume out of sheer hunger, but then they saw an ill-looking woman. The two other women told her to gather wood for a fire. She later saw that they had killed the woman and were planning to cook her meat. The investigation concluded that all three had played a role in the murder; therefore, 'Abbas Quli Khan ruled that all three women should be taken to a room, and "an arch was demolished over their heads."[118] A shorter yet similar case involving a Nishapuri woman who confessed to having eaten seven children out of hunger ended in a similar manner: Navvab Hisam al-Saltanah ordered for her to be killed.[119]

Children sometimes collaborated with women's networks in abducting and eating other children. Since they acted under the authority of adults, the degree of their criminal liability was in question. A fourteen-year-old boy abducted the child of a dyer who had a shop in the Lab-i Chal area in Qum.[120] When the child started screaming, his father seized his son and presented the older boy to the court of Mullah Muhammad Sadiq. A report was prepared based on the incident. Sadiq warned the youth and intended to chastise him. The youth confessed that there were five women in the Imamzadah Shah Hamzah neighborhood, including his own mother, who for some time had been gathering children from the city streets through deception and trickery. These children would then be consumed at nightly meals. Several people were dispatched to find these women so that "they could be punished according to the shariʻah" (hadd-i sharʻi jari namayand). But once the women heard of this, they ran away and never returned to their usual haunt. Since the youth was not criminally responsible (mukallaf), having not reached the age of maturity, he was chastised and released instead of receiving a punishment.[121]

Famine pushed ordinary people to violate social norms of bodily sanctity through cannibalism and spot questioning and inspections. Given the previous decade's emphasis on community policing, ordinary subjects proactively monitored and scrutinized strangers. The extraordinary circumstances emboldened ordinary subjects to collectively make decisions over life and death through rough justice, thus crossing into a moral and legal universe in which ordinary subjects acted as judges and executioners, often in highly ritualized and symbolic forms and with impunity.

Murder, *Bast*, and Jurisdiction under Iʻtizad al-Dawlah

Between the 1870s and 1890s, Qum was mainly governed by Iʻtizad al-Dawlah. He was married to the daughter of Nasir al-Din Shah, Fakhr al-Muluk, who was occasionally the de facto governor of the city. Iʻtizad al-Dawlah applied similar principles as Adib al-Mulk when it came to monitoring neighborhoods, keeping detailed records, and neutralizing the power of *mutavallibashi* and his servants, although he did not leave behind a firsthand summary account of his tenure. Instead, numerous letters, telegrams, and reports reveal his (and his successors') overall approach to crime and *bast* in the city.[122] These sources reveal the overlapping jurisdiction and, at times, strained relations between the courts of the shah, governor, and local ʻulama; the persistent significance of the *bast* in criminal cases, despite repeated efforts to regulate it; the continued involvement of shrine servants in local crime; and the use of spectacles of punishment.

I'tizad al-Dawlah continued the textual practices of his predecessor, in which events in the city, especially crimes, petitions, and legal cases, were recorded and forwarded to the imperial court in Tehran. In a letter dated 1873/74 (1290 H.), he mentioned writing a regular "report [*ruznamah*] of the city's conditions and urban events" in two booklets that were forwarded to the shah; the report included all "petitions and cases" (*'ara'iz va da'avi*) involving the people as well as the cases heard by the assistant governor, 'Ali Khan.[123] In response to an accusation that I'tizad al-Dawlah was negligent in tending to people's affairs, dated July/August 1879 (Sha'ban 1296 H.), he described the lengths he went to for "ordinary people" (*'ammah-i mardum*) without exception, "from the morning until three hours into the night," while suffering in the "stifling hot weather."[124]

Like his predecessors, I'tizad al-Dawlah had to contend with the power of the *mutavallibashi*, the criminal activities of his servants, and the legally exceptional status of sanctuary zones in the city. In an undated letter to Nasir al-Din Shah, he complained about the *mutavallibashi*'s reticence in punishing certain shrine servant "evildoers." The governor employed a familiar technique: he asked that the "troublemaker" (*mufsid*) servants be identified. Although the *mutavallibashi* tried to delay this, he eventually identified them and banished them from the "assembly of servants" (*jirgah-i khuddam*). I'tizad al-Dawlah also made the *mutavallibashi* sign a document making him the guarantor of the remaining shrine servants.[125]

Accused murderers continued to take asylum at the Ma'sumah Shrine, given the reticence of officials to forcibly remove them. This resulted in jurisdictional friction between the central government, the local government, and the *mutavallibashi*. For the central government, its ability to deliver justice in murder cases was a key expression of its authority, especially when the victims' heirs invoked their jurisdiction because the governor and *mutavallibashi* were unable or unwilling to act. In many of the telegraphic exchanges between the central government—including the prime minister and Na'ib al-Saltanah—and the *mutavallibashi*, both sides articulated competing shari'ah discourses: the former was mainly concerned with carrying out *hudud* and *qisas*, while the latter emphasized respecting the sanctity of the shrine. Since asylum often bought time to negotiate a settlement or other alternatives to *qisas*, it became a flashpoint for the enactment of multiple jurisdictions over the issue of the inviolability of the sanctuary and the universal applicability of the law (in this case shari'ah), which usually worked in favor of the accused.

In 1879, Rajab 'Ali Yazdi murdered an unnamed Zoroastrian in Yazd before taking refuge at the Ma'sumah Shrine. On April 3, 1879, Mirza Husayn Khan Sipahsalar informed the *mutavallibashi* that the shah wanted the man imprisoned in the sanctuary until he could face justice in Tehran.[126] In his response, the *mutavallibashi* confirmed that Rajab 'Ali Yazdi was being held firmly in place but that this confinement had caused the 'ulama of Qum and Tehran to mock, bother, and complain about him for this violation of *bast* principles. Sipahsalar responded sharply by reminding the *mutavallibashi* that the shari'ah called for the punishment (*hudud*) of those who commit murder and disorderly (*mufsidah*) actions; therefore, such opinions should not bother him.[127] Kamran Mirza Na'ib al-Saltanah later requested that the governor, I'tizad al-Dawlah, send Rajab 'Ali to Tehran under armed escort for further investigation.[128] The governor refused on the grounds that this would violate the sanctity of the shrine: "How can he be brought out the sanctuary since the shah would not be pleased with him being dragged out [forcibly] and sent to Tehran?"[129] The delay tactic worked in Rajab 'Ali's favor: roughly a week later, the Zoroastrian heir to the murdered person agreed to accept *diyah* on the condition that Rajab 'Ali be banished (*ikhraj-i balad*) permanently from Yazd. Failure to do the latter would mean that the heirs would kill him with impunity.[130] The payment of compensation included not only the Islamically prescribed *diyah* for a Zoroastrian, which amounted to forty tumans, but also the collective contribution of the shah, the governor, and others in Qum of roughly 100–150 tumans to the heirs as a condition for Rajab 'Ali's release. Rajab 'Ali also signed a guarantee not to return to Yazd.[131]

In another instance, the *mutavallibashi* brought about a settlement to avoid *qisas* for people under his authority. On August 25, 1889 (27 Zi

Hijjah 1306 H.), a camel driver of the *mutavallibashi* fought with an imperial camel driver over a "trifling matter" that resulted in the former shooting the latter to death. The *mutavallibashi* resolved the matter by agreeing to pay thirty tumans in compensation.[132]

A man by the name of Shaykh ʿAli was injured and came to Qum after a general brawl in 1879. The man died of his wounds three days later. The case involved Shaykh ʿAbbas, the headman (*raʾis*) of the Imam Jumʿah, who had fought with several farmers. The murderer, a man named Haydar, took refuge in the Shah Hamzah Shrine. The governor put several attendants on duty to catch the man as soon as he left the shrine. In the meantime, another man, named Husayn ʿAli, also died. Shaykh ʿAbbas took refuge at the Maʿsumah Shrine, fearing implication in one or both of the murders. The *mutavallibashi* was ordered to imprison Shaykh ʿAli in the shrine and put the suspect in chains. Since this was "murder on the basis of a strong suspicion" (*qatl-i laws*), the case was to be heard by a shariʿah court.[133]

In October/November 1885 (Muharram 1303 H.), Mahdi Naʿlband murdered his wife. He then took refuge at the Maʿsumah Shrine. The prime minister sent a telegram to the *mutavallibashi*, accusing him of defying a government order to capture Naʿlband and allowing the shrine servants to help him escape.[134] He claimed that the *mutavallibashi* had "protected and harbored a murderer," which was not sanctioned by either "shariʿah or local custom [*ʿurf*]" and would only lead to "infamy and trouble." He then commanded the *mutavallibashi* to capture and bring Naʿlband to the government, "even if he had taken refuge at the house of a shrine servant."[135] The *mutavallibashi* vigorously denied the accusations. Instead, he claimed that Naʿlband had been captured by a government attendant (*farrash-i hukumat*) tasked by the assistant governor to do so when he exited the residence of a certain Aqa Husayn. Since it was the month of Muharram, Naʿlband was lost in the crowd of ritual mourners. The *mutavallibashi* then sent a servant, who, along with the assistant governor's servant, searched for the man in the environs of Maʿsumah's grave (Rawzah-i Mubarakah), but their search turned up nothing.[136] The prime minister followed up, saying that the *mutavallibashi*'s version of the events had been relayed to the shah, adding that the search for the murderer should continue.[137]

Despite the best efforts of Adib al-Mulk and later governors, Qum's sanctuaries continued to act as inviolable spaces, which attracted all manner of criminals, including murderers. Although the *mutavallibashi* and governor agreed to keep accused murderers imprisoned in the shrine until they could face justice, others worked toward a settlement to avoid execution. All legal authorities invoked the shari'ah, whether to claim that forcibly removing a refugee from a shrine was a violation of it or to say that carrying out its punishments was essential. These arguments, fissures, and issues came to a head in the explosive 'Abdullah Sultan murder case in early 1882.

The 'Abdullah Sultan Murder Case

'Abdullah Sultan's murder of his wife, Shahzadah Bigum, in Mahallat, a town close to Qum, in 1882 stands out as one of the most well-documented legal cases of the era. Contemporary telegrams between the shah, prime minister, and governor and diaries and memoirs of court officials, next-of-kin of the murdered, and others provide us with multilayered perspectives about the significance of the event. The trial and ultimate decision to execute the murderer involved multiple jurisdictions, including that of Hajji Sayyid Javad, who issued the ruling of *qisas*; the governor and the *mutavallibashi*, who tried to forestall the ruling since the murderer had taken asylum at the Ma'sumah Shrine; and the shah, who confirmed the ruling and insisted on its implementation.

Like many small towns in Iran, Mahallat was composed of two main lineage groups, the Sayyids and the Qal'ahs, between whom there were tensions and conflicts. Two local 'ulama decided to reconcile them through a common and often effective means: intermarriage. They persuaded Sadr al-Din, the father of Shahzadah Bigum, to give his fifteen- or sixteen-year-old daughter to 'Abdullah Sultan, a fifty-year-old man. Despite Shahzadah Bigum's objections, she was married to the man and joined his household with her slave boy, Haqq Virdi; her Black female slave Yasaman; and Yasaman's daughter, Bilgis.[138] The couple had a baby girl named Gawhar but fought often. 'Abdullah Sultan started acting erratically by barricading himself in his home and not allowing anyone to leave, including his wife, who wanted to visit her father's house, claiming that people in his lineage group were out to get him. One night, while fighting over dinner, ʿAbdullah Sultan threatened to bring the decapitated heads of his wife's father and uncle, to which Shahzadah Bigum responded by calling him a dog incapable of doing such a thing. After the couple went to bed, a gunshot was fired. Yasaman rushed to the door of their bedroom to see what had happened: standing with a gun in hand in the smoke-filled bedroom, ʿAbdullah Sultan told her, "Leave, you black dog! If you scream, I will kill you!" When the slaves felt it was safe, they came out to find the gruesome, lifeless body of Shahzadah Bigum next to her breathing forty-day-old infant.[139]

Subsequent investigation demonstrated that she had been shot from under the chin, with the bullet exiting through her brain, and stabbed thirty-three times in various parts of her body.[140] One of the two ʿulama who had arranged for her marriage, who was also her kinsman (and thus able to see the body), Hajj Mullah Muhammad Taqi, along with several women, went to record and produce testimony about the precise nature of the wounds.[141] One of the shah's close courtiers, Iʿtimad al-Saltanah, provided a contemporary account of the nature of the wounds that was more graphic: "Her husband [ʿAbdullah Sultan] apparently disfigured [maslah] her, cut off her head, and cut off her nipples."[142]

When the bereaved family took the body of Shahzadah Bigum to Qum for burial, they learned that ʿAbdullah Sultan had taken sanctuary at the Maʿsumah Shrine. From Qum, they sent telegrams to the shah, the prime minister, and the sister of the shah, ʿIzzat al-Dawlah, about the murder since there was no telegraph office in Mahallat.[143] Mustawfi al-Mamalik immediately wrote to the governor and to the mutavalli-bashi, informing them to put chains around ʿAbdullah Sultan's neck and to keep him imprisoned until a ruling could be made.[144] The Shah issued a direct telegraphic imperial order to Iʿtizad al-Dawlah and the mutavallibashi, commanding them to keep ʿAbdullah Sultan imprisoned and threatening that they and the shrine servants would be held criminally responsible if they allowed him to escape.[145] Subsequent cables reinforced this and added that he should be guarded day and night.[146]

Sadr al-Ashraf's memoirs provide crucial details about the trial proceedings. The father of the murdered woman brought the case before the famous Sayyid Javad; 'Abdullah Sultan had a representative (*vakil*) while he was imprisoned in the shrine. The trial, which lasted roughly forty days, concluded that there was much circumstantial evidence (*qara'in*) for intentional homicide, but since there were no eyewitnesses to the murder itself, it fell short of being proven. As such, an oath procedure (*qasamah*) was initiated in the judge's presence that resulted in the judge ruling that the murder had been proven.[147] Despite the best efforts of the governor of Isfahan, Zill al-Sultan, to bring about a reconciliation and offer a hefty blood price, the heirs refused and insisted on *qisas*.[148]

The willingness of the heirs to carry out retaliation did not translate into immediate action, since 'Abdullah Sultan was still in the sanctuary. Furious, the shah issued the following telegraphic imperial order: "The man who is determined to be a murderer is commanded by God to be beheaded; despite God's ordinance, why are you giving him asylum in the sanctuary? If Ma'sumah were alive today, she would rule that this burnt father [*pidar sukhtah*] should be executed. What buffoonery [*lutibazi*] is this that they do?" He ended the decree by threatening to depose and summon both the governor and the *mutavallibashi* to Tehran if they did not bring the murderer out of the sanctuary for execution.[149] In response, the governor asked for a ten-day delay so that the sanctity of the shrine would not be violated (*hatk-i ihtiram*) and no insult be made to the holy precincts, which might lead to a tumult, but the shah restated his threat if *qisas* was not immediately carried out.[150]

On April 14, 1883, Shahzadah Bigum's family and the governor, dressed in red, "wrathful" (*ghazab*) garb, along with several executioners (*mir ghazabs*) and attendants (also dressed in red), entered the precincts of the shrine. The bereaved Sadr al-Din deputized his brother to carry out *qisas* on his behalf. At first, the governor and assistant shrine guardian (*na'ib al-tuyulah*) tried to persuade the deputized brother to carry out *qisas* in a sheltered courtyard, the Hayat-i Shahi, but the latter insisted that retaliation must be done among the general public (*dar mala'-yi 'amm*). The shrine servants dragged the condemned man from the shrine in chains and handed him over to the heirs.[151] The official telegraphic report is suggestive of the way the aforementioned account may have tried to distance the family from violating the *bast*: in it, it was

Sadr al-Din who directly dragged 'Abdullah Sultan from his shrine chamber rather than the shrine servants.[152] Both accounts agree that he was taken to a nearby river, where *qisas* was carried out before a large crowd. Sadr al-Ashraf added that his father did not merely behead 'Abdullah Sultan: this was preceded by knife wounds to the stomach (mirroring the murder itself) before two other kinsmen delivered fatal blows that severed his head.[153]

The shah expressed delight upon hearing of the faithful implementation of his order and promised both the governor and the *mutavalli-bashi* robes of honor (*khal'ats*).[154] And yet, the issue of the *bast*'s sanctity lingered. Had the shah violated the *bast* by having 'Abdullah Sultan forcibly removed from the sanctuary, and if so, what were the implications? To Hajj Sayyah, a Mahallati traveler whose patron Zill al-Sultan tried to negotiate for a blood price instead of execution, the shah's order set a bad precedent. He described the "shameful" violation of the *bast* of 'Abdullah Sultan as one of the major events of 1882–83 (1300 H).[155] Eight years later, the shah ordered that Hajj Sayyah's close friend, the pan-Islamist Jamal al-Din Asadabadi (aka al-Afghani), be violently dragged out of the Shah 'Abd al-'Azim Shrine bareheaded and half-naked in the snow before being unceremoniously banished from the country.[156] Ironically, the shah who had deposed his first prime minister, Amir Kabir, for violating the *bast* now ordered the same quite regularly.

Baha'is before the Law

Scholars such as Leslie Peirce and Nobuaki Kondo have studied the Jewish and Christian use of shari'ah courts in the Ottoman Empire and Qajar Iran, respectively.[157] What has largely been unexplored is how so-called apostates, such as Babis and Baha'is, made use of shari'ah and government courts.[158] Shi'i jurisprudence required a high evidentiary bar for apostasy conviction, making it possible to avoid punishment so long as one did not make secret beliefs too public. Secret beliefs, like secret acts, were considered inviolable. Despite this, there were repeated efforts to prove the apostasy of Baha'is in Qum and surrounding areas by neighbors, competing elements in the bazaar, and those who generally considered Baha'is to be a polluting and dangerous presence. Those who made apostasy accusations invoked the jurisdiction of like-minded 'ulama and/or governors, while Baha'is typically invoked the shah's jurisdiction through petitions and the jurisdiction of sympathetic 'ulama who produced legal evidence for the "soundness of their beliefs."[159] Despite certain jurists issuing death sentences for Baha'is in Qum, these were not necessarily carried out: typical punishments included imprisonment or banishment as forms of moral containment.

THE GHULAM RIZA JASBI APOSTACY CASE

On April 14, 1882 (25 Jumada al-Avval 1299 H.), a group of villagers from Jasb, an agricultural district, traveled to nearby Qum. They complained to the *mujtahid* Sayyid Javad that a fellow villager, Mirza Ghulam Riza, was a Baha'i and provided testimony (*shahadat*) to that effect at Sayyid Javad's shari'ah court.[160] By doing so, they invoked the court's jurisdiction because being a Baha'i constituted a violation of the shari'ah. It was two of these villagers, 'Abd al-Vahhab Kadkhuda (Ghulam Riza's brother-in-law and sworn enemy) and Muhammad Riza Sayf al-Shari'ah, who provided as evidence Baha'i books and scriptures obtained ostensibly by violating the sanctity of Ghulam Riza's domicile.[161] Representatives from all seven villages that constituted Jasb provided testimony. Based on this evidence, Sayyid Javad and other 'ulama issued a ruling that Ghulam Riza and his brother Aqa Muhammad Javad were Baha'is.[162] Sayyid Javad wrote in his ruling that Ghulam Riza "had many books of the wayward group [*ta'ifah-i zallah*] in his house," which convinced the governor that he had been a Baha'i for many years.[163] Sayyid Javad also asked the governor to send an official (*ma'mur*) to detain Ghulam Riza and his brother and to bring them to Qum in chains to be imprisoned.[164]

Kamran Mirza Na'ib al-Saltanah and I'tizad al-Dawlah subsequently interrogated Ghulam Riza, during which time he confessed (*i'tiraf*) in their presence that he was a Baha'i.[165] I'tizad al-Dawlah reiterated in his telegrams that Ghulam Riza's conviction was partly because he was well-known—meaning publicly known—as a Baha'i. He described Ghulam Riza as among the community's famous people (*ma'arif*), on the basis of shari'ah and local government (*shar'an va* 'urfan) investigations, and the entire matter as "having become public and exposed" (bih shuyu' va istifazah risidah).[166] Their crime was referred to as holding "corrupt beliefs" (fasad-i 'aqidah and elsewhere 'aqa'id-i fasidah) rather than the technical term for apostasy (irtidad).[167] But this was not a ta'zir case that was prosecuted on the basis of probabilities; instead, the issue of lack of doubt came up often, suggesting that it was categorized as a hadd case. I'tizad al-Dawlah repeatedly said that there was no doubt (shubhah) of Ghulam Riza's guilt, shubhah being a category of doubt in Islamic jurisprudence that nullified a hadd punishment.[168] These sources reveal that the basis of apostasy was the eyewitness testimony of Ghulam Riza's fellow villagers, books and writings found in his home indicating his Baha'i affiliation, his public notoriety as a Baha'i, and a confession in the presence of government officials.

Legal authorities disagreed on the appropriate punishment. Sayyid Javad and another 'alim, Mirza Hasan, had initially issued a death sentence, for which "a foolish repentance" (tawbah-i sarsar) was unacceptable.[169] I'tizad al-Dawlah believed that the crime was deserving of "all manner of humiliations [khijalat] according to both shari'ah and local practice [shar'an va 'urfan]," which presumably meant a publicizing ritual of some sort.[170] Despite the 'ulama issuing a death sentence, the shah, who had final authority on such rulings, ordered a punishment of "life imprisonment" (habs-i mu'abbad).[171] The governor understood life imprisonment as moral containment, describing "this city [i.e., Qum] and all of the agricultural districts . . . [as] free from the evil of this abased group [ta'ifah-i razilah]" as a result of it.[172]

With Ghulam Riza facing a death sentence, his family and friends (and even Ghulam Riza himself) petitioned the shah directly, invoking his jurisdiction over that of local courts. According to Baha'i accounts, a Jasbi Baha'i, Aqa Mir, petitioned the shah in Tehran and received an imperial decree for the release of Ghulam Riza and his brother, but this did not occur, since the governor wrote Na'ib al-Saltanah, claiming that their release would lead to an uprising in Qum.[173] Aqa Mir constantly petitioned Na'ib al-Saltanah for their release nine months into their imprisonment. Both Aqa Mir and Na'ib al-Saltanah went to Qum, where

the latter personally questioned the two brothers in the presence of
I'tizad al-Dawlah. Na'ib al-Saltanah released Muhammad Javad and
promised to eventually secure the release of Ghulam Riza upon his return to Tehran, although this did not immediately happen.[174] Official
telegrams mention Ghulam Riza's sister and brother, Muhammad Javad, petitioning the shah, claiming the accusations were motivated by
enmity.[175] I'tizad al-Dawlah dismissed the protestations of Aqa Mir on
the grounds that he too was a Baha'i who presented himself as an upright sayyid.[176] After nine months of imprisonment, Ghulam Riza petitioned the shah, stating that the accusation had an ulterior motive; he
asked for clemency because he had fallen ill.[177] Switching tactics, Baha'is
appended testimonies (*shahadat*)—including by the *'alim* Hajji Mirza
Fakhr al-Din—demonstrating the "soundness of beliefs" (*sihhat-i
'aqa'id*) of Ghulam Riza, to their petitions to the central government.
This prompted Mustawfi al-Mamalik to call on I'tizad al-Dawlah to
hold a gathering (*majlis*) to clarify the nature of his beliefs.[178] The governor merely restated that the local 'ulama had already determined that
he was a Baha'i, so Mustawfi al-Mamalik wrote Ghulam Riza directly,
saying, "If your belief and intention is righteous, then distance yourself
from this blameworthy accusation [*nisbat-i mazmum*] through Aqa
Sayyid Javad and Aqa Hasan," which would have been highly unlikely.[179] Ghulam Riza was finally released, either sixteen months or
nearly three years after his initial imprisonment, according to different historical accounts, apparently because the repeated Baha'i petitions proved effective.[180]

Ghulam Riza and Muhammad Javad's apostasy case started with
the suspicions and actions of fellow villagers in Jasb but, like many similar rural crimes, ended up before a court in the nearest city. Both parties invoked multiple jurisdictions: the 'ulama, the governor, and the
shah's court all became involved, either to issue a ruling or to reverse
and amend previous ones or to provide documentary evidence of guilt
or innocence. While the accused were certainly disadvantaged, they and
their supporters managed to navigate the overlapping legal jurisdictions
to bide time, to change a death sentence into one of life imprisonment,
and ultimately to secure release.

The Ghulam Riza apostasy case set the stage for a similarly complex series of cases involving the Baha'i Naddaf brothers, Muhammad Husayn and Muhammad Riza, and their respective families over a roughly
nine-year period (ca. 1888–97) (figure 20). The Naddaf brothers were cotton carders (*naddafs*) who settled in the Chahar Mardan neighborhood
of Qum in 1861. They opened up a commercial office (*hujrah*) and became relatively prosperous through their trade.[181] Given the sanctity associated with Qum, the opponents of the Naddafs viewed their presence
as morally polluting.[182] It was often their neighbors, their rivals in the
bazaar, or the 'ulama who charged them with apostasy and produced
testimonies as evidence. Given the overlapping nature of jurisdiction,
the 'ulama's death sentences were not carried out, despite the efforts of
some of their followers. The Naddafs, like Ghulam Riza before them,
turned to alternative authorities, especially the shah and the prime minister, for redress but found themselves caught in a three-way struggle
between the central government, the local government, and hostile
'ulama. They also turned to sympathetic local 'ulama, who not only
vouched for the "correctness" of their beliefs through testimonies but
mobilized their supporters in their defense.

In December 1888/January 1889 (Rabi' al-Sani 1306 H.), the Naddaf brothers faced a powerful network of bazaaris, the 'ulama, and even
the governor, who wanted to expropriate their property. A fellow cotton carder, Muhammad 'Arabistani Hallaj, sent a message to a member
of the Naddaf family threatening to cut off his head with his own hands
on account of him being a "Babi." Meanwhile, Na'ib Mahdi of the Chahar Mardan neighborhood saw an opportunity to appropriate the Naddaf family's wealth, so he contacted the prayer leader Sayyid Zakariyya
Pishnamaz.[183] Pishnamaz drafted a testimony (*shahadatnamah*), which
was signed by a number of individuals, stating that the brothers' execution was "legally incumbent" (*qatlishan vajib*) for being Babis.[184] Economic competition in the bazaar seemed to have been a major motivation
for the initial accusation against the Naddafs since the signatories to the
testimony included merchants, heads of guilds, and a fellow cotton
carder.[185] Na'ib Mirza took this signed document to the governor, I'tizad

Figure 20: The Baha'i Naddaf brothers,
Muhammad Riza and Muhammad Husayn.
(Source: Muhammad Husayni, *Tarikh-i Amr-i Baha'i dar Shahr-i Qum*, n.p.)

al-Dawlah, hoping to expropriate the brothers' wealth. The governor had
the two Baha'i men detained. During the course of their interrogation,
they were asked to prove their innocence through disassociation (*tabarri*)
by saying "unseemly words," meaning ritual cursing of Baha'i authorities, in addition to providing bribes (*rishvah*) in exchange for their safety,
but the brothers refused. As a consequence, they were put into chains
and repeatedly tortured while ruffians circled their house and shop.[186]
In the meantime, the family of the Naddaf brothers petitioned Nasir al-
Din Shah from the imperial telegraph office and also asked Aqa 'Ali
Haydar Shirvani, a Russian Baha'i merchant in Tehran, to intercede on
their behalf at the court. The shah responded by commanding that the

Naddafs be released, not a single *dinar* of theirs touched, and the claims against them dismissed for being without merit.[187] The shah's ruling effectively overturned Pishnamaz's death sentence, and the governor's support for it.

Two years later, the *mujtahid* Hajji Sayyid Sadiq ruled that the Naddafs were apostates. His ruling not only accused them of being infidels (*kufr*) but also banned commercial transactions with them. He declared their "hindrance and repulsion" (*ta'aruz va daf'*) a "shari'ah obligation" (*farizah-i shar'i*) that would ensure that the person that carried it out "would attain paradise," opening the path for legally sanctioned violence against them without government authorization. As a result, bazaaris refused to sell them necessary commercial goods, and the Naddafs were barred from entering the bathhouse (hammam) and from having their beards trimmed and shaved by bath attendants. Ruffians also pulled the veils (*chadurs*) off the heads of their female family members as part of the harassment. On April 25, 1891 (16 Ramazan 1308 H.), a band of seminarian primary-school children and ruffians affiliated with Sadiq attacked the Naddafs' shop and threw stones at it. Sayyid Husayn, a leading ruffian, entered the Naddafs' shop with a bayonet, threatening them with death because he wished to implement the *mujtahid*'s ruling. He was stopped, however, by the Naddafs' neighbors, who saved their lives. Shortly thereafter, five ruffian sayyids attacked Mirza Muhammad Ibrahim ibn Naddaf with a knife, ripped his clothing, and dragged him into the bathhouse to kill him, but he was saved once again by his neighbors.[188]

The Naddaf family turned to Tehran for help via telegraph and received a favorable ruling from the shah, which effectively trumped the local shari'ah ruling. Prime Minister Amin al-Sultan relayed the shah's command: he contradicted Hajji Sayyid Sadiq by stating that the Naddafs were Muslims and believers in Muhammad. The prime minister also forbade the local government from allowing them to be harassed.[189] News of the shah's ruling infuriated Sayyid Sadiq, who mounted the pulpit during the Friday prayers and asked if there was a "man in the Muslim congregation" who would deal with these "two felt-hatted cotton carders." Although Sadiq managed to mobilize some ruffians, the local government punished them before they could do any harm.[190]

Tensions once again came to the fore in 1894, when Ibn Naddaf found himself at odds with Mashhadi Ramazan, an attendant (*farrash*) of the Ma'sumah Shrine. Ibn Naddaf had previously bought property from Mashhadi Ramazan, but now the latter lived across from them. Upon learning that the men were Baha'is, he would insult them and try to force them to pay him an extortionate "tax" (*madakhil*). He even issued an ultimatum to the Naddafs: either leave the neighborhood or face constant torment. When neighbors sympathetic to the Naddafs confronted him about his behavior, he claimed to be a servant of the prime minister. The Naddafs eventually petitioned the prime minister directly. On August 4, 1894 (2 Safar 1312 H.), the prime minister commanded Hajji Amin al-Tuliyah Mirza Sayyid 'Ali to punish the attendant harshly and asked the governor, Muhammad Hasan Khan Amir Tuman, to do the same and banish him from the city. In response, Mashhadi Ramazan showed contrition and asked an intermediary to bring about a reconciliation between himself and the Naddafs so that he could stay in the city.[191]

A year later, Sayyid Sadiq heard of the Naddaf brothers sending Baha'i funds (*huquq Allah*) to 'Akka. He mobilized local ruffians and "zealots" (*mu'tasibin*) against them by issuing an "apostasy [*takfir*] and death ruling." The Naddafs contacted the prime minister, who employed shari'ah reasoning in his ruling: "According to the shari'ah, you cannot spy on the interior state of a person [*tajassus-i batin*]. They swear [*qasam*] [to their Islamic orthodoxy] on the outside [*zahir*]."[192] He then commanded that the Naddafs be left alone, but since the governor was sympathetic to Sayyid Sadiq and his supporters, he neglected to protect the brothers. Instead, the Naddafs were defended by two local 'ulama, Aqa Sayyid 'Abdullah and Aqa Shaykh Muhammad. Although not explicitly stated, their motivation in doing so appears to have been to demonstrate the superiority of their juridical authority over that of their 'ulama rivals. Hajji Sayyid Sadiq reacted by mounting the pulpit once more to deliver a fiery sermon against the Naddafs. The prime minister's next telegram, dated June 1, 1896 (19 Zi Hijjah 1313 H.), used the support and testimony of these 'ulama as evidence of "the soundness of [the Naddafs'] beliefs." The governor was this time compelled to prevent people from harassing the Naddafs. Despite this, Mirza Abu al-Hasan

Pishnamaz commanded a group of seminarians to attack the Naddafs' home and enter it forcibly, in violation of Islamic privacy norms. The Naddafs then petitioned Aqa Sayyid ʿAbdullah, who sent someone to counsel Hajji Sayyid Sadiq to stop his mobilizations, but this failed. Finally, Muzaffar al-Din Shah himself ruled that the Naddafs should not be bothered according to "the scale of the shariʿah" (mizan-i sharʿ).[193]

In January/February 1896 (Shaʿban 1313 H.), a neighborhood dispute snowballed into a death sentence and a still-larger mobilization against the Naddafs. Ustad Abu al-Qasim Banna, a neighbor of a member of the Naddaf family, regularly ascended the roof of his house, where he would curse and utter death threats against them. The Naddafs complained to people in authority over Banna, which led to a sayyid warning him that he would be punished if he repeated his behavior. Banna then went to the house of Hajji Sayyid Sadiq, where he testified that the Naddafs disliked the sound of the call to prayer and wanted to prevent it, on the basis of which the latter once again declared them apostates and prepared another testimony signed by himself, several other ʿulama, Banna, and a group of seminarians, traders, and merchants.[194]

Meanwhile, Muhammad ʿArabistani Hallaj gathered with a group of other men armed with sticks and maces to confront Ibn Naddaf in a local caravanserai, where he was with the Christian merchant Khwajah Haratun; Haratun saved his life by pointing a gun at the crowd. Haratun then arranged for an attendant to deliver him to the English Telegraph Office, where he could take refuge. While several male Naddaf family members were imprisoned in the house of Aqa Sayyid Ishaq, a rumor spread that Ibn Naddaf had been killed. This led his mother to enter the house of Sayyid ʿAbdullah, wailing that her son had been murdered. Moved by this, Sayyid ʿAbdullah, who was holding a seminar at the time, threw his turban to the ground and marched out of his house barefoot with sayyids, seminarians, and later merchants and craftsmen in tow. Half of the merchants and craftsmen of the bazaar who were his followers closed their offices and shops in support. He addressed the large crowd, saying, "Islam has been trampled upon," before leaving the city with his followers. A group started tugging at his hands and feet, begging him to give them an order to retrieve the detained Naddafs. He responded as follows: "Oh sayyids! Today is the day of jihad. You will

march inside the house of Sayyid Ishaq and raid it. You will put his turban on his shoulders, and you will drag him on the floor. You will beat
him severely and bring his corpse to me. And you will release these Muslims [i.e., the Naddafs]." A group of sayyids armed with sticks and
maces started assembling to carry out his order. Hearing of this, the *mutavallibashi* feared the potential violence, so he sent his servants to tact-
fully stop the sayyids. He also granted the Naddafs and their in-laws
asylum at his house. Ibn Naddaf was first taken to the government house
before joining his family at the *mutavallibashi*'s house in asylum.[195]

The governor facilitated a meeting of the city's 'ulama, seeking a
resolution. The 'ulama aligned against the Naddafs agreed to let the Naddafs go free on the condition that they be banished, a compromise
that protected their vision of community moral purity. The governor
informed the Naddafs that they should leave voluntarily to be left in
peace, leading to their subsequent safe passage to Tehran in 1896/97
(1314 H.).[196]

After a ten-month stay in Tehran, the Naddafs returned to Qum,
where they were scapegoated in an unrelated conflict between the 'ulama
and the government. One day, a sayyid beat up a government servant
(*nawkar*), leading the government to detain him and beat him in turn.[197]
The bold sayyid hit another official, leading to a harsh response. The
'ulama gathered at the Ma'sumah Shrine, where Aqa Sayyid Ishaq bad-
mouthed the government. The central government summoned Ishaq to
Tehran as a result. In the ensuing protests, the governor took refuge in
the surrounding villages, which allowed certain 'ulama to act with impunity toward the Naddafs. The Naddafs sought help from the local
central-government court (Divankhanah) representative, Na'ib Husayn,
but he could not guarantee safety, so they hid at the house of Muhammad Riza Big Dustaqban for twenty days. Since the prime minister's
decree was not enough to ensure safety, Ibn Naddaf stayed with
Sayyid 'Abdullah.[198] Sayyid Sadiq approached the governor and asked
for the Naddafs' banishment once more. The governor's court summoned the Naddafs for interrogation and threatened them with property seizure. They were then whipped, bastinadoed, and imprisoned. The
Naddaf brothers defended themselves by using two *fatvas* from Sayyid
'Abdullah and Aqa Shaykh Husayn testifying to their belief in the Quran,

the Imams, and the Day of Resurrection. The latter *fatva*, which was dated October 10, 1897 (13 Jumada al-Avval 1315 H.), was even endorsed by the famous Tehrani *mujtahid* Shaykh Fazlullah Nuri.[199] These two *fatvas* were secured by paying large sums of money, since, by establishing legal facts, it could afford them a measure of protection.[200]

The Baha'i experience with various legal venues in Qum suggests that far from being hapless victims, Baha'is made strategic use of imperial, local, and Islamic legal venues to ensure a measure of self-preservation. Although Islamic privacy norms made it difficult to prove apostasy, accusers made their case through testimony, possession of books and scriptures, and the accused's refusal to engage in ritual cursing. Baha'is produced their own legal facts by way of testaments to their "correct beliefs" endorsed by the 'ulama. They further appealed to alternative jurisdictions, especially that of the shah, with mixed results; the harshest rulings, such as execution or life imprisonment, were not necessarily implemented, nor did a ruling clearing one's name guarantee safety.

Conclusion

In Qum, crime, policing, authority, and punishment revolved to a great degree around the nexus of sanctity, inviolability, and privacy. The sacred shrines of the city provided sanctuary for criminals that had ballooned into a sizeable asylum zone, facilitating extortion rings, prostitution rackets, and robbing pilgrims by the 1860s. The famine of the early 1870s also brought to the fore inviolability and sanctity in relation to crime and policing but in unexpected ways: first, cannibalism constituted a grotesque violation of bodily sanctity, one that provoked fear, suspicion of outsiders, and anger toward those who did it; second, both government officials and ordinary subjects intrusively policed the bodies of suspected cannibals for body parts. The rough justice that sometimes ensued pointed to a popular understanding of legality in which ordinary subjects carried out unmediated violence. In later decades, murderers used the inviolability of the Ma'sumah Shrine to prevent forcible removal by government officials or angry heirs and to gain an opportunity to negotiate a settlement and evade execution.

'Abdullah Sultan's case violated this pattern insofar as he was forcibly removed by the shah's order and subsequently executed. Finally, the case of Baha'i apostasy in Qum points to yet another valence of privacy and inviolability: the privacy of heretical thoughts and ideas. Cases against Baha'is first had to "publicize" Baha'is by amassing evidence of their heterodox beliefs through seized private documents and testimonies of credible witnesses, leading to conviction.

Crime in Qum also had much to do with moral pollution. The shrine embodied purity that was in tension with the prohibited acts that occurred within and around it. One strategy to police vice, then, was to reconstitute tried and true methods of spatial surveillance through guarantorships and the *kadkhuda* system. Ordinary subjects occasionally policed vice directly, as witnessed in the cases of cannibalism and apostasy, which entailed overstepping cultural privacy norms. Finally, the presence of the criminal, especially the murderer, in the precincts of the shrine led to a paradoxical relationship between sanctity/purity and the polluted: Did the sanctity and inviolability of the shrine trump the polluted figure of the defiled criminal, or vice versa? The answer often depended on one's position and understanding of jurisdiction.

Legal jurisdiction in Qum operated at three major levels: the authority of the *mutavallibashi*, the authority of the local governor, and the authority of the shah and the royal court. These three juridical poles of power formed multiple possible configurations and alliances depending on the legal case in question: when the local governor and the *mutavallibashi* formed an alliance, this posed the greatest threat to the authority of the central government, given the latter's remoteness. The shah's court also sometimes sought to confirm a governor's ruling against a *mutavallibashi* who protected or hid criminals in the *bast* zone. Seen from the perspective of the accused, these overlapping jurisdictions allowed the possibility of negotiating a settlement, delaying a death sentence, overturning a ruling of life imprisonment, and ideally, securing freedom.

Epilogue

In the aftermath of the long nineteenth century, Iran underwent its first of two twentieth-century revolutions. The immediate spark for the Constitutional Revolution (1905–11) was a penal act: Tehran's governor, 'Ala al-Dawlah, had two merchants publicly bastinadoed for raising the price of sugar on December 12, 1905, in a manner reminiscent of the *hisbah* regulations enacted by Adib al-Mulk in Qum nearly half a century earlier. Prior to this punishment, the prime minister had enacted strict customs reforms that adversely affected merchants. A large crowd responded by closing the bazaar, gathering at the Masjid-i Shah, and making a series of demands, including the governor's deposition. The crowd then took asylum at the Shah 'Abd al-'Azim Shrine to protest the injustice. It also demanded a house of justice (*'adalatkhanah*), which eventually became a parliament (*majlis*), both terms that had been used in the previous century to refer to local participatory legal forums for redress beyond the governor's court. Popular sentiment in 1905 called into question the governor's punitive authority in a specific case, which set into motion a demand to revamp legal redress altogether. Ironically, this revolutionary demand was articulated through the language of reform.[1]

The 1979 Islamic Revolution also bears the indelible traces of crime and punishment, not only in its immediate triggers but also in its claims to juridical sovereignty. When the official Iranian newspaper *Ittila'at* published a negative editorial about Ayatullah Ruhullah Khomeini, protestors closed the bazaar and attacked monarchical symbols. Security forces enacted police measures, resulting in five deaths. Like the bastinadoing of the sugar merchants, these measures kicked off further protests in the form of rolling mourning rituals throughout the country that eventually toppled the monarchy. Ayatullah Khomeini emerged as the country's supreme leader and champion of an Islamic state (*hukumat-i Islami*) in which a monarch had no place.[2] Of all world historical revolutions, arguably none has called into question simplistic secular narratives of progress and change more than the Iranian Islamic Revolution.[3]

Private Sins, Public Crimes has made every effort to "unthink" the present. It is tempting to reduce nineteenth-century Iran to a mere prologue to the Constitutional Revolution, Pahlavi-era modernity, and especially the events of the 1979 Revolution. For instance, nineteenth-century doctrinal transformations in Shi'ism that granted greater authority to jurists partially paved the way for Khomeini's concept of the Guardianship of the Jurist (*Vilayat-i Faqih*) in the run-up to the Islamic Revolution.[4] Shi'i jurists' approach to criminal law under the Islamic Republic could be read anachronistically as a "medieval" and "barbaric" reaction to a "failed" project of modernity with nineteenth-century origins.

Although this book has focused on the nineteenth century, its contributions to understanding near-contemporary developments in Iran lay not in seeing the Islamic Revolution as a religious reaction to secularism and modernization or as solely the product of Shi'i doctrinal changes. Instead, its implications address an abiding paradox of the revolution: How did predominantly Shi'i Iran shift from seeing religiously sanctioned violence of "fixed mandatory punishments" and "forbidding wrong" as being solely the prerogative of the Shi'i Imams to something that Shi'i jurists could not only implement but codify and make state law? The answer lies in the enduring interactions between *fiqh*, advice literature, government directives, and everyday policing and penal practices of the nineteenth century. Seen in this light, the resurgence of judicial torture, public spectacles of state-sanctioned violence, and appeals to religious justifications for policing in the Islamic Republic of Iran should not be viewed as an anomalous rupture but rather as a continued synthesis of everyday practices, religious doctrines, and government legal techniques.

The continuities of past practice and current realities are not lost on contemporary Iranians who read Qajar-era primary sources. One such source, 'Ali Akbar Sa'idi-Sirjani's collection of Persian-language reports that deal extensively with crime, policing, and punishment in Shiraz, was published just three years after the revolution. When the anthropologist Setrag Manoukian frequented bookstores in Shiraz in the course of fieldwork, locals admonished him to take note of it: "Did you read it? Did you see? Did you see how things were? They were like they are today! Read!"[5] What about reports on 'ulama and seminarian raids, bribe-taking police and government officials, judicial torture, and public spectacles of punishment resonates so strongly with Iranians under the Islamic Republic?

Shahs, Jurists, and Jurisdiction

Over the course of the twentieth century, the question of who had the authority to issue rulings, to police, and ultimately to punish continued to be debated in Iran. Jurisdiction became increasingly territorialized and organized into a clearer hierarchy in ways that left little room for earlier overlapping jurisdictions. While in advice literature, the two "brothers" of "religion and government" (din va dawlat) had a shared role in authority, the Islamic Revolution's reversal of the Pahlavi state's steady expansion of its jurisdiction at the expense of Shi'i jurists swapped the "turban for the crown."[6]

Since the nineteenth century, politico-legal keywords have undergone profound changes and erasures, demonstrating the novel reconfigurations of governance, law, and authority. Siyasat, which earlier could mean harsh (and often capital) punishment administered by the state, now only retains the connotation of politics. Shari'ah too underwent a similar narrowing: under the Qajars, government officials often claimed to be implementing the shari'ah without reference to Islamic jurisprudence, but over the course of the twentieth and twenty-first centuries, shari'ah increasingly became synonymous with *fiqh*. *Hukumat* once described any court with the authority to issue a ruling (*hukm*), such as a local government court (*hukumat-i 'urfi*) or a shari'ah court (*hukumat-i shar'i*), while now only its meaning as "government" prevails. To contemporary ears, *hukumat-i shar'i* has lost this legal meaning; instead, it is synonymous with Khomeini's term for an Islamic government (*hukumat-i Islami*), suggesting another slippage from the legal to the political.[7]

The professionalization of the judiciary, codification, and the formation of modern police undid the overlapping jurisdictions of governors, shahs, and Shi'i jurists. This shift was predicated on seeing such overlaps as inconsistencies and inefficiencies in need of modern remedies, criticisms articulated in the nineteenth century but systematically implemented only in the twentieth century. Under the Pahlavis, the place of shari'ah was relegated to the realm of personal status law, much as it was in many other majority-Muslim countries; penal law continued to draw inspiration from French models.[8] Criminal jurisdiction appeared more in line with modern understandings of it: courts were hierarchically and territorially arranged, and the state held all legal power. Despite differences in ideological content, the Islamic Republic continued this pattern while claiming that God's sovereignty legitimizes state authority as mediated and interpreted by Shi'i jurists committed to the revolution.

Seen from the perspective of the marginalized and the accused, legal formalization and systemization were a mixed blessing. On the one hand, they promised transparent rules, due process, and clear jurisdictional boundaries between various types of courts; on the other hand, these rulings were more definitive, with fewer avenues for appeal. In the nineteenth century, condemned criminals could pit different jurisdictions against one another to seek stays of execution or punishments or to overturn long-term or life prison sentences. Intercession and asylum at sanctuaries also provided ordinary Iranians more room for maneuver than in a bureaucratized legal system.

Private/Public in an Era of Transformation

Part of the overall challenge of historical analysis of Iran has been its emphasis on change over time: revolutions, coups, scientific transformations, and modern institutions—these are all the ligaments of a good story, and Iran has had no shortage of change since the nineteenth century. As a corollary to this approach, there has also been emphasis on the embodiments of such change: the modernized middle and working classes, the modern armed forces, lawyers, judges, and police.[9] But equally consequential for our purposes is the durability of certain modes of thinking about justice, crime, punishment, legality and their connection to understandings of public and private, specifically as it pertains to Islamic jurisprudence. How, then, are we to think about legal continuities embodied within the great transformations and ruptures of Iranian history?

Science, technology, and capitalism have played a crucial role in twentieth- and twenty-first-century shifts in understandings of private/public, sin/crime, policing, and punishment in Iran. Scientific innovations have been credited for a transformation in the doctrines of legal proof and policing in many countries through the use of forensic evidence, autopsies, fingerprinting, and photography as means of identifying the cause of death, the probability of criminal involvement, and the identification of suspects. New technologies also force authorities to reconsider the relationship between private and public: Are cars considered private and inviolable like the home and body, or are they public and subject to police inspections? Even the role of new media has significant legal implications: Can audio and video recordings of illicit acts or ideas, transmitted beyond the intended audience, constitute definitive evidence in place of consistent witness testimonies or confessions?

In the twentieth century, the formal police expanded beyond Tehran and became increasingly professionalized, and it remains a crucial expression of state power. And yet nonstate actors, including seminarians, ruffians, and ordinary subjects, continued to police morality in ways reminiscent of their nineteenth-century predecessors. Ordinary subjects in the 1910s and 1920s, for instance, took umbrage at the formation of a red-light district in their backyard, leading them to petition members of parliament and other government officials to have prostitutes exiled from their neighborhood, a recurring solution to moral pollution in the nineteenth century.[10] After the 1979 Revolution, vice squads, known since 2002 as the Gasht-i Irshad, embarked on moral policing that highlighted the contested boundaries between private and public. They, like their nineteenth-century analogues, saw themselves as operationalizing forbidding wrong with a special focus on "incorrectly" worn hijabs and the public mingling of unrelated men and women. But as in the nineteenth century, those who engaged in moral policing did not limit their surveillance to public spaces: private parties, scripted as "Western" and thus "immoral," became the object of contemporary *hisbah* raids, with sometimes dire consequences for their attendees.[11] Contemporary entertainment music, such as rock, metal, and rap, was similarly forced to go "private." The underground music scene has thrived by playing in unusual venues away from prying eyes, such as abandoned warehouses or secluded farmhouses, as famously depicted in the semifictionalized documentary *No One Knows Persian Cats*.[12] The constantly renegotiated boundaries between public and private, crime and sin, legal and moral, have led to intrusive policing but also fierce resistance. Despite Islamic law's strong privacy norms, Iranian police regularly violate the home's sanctity on the basis of suspicion of immorality. That those who drink alcohol, throw mixed-gender parties, and listen to and/or perform entertainment music have done so primarily within the home as an act of resistance suggests the durability of tactics with a much older pedigree. Even in the realm of modern technologies, the clandestine circulation of cassettes and videos and later the use of encrypted or anonymous internet pages, websites, and messaging tools have sought to ensure a level of privacy and protection from state sanctions.

Codification and Its Afterlife

Codification is an illuminating vector through which to understand legal continuities and ruptures. Much of the scholarship on codification in Muslim societies treats it as a colonial import, one that, when it did deal with shariʻah, led to its instrumentalization first for colonial and later for secular state-building purposes that were antithetical and incompatible with the shariʻah's internal logics.[13] And yet this reading of codification as an authoritarian or colonial project ignores its potential use by popular and democratic movements.[14] The makers of the Iranian Constitutional Revolution similarly argued that constitutionalism and legal codification were potent instruments for delivering justice, equality, and rights compatible with Islam, which echoed similar ideas proposed by Mustashar al-Dawlah and others.[15] The Pahlavi-era state continued the project of codification, albeit in an authoritarian form. The penal codes of the constitutional, immediate postconstitutional, and Pahlavi eras were adaptations of the Napoleonic penal code, possibly through Ottoman Turkish translations.[16] The specter of earlier draft penal codes surveyed here has all but been forgotten in telling this story.

Most studies of the Islamic Republic's Iranian Criminal Code treat it as a rupture from its "secular" Pahlavi-era predecessors insofar as it systematized Islamic jurisprudential categories of *qisas*, *hudud*, *taʻzir*, and *diyah*.[17] And yet, nineteenth-century Iranian codification efforts complicate this narrative. The Military Code, for instance, included articles on *hudud* punishments alongside military punishments. The later Police Code similarly included articles about *qisas* that was to be handled at a shariʻah court. Administrative manuals and imperial *farmans* also consistently invoked *hudud*, *qisas*, and adherence to the shariʻah more generally, sometimes in a code-like structure. When considering the draft codes and proposals of the nineteenth century, the codification of Islamic jurisprudence appears to be even less of a twentieth- and twenty-first-century innovation. For instance, the draft translation of the 1851 Ottoman Penal Code included references to *qisas*, *diyat*, *hadd*, and *tazʻir*. But the closest approximation to an Islamic penal code were the chapters in the *Jamiʻ-i Nasiri* on *hudud*, *taʻzir*, *qisas*, and *diyat*. Written in plain Persian and as straightforward rules, the *Jamiʻ-i Nasiri* referred to itself as the law of Islam (*qanun-i Islam*) and was almost adopted by Nasir al-Din Shah as an alternative to European-style codes. Seen in this light, the Islamic Republic's Criminal Code is a culmination of multiple strands of nineteenth-century thinking about codification.

Codification also reshaped how intentional murder was punished. In the nineteenth century, murder victims' families often had the final say in whether the convicted murderer lived or died. Under Pahlavi-era laws, murder was redefined more narrowly as an offense against the state, thus making any punishment against the murderer a question solely for the courts to decide. The Islamic Republic's Criminal Code, on the other hand, includes provisions that restored elements of a victims-centered approach to intentional homicide, one in which the heirs can choose retribution or forgiveness and compensation. Arzoo Osanloo's recent ethnography delves into the how and why of families deciding to forgo retribution, paying close attention to the court's role in advocating for the latter. Her study demonstrates the central role of victims' mothers in making the final decision in *qisas* cases.[18] Women sometimes appear as decision-makers in nineteenth-century sources as well, although they also implemented *qisas* directly without reliance on male relatives or a hired executioner for a brief period.

Sanctity, Honor, and the End of the Spatial Exception

Studies of criminal law in Iran have largely explored one facet of honor: namely, the concept of sexual honor and honor killings. The philosopher Kwame Anthony Appiah has explored how the protection of one such form of honor, known as *ghayrat*, might entail extrajudicial violence against a female family member who is considered to have brought shame to the family through illicit sex.[19] Along similar lines, Irene Schneider has compared the penal codes of the Pahlavi and Islamic Republic eras for their use of the terms *namus* and *'ismat* to mean sexual honor.[20] And yet these forms of honor fail to capture the much more historically consequential and expansive ethico-legal notion of *hurmat* (sanctity/honor), which was a closer precedent to an inalienable legal right.[21]

As with much of the world, especially after the 1948 United Nations Universal Declaration of Human Rights, Iranians vigorously debated the validity of human rights. Advocates embrace its validity for the full spectrum of categories of personhood, including women, sexual minorities, religious minorities, ethnic groups, atheists, agnostics, and beyond. The commonly used contemporary terms for human rights (*huquq-i bashar* or *huquq-i insan*) and their violation (*naqz*), which has the connotation of breaking a treaty, suggest how much the term *haqq* has changed. *Haqq* was used in nineteenth-century petitions calling on the government to "administer justice" (*ihqaq-i haqq*; literally, restoring a right). In Islamic jurisprudence, the "Rights of Humans" (*Huquq al-Insan*) referred not to human rights as understood today per se but to the rights and obligations of individuals to one another, say, in commercial transactions and matters of retribution and compensation for injury and death, as opposed to "the Rights of God" (*Huquq Allah*), which included *hudud* and *ta'zir* punishments, as well as alms, Friday worship, and "conquered property belonging" to the Muslim community.[22] There have been many efforts to draw on the former terminology to articulate some notion of indigenous Islamic rights by scholars of Islam law and ethics, given the overlap in connotations, and much ink has been spilled about the compatibility of Islamic human rights with a universal notion of human rights.[23] Part of what this book suggests, however, is that in the nineteenth century, Iranians drew on the language of *hurmat*, that inviolable dimension of their body, their homes, their property, their dignity, and even their lives, which had been violated, ripped, or exposed, to articulate an analogous notion to what we would call a right. A reinvestigation of the category of *hurmat*, a notion invoked repeatedly by the wronged, irrespective of status group, may serve as a more fruitful starting point for the often fraught activity of cross-cultural and transhistorical translation.

Throughout the nineteenth century, the sanctuary was a significant place of asylum for people accused of crimes, and its inviolability caused consternation for Amir Kabir, Nasir al-Din Shah, and many local governors. When government officials tried to curtail and ban the practice, they claimed that the government was just, the accused would be treated fairly, and that "just" laws (including the *hadd* and *qisas*) should be implemented universally. Opponents argued that to violate the sanctity of the sanctuary was itself a violation of the shari'ah, an expression of injustice, and an act that would have dangerous effects. Although the practice of taking sanctuary continued into the constitutional, post-constitutional, and more rarely in the Pahlavi periods, the centralization and systematization of legal institutions under the Pahlavis put an end to the practice. In 1924, a deserting soldier was dragged out of the *bast* at Shah 'Abd al-'Azim, an act for which Riza Khan apologized in a letter. But by 1935, when Shaykh Taqi Buhlul and others protested the sartorial changes implemented by Riza Shah, the latter reacted by violating the sanctuary of the Gawharshad Mosque.[24] Over the course of the twentieth century, *bast* and *bast nishini* therefore lost their legal connotation of asylum and increasingly came to mean a sit-in and protest as a specific location. The Pahlavi and Islamic Republic banning of sanctuaries for criminals appears to have been justified on similar grounds as their nineteenth-century antecedents: the criminal has rights to due process, the law is just, and it must be applied universally to all subjects within the borders of the state.

Learning the Lessons of Torture and Past Punishments

In 2002, the Islamic Republic opened the 'Ibrat Museum, the site of a former Pahlavi prison founded in 1932 and used by the shah's secret service, SAVAK, to interrogate and torture political opposition groups (including Islamists) in the 1960s and 1970s.[25] 'Ibrat, which meant "exemplary deterrent punishment" in the Qajar era, now conveys lessons about the Pahlavi state's crimes, brutality, and torture against innocent citizens, lessons that, if one believes state propaganda, have been learned, heeded, and avoided by adherence to shari'ah justice. Around the same time as the erection of the original prison structure, the Pahlavi state founded the Museum of Anthropology (Muzah-i Mardumshinasi) in 1935. One of the wax statues portrays an executioner from the Nasiri era named Qadir about to behead a criminal. Qadir is portrayed standing over a condemned man, whose hands are bound from behind and who is kneeling on the ground. Qadir is holding his head back by the nose and has a dagger approaching his neck (figure 21).[26] Much like representations found in the 'Ibrat Museum, this Pahlavi-era depiction was intended to portray the backward and barbaric practices of a bygone era. In both cases, museumization signified something left behind as a "bad" tradition that was to be replaced by just practices. Put another way, public beheadings for the Pahlavis and secret torture and interrogation

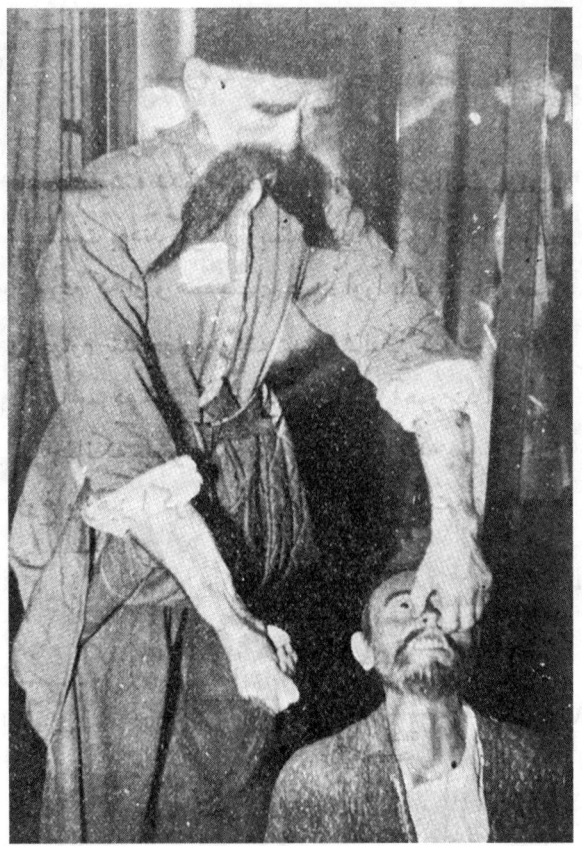

Figure 21: Wax figure in the Iranian Museum
of Anthropology of a Nasiri-era chief executioner,
Qadir Mirza, about to behead a criminal.
(Source: Amir 'Ala'i, *Mujazat-i I'dam*, 33)

for the Islamic Republic had become polluted symbols of legal practices
associated with the governments they replaced. But victims of both
states would probably tell a different story.

Efforts to curtail or abolish torture and public executions in Iran
do not map onto tidy schemas of historical narratives moving effortlessly
from tradition to modernity. Capital punishment under the Pahlavis, especially from the 1930s onward, initially followed a familiar trajectory:

it was increasingly "privatized," in the sense of being hidden from public view. In Michel Foucault's classic work on prisons in western Europe, he traced the transformations in punishments over the course of the eighteenth and nineteenth centuries, which started with public spectacles of violence expressing sovereign power, moved on to the privatization of punishments, and ended with the production of docile bodies through prisons.[27] On the surface, at least for most of the Pahlavi period, his analytical insights would seem to hold: Qajar-era public spectacles of punishments were eventually replaced by secret executions (mostly of political dissidents) and by an ever-expanding prison system.

And yet there were striking exceptions, such as the execution of the serial murderer 'Ali Asghar Burujirdi on June 27, 1934. 'Ali Asghar had raped and murdered numerous young children in both Iraq and Iran. He was executed before throngs of spectators in Tehran's Sipah Square.[28] As with so many facets of twentieth-century Iranian history, this episode has been subsumed under the modern: modern middle-class sensibilities, the rise of modern criminology, and modern infrastructural shifts. A detail about his execution, which has been passed unremarked, provides a clue to how developments dating from the Qajar era found their ultimate expression in the Pahlavi era. It will be recalled that in the draft translation of the 1858 Ottoman Penal Code and Malkam Khan's proposed penal code, both of which had been inspired by the Napoleonic Code, a criminal sentenced to death was to be executed in public view with a placard stating the criminal's name, the crime, and the punishment, not only to convey a deterrent lesson but also so as to render them infamous. Displayed prominently on the gallows from which 'Ali Ashgar was hanged, we see precisely such a placard, which read, "The execution of 'Ali Asghar, the murderer" (*I'dam-i 'Ali Asghar-i Qatil*) (figure 22).[29] Unlike the symbolism and ritualistic parade of nineteenth-century public executions, the use of the placard assumed that a literate audience who could literally "read" the meaning conveyed by the public punishment. And indeed, the spread of official education at all levels in the 1920s and 1930s made it likely that more spectators could understand such a placard than in the 1880s, when such draft penal codes were being proposed.

Figure 22: Serial murderer 'Ali
Asghar Burujirdi's execution.

(Source: "Tihran, Maydan-i Tupkhanah, I'dam-i Asghar-i Qatil,"
Pazhuhishkadah-i Tarikh-i Mu'asir, no. 'ayn-1-424)

Under the Islamic Republic, public executions (and corporal punishments) have regained prominence, calling into question both liberal
and Foucauldian narratives regarding their disappearance in the face of
modern science, penal codification, and prison expansion. Despite modernization, industrial development, the expansion of public health and
educational institutions, and a modern military—all the components
that emerged in lockstep with the prison in Foucault's rendering, pub-

lic spectacles of violence were back with a vengeance.[30] The new republic had no qualms about public executions, although there were many more secret executions in prisons as well. This did not mean that Iran had demodernized or somehow turned back the clock. Instead, the problem is with the theory itself and its application as a universal explanatory paradigm.

The reemergence of public executions, which typically included hangings from makeshift gallows in public squares or stadiums and, less typically, stonings and beheadings intended as deterrent lessons, is unmistakably a legacy of nineteenth-century practices. Public corporal punishment carried out by Revolutionary Committees was intended not just as deterrence but as a means of "cleansing" Iran of the traces of the previous regimes, indicating a politicization of pollution. Only through the sovereign display of violence, carried out by the ordinary defenders of the regime forming committees, could it be purged from society.[31] In some instances, people sentenced to death had pictures taken with neck placards stating their supposed crimes, which was reminiscent of 'Ali Asghar's execution scene and the long history of draft penal codes that informed it.[32]

I would like to end by considering why state violence as punishment, even when justified, legitimized, and supported by large segments of the population, has by and large remained private, not only in Iran but also in otherwise-democratic polities such as the United States. In the nineteenth century, a private punishment was a missed opportunity for society to "see" justice done, the sensory experience of which was intended to bring the community together, deter others from committing the same crime, and expiate sin. Certainly, the history of emotions is significant: changing sensibilities toward the sight of pain, suffering, and ultimately death have resulted in the sanitation of violence. And yet, there is something brutally honest about a state that performs its violence in full view of spectators. Twentieth- and twenty-first-century privatized punishment has the structure of a premodern sin: it is performed secretly, away from eyes that might emulate, condemn, or misread it. We may ask ourselves why we are collectively outraged by leaked videos and pictures of legally sanctioned punishments occurring privately, brought before our eyes through an array of technological media, but less moved to condemn when such reports are meticulously documented by witness and survivor accounts of state violence, whether in the form of brutal prison conditions or secret executions. We might ask ourselves if this is the original sin of a state sovereignty that still ultimately rests on violence.

Glossary

Amrad: A "beardless male youth" who was the object of male desire; often a young male prostitute in a criminal context.

'Arizah (pl. 'Arizijat): A petition made to an authority, such as a governor or a shah, with the goal of a settlement or legal ruling.

Bast: Taking sanctuary or asylum; a criminal asylum seeker typically could not be forcibly removed from a sanctuary.

Biglarbigi: A police magistrate or mayor of a city or town.

Darughah: An urban police chief often associated with the bazaar.

Divankhanah: A court associated with the shah and the central government, which issued legal rulings; *Divankhanah-i 'Adliyah* became the early term used for the Ministry of Justice.

Diyah (or diyat): Financial compensation for injury or death in Islamic jurisprudence.

Farman: An imperial decree, command, or ruling, often in response to a petition.

Farrash: An attendant whose functions could include policing, guarding, and punishing; the head attendant (*farrashbashi*) was active in urban policing.

Fatva: A responsa issued by an Islamic jurist to a question posed by a Muslim inquirer that was technically not binding (see *Hukm*).

Fiqh: Islamic jurisprudence, or the collective 'ulama endeavor to understand shari'ah based on certain methodologies.

Hisbah: See *Ihtisab*.

Hadd (pl. Hudud): Fixed mandatory punishment for a specific crime mentioned in the Quran and hadith in Islamic jurisprudence.

Hukm: A binding ruling made in a specific case; this term was used to describe a legal ruling made by a jurist, a governor, or the shah.

'Ibrat: A deterrent exemplary punishment.

Ihtisab: The administrative duty to "forbid wrong," which could include moral policing and/or market regulations.

Iltizam: A legally binding promise or guarantee taken from someone to take responsibility for the actions of a third person or persons.

Kadkhuda: A neighborhood or village headman who was responsible for local policing and crime reporting in addition to other administrative duties.

Kalantar: A mayor or chief magistrate; often used interchangeably with *biglar-bigi*.

Luti: An urban ruffian usually connected to a particular neighborhood.

Mir ghazab: An executioner responsible not only for executions but also for the torture and disfigurement of suspects or convicted criminals.

Mujtahid: A Shi'i jurist authorized and qualified to apply their understanding of shari'ah to new circumstances.

Mutavalli: A guardian of a shrine, particularly of an Imam, his descendants, or another revered religious figure.

Qanun: A law, code, or constitution.

Qaravul: A night watchman responsible for monitoring and reporting on the movements of individuals and apprehending suspected criminals.

Qasamah: An oath procedure by which the heirs of a homicide victim established guilt when there was strong suspicion but insufficient evidence.

Qisas: Legal retribution for intentional homicide or injury determined after a shari'ah trial.

Shafa'at: Intercession, usually by someone with influence over the person issuing a ruling, to reduce a sentence or forgive a criminal.

Shari'ah: The ethically, ritually, and legally incumbent and prohibited dimensions of Islam.

Siyasat: A harsh punishment, often capital, inflicted on the basis of government authority; politics or administration.

Sulh: An amicable settlement reached in a case of injury or death to avoid *qisas*.

Tashhir: A punishment involving ignominious parading with the purpose of public exposure.

Ta'zir: A discretionary punishment for a violation of the shari'ah without a fixed mandatory punishment (*hadd*).

Tavasut: See *Shafa'at*.

'Urf: Custom or local practice; a ruling made on the basis of the local executive authority, especially that of a governor.

Varasah: The heirs of someone killed intentionally or unintentionally who have the choice of compensation, retribution, or forgiveness in the former case and compensation or forgiveness in the latter.

Zimanat: See *Iltizam*.

Zina: Sexual penetration by a man of a woman outside of a licit permanent or temporary marriage or master-slave relation.

Abbreviations

Encyclopaedia of Islam, 2nd ed. = *EI2*
Encyclopaedia Iranica = *EIr*
Sazman-i Asnad va Kitabkhanah-i Milli = *SAKM*

Notes

Where applicable, these notes provide citations to the original sources, and unless otherwise indicated, the translation of the quoted material is mine.

Introduction

1. This episode will be discussed further in chapter 4.

2. Enayat, *Law*, 2, 34, 45–46; Karny, "Mirza," 17; Lambton, "Hukuma"; Floor, "Change," 116.

3. Algar, *Malkum*.

4. Schayegh, *Who*, 8, 22; Nikpour, "Prison," 26, 85, 89.

5. F. Ahmed, *Afghanistan*.

6. Enayat, *Law*, 23–24.

7. See, for example, Sheikholeslami, *Structure*.

8. Hallaq, *Sharī'a*, 308–23.

9. Emon, "Quadrants," 1100.

10. Weber, *Basic*, 75.

11. Schmitt, *Concept*.

12. Crone, *God's*.

13. Cook, *Commanding*; Rabb, *Doubt*; Mottahedeh and Stilt, "Public"; Stilt, *Islamic*; Johansen, "Secular"; El Shamsy, "Shame."

14. Habermas, *Structural Transformation*; Calhoun, *Habermas*. Michael Warner also presents a theoretical articulation of public, which, like Habermas and his interlocutors, links its formation to modernity. Warner, *Publics*. Such an insistence on coupling private/public to the historical shift of modernity closes off the horizon of possible premodern meanings associated with these terms.

15. For a useful summary of the potential equivalents of such terms in Arabic, see Ammann, "Private." Shahab Ahmad has also articulated a comprehensive private/public model for Muslim societies. Ahmed, *What*, 377–86.

16. Khan, *Self*, 29.

17. Friedland, *Seeing*, 36. In medieval Christian theology, a dictum stated that secret sins required secret penance, while public sins required public penance. Similarly, in English common law, a murder committed in secret required an inquiry and trial, while a manifest murder could be punished on the spot. Mansfield, *Humiliation*, 116.

18. For spying, see Reza, "Islam's," 705, 723–27. For torture, see Reza, "Torture"; Rejali, *Torture*.

19. Ahmed, *What*, 385; Ammann, "Private," 87–88.

20. Opwis, *Maṣlaḥa*.

21. Johansen, "Claims." *Huquq Allah* had an expansive set of connotations, especially in Hanafi jurisprudence, which included "the punishment of crimes, alms, the Friday worship and conquered properties which belongs to the Islamic community (*al-hudud wa al-sadaqat wa al-jumuʿat wa al-fayʾ*)." Hoexter, "Huquq Allah," 134.

22. My primary concern is not purity and pollution in Islamic law more broadly, although often there are notable intersections and implications, such as in the case of non-Muslim populations. For purity and pollution in Islamic ritual, ethics, and law, see Reinhart, "Impurity"; Katz, *Body*.

23. Durkheim, *Elementary*, 241.

24. Durkheim, 263.

25. Han, *Topology*, 8–9. On why the state had to punish certain crimes, like adultery, so that others did not mimic it, see also Friedland, *Seeing*, 36–37.

26. A hadith states that a hidden sin is immune from the duty to forbid wrong. Khan, *Self*, 29.

27. Weber, "Politics."

28. Schmitt, *Dictatorship*, 2.

29. See especially Hallaq, *Impossible*.

30. Cohen, *Crossroads*, 156.

31. E. P. Thompson, "Moral." For the application of Thompson's ideas to various facets of Qajar Iran's social history, see Khazeni, *Tribes*; Cronin, *Social*.

32. E. P. Thompson, "Rough."

33. Ford, "Law's."

34. Cormack, *Power*; Dorsett and McVeigh, *Jurisdiction*; Richland, "Jurisdiction."

35. Nielsen, *Secular Justice*; Tillier, "Mazalim in Historiography." Another recent articulation of jurisdiction, which is less relevant to the current study, considers the difference in Islamic jurists' authority to issue rulings in the "Abode of Islam" (*Dar al-Islam*) versus the "Abode of War" (*Dar al-Harb*). Albrecht, *Dār Al-Islām Revisited*.

36. Arjomand, *Shadow*, 9, 21, 248, 257–58, 261, 264–65; Schneider, "Religious."

37. In this understanding, my argument is closer to James Baldwin's characterization of eighteenth-century Egypt's legal system as composed of three poles: the Divan al-'Ali, Divan-i Humayun, and shari'ah courts. Baldwin, *Islamic Law*, 66. Francis Steingass captures the expansive meaning of *hukumat* as "dominion, sovereignty, absolute power; jurisdiction; a principality; the sentence of a judge." See "Hukumat" in Steingass, *Comprehensive Persian-English Dictionary*. *Valayat, qalamru,* and *davari* are other terms with the connotation of jurisdiction, although the latter two appear less frequently with this connotation in Qajar sources.

38. For works addressing inequalities based on some of these categories of personhood in Qajar Iran, see Tsadik, "Legal Status"; Najmabadi, *Women*; A. Amanat, *Resurrection*; Mirzai, *History*.

39. Douzinas, "Metaphysics," 26.

40. Floor, "Police"; Floor, "Office"; Lambton, *Islamic Society*, 12–13; Lambton, "Evolution." For the Ottoman Empire, see Başaran, *Selim III*. For Arab societies, see Lafi, "Policing."

41. Lambton, "Mahkama."

42. Lambton, *Islamic Society*, 10–11.

43. Floor, "Police," 294, 297–99.

44. This has been demonstrated by the scholarship of Tuğ, *Politics*, 163; Semerdjian, *Straight*, 86.

45. Petry, *Criminal Underworld*, 123, 176.

46. Alshech, "Out of Sight," 270; Hamadeh, "Mean," 261–62.

47. Klein, "Public"; Stilt and Saraçoğlu, "Hisba."

48. Campo, *Other Sides*.

49. If God's jurisdiction was over private sins, the opposite was true of worldly authorities: the *muhtasib*'s jurisdiction in medieval Egypt, for instance, was over *visible* illicit acts. Stilt, *Islamic*, 72, 83, 94, 130–31.

50. For the related notion of surety in Islamic law, see Hallaq, *Shari'a*, 259; Peters, *Crime*, 81–83, 84, 193. For the use of guarantorship in the Ottoman Empire, see Turna, "Pandemonium," 169, 171–72; K. Fahmy, *Quest*, 100–102.

51. My reading of this has been informed by K. Fahmy, *Quest*, 190, 200–201; Marcus, "Privacy"; Raymond, "Role."

52. Along similar lines, David Garland has argued that public punishment was a repetition of what had occurred in secret, namely, the torture of the condemned man and his confession, which thus revealed it to the public. Garland, *Punishment*, 140.

53. Garland, 167.

54. Friedland, *Seeing*, 203–4; Smith, *Punishment*, 170.

55. Friedland, *Seeing*, 100.

56. E. P. Thompson, "Rough," 480.

57. E. Cohen, *Crossroads*, 180.

58. Friedland, *Seeing*, 30; Smith, *Punishment*, 1–2.

59. René Girard makes this point in discussing the *pharmakos*, a criminal who was considered a "polluted object" and whose expulsion or execution cleansed the community. Girard, *Violence*, 95.

60. Smith, *Punishment*, 38.

61. Friedland, *Seeing*, 56.

62. E. Cohen, *Crossroads*, 171, 173.

63. Lange, "Legal," 83–84.

64. Aghaie, *Martyrs*; Khazeni, *Tribes*; Werner, *Iranian Town*; Walcher, *Shadow*.

65. E. Cohen, *Crossroads*, 189.

66. For similar practices in early modern Amsterdam, see Spierenburg, *Spectacle*, 57.

67. Therefore, those who attacked and pillaged cemeteries and sanctuaries or plundered on holy days would risk God's wrath. Duby, "Introduction," 26.

68. Duby, 27–28.

69. See Eshaghi, "Quietness"; Khalisi, *Tarikhchah-i Bast*.

70. See, for instance, Abrahamian, *Tortured*; Floor, "Change"; Nikpour, "Prison."

71. Matthee, *Pursuit*.

72. For the latter approach, see Martin, *Qajar*.

73. Gulbun, "Lughat."

74. Schneider, *Petitioning*.

ONE Sin, Crime, and Punishment in Shiʿi Jurisprudence

1. Peters, *Crime*, 53–65.

2. Michael Cook mentions this idea in relation to the Hanafi School in *Commanding*, 7, 9, 308. See also Hallaq, "God," 70.

3. Mottahedeh and Stilt, "Public"; Stilt and Saraçoğlu, "Hisba."

4. Cook, *Commanding*, 479–80. It should be noted that a minority of Shiʿi jurists believed that this obligation was still incumbent on the head of household within the domicile.

5. M. Ayoub, "Repentance,"; Peters, *Crime*, 30, 41; Powers, "Offending Heaven."

6. El Shamsy, "Shame"; Kadivar, "Introduction."

7. Cook, *Commanding*, 480–81.

8. Emon, "Huqūq Allāh," 329.

9. Johansen, "Sacred," 298.

10. Johansen, 298–99. See also Emon, "Huqūq Allāh," 326, 329; Vikør, "Muslim Subjects," 275–76.

11. Shaykh Baha'i, *Jamiʿ*; Majlisi, *Hudud*.

12. Najafi, *Jawahir*. For a discussion of this work's significance, see A. Amanat, *Iran*, 203–4.

13. Shafti, *Maqalah*.

14. M. Qummi, *Jamiʿ*.

15. Johansen, "Valorization."

16. Elizabeth Thompson, "Public"; Grehan, *Everyday Life*, 192–95.

17. Faruqi, "Music"; Klein, "Music"; Shiloah, "Music." For Safavid Shi'i jurists' views, see Newman, "Clerical Perceptions."

18. Cook, *Commanding*, 80.

19. Mottahedeh and Stilt, "Public," 737–38; Johansen, "Valorization," 75.

20. Mottahedeh and Stilt, "Public," 741.

21. Klein, "Public," 58–59.

22. Alshech, "Out of Sight," 268.

23. Alshech, 270–71.

24. Alshech, 271–72, 288.

25. Najafi, *Jawahir*, 29:63–102.

26. Hamoudi, "Sex," 61.

27. Hamoudi, 61.

28. Hamoudi, 62.

29. Najafi, *Jawahir*, 29:97; Hamoudi, "Sex," 62.

30. Shaykh Baha'i, *Jami'*, 1:39. For a similar discussion in the context of the Ottoman imperial harem, see Ergin, "Ottoman," 103–4.

31. Klein, "Music," 215–16.

32. Klein, 221.

33. Mottahedeh and Stilt, "Public," 738.

34. Najafi, *Jawahir*, 22:44.

35. Najafi, 22:45.

36. Najafi, 22:55.

37. Najafi, 22:46.

38. Najafi, 22:51.

39. Najafi, 14:264. For a study of the ideal of self-control, see Elias, *Civilizing*.

40. Najafi, *Jawahir*, 22:46, 48.

41. Najafi, 22:49–50.

42. Najafi, 22:47, 54–55.

43. Najafi, 22:51.

44. Najafi conceded that there was no evidence that *ghina'* was forbidden in and of itself. Najafi, 22:49.

45. Najafi, 22:49. Shaykh Baha'i similarly forbade the buying and selling of instruments of diversion (*lahv*), such as the *daff, nay*, and *'ud*. Shaykh Baha'i, *Jami'*, 2:199.

46. Najafi, *Jawahir*, 22:48–49; Shaykh Baha'i, *Jami'*, 2:199.

47. Najafi, *Jawahir*, 22:49.

48. Najafi, 22:56.

49. Shaykh Baha'i, *Jami'*, 2:230.

50. Shaykh Baha'i, 2:417.

51. Shaykh Baha'i, 2:367.

52. Shaykh Baha'i, 41:47.

53. Najafi, *Jawahir*, 36:468, 22:111.

54. Najafi, 41:44.

55. Peters, *Crime*, 12–16.

56. Majlisi, *Hudud*, 20, 24.

57. Majlisi, 31. Some legal authorities claimed that one confession was sufficient.

58. Majlisi, 50.

59. Majlisi, 87.

60. Majlisi, 88.

61. Majlisi, 89.

62. Majlisi, 91.

63. Johansen, "La découverte," 8; Johansen, *Contingency*, 356; K. Fahmy, *Quest*, 104, 108. According to Peters, Hanafis, Shafi'is, and Shi'is consider the *qadi's* knowledge (*'ilm al-qadi*), regardless of how it was acquired, as sufficient proof in criminal matters. Peters, *Crime*, 12. Hossein Modarressi similarly argues that there were both early Sunni (mostly Hanafi and Ibn Hazm) and Shi'i jurists who argued for this doctrine, but he perceptively notes that it had the "potential to substantially expand the jurisdiction of a judge and his ability to go beyond the traditional framework of an Islamic court." Modarressi, "Circumstantial," 19.

64. Najafi, *Jawahir*, 40:10–11, 13, 20.

65. Majlisi, *Hudud*, 117. For the original passage, see Tusi, *Tahdhib*, 10:221.

66. Majlisi, *Hudud*, 117.

67. Majlisi, 20; Shafti, *Maqalah*, 46, 79.

68. Shafti, *Maqalah*, 82.

69. Shafti, 134–35. He summarized some of the views of classical authors in other passages, including those who said it was the judge's prerogative even in the absence of the Imam. Shafti, 143–45.

70. Najafi, *Jawahir*, 40:86–87.

71. Najafi, 41:366–67.

72. Najafi, 40:119–20. This is similar to the Maliki School's position that giving birth to a child could be used as evidence for *zina* having occurred. Katz, "Hadd," 368.

73. Najafi, *Jawahir*, 40:87.

74. Najafi, 40:88.

75. On secrecy in Islam, see Dakake, "Hiding"; Khan, *Self*.

76. Arjomand, *Shadow*, 209.

77. See Heern, *Emergence*, 222–23.

78. Shafti, *Maqalah*, 130.

79. Shafti, 169.

80. Shafti, 181. This, he stated, was even the case during the greater occultation, which marked a period from 941 (329 H.) onward, when there was no longer any communication with the Hidden Imam via his agents. Shafti, 182.

81. Interestingly, al-Ghazali argued against granting Shi'is protections and rights on the basis of the Shi'is' belief in this abeyance. Cook, *Commanding*, 430.

82. Shafti, *Maqalah*, 186.

83. For one such exclusively ritualistic reading of *hudud* punishments, see Gleave, "Public."

84. Shafti, *Maqalah*, 189.

85. Shafti, 192.

86. Shafti, 192.

87. Shafti, 194.

88. Cook, *Commanding*, 479–80.

89. Cook, 480.

90. Cook, 480.

91. Cook, 300.

92. M. Qummi, *Jami'*, 1:419.

93. M. Qummi, 1:420.

94. Cook, *Commanding*, 32–35.

95. For classical Imami *fiqh*, see Cook, 263–66.

96. Cook, 285. Shaykh Baha'i expressed a similar view in his widely read *Jami'-i 'Abbasi* and suggested that it should not be practiced with violence. Shaykh Baha'i, *Jami'*, 2:146; Arjomand, *Shadow*, 175.

97. M. Qummi, *Jami'*, 1:417–8.

98. M. Qummi, 1:422. He was careful to specify that such an act was not for-bidding wrong with violence.

99. Gleave, "Jihad," 44, 49, 57.

100. Kashif al-Ghita', *Kashf*, 419–21; Cook, *Commanding*, 287.

101. Tunakabuni, *Qisas*, 414.

102. Najafi, *Jawahir*, 21:361.

103. Najafi, 21:383–85.

104. Najafi, 21:385.

105. Cook, *Commanding*, 482. Cook does not address in detail the role of the father, husband, and master within the domicile in forbidding wrong.

106. To my knowledge, Patricia Crone is the only scholar to have pointed out this phenomenon. She refers to this figure as the "domestic tyrant." I have used the term "patriarch" to capture these three specific roles. Crone, *God's Rule*, 67, 296.

107. M. Qummi, *Jami'*, 1:417.

108. M. Qummi, 1:424.

109. Najafi, *Jawahir*, 21:386–90; Shaykh Baha'i, *Jami'*, 2:163.

110. Shaykh Baha'i, *Jami'*, 2:163.

111. Shafti, *Maqalah*, 50, 51.

112. Shafti, 51.

113. Shafti, 52.

114. Shafti, 59–84.

115. Shafti, 59–60.

116. Shafti, 67–68.

117. Shafti, 83.

118. Shafti, 84.

119. Shafti, 74.

120. Shafti, 80.

121. Shafti, 85–125.

122. Quran 4:15.

123. Quran 24:2.

124. Shafti, *Maqalah*, 88.

125. Shafti, 89.

126. Shafti, 95.

127. Shafti, 94.

128. In other interpretations of this issue by jurists, the husband had the choice of staying with his wife, divorcing her, or carrying out the *hadd* on her. Shafti, 90.

129. Shafti, 108.

130. Shafti, 116.

131. Shafti, 115–16. He considered this authority in cases of adultery as "absolutely permissible" (*al-jawaz mutlaqan*). Shafti, 119.

132. Shafti, 126–29.

133. Shafti, 129.

134. M. Cohen, "Pact"; Levy-Rubin, "Shurut 'Umar."

135. Afary, "Outcastes," 143, 147.

136. Tsadik, *Foreigners*, 30. For another notable scholar to engage with Shi'i sources, albeit often of a much earlier period, see Soroudi, "Concept," 142–47. In Laurence Loeb's study of Jews in southern Iran, he relies on *Jami'-i 'Abbasi* as a significant source of Shi'i jurisprudence on Jews relevant to the nineteenth-century. Loeb, *Outcaste*, 292.

137. Najafi, *Jawahir*, 21:265–67, 276–77, 43:40–41; Qummi, 1:402–3, 409–14; Tsadik, *Foreigners*, 24–25.

138. Najafi, *Jawahir*, 21:267–69; Tsadik, *Foreigners*, 27.

139. Najafi, *Jawahir*, 21:318, 41:335–36; Tsadik, *Foreigners*, 24.

140. Najafi, *Jawahir*, 41:379; Tsadik, *Foreigners*, 24.

141. Najafi, *Jawahir*, 41:313; Tsadik, *Foreigners*, 24.

142. Najafi, *Jawahir*, 41:336; Tsadik, *Foreigners*, 24.

143. Najafi, *Jawahir*, 41:379; Tsadik, *Foreigners*, 24.

144. Najafi, *Jawahir*, 21:269–70, 317–18; Tsadik, *Foreigners*, 27; Tsadik, "Legal," 400.

145. See Najafi, *Jawahir*, 37:44–45, 43:400–401; Tsadik, "Legal," 397.

146. Majlisi, *Hudud*, 163.

147. Majlisi, 41.

148. Tsadik, *Foreigners*, 27.

149. Najafi, *Jawahir*, 21:286–87. The Hijaz was also prohibited. Najafi, 21:289–91; Tsadik, "Legal," 395. For general discussions of this restriction in Islamic texts, see Maghen, "Close Encounters," 364, 367.

150. Tsadik, *Foreigners*, 27.

151. Najafi, *Jawahir*, 21:271–73, 247–48. For other *dhimmi* regulations, see Najafi, 21:273–6; Tsadik, *Foreigners*, 28. For further discussion of the issue of differentiation in hairstyles for men, see Kister, "'Do Not Assimilate."

152. Tsadik, *Foreigners*, 16–17; Ebrami, "Impure."

153. Tsadik, *Foreigners*, 18.

154. Majlisi, for example, saw the function of crucifying a *muharib* as deterrence for others. Majlisi, *Hudud*, 45.

155. Gleave, "Crimes," 93–94.

156. Majlisi, *Hudud*, 17.

157. Majlisi, 66.

158. Lange, "Legal."

159. Majlisi, *Hudud*, 24.

160. Najafi, *Jawahir*, 41:400–401.

161. Majlisi, *Hudud*, 16.

162. Majlisi, 63. For more on speech acts as crimes in Islamic law, see Rabb, "Society."

163. Majlisi, *Hudud*, 64.

164. Majlisi, 45. For broader discussions of rebels and crucifixion, see Abou El Fadl, *Rebellion*.

165. Majlisi, *Hudud*, 44. A person could not be left on the crucifix for longer than three days before being taken down and ritually washed. Majlisi, 46.

166. Majlisi, 21.

167. Majlisi, 15. For a discussion of what this ordering meant, see Gleave, "Public," 265–72.

168. Majlisi, *Hudud*, 21–22.

169. Majlisi, 26.

170. Majlisi, 21.

171. Majlisi, 100.

172. Najafi, *Jawahir*, 42:299. Majlisi suggested that a beheading would be preferable in all three circumstances. Majlisi, *Hudud*, 100.

173. Majlisi, *Hudud*, 100.

174. Majlisi, 21, 44, 14, 15, 63.

175. In both cases, this involved cutting off the right hand and the left foot. Majlisi, 21, 44.

176. Majlisi, 37.

177. Majlisi, 37.

178. Majlisi, 37.

179. Majlisi, 63.

180. Majlisi, 65.

181. Majlisi, 22.

182. Majlisi, 14.

183. Majlisi, 28.

184. Some 'ulama said a slave receives forty lashes, half that of a free person's due, and that on the third or fourth time, they would be executed. Majlisi, 31.

185. Majlisi, 59. For more on *ta'zir* in Islamic penal law, see El-Awa, "Ta'azir."

186. Majlisi, *Hudud*, 59. For the last definition, this would mean that in matters similar to *zina*, it has to be under one hundred lashes for a free person and less than fifty for a slave. For eating and drinking prohibited things, it should be less than eighty lashes, and for false accusations, less than the prescribed *hadd* for defamation (*fuhsh*). Majlisi, 59.

187. Majlisi, 13.

188. A half-free male or female slave (*ghulam* or *kaniz*) who engaged in *zina* would receive seventy-five lashes. If they were more free, then their *hadd* went up accordingly. Majlisi, 16.

189. Majlisi, 66.

190. Majlisi, 60.

191. Majlisi, 19.

192. Majlisi, 64.

193. Majlisi, 64–65.

194. Majlisi, 17. Gleave notes that the person receiving *hadd* punishments should not be sick; if they were, then they received this symbolic punishment. Gleave, "Crimes," 91–92.

195. Majlisi, 18.

196. Majlisi, 21.

197. Others say that one hundred lashes should be given in this situation. Majlisi, 21.

198. Majlisi, 21.

199. Majlisi, 22.

200. Majlisi, 23.

201. Majlisi, 24.

202. Majlisi, 25.

203. Majlisi, 60.

204. Majlisi, 61.

205. Majlisi, 62.

206. Schneider, "Imprisonment."

207. Majlisi, *Hudud*, 37.

208. Majlisi, 48–49.

209. Majlisi, 66.

210. This was a form of *ta'zir* punishment. Majlisi, 62.

211. Others claimed that if the judge suspects that the person is the murderer, then they can be imprisoned for six days. Majlisi, 95.

212. Majlisi, 72.

213. Majlisi, 44. Another *hadd* punishment for a *muharib* who unsheathed a sword but did not hurt anyone was that they would be exiled from the city. Majlisi, 45.

T W O   Sovereignty and Law in Advice and Reform Literature

Epigraph: Kashifi, *Akhlaq-i Muhsini*, 288.

1. Hallaq, *Impossible*.

2. See, for instance, Gleave, "Jihad,"; Kondo, *Islamic*, 34.

3. Arjomand, "Political Ethic."

4. Those who wrote advice literature encompassed government ministers, scribes, officials, Sufis, Shaykhis, Sunnis, and even Shiʻi jurists. Zargarinizhad, "Dara-mad," 15–16.

5. Gleave, "Jihad," 47. Gleave makes this remark with reference to Ahmad Naraqi, who wrote works of jurisprudence, advice literature, and mysticism that lacked consistency on matters such as political authority. See also Gleave, "Two."

6. Lange and Fierro, "Spatial," 1–3.

7. Arjomand, *Shadow*, 100.

8. The earliest documented usage of the term is by the mystic Ibn al-ʻArabi. Belhaj, "Law," 403. For further discussion, see Johansen, "Signs"; Rapoport, "Royal."

9. Arjomand, "Perso-Islamicate," 83.

10. Najafi does use this term once but to refer to a shariʻah-bound policy carried out by a judge and not a government official. Najafi, *Jawahir*, 31:214.

11. Rizvi, "Shiʻi."

12. Kashfi, *Tuhfat*, 896.

13. Other Qajar-era mirrors for princes invoked the idea of the just sultan in reference to the shah. Hajji Mirza Aqasi composed one such work in 1830, in which he referred to Sufi themes alongside the importance of shariʻah ordinances (*ahkam*). He described governance in terms of practical wisdom (*hikmat-i ʻamaliyah*) and stressed the just king's role in protecting subjects, providing redress, and stamping out moral corruption and conflicts. Hajj Mirza Aqasi, "Chahar," 233, 238, 241, 249, 252–53.

14. Kashfi, *Tuhfat*, 898. For a discussion of this idea and similar passages in Kashfi by scholars more interested in the issue of political legitimacy, see Arjomand, "Shiʻite Hierocracy," 53–54; Hairi, "Legitimacy," 282–83. Ahmad Kazemi Moussavi argues that this work did not conform to the structures of Imami thought and, by implication, was illegitimate as a guide for understanding Shiʻi jurisprudence. Kazemi Moussavi, *Religious*, 252.

15. Kashfi, *Tuhfat*, 899. Kashfi ended his politics section with a Persian translation of ʻAli bin Abi Talib's letter to Malik bin Ashtar, the governor of Egypt, which he argued contained a justification for not only vicegerency (*niyabat*) of both a particular (*khass*) and universal (*ʻamm*) type but also the implementation of "administrative laws" (*qavanin-i siyasatiyah*). Kashfi, 920.

16. Kashfi, 495.

17. Yilmaz, *Caliphate*, 51, 85–86, 335.

18. Kashfi, *Tuhfat*, 506.

19. Lambton, "Some New Trends," 121.

20. Kashfi, *Tuhfat*, 915.

21. Kashfi, 917.

22. Kashfi, 916–17.

23. Rustam al-Hukama, "Shams," 303.

24. Rustam al-Hukama, 316; Dakake, "Hiding," 342; Hairi, "Legitimacy," 274–75. In fact, Fath 'Ali Shah attempted to use the term *ulu al-amr* to justify his rule. The Shi'i jurist Mirza Abu al-Qasim Qummi, however, objected to it. Kazemi Moussavi, *Religious*, 250.

25. Rustam al-Hukama, "Shams," 318. This, like his previous claim, placed kingship on the plane of the universal. In fact, he saw no reason why a minister could not be Jewish, Christian, or Zoroastrian, so long as they were rational people (*'uqala*). Rustam al-Hukama, 326.

26. Rustam al-Hukama, 313.

27. Rustam al-Hukama, 315.

28. Rustam al-Hukama, 333.

29. For Rustam al-Hukama's interpretation of a Quranic verse prohibiting lewdness (*fahsha*), prohibited acts (*munkar*), and rebellion (*baghi*) to similarly justify the sovereign's authority, see Rustam al-Hukama, 317.

30. Rustam al-Hukama, 354.

31. Rustam al-Hukama, 355.

32. Rustam al-Hukama, 358–59. With respect to soldiers, he made a similar claim elsewhere. Rustam al-Hukama, *Rustam al-Tavarikh*, 329–31; Perry, *Karim Khan Zand*, 287. His arguments parallel those of later authors justifying the legalization of prostitution in the late Ottoman and early Republic of Turkey. Wyers, *Wicked*, 81–110.

33. Rustam al-Hukama, "Shams," 346.

34. Rustam al-Hukama, 346.

35. Rustam al-Hukama, 351. He then cited Hafiz's famous line of poetry in which he advised his readers to use caution when drinking and listening to music privately with a friend. Rustam al-Hukama, 351. See Cook, *Commanding*, 436. For overviews of *hisbah* manuals, see Stilt, *Islamic*, 38–72; Musallam, "Ordering."

36. Rustam al-Hukama, "Shams," 351.

37. For the *muhtasib*'s stand and instruments of punishment in medieval Cairo, see Stilt, *Islamic*, 50–53.

38. Rustam al-Hukama, "Shams," 369. For the use of demeaning hats in punitive parades, see Lange, "Legal," 83–84.

39. Rustam al-Hukama, "Shams," 369.

40. Rustam al-Hukama, 367–68. This was not a punishment typically found in Islamic jurisprudence unless the person carrying the arms was labeled a *muharib* because they threatened the lives of Muslims with instruments of war. The proposed prohibition reflected a tendency in Iranian theories of kingship to see public violence as a personal offense against the sovereign requiring government punishment. Lange, *Justice*, 9.

41. Rustam al-Hukama, "Shams," 368. Likewise, the punishment for fighting described here is not to be found in Islamic jurisprudence. If anything, injuries would have to be settled either through retaliation or compensation.

42. Rustam al-Hukama, 368. Rustam al-Hukama apparently had in mind the penalties for slander, which were closely related to punishments for giving false testimony.

43. Lange, "Torture"; Reza, "Torture."

44. Rustam al-Hukama, "Shams," 355–56. For a similar actual case of insects, in this case bees, being used as a punishment, see "Tawqif-i Shikanjah," 1302 H. / [1884/85], SAKM, no. 295/6456.

45. Rustam al-Hukama, "Shams," 371.

46. Rustam al-Hukama, 373.

47. Damavandi, "Tuhfat," 35; Zargarinizhad, "Daramad," 64. Although the text was published in the Nasiri era, Damavandi referred to Muhammad Shah as the "just king" and stated that the text had been edited by Muhammad Shah's prime minister, Hajji Mirza Aqasi. Damavandi, "Tuhfat," 37. His praise of Muhammad Shah had messianic undertones, insofar as he claimed that the appearance of a just king could usher in the appearance of the Hidden Imam. Damavandi, "Tuhfat," 56. For further discussions of Ibn Damavandi, see Sohrabi, *Revolution*, 293–94; A. Amanat, *Pivot*, 70; Zargarinizhad, "Daramad," 63–67.

48. Damavandi, "Tuhfat," 61.

49. Damavandi, 72.

50. Damavandi, 56; Zargarinizhad, "Daramad," 66–67.

51. Damavandi, "Tuhfat," 59.

52. Damavandi, 59.

53. Damavandi, 59.

54. Zargarinizhad, "Daramad," 14, 18, 22.

55. "Mishkat-i Muhammadiyah," 27. For the retention of hard labor in early nineteenth-century penal codes, see Durkheim, "Two Laws," 46.

56. Kashfi, "Mizan," 125.

57. Kashfi, 110, 123. The shahs and sultans had to abstain from vice themselves to have the moral authority to forbid wrong; otherwise it would open the door to the spread of "vice and immorality." Kashfi, 141–43.

58. Kashfi, 128.

59. For a discussion of this understanding of the "legal" in Islamic jurisprudence, see Emon, "Quadrants," 1100; Kamali, *Principles*, 44–46.

60. Kashfi, "Mizan," 127, 133.

61. Kashfi, 134, 140.

62. Savuji, "Siyasat," 298.

63. Savuji, 243, 257.

64. Savuji, 255.

65. Savuji, 242. If the sovereign failed to follow and implement shari'ah rulings, a calamity would occur. Savuji, 254.

66. Savuji, 247.

67. Savuji, 250.

68. The maxim states, "He who exceeds in carrying out the fixed mandatory punishments of God transgresses against himself" (*man yata'adda hudud Allah faqad zalama nafsahu*). Savuji, 265. For the definitive study of doubt as it pertains to Islamic criminal law, see Rabb, *Doubt*.

69. Savuji, "Siyasat," 265.

70. Savuji, 265.

71. Savuji, 259. In fact, this role-reversal idea probably had its origins in al-Ghazali's discussion of sovereignty in his famous *Kimiya-yi Sa'adat*. Hillenbrand, "Little-Known," 595.

72. Savuji, 260.

73. Savuji, 262.

74. Tihrani, *Dastur*, 3; Qazvini, *Qanun*, 114.

75. Arjomand, "Political," 34.

76. Tihrani, *Dastur*, 192.

77. Tihrani, 195.

78. Tihrani, 197.

79. There does not appear to be any consensus about the date of composition of this work. Firoozeh Kashani-Sabet argues that it was published in 1853 (1270 H.), while Juan Cole claims that it was composed sometime after 1868. For representative scholarship on the author and the book, see Arjomand, "Political," 36; Cole, *Modernity*, 88; Kashani-Sabet, *Frontier*, 80–81.

80. Qazvini, *Qanun*, 37. This position strayed from the *fiqh* position that a master could punish their slave in the domestic sphere for a *hadd* crime.

81. Qazvini, 89. He contrasted this situation with foreign governments, where "there is one legal court, rulings are one [*ahkam yaki*], and not even 100 dinars are taken from anyone oppressively." Qazvini, 89.

82. Qazvini, 96–97.

83. Qazvini, 97–98.

84. Qazvini, 97. Qazvini used the term *qisas* to mean execution in this context, although within *fiqh*, this term was used to mean lex talionis and not execution per se.

85. Qazvini, 98.

86. Qazvini, 120.

87. Qazvini, 120. Qazvini's punishments did not match those found in *fiqh* for these crimes; instead, he seems to have constructed his own original schema.

88. Qazvini, 120.

89. Qazvini, 121–22.

90. Qazvini, 108.

91. Qazvini, 122; Najmabadi, *Women*, 143. Some Muslim jurists did in fact argue that beardless youth should veil in public. El-Rouayheb, *Homosexuality*, 112.

92. Qazvini, *Qanun*, 123; Najmabadi, *Women*, 144. For shaving as punishment in Shi'i *fiqh*, see Hamoudi, "Sex," 56.

93. Qazvini, *Qanun*, 122.

94. Qazvini's argument parallels discussions found in Sunni legal texts about Muslim women having to cover their faces and body parts in front of non-Muslim women out of regard for informational privacy. Alshech, "Out of Sight," 283.

95. Qazvini, *Qanun*, 124.

96. Malkam Khan, "Kitabchah-i Ghaybi," 14.

97. Malkam Khan, 36.

98. Malkam Khan, 37.

99. Malkam Khan, 26.

100. Malkam Khan, 29.

101. Malkam Khan, 30.

102. For further scholarship on the author and this treatise, see Bakhash, *Iran*, 38–40; Hairi, *Shi'ism*, 32–37; Algar, *Malkum*, 139, 204. For an English translation of the text, see Mustashar al-Dawlah, *One Word*.

103. Sohrabi, *Revolution*, 303.

104. Mustashar al-Dawlah, *Yak*, 101.

105. Mustashar al-Dawlah, 90.

106. Mustashar al-Dawlah, 91–92. He did, however, draw a clear line between what might or might not be considered harmful and on what grounds. For more on this issue, see Cook, *Commanding*, 531.

107. Mustashar al-Dawlah concluded that all of these laws were fully in line with the nineteen principles of the French constitution. Mustashar al-Dawlah, *Yak*, 90.

108. Mustashar al-Dawlah, 89–90.

109. Mustashar al-Dawlah, 90. For the theme of sexual violation in Islamic law, see Azam, *Sexual*.

110. Mustashar al-Dawlah, *Yak*, 88.

111. Mustashar al-Dawlah, 88–89.

112. Mustashar al-Dawlah, 88.

113. Mustashar al-Dawlah, 101–2.

114. Mustashar al-Dawlah, 102.

115. Mustashar al-Dawlah, 103. The European equivalent of this leniency was the right of the king to pardon or commute sentences. For example, a European king could commute a death sentence to life imprisonment. Mustashar al-Dawlah, 103.

116. In a letter to Mustashar al-Dawlah, Akhundzadah points out several respects in which he views the shari'ah as being fully incompatible with modern laws. Akhundzadah, *Maqalat*, 33–40. For Akhundzadah's ideas on the rule of law and constitutionalism, see Adamiyat, *Andishahha*, 136–71.

117. Akhundzadah, *Maqalat*, 33.

118. Akhundzadah, 33.

119. Akhundzadah, 39.

120. Akhundzadah, 40.

121. Akhundzadah, 39.

122. This appears to be a reference to Quran 4:15, in which a female fornicator is to be confined for life. Akhundzadah conveniently did not mention that this verse was abrogated by Quran 24:2, which mentioned one hundred lashes for *zina*. In *fiqh*, the punishment was either lashings or stoning, depending on the status of the adulterers.

123. Akhundzadah, *Maqalat*, 34.

124. This, in his mind, was not equality. Akhundzadah, 35.

125. Akhundzadah, 35.

126. Akhundzadah, 36.

127. Akhundzadah, 37.

128. Akhundzadah, 37–38.

129. Akhundzadah, 38.

130. Akhundzadah, 38.

131. For more on Bentham, see Bedau, "Bentham's Utilitarian Critique."

132. Akhundzadah, *Maqalat*, 39. Akhundzadah presumably had the *hadd* punishment for apostasy in mind for this latter case.

133. The book was distributed in Iran and eventually printed in Bombay in 1883. Momen, "Bahá'í Influence," 48–49, 52. It was published just two years after Baha'u'llah's *The Most Holy Book* (*Kitab-i Aqdas*) and similarly touched on legal themes. 'Abdu'l-Baha justified withholding his name so no one would attribute any motive to it except for improving general welfare (*khayr-i kull*). 'Abdu'l-Baha, *Madaniyah*, 8. For further discussion of this text's significance, see A. Amanat, "Constitutional Revolution."

134. 'Abdu'l-Baha, *Madaniyah*, 8, 14, 81. Throughout the text, he emphasized justice and the hope for a "just government" (*hukumat-i 'adilanah*). 'Abdu'l-Baha, 15.

135. This essentially established a baseline for the legitimate use of violence. 'Abdu'l-Baha, 112. The Quranic verses cited were as follows: Quran 3:110, 3:100, 16:92.

136. 'Abdu'l-Baha, *Madaniyah*, 115.

137. 'Abdu'l-Baha, 115.

138. 'Abdu'l-Baha, 116.

139. 'Abdu'l-Baha, 19–20.

140. 'Abdu'l-Baha, 118.

141. 'Abdu'l-Baha, 20.

142. Sayyid 'Ali Al-i Davud, for instance, indicates that the text was probably a translation from Ottoman Turkish because the translator describes himself as a Turkish translator. Al-i Davud, *Nukhustin*, 151. The other two editors provide no indication that these were translations of penal codes.

143. The translation omits the preface, with the exception of a brief introduction to the three chapters (*fasl*) that it will address, and stops abruptly in chapter 2, article 2. It is entirely possible that the existing manuscript on which this text was based was incomplete. Mushir al-Dawlah, "Kitabchah." For the original Ottoman

Kanun-i Ceza, see "Kanun." Although the booklet is undated, internal evidence suggests that it was written in the final months of the premiership of Mirza Aqa Khan Nuri and at the same time as the formation of the Ministry of Justice (Divankhanah-i 'Adliyah). Mushir al-Dawlah, "Kitabchah," 485, 489. For further discussion of the Ministry of Justice being formed in that year, see Bakhash, *Iran*, 84; Nashat, *Origins*, 44.

144. Mushir al-Dawlah, "Kitabchah," 488.

145. Mushir al-Dawlah, 489. Mushir al-Dawlah translated the three terms out of order, which in the original code were *fasl-i can*, *fasl-i 'irz ve namus*, and *fasl-i mal*, although the translation as a whole preserves the order of the original text. "Kanun," 152.

146. Mushir al-Dawlah, 492; "Kanun," 158. For *taqsir* as a translation for *cunha*, see Mushir al-Dawlah, 490; "Kanun," 154. In an account of a pledge Nasir al-Din Shah made before notables and foreign dignitaries, the shah is said to have promised to ban the government from punishing anyone before first proving their crime (*jurm va jinayat*), suggesting that *jurm* was a more commonly used synonym for crime in Persian. Mushir al-Dawlah, 486.

147. Mushir al-Dawlah, 492; "Kanun," 160. Kent Schull attributes this wide inclusion of *qisas*, *hadd*, and *ta'zir* alongside *siyasat* crimes and punishments to the 1840 (*sic*: 1839) Ottoman Penal Code, when in fact *hadd* and *ta'zir* appear to be absent in this earlier code. Instead, these terms appear for the first time in the 1851 *Kanun-i Cedid*. Schull, "Criminal," 159.

148. Mushir al-Dawlah, "Kitabchah," 490–91; "Kanun," 155–56. The Ottoman terms used here were *kürek* for "hard labor" and *pranga* for "shackles." For further discussion of these terms, see Peters, *Shari'a*, 120.

149. Note that the use of the term *qanun-i siyasat* to mean "penal code" would probably have been more comprehensible in the Iranian context than *qanun-i jaza*, the latter being closer to contemporary Ottoman Turkish usage.

150. Mushir al-Dawlah, "Kitabchah," 489; "Kanun," 153. During the Tanzimat, a provincial council was referred to as a *majlis*, which was another allusion to contemporary Ottoman terminology.

151. Mushir al-Dawlah, "Kitabchah," 489–90; "Kanun," 153.

152. Mushir al-Dawlah, "Kitabchah," 489; "Kanun," 152. The Ottoman Turkish text simply states, "without exception."

153. Mushir al-Dawlah, "Kitabchah," 491; "Kanun," 158.

154. Mushir al-Dawlah, "Kitabchah," 492; "Kanun," 160.

155. "Qanun-i Jaza," Majlis Library, no. 10-32094.

156. Hasanzadah, Zargarinizhad, and Samaghabadi, "Dar al-Tarjumah," 70. For a list of his published works, see Afshar, "Aghaz," 92, 103–4. He translated a number of Ottoman texts including the Gülhane Hatt-ı Şerif, Ottoman ceremonial protocols, a text pertaining to the organization of Ottoman ministers, an Ottoman postal budget, and a set of regulations for the Iranian armed forces (which was possibly an original composition). "Kurrasat al-Ma'i," Majlis Library, no. 9452, 1490–95, 1498–1503, 1538–159, 1632–44; "Kurrasat al-Ma'i," Majlis Library, no. 9451, 1392–98.

157. "Qanun-i Jaza," 8, 11.

158. I'timad al-Saltanah, *Ruznamah*, 669–70.

159. I'timad al-Saltanah, 265.

160. "Qanun-i Jaza," 11. For a useful summary of these ideas among early Islamic thinkers, see Crone, *God's Rule*, 259–66.

161. "Qanun-i Jaza," 10.

162. "Qanun-i Jaza," 7.

163. "Qanun-i Jaza," 2–4.

164. "Qanun-i Jaza," 4, 6.

165. "Qanun-i Jaza," 10.

166. "Qanun-i Jaza," 13.

167. "Qanun-i Jaza," 14–15; *Ceza Kanunname*, 2. In this same article, the Ottoman Penal Code referred to government as *dawlat*, while the Persian translation used the term *Divankhanah-i 'Urfi*, once again making it clear that this was not to be confused with a shari'ah court.

168. "Qanun-i Jaza," 15; *Ceza Kanunname*, 3. On the difficulties of finding precise Ottoman (and English) translations for these three French terms, see Bucknill et al., *Imperial*, 5.

169. See articles 3–5 in both codes. "Qanun-i Jaza," 15–16; *Ceza Kanunname*, 3. For the translations of terms used here, see Bucknill et al., *Imperial*, 6–7.

170. "Qanun-i Jaza," 15. The Ottoman terms used for these were *katl, kürek, kalabandlik, nafi, memuriyetden mahrumiyet, hukuk-i medeniyetten iskat. Ceza Kanunname*, 3. At first glance and without an understanding of the Ottoman Penal Code, some of the Persian terms appear quite confusing. For example, *tab'id* and *nafy* both mean "exile," while *taqyid* simply means "being bound" but does not have the connotation of hard labor. *Hirman* means "prohibition," while *isqat* means "dropped" and, more commonly, "abortion." What was being prohibited or aborted was left ambiguous in the translation of this article.

171. "Qanun-i Jaza," 15–16. The Ottoman code elaborated on public exposure in article 19. *Ceza Kanunname*, 5. For the relevant passages in the Napoleonic Code and discussion of public exposure's abolishment in France in 1848, see Bucknill et al., *Imperial*, 16.

172. "Qanun-i Jaza," 16; *Ceza Kanunname*, 3.

173. "Qanun-i Jaza," 16. In the Ottoman Penal Code, this fine amount was one hundred piastres. *Ceza Kanunname*, 3.

174. Malkam Khan, "Daftar," 121. For further discussion, see Bigdeli, "Legal," 178.

175. Malkam Khan, "Daftar," 127.

176. Malkam Khan, 127.

177. Malkam Khan, 127–28. Viewing Iran through a European gaze, Malkam Khan considered this to be the reason why Europeans viewed Iran as barbaric: because it was not clear if the government would punish any crime. In London, he claimed,

whoever commits a crime knows its punishment, while in Iran, no one knows how a crime will be punished. Malkam Khan, 128.

178. Malkam Khan, 128.

179. Malkam Khan, 137.

180. Malkam Khan, 140. In some ways, this was an extension of the logic of the guarantorship that undergirded other arrangements throughout Iran.

181. See Hamid Algar's brief discussion, which is so fixated on the supposed incongruence of codification and shari'ah that it fails to substantially analyze and situate the text within the context of comparable efforts in the Ottoman Empire and Egypt. Algar, *Malkum*, 190–91. Fereshteh Mangeneh-Nourai suggests that the penal code proposed by Malkam Khan was based on a "French pattern" but provides no evidence. Mangeneh-Nourai, "Life," 85.

182. Malkam Khan, "Daftar," 130.

183. Malkam Khan, 129. Interestingly, the term *siyasat* had the connotation of harsh punishment or, more commonly, execution in Qajar-era texts. *Tadib* appeared in the Ottoman Penal Code but as the second-most-severe form of punishment and not the least severe. Malkam Khan redefined commonly used terminology to suit his vision of a penal law.

184. Malkam Khan, 129. Note that seizure of goods was not a punishment found in the 1858 Ottoman Penal Code or its Persian translation. Malkam Khan elaborates on the productive labor involved in each type of imprisonment.

185. Malkam Khan used *fatva-yi qatl* to refer to a death sentence. Typically, a death sentence, whether in government documents or in shari'ah ones, was called a *hukm-i qatl*, since *fatva* was a nonbinding legal responsum.

186. Malkam Khan, 130–31. It was also stated that *zajr* entailed government disgrace and exposure in the city square as a public deterrent. Malkam Khan, 131–32.

187. Malkam Khan, 130. Those who were given temporary time in the penitentiary, between five and twenty years, would be bound by the same labor requirements and conditions as those who received a life sentence. Malkam Khan, 131.

188. The duration of *ghazab-i zindan* was between five and twenty years. Malkam Khan, 131.

189. Malkam Khan, 132.

190. Malkam Khan, 132.

191. Malkam Khan, 132.

192. Malkam Khan, 133.

193. Malkam Khan, 133.

194. Malkam Khan, 133. Malkam Khan explained that the various charges would be clarified in further chapters that would need to be written in the code. Malkam Khan, 134. Elsewhere, he explained that detention was used in Iran as a debtor's prison by lenders because Iran did not have any laws addressing this issue, which led to the "worst form of disorder." Malkam Khan, 135.

195. Malkam Khan, 134.

196. Algar, *Malkum*, 190.

197. For a discussion of this Islamization of the mirror for princes genre, see Al-Azmeh, *Muslim Kingship*, 99–100; Tor, "Islamisation."

198. Bihbahani, "Minhaj al-'Ali," 143, 156–61. 'Abdu'l-Baha also made a very similar claim but reached a very different conclusion: since Europeans borrowed to bring about reforms, there was no shame in Muslims borrowing in turn. 'Abdu'l-Baha, *Madaniyah*, 17.

199. Bihbahani, "Minhaj al-'Ali," 203.

200. In doing this, he needed to work with a consultative assembly (*majlis-i shura*). Bihbahani, 204. The idea that the shah had to act as a supreme arbiter in shari'ah matters parallels the claims made by Emperor Akbar in weighing competing religious claims. Richards, *Mughal Empire*, 39–40.

201. Bihbahani, "Minhaj al-'Ali," 214.

202. Bihbahani, 214–15. Bihbahani stood out from other reformists by discussing the disparities in punishments for various religious groups.

203. Bihbahani, 240.

204. Bihbahani, 219.

205. Bihbahani, 215–16.

206. "Ruh al-Islam," 359; Zargarinizhad, "Daramad," 73. The author of its introduction, Muhammad Kazim Tabataba'i, suggested that the work was composed in 1853/54, but the author feared revealing his name because of an oppressive prime minister, meaning Mirza Aqa Khan Nuri. "Ruh al-Islam," 325; Zargarinizhad, "Daramad," 71. The introduction claimed that the treatise helped explicate the meaning of humanity (*ma'ani-i adamiyat*), suggesting a possible connection to Malkam Khan's secret society modeled on Masonic lodges, known as the "House of Oblivion" (Faramushkhanah), either by the author of the preface or the author. "Ruh al-Islam," 326. The author spent the early part of his work invoking hadith and the works of al-Ghazali and Sa'd al-Din Taftazani, perhaps as a means of establishing his own Islamic orthodoxy. "Ruh al-Islam," 335, 345–46.

207. "Ruh al-Islam," 358.

208. "Ruh al-Islam," 335.

209. Occasionally, there were references to common maxims found in advice literature. Citing a common maxim connected with mirrors for princes, the author stated that the kingdom will last despite infidelity but not with oppression. "Ruh al-Islam," 368.

210. "Ruh al-Islam," 376.

211. The forms of punishment described were as follows: confinement, punishment, discretionary punishment, or regular punishment (*zajr va siza va ta'zir va tanbih*). What is unique about this usage of *hadd* is that it meant punishment more generally rather than fixed mandatory punishments.

212. "Ruh al-Islam," 362. The principle of equality was emphasized in the Ottoman penal codes as well. Elsewhere, the author stated that rewards and punishments

had to be based on the rights of all individuals, irrespective of their high or low status, being learned or illiterate, or being a leader or a poor person. "Ruh al-Islam," 376.

213. "Ruh al-Islam," 376.

214. "Ruh al-Islam," 359.

215. On this idea, see Girard, *Violence*, 7, 212–14.

216. "Ruh al-Islam," 360.

217. "Ruh al-Islam," 360.

218. "Ruh al-Islam," 360.

219. "Ruh al-Islam," 363–64. Its absence was considered to be a hindrance to Iran's progress. "Ruh al-Islam," 365.

220. "Ruh al-Islam," 368.

221. "Ruh al-Islam," 369.

222. "Ruh al-Islam," 370.

223. "Ruh al-Islam," 370.

224. "Ruh al-Islam," 370. It was left ambiguous, however, as to whether people were free to change religion, since this, in the case of conversion out of Islam, would be considered an act of apostasy.

225. "Ruh al-Islam," 371.

226. Nazim al-Islam Kirmani, *Tarikh*, 146.

227. Hajj Mullah 'Ali Shari'atmadar, "Jami'-i Nasiri," Kakh-i Gulistan, no. 2973, 1279b; Danishpazhuh, "Jami'-i Nasiri," 510; Nazim al-Islam Kirmani, *Tarikh*, 146–47; I'timad al-Saltanah, *Al-Ma'asir*, 201.

228. Fleischer, "Lawgiver."

229. Kohlberg, "Bahā'-al-Dīn 'Āmelī."

230. Danishpazhuh, "Jami'-i Nasiri," 503.

231. Shari'atmadar, "Jami'-i Nasiri," 1445b.

232. Shari'atmadar, 1449b. See also Shari'atmadar, 1281b.

233. Ansari, "Qanun-i Nasiri," 305, 307, 309.

234. Ansari, 313, 324.

235. Ansari, 309.

236. Ansari, 314.

237. Ansari, 359.

238. Mu'allim Habibabadi, *Makarim*, 4:1170–71; al-Tihrani, *al-Dhari'ah*, 5:70, 75; Nazim al-Islam Kirmani, *Tarikh*, 145.

239. Shari'atmadar, "Jami'-i Nasiri," 1283b.

240. Shari'atmadar, 1281b, 1282a.

241. Shari'atmadar, 1443b.

242. Shari'atmadar, 1460a.

243. Shari'atmadar, 1460b, 1462b.

244. Shari'atmadar, 1482b.

245. Shari'atmadar, 1459a.

246. Shari'atmadar, 1443a–b.

247. Shari'atmadar, 1282b, 1450b.

248. al-Tihrani, *al-Dhari'ah*, 5:75; Mu'allim Habibabadi, *Makarim*, 4:1171; Nazim al-Islam Kirmani, *Tarikh*, 144, 147; Danishpazhuh, "Jami'-i Nasiri," 514.

249. Nazim al-Islam Kirmani, *Tarikh*, 147.

THREE   Policing and Punishments through *Farmans*, Codes, and Regulations

Epigraph: "Undated letter from Nasir al-Din Shah to Amin al-Mulk," in Bayani, *Panjah*, 190.

1. For critiques of Michel Foucault because he does precisely this, see Piacentini, "Punishment."

2. Fragner, "Farmān."

3. Hallaq, *Impossible*.

4. Kondo, *Islamic*, 4, 23; Werner, *Iranian*, 235.

5. Assef Ashraf has observed this dynamic with regard to petitions and *farman*s. Ashraf, "Copied."

6. Enayat claims that Amir Kabir started his own reforms by borrowing from the Ottoman Tanzimat and having a work translated from Ottoman Turkish into Persian in 1853. Enayat, *Law*, 51. He relies on a Persian article for this claim, but the citations for this assertation do not substantiate the existence of such a work. See Fath-'Alizadah, "Vazhah."

7. On the *mecelle*, see S. Ayoub, "Mecelle."

8. The Aqqoyunlu Sultan Uzun Hasan seems to have been a slightly earlier fifteenth-century exception since he had a *kanunname* dealing mostly with agricultural issues. See Peirce, "Domesticating," 121. The Safavid Shah Tahmasp issued a decree, referred to as the "law of sovereignty" (*qanun-i saltanat*), which included sixty-nine separate ordinances, including several pertaining to criminal matters. For the translation of this text, see Arjomand, *Sociology*, 159–65. This is possibly the closest Safavid equivalent to an Ottoman *kanunname*, although it does not appear to have been systematically implemented.

9. See the translation of three such decrees by the Safavid Shah Tahmasp. These decrees used the term "immoral acts" (*a'mal-i shani'*) as a way to categorize these prohibitions in a way that paralleled the terminology of Muhammad Baqir Majlisi in his Persian legal compendium. Arjomand, *Sociology*, 151–65. For Shah Tahmasp's and Shah Sultan Husayn's Persian *farman*s, see Ja'fariyan, *Din*, 434–45.

10. Cook, *Commanding*, 252–300, 531.

11. Lambton, "Hisba"; Floor, "Office."

12. Floor, "Marketpolice."

13. I'timad al-Saltanah, *Al-Ma'asir*, 163.

14. I'timad al-Saltanah, 163.

15. I'timad al-Saltanah, 163–64.

16. Enayat, *Law*, 42, 208; Kondo, *Islamic*, 17, 25.

17. I'timad al-Saltanah, *Al-Ma'asir*, 164.

18. I'timad al-Saltanah, 164.

19. Zhukovskii, *Ash'ar*, 70.

20. Zhukovskii, 70.

21. I'timad al-Saltanah, *Al-Ma'asir*, 164.

22. I'timad al-Saltanah, 165.

23. Mustawfi, *Sharh*, 3:229.

24. Mustawfi, 3:230.

25. Mustawfi, 3:230.

26. Mustawfi, 3:230.

27. Mustawfi, 3:230.

28. Martin, "Evaluation,"; Cronin, "Importing"; Rabi and Ter-Oganov, "Military."

29. On the *darughah*, see Lambton, "Evolution." On the *biglarbigi*, see Jackson, "Beglerbegī."

30. For this transformation, see Kafadar, "Janissaries."

31. Mirza Muhammad Khan Qajar Sipahsalar composed the lengthy Military Code in 1865, and it appears to have been an updated and amended version of a text written as far back as 1858. I have used the 1865 version from the Majlis Library here. Mirza Muhammad Khan Qajar Sipahsalar, "Kitabchah-i Qanun-i Nizamiyah," Majlis Library, 1865 (1282 H.), no. IR 10-49188. There was a brief notice about this code in the official government newspaper. *Ruznamah-i Dawlat-i 'Illiyah-i Iran*, n.576 (8 Jumada al-Avval 1282 H. / [September 29, 1865]). I'timad al-Saltanah referred to a military code (*qanun-i nizami*) dated 1274 H. / [1857/58] that was published in various newspapers and histories, but I have not been able to find such a code in the official newspaper for that year. I'timad al-Saltanah, *Al-Ma'asir*, 163. There was, however, a very similar version of the military code composed in April–May 1861 (Shaval 1277 H.) consisting of six rather than seven chapters. It too started with the shah's *dastkhatt* addressed to Sipahsalar, endorsing its contents and promising to punish anyone who opposed it. The catalog lists Muhammad 'Ali Jarrah-i Nizam as the author of the code, but this appears to be the copyist. Muhammad Ali Jarrah-i Nizam, "Qanun-i Qushun," Majlis Library, 1861 (1277 H.), no. 11-9884. In a letter to the shah, there is an indication that a military law was composed in which "all of the punishments are in line with French regulations [*qava'id*]," a possible partial basis for the later Military Code. "Undated letter to Nasir al-Din Shah," SAKM, no. 295/7428, folio 83. In another letter, several punishments for a Khanlar Khan were proposed to be added to "the code book of the punishment of crimes committed by a sarhang" (*kitab-i qanun-i tanbih-i taqsirat-i sarhang*) since the code did not include such punishments. "Letter," Ramazan 1278 H. / [March 1862], SAKM, no. 295/7428, folio 133. This suggests that versions of the later Military Code were being amended and expanded before 1865.

32. Sipahsalar, "Kitabchah," 52.

33. Sipahsalar, 1. Such a printed version of the text does not seem to exist.

34. Sipahsalar, 18–19.

35. Sipahsalar, 35.

36. Sipahsalar, 38–39.

37. Sipahsalar, 26.

38. Sipahsalar, 25.

39. Sipahsalar, 29.

40. Sipahsalar, 39.

41. Sipahsalar, 40.

42. Sipahsalar, 41.

43. Sipahsalar, 41.

44. Sipahsalar, 48.

45. Sipahsalar, 41.

46. Sipahsalar, 48. For a similar use of *hudud* to describe the non-*hadd* crime of desertion from the war front or a fortress, possibly because it was seen as a form of treachery in warfare (*riddah*), see Sipahsalar, 48.

47. Sipahsalar, 41. In *fiqh*, the injured party would have had the option of retaliation, compensation, or forgiveness, but the Military Code reduced the options to punishment only.

48. Sipahsalar, 43.

49. Sipahsalar, 42–43.

50. Sipahsalar, 25.

51. Sipahsalar, 45.

52. Sipahsalar, 13.

53. Sipahsalar, 14. Similar tactics were used against criminals refusing to leave a sanctuary. For a case in which the authorities in Shiraz threatened a refugee at a shrine with punishing the people attached to him and property seizure, see Vejdani, "Urban," 1199.

54. Sipahsalar, "Kitabchah," 47.

55. Sipahsalar, 47.

56. Sipahsalar, 34, 47.

57. Sipahsalar, 48.

58. [Mirza Yusuf Khan Mustawfi al-Mamalik], "Takalif-i Hukkam," SAKM, no. 295/7491, folios 75–85. Although Mustawfi al-Mamalik did not sign this administrative manual, the shah referred to its drafter as Jinab Aqa, his well-known title. For a collection of letters between the shah and Mustawfi al-Mamalik that demonstrates this, see Sa'idi, *Shah va Jinab.*

59. "Takalif-i Hukkam," 75, 85.

60. "Takalif-i Hukkam," 76.

61. "Takalif-i Hukkam," 77–78. This emphasis on provincial councils mirrored the terminology of the 1851 Ottoman Penal Code and its Persian translation.

62. "Takalif-i Hukkam," 79.

63. "Takalif-i Hukkam," 80.

64. "Takalif-i Hukkam," 83.

65. "Takalif-i Hukkam," 82.

66. "Takalif-i Hukkam," 82.

67. "Takalif-i Hukkam," 82.

68. Mustawfi al-Mamalik, "Dastur al-'Amal," 451.

69. Mustawfi al-Mamalik, 452.

70. Sipahsalar sent out a copy of the duties (*takalif*) of the guard barracks (*qaravulkhanah*s) of Tehran and referred it to Mirza Vajihullah Mirza Pishkhidmat-i Khassah, who appears to have been in charge of this institution in Tehran. *Ruzna-mah-i Iran* n.351 (18 Rabi' al-Sani 1295 H. / [April 21, 1878]). All of the citations in the following notes are to this version of the Guard Barracks Code, which was published in 1878. An earlier version with slightly different wording was published in a military newspaper in 1877. *Ruznamah-i Nizami-i 'Ilmiyah va Adabiyah*, n.4 (20 Zi Hijjah 1293 H. / [January 6, 1877]), reproduced in Sartip, "Nazm-i Qaravulkhanahha."

71. *Ruznamah-i Iran* n.351, article 12.

72. Article 5.

73. Article 1.

74. Article 15.

75. Article 7.

76. Article 7.

77. Article 17.

78. Article 18.

79. Article 18.

80. Article 18.

81. Article 18.

82. Article 11.

83. Wishnitzer, "Into the Dark," 514, 517.

84. *Ruznamah-i Iran* n.351, article 8.

85. Article 8.

86. Article 10.

87. Article 10.

88. Article 16.

89. Conte di Monteforte, "Kitabchah-i Qanun," Majlis Library, 1879 (1296 H.), no. 6, 2-20359.

90. *Ruznamah-i Iran*, n.382 (12 Rabi' al-Sani 1296 H. / [April 4, 1879]) (hereaf-ter Summary Code). The reason for two separate codes was never explained in the newspaper.

91. Kondo, *Islamic*, 25.

92. See K. Fahmy, "Anatomy."

93. Monteforte, "Kitabchah," 1.

94. Monteforte, 4.

95. Monteforte, 4–5.

96. Monteforte, 2. See also Summary Code, article 6. The codes also articu-lated the idea of spreading "justice and rights" and protecting public safety as part of shari'ah ordinances. Monteforte, "Kitabchah," 4; Summary Code, article 20.

97. Summary Code, article 18.

98. Monteforte, "Kitabchah," 4. The intention of implementing the shari'ah was so that people would further be obedient to it. Summary Code, article 6.

99. Monteforte, "Kitabchah," 5. The police were also bound to respect the 'ulama. Monteforte, 6.

100. Summary Code, article 20.

101. Summary Code, article 21. The Summary Code listed rules without always including exact punishments. It did, however, state that the government intended to announce the responsibilities of the people of Tehran with respect to the code. Summary Code, article 9.

102. Monteforte, "Kitabchah," 4, article 13.

103. Monteforte, 6–7.

104. Fahmy points out how the use of circumstantial evidence for conviction was a key feature of the *siyasah* councils in nineteenth-century Egypt. K. Fahmy, *Quest*, 83, 109.

105. Monteforte, "Kitabchah," 8, article 6.

106. Monteforte, 10, article 12.

107. Monteforte, 8, article 5.

108. Summary Code, article 3.

109. Monteforte, "Kitabchah," 7, article 3.

110. Monteforte, 8, article 4.

111. Monteforte, 7, article 1.

112. Monteforte, 7, article 2.

113. Monteforte, 13, article 20.

114. Monteforte, 13, article 24.

115. Monteforte, 12–13, article 22.

116. Monteforte, 13, article 25.

117. Monteforte, 13, article 23.

118. Monteforte, 9, article 9.

119. Monteforte, 8, article 8.

120. Monteforte, 11, article 17.

121. Monteforte, 9–10, article 11.

122. They would be imprisoned for one month to a year and fined five to ten tumans. Monteforte, 12, article 21.

123. Monteforte, 10. In *fiqh*, a sexual violator would also be responsible for monetary compensation in place of her bride-price.

124. Monteforte, 10, article 14.

125. This proprietary understanding of rape was common in pre-Islamic Near Eastern law and later in the Maliki school. Azam, *Sexual*, 24, 104–11, 115, 142, 159, 233–34.

126. Monteforte, "Kitabchah," 11, article 14.

127. Monteforte, 11, article 15.

128. Summary Code, article 10. This is the closest that code comes to discussing prostitution.

129. Monteforte, "Kitabchah," 12, article 19.

130. Monteforte, 12, article 21.

131. Monteforte, 20, article 41. See also Najmabadi, "Types," 283–84.

132. Injuring or murdering someone in the *haram* warranted a one-third increase in compensation compared to the same crime committed elsewhere. Majlisi, *Hudud*, 112; Shaykh Baha'i, *Jami'*, 2:442.

133. Monteforte, "Kitabchah," 21, article 46.

134. Summary Code, article 17.

135. Monteforte, "Kitabchah," 17, article 33.

136. Monteforte, 20, article 42.

137. Monteforte, 8, article 7; Kazemi, "Doctoring"; Rosenthal, "Herb."

138. Monteforte, "Kitabchah," 17, article 32.

139. Summary Code, article 8. For gambling in Islam, see Rosenthal, "Gambling."

140. Monteforte, "Kitabchah," 19, article 40.

141. They would receive between forty-eight hours and a month in prison and pay a fine of one to ten tumans. Monteforte, 17, article 34. A *qahvahkhanah*, despite its name, typically served tea, while a *chilupazkhanah* was a rice and kabab stall often found in the bazaar.

142. Monteforte, 17–18, article 34.

143. Monteforte, 18, article 35.

144. Monteforte, 18, article 36.

145. Monteforte, 15, articles 27–28.

146. Monteforte, 16, article 30.

147. Monteforte, 17, article 31.

148. Monteforte, 24, article 57.

149. Monteforte, 24, article 58.

150. Summary Code, article 19.

151. K. Fahmy, *Quest*, 101–3, 113, 128, 130, 187, 279, 307.

152. See Turna, "Pandemonium."

153. Monteforte, "Kitabchah," 22, article 49.

154. Monteforte, 22, article 50.

155. Summary Code, articles 11–13.

156. Summary Code, article 16.

157. Summary Code, article 14.

158. Summary Code, article 15.

159. Monteforte, "Kitabchah," 19, article 37.

160. Adamiyat and Natiq, *Afkar*, 454. For a comprehensive biography of Zill al-Sultan, see Walcher, *Shadow*.

161. Amin al-Sultan, "Dastur," 458.

162. In Ottoman usage, *'urf* meant not only custom but also political and executive authority, especially of the sultan. Heyd, *Studies*, 168–71. In Qajar usage, *'urf* was usually an executive decision or ruling made by the local government (*hukumat*) rather than the shah.

163. Amin al-Sultan, "Dastur," 458.

164. Amin al-Sultan, 460.

165. Amin al-Sultan, 460.

166. Amin al-Sultan, 461.

167. Amin al-Sultan, 461.

168. For the full text of this *farman*, see Adamiyat, *Amir*, 314. Adamiyat claims that the central government was weak, so the governors ignored this *farman*, without further evidence. Lambton claims that there was a similar *farman* outlawing torture in 1844 but does not provide a source. Lambton, "Mahkama."

169. Adamiyat, *Amir Kabir*, 314.

170. Adamiyat, 315.

171. Adamiyat, 315.

172. *Vaqayi'-i Ittifaqiyah*, n.32 (14 Zi Qi'dah 1267 H. / [September 10, 1851]). See also Adamiyat, *Amir*, 316.

173. *Vaqayi'-i Ittifaqiyah*, n.202 (23 Rabi' al-Avval 1271 H. / [December 14, 1854]).

174. This was published in *Ruznamah-i Iran*, n.26 (2 Jumada al-Avval 1288 H. / [July 20, 1871]). For further discussion, see Bakhash, *Iran*, 88–89; Karny, "Mirza Hosein," 255–56.

175. I'timad al-Saltanah, *Al-Ma'asir*, 174–75.

176. *Ruznamah-i Iran* n.26 (2 Jumada al-Avval 1288 H. / [July 20, 1871]).

177. Singha, *Despotism*, 7. A similar principle was reiterated in a 1594 Mughal administrative manual. Akbar and Abū al-Faẓl, *Mukātabāt*, 80.

178. *Ruznamah-i Iran*, n.26 (2 Jumada al-Avval 1288 H. / [July 20, 1871]).

179. "Takalif-i Hukkam," 83.

180. Singha, *Despotism*, 74.

181. *Al-Muntabi'ah Fi al-Fars*, y.1, n.10 (24 Sha'ban / [October 17, 1872]).

182. Bayani, *Panjah*, 27.

183. Bayani, 139. The shah was fearful that such practices would spread throughout the province and threatened the governor with personally punishing him if he did not stop it from happening again. Bayani, 140.

184. Ashraf, "Copied."

185. For a pathbreaking study of the Astrakhan code, see Berberian, "'Unequivocal.'"

186. Ra'in, *Iraniyan*, 120.

187. Bore, "Missions," 321. Bore translated the *farman* quoted here into English. Among the examples given were the building and repairing of places of worship, burial of the dead, building colleges for youth, contracting marriages, and transfers of power. Bore, 321–22.

188. Bore, 322.

189. Bore, 322.

190. *Vaqayi'-i Ittifaqiyah*, n.338 (1 Zi Qi'dah 1273 H. / [June 23, 1857]). The published text was clearly a *farman* since it referred to its contents as being "based on the
holy imperial command" (*'ala hasab al-amr-i aqdas al-a'la*).

191. See Abu-Mannah, "Islamic"; Ueno, "Fatherland."

192. Abu-Mannah, "Islamic."

193. *Vaqayi'-i Ittifaqiyah*, n.338.

194. *Vaqayi'-i Ittifaqiyah*, n.338.

195. Lambton argued that the basis of guarantorship among guilds was modeled on the agnate clan (*'aqilah*) system of liability. Lambton, *Islamic*, 20.

196. *Vaqayi'-i Ittifaqiyah*, n.338. The use of the term "humanity" may have
been an allusion to Mirza Malkam Khan's philosophy, which was connected to his
secret society, the "House of Oblivion" (*faramushkhanah*). See Algar, "Introduction";
A. Amanat, *Pivot*, 363–64, 384–85, 391–93.

197. I have used the full text of this document, which is reproduced in Bayani,
Panjah, 465.

198. Bayani, 466.

199. Bayani, 467.

200. Bayani, 469.

201. Bayani, 468.

202. Bayani, 466.

203. Bayani, 279. The version of the administrative manual used here, however,
was dated 1868/69 (1285 H.).

204. Bayani, 274.

205. Bayani, 274.

206. Bayani, 275.

207. A. Amanat, *Pivot*, 82, 306–7; Tsadik, *Foreigners*, 60, 66–67, 69, 74, 78, 104–6.

208. Bayani, *Panjah*, 277, article 21. Article 13 addressed the issue of single
women (*zanan-i bivah*) being taken for labor (*fi'ligi*). The *dastur al-'amal* defined
labor as a task reserved for men only. Bayani, 276.

209. Bayani, 277, article 22.

210. Bayani, 278.

211. Bayani, 278, article 24.

212. "Qanun-i Hukumat," 136. Lambton argues that from the middle of the
nineteenth century, the Qajars embarked on a project of transferring disputes between Muslims and *zimmi*s from shari'ah courts to the Divan. Lambton, "Mahkama."

213. Tsadik, "Legal," 405. In 1881/82 (1299 H), Nasir al-Din Shah relieved the
Zoroastrians of Yazd and Kerman from paying extortionate taxes. I'timad al-
Saltanah, *Al-Ma'asir*, 165. This was apparently a reference to the abolishment of the *jizyah*, although I'timad al-Saltanah did not frame it as such so as not to offend religious
sensibilities. For further context regarding this abolishment, see Farridnejad, "Royal."

214. "Takalif-i Hukkam," 83.

215. *Farhang* n.377 (Zi Qiʻdah 1303 H. / [August 1886]), reproduced in Rajaʼi, *Tarikh*, 324–26. For a study of a similar dynamic between foreign missionaries and proponents of the state on the question of religion, see Makdisi, *Culture*.

216. For studies of sanctuaries in Judaism, Christianity, and Islam, see Rabben, *Sanctuary*, 31–34; Shoemaker, *Sanctuary*; Khalisi, *Tarikhchah*.

217. See especially Westermarck, "Asylum." Asylum was also a significant theme discussed by the prominent sociologist Émile Durkheim. Durkheim, *Elementary*, 97, 207, 229, 237. René Girard elaborates on the cessation of violence and the sanctuary. Girard, *Violence*, 221.

218. See Cahen, "Himaya"; Watt, "Idjara"; Wensinck, "Al-Masjid al-Haram"; Schact, "Aman"; Savory, "Bast"; Munt, *Holy City*.

219. See Vejdani, "Urban," 1189; Eshaghi, "Quietness," 501–2.

220. Beccaria, *Beccaria*, 92.

221. Lorentz, "Iran's Great Reformer," 97; Algar, *Religion*, 133–35; Karny, "Premiership," 26–27; Khalisi, *Tarikhchah*, 20, 29, 132–33, 135–43; A. Amanat, *Pivot*, 237–38.

222. A. Amanat, *Pivot*, 150.

223. Lisan al-Mulk, *Nasikh*, 1152.

224. Lisan al-Mulk, 1152.

225. Lisan al-Mulk, 1152.

226. Lisan al-Mulk, 1153; A. Amanat, *Pivot*, 148–49.

227. Lisan al-Mulk, *Nasikh*, 1154; A. Amanat, *Pivot*, 150–51.

228. A. Amanat, *Pivot*, 118.

229. *Vaqayiʻ-i Ittifaqiyah*, n.56 (5 Jumada al-Avval 1268 H. / [February 26, 1852]).

230. *Vaqayiʻ-i Ittifaqiyah*, n.158 (11 Jumada al-Avval 1270 H. / [February 9, 1854]).

231. Shoemaker, *Sanctuary*.

232. *Vaqayiʻ-i Ittifaqiyah*, n.407 (11 Rabiʻ al-Sani 1275 H. / [October 19, 1858]).

233. "Vaqayiʻ-i Ittifaqiyah-i Dar al-ʻIlm-i Shiraz," in Bayani, *Panjah*, 42–43. See also Bayani, 48–49.

234. *Ruznamah-i Dawlat-i ʻIlliyah-i Iran*, n.499 (10 Rabiʻ al-Avval 1278 H. / [September 16, 1861]).

235. *Ruznamah-i Dawlat-i ʻIlliyah-i Iran*, n.545 (10 Muharram 1280 H. / [June 27, 1863]).

236. This implies that they did not have the right to carry out *qisas* in the shrine itself since this was taboo.

237. Fahmy points out a similar logic in nineteenth-century Egypt. K. Fahmy, *Quest*, 96, 122.

238. Bayani, *Panjah*, 44. See also Bayani, 49–50. Similarly, in *fiqh*, criminals who had taken sanctuary in the *haram* in Mecca were not to be removed violently; instead, they were to be deprived of food and water until they came out. Najafi, *Jawahir*, 41:344, 42:299–300.

239. "Takalif-i Hukkam," 83; Mustawfi al-Mamalik, "Dastur," 452–53.

FOUR Violence, Lawmaking, and Law Maintenance in Isfahan, "The Abode of Sovereignty"

1. Graeber and Sahlins, *On Kings*, 73.
2. Benjamin, *Reflections*, 283.
3. Tilly, "War Making."
4. Benjamin, *Reflections*, 283.
5. Benjamin, 284–85.
6. Muhammad Baqir Shafti, "Su'al va Javab," ms., n.d., Majlis Library, no. 11-01179. While there are similar studies of the way murder cases were handled in shari'ah court documents in other Muslim societies, nothing similar has been attempted for Qajar Iran. Peters, "Murder on the Nile"; Müller, "Crimes."
7. For the printed version, see Shafti, "Su'al va Javab," printed, 1247 H. / [1831], Majlis Library, no. 07-01311.
8. I have mostly utilized the aforementioned version of the manuscript from the Majlis Library for the cases here, although there are other versions with additional murder cases discussed later.
9. Shafti, "Su'al va Javab," ms., 322.
10. Such a conviction was on the basis of "circumstantial or incomplete evidence." Peters, *Crime*, 193.
11. Shafti, "Su'al va Javab," ms., 358. For a valuable study of the oath procedure, see Peters, "Murder in Khaybar."
12. Quran 17:33.
13. Shafti, "Su'al va Javab," ms., 358–59.
14. Shafti, 360.
15. The full text of the case discussed here is found in Ja'fariyan, *Kilk*, 184–85. Although not mentioned in Ja'fariyan's publication, the original source of the death sentence is from Muhammad Baqir Shafti, "Su'al va Javab," ms., n.d., Ayatullah Burujirdi Library, no. 424, folio 168b–169b. This version of the manuscript included this *qisas* case at the very end of the text, unlike the Majlis manuscript used here, which discusses *qisas* cases under the heading of *hudud*.
16. Tēr Hovhaneants', *Tarikh*, 321. The *Tarikh-i Bakhtiyari* traces the lineage of this group back to a group of Lurs who were taken by Nadir Shah to Khurasan and who settled in Isfahan after the shah's murder. Sipihr and Sardar As'ad, *Tarikh-i Bakhtiyari*, 491. Tahvildar mentioned that the city-dwelling Lurs resided predominantly in Lunban and Bidabad neighborhoods, while others lived in the surrounding areas of Juzdan and Sha'ish. They were typically engaged in peddling, making earthen vessels for bread, working as hired laborers in agricultural areas and the outskirts of the city, and working in various government capacities as soldiers, cavalry, and servants. Tahvildar, *Jughrafiya*, 74, 94.
17. Fasa'i, *Farsnamah*, 1:725. For an instance in which Hajji Hashim Khan and his men stole from the house of a notable (*ashraf*) who had left his home for pilgrimage, see Maftun Dunbuli, *Ma'asir*, 386–87.

18. Lisan al-Mulk, *Nasikh*, 355.

19. Lisan al-Mulk, 355. He had newlywed brides brought to him before going to the house of the groom, suggesting that he raped them. Jabiri Ansari, *Tarikh* (1999), 312.

20. Fasa'i, *Farsnamah*, 1:726; Shirazi, *Tarikh*, 595.

21. Chamich, *History*, 538.

22. Fasa'i, *Farsnamah*, 1:725.

23. Chodźko, *Specimens*, 445–46. This popular poem, which I have quoted here, was translated by Chodźko directly. In his work, he did not include the original Persian poem.

24. Tēr Hovhaneants', *Tarikh*, 323; Wolff, *Missionary*, 90–91.

25. Tēr Hovhaneants', *Tarikh*, 321; Wolff, *Missionary*, 90–91.

26. Chamich, *History*, 538–45. This episode is also mentioned in Tēr Hovhaneants', *Tarikh*, 322–25. For more on the life of Amin al-Dawlah, see A. Amanat, "Amīn-al-Dawla."

27. Lisan al-Mulk, *Nasikh*, 356. For further discussion about the precise kinship connection between Amin al-Dawlah and Hajji Hashim Khan's father, Hajji Rajab 'Ali, see Tahvildar, *Jughrafiya*, 74; Fasa'i, *Farsnamah*, 1:725.

28. Fasa'i, *Farsnamah*, 1:726. The original source of this passage appears to be Shirazi, *Tarikh*, 594–96.

29. Maftun Dunbuli, *Ma'asir*, 326–27.

30. Shirazi, *Tarikh*, 595; Maftun Dunbuli, *Ma'asir*, 387–88.

31. Jabiri Ansari, *Tarikh* (1999), 89.

32. Jabiri Ansari, 89; Tēr Hovhaneants', *Tarikh*, 327.

33. Maftun Dunbuli, *Ma'asir*, 388; Tēr Hovhaneants', *Tarikh*, 326; Fasa'i, *Farsnamah*, 1:726; Lisan al-Mulk, *Nasikh*, 326; Chamich, *History*, 545–49; Tahvildar, *Jughrafiya*, 75.

34. *Oriental Herald* 9 (1826): 171. For a similarly detailed account, see *Asiatic Journal* 21 (1826): 402.

35. Bamdad, *Sharh-i Hal*, 5:328.

36. Lisan al-Mulk, *Nasikh*, 356.

37. Lisan al-Mulk, 356; Jabiri Ansari, *Tarikh-i Isfahan va Ray*, 42–44. For further elaboration, see Lambton, *Landlord*, 440–41.

38. Tēr Hovhaneants', *Tarikh*, 330–31.

39. See Nasiri, Rahmanian, and Khurasani, "Lutiyan," 110; Algar, *Religion*, 110.

40. Bore, "Missions," 320.

41. De Bode, *Travels*, 1:49.

42. Graeber, *Debt*, 226–27.

43. Tēr Hovhaneants', *Tarikh*, 333.

44. De Bode, *Travels*, 1:49.

45. For background on Shafti, see Iqbal, "Hujjat"; Schneider, "Muḥammad Bāqir Šaftī."

46. Tunakabuni, *Qisas*, 357; Arjomand, *Shadow*, 232–33.

47. Tunakabuni, *Qisas*, 352–53, 356, 368–69; Arjomand, *Shadow*, 238–39. The Qajars sought other ways to make strategic alliances in the city, most notably through intermarriage with local elites. See Ashraf, "Khan," 151–52.

48. Fraser, *Travels*, 283.

49. De Bode, *Travels*, 1:49.

50. De Bode, 1:50.

51. Lisan al-Mulk, *Nasikh*, 597.

52. Duindam, *Dynasties*, 194.

53. Lisan al-Mulk, *Nasikh*, 597–98.

54. Hambly, "Farmānfarmā."

55. Lisan al-Mulk, *Nasikh*, 598. See also Tēr Hovhaneants', *Tarikh*, 333.

56. Tēr Hovhaneants', *Tarikh*, 333.

57. Tēr Hovhaneants', 335–37.

58. Bamdad, *Sharh-i Hal*, 4:161–2. See also Nasiri, Rahmanian, and Khurasani, "Lutiyan," 112. A recent critical edition and scholarly introduction to a series of poems dedicated to Manuchihr Khan shed further light on him. Muzahhab Isfahani, *Muqaddamah*.

59. Flandin and Coste, *Safarnamah*, 134.

60. Lisan al-Mulk, *Nasikh*, 741; Hidayat, *Fihris*, 453; Sercey, *Iran*, 195; I'timad al-Saltanah, *Tarikh*, 1647.

61. Heern, *Emergence*, 225–26.

62. Flandin and Coste, *Safarnamah*, 134.

63. Flandin and Coste, 119–20.

64. Hidayat, *Fihris*, 453; Tilly, "War Making."

65. A. Amanat, *Pivot*, 28–29; A. Amanat, *Resurrection*, 79–80; Algar, *Religion*, 105–7.

66. Lisan al-Mulk, *Nasikh*, 741.

67. Zill al-Sultan, *Tarikh*, 383. Zill al-Sultan mentions Mirza 'Abd al-Husayn Shamsabadi as the scion of the Safavid dynasty, but contemporary sources that mention him do not connect him to the Safavids. He did, however, ally himself with the Safavid *navvabs* in a later episode against the governor, Ghulam Husayn Sipahdar.

68. Lisan al-Mulk, *Nasikh*, 742; I'timad al-Saltanah, *Tarikh*, 1648. See also Calmard, "Moḥammad Shah."

69. Flandin and Coste, *Safarnamah*, 134; Sercey, *Iran*, 195–96. For a discussion of this episode, see Nasiri, Rahmanian, and Khurasani, "Lutiyan," 113.

70. Hidayat, *Tarikh*, 10:8272; Flandin and Coste, *Safarnamah*, 134.

71. Flandin and Coste, *Safarnamah*, 134; Sercey, *Iran*, 191–92.

72. See Lisan al-Mulk, *Nasikh*, 742; I'timad al-Saltanah, *Tarikh*, 1648; Hidayat, *Tarikh*, 10:8272; Sercey, *Iran*, 191–92.

73. Tēr Hovhaneants', *Tarikh*, 337.

74. Flandin and Coste, *Safarnamah*, 141. According to Tēr Hovhaneants', the shah blamed the Imam Jum'ah for this event and wanted to ensure that he "did not overstep his boundaries." Tēr Hovhaneants', *Tarikh*, 337.

75. Flandin and Coste, *Safarnamah*, 141.

76. De Bode, *Travels*, 1:450–51.

77. There are few studies of Manuchihr Khan. For a brief biography, see Bam-dad, *Sharh-i Hal*, 4:159–63.

78. For this episode, see Lisan al-Mulk, *Nasikh*, 767–77; Bamdad, *Sharh-i Hal*, 4:162; Khazeni, *Tribes*, 50.

79. Floor, "Judicial."

80. Bamdad, *Sharh-i Hal*, 4:162.

81. Bamdad, 4:159.

82. Jabiri Ansari, *Tarikh* (1999), 45.

83. Tēr Hovhaneants', *Tarikh*, 339–40.

84. Flandin and Coste, *Safarnamah*, 240–42.

85. Flandin and Coste, 243.

86. Flandin and Coste, 243.

87. Tēr Hovhaneants', *Tarikh*, 341–42.

88. Isfahani, *Vajizat*, 19.

89. "Vaqayi'-i Dar al-Saltanah-i Isfahan I," ms., 1256 H. / 1840, Malik Library, no. 2256133 (August 2, 1840 / 4 Jumada al-Sani, 1256 H.).

90. "Vaqayi' I" (August 5, 1840 / 7 Jumada al-Sani, 1256 H.).

91. "Vaqayi'-i Dar al-Saltanah-i Isfahan II," ms., 1257 H. / 1841, Malik Library, no. 1080902 (June 5, 1841 / 15 Rabi' al-Sani, 1257 H.).

92. "Vaqayi' I" (July 30, 1840 / 1 Jumada al-Sani, 1256 H.; August 6, 1840 / 8 Jumada al-Sani, 1256 H.).

93. "Vaqayi' I" (August 7, 1840 / 9 Jumada al-Sani, 1256 H.).

94. "Vaqayi' I" (August 4, 1840 / 6 Jumada al-Sani, 1256 H.).

95. "Vaqayi' I" (August 3, 1840 / 5 Jumada al-Sani, 1256 H.).

96. "Vaqayi' II" (May 30, 1841 / 9 Rabi' al-Sani, 1257 H.).

97. "Vaqayi' II" (May 24, 1841 / 3 Rabi' al-Sani, 1257 H.).

98. "Vaqayi' II" (May 24, 1841 / 3 Rabi' al-Sani, 1257 H.).

99. For the parallel use of "guarantee" (*daman*) in early nineteenth-century Alexandria, see K. Fahmy, "Social," 296–98.

100. "Vaqayi' I" (August 4, 1840 / 6 Jumada al-Sani, 1256 H.).

101. "Vaqayi' I" (August 8, 1840 / 10 Jumada al-Sani, 1256 H.).

102. "Vaqayi' I" (August 3, 1840 / 5 Jumada al-Sani, 1256 H.).

103. "Vaqayi' I" (August 4, 1840 / 6 Jumada al-Sani, 1256 H.).

104. "Vaqayi' I" (August 8, 1840 / 10 Jumada al-Sani, 1256 H.).

105. Najmabadi notes that a man who shaved his beard in nineteenth-century Iran was referred to as *amradnuma*, meaning "looking like an *amrad*." Najmabadi, *Women*, 16.

106. "Vaqayi'-i Dar al-Saltanah-i Isfahan III," ms., 1257 H. / 1841, Malik Library, no. 1080909. (April 22, 1841 / 29 Safar, 1257 H.).

107. "Vaqayi' I" (August 4, 1840 / 6 Jumada al-Sani, 1256 H.).

108. "Vaqayi' III" (April 9, 1841 / 16 Safar, 1257 H.).

109. "Vaqayi' III" (April 10, 1841 / 17 Safar, 1257 H.).

110. "Vaqayi' I" (August 7, 1840 / 9 Jumada al-Sani 1256 H.).

111. "Vaqayi' I" (August 5, 1840 / 7 Jumada al-Sani, 1256 H.).

112. "Vaqayi' II" (May 29, 1841 / 8 Rabi' al-Sani, 1257 H.).

113. "Vaqayi' II" (May 28, 1841 / 9 Rabi' al-Sani, 1257 H.).

114. "Vaqayi' III" (April 11, 1841 / 18 Safar, 1257 H.).

115. Tēr Hovhaneants', *Tarikh*, 344.

116. Tēr Hovhaneants', 351, 354. The account of Rustam Big's murder produced here is based on two firsthand, Armenian-language reports published in the Calcutta journal *Azgasar* in 1848. The text of both accounts in Persian translation is provided in Tēr Hovhaneants', 351–53, 354–59.

117. Tēr Hovhaneants', 354–56.

118. Tēr Hovhaneants', 357.

119. Tēr Hovhaneants', 352–53, 358–59.

120. Lisan al-Mulk, *Nasikh*, 1001–2; Hidayat, *Tarikh*, 10:8519; Khurmuji, *Haqa'iq*, 55. The term *manshur* was often used interchangeably with *farman* and *hukm* in Qajar sources.

121. Lisan al-Mulk, *Nasikh*, 1002.

122. Zanganah, "Vaqayi'," 192.

123. Tēr Hovhaneants', *Tarikh*, 345–50.

124. Mu'allim Habibabadi, *Makarim*, 5:1803–4.

125. Zanganah, "Vaqayi'," 191.

126. Zanganah, 191; Lisan al-Mulk, *Nasikh*, 1002; Hidayat, *Tarikh*, 10:8519.

127. Zanganah, "Vaqayi'," 192.

128. Zanganah, 192; Lisan al-Mulk, *Nasikh*, 1002.

129. Zanganah, "Vaqayi'," 192–93; Lisan al-Mulk, *Nasikh*, 1002; Hidayat, *Tarikh*, 10:8520.

130. Zanganah, "Vaqayi'," 193.

131. Zanganah, 193.

132. Zanganah, 193.

133. A. Amanat, *Pivot*, 123–24; Algar, *Religion*, 126.

134. This episode is explored by a number of scholars, although none of them fully explores its implications for sovereignty and juridical authority. Algar focuses on the relationship between the state and the 'ulama in the episode and rightfully points out that there were clear divisions among the 'ulama as to whether they should support the state or the opposition. Martin, on the other hand, is interested in how the episode illustrates the tendency of the state to negotiate with social movements. Her account incorrectly identifies 'Abd al-Husayn Vazir as a member of the Safavid navvab family, when, in fact, he was merely allied with them. Finally, Walcher sees the episode as an example of how local Isfahani factions resisted Qajar state centralization, although it is clear that there were local elements that were willing to cooperate with the state in order to bolster their power vis-à-vis their enemies. Algar, *Religion*, 126–28; Martin, *Qajar*, 76–77; Walcher, "Isfahan." For a detailed and accurate account

of the episode, one that closely parallels the account provided here, see Tulabi and Zargarinizhad, "Daramad," 435–42.

135. Lisan al-Mulk, *Nasikh*, 1078; Khurmuji, *Haqa'iq*, 77. Hidayat provides the wrong year (1266 H. instead of 1265 H.) for the start of his governorship. Hidayat, *Tarikh*, 10:8520.

136. Hidayat, *Tarikh*, 10:8520; Khurmuji, *Haqa'iq*, 77.

137. Farajullah Munshi, "Tarikh," 444.

138. Hidayat, *Tarikh*, 10:8520.

139. Khurmuji, *Haqa'iq*, 77; Lisan al-Mulk, *Nasikh*, 1078; Abbott, *Cities*, 127.

140. Khurmuji, *Haqa'iq*, 77.

141. Hidayat, *Tarikh*, 10:8521.

142. Khurmuji, *Haqa'iq*, 77; Lisan al-Mulk, *Nasikh*, 1078–79; Hidayat, *Tarikh*, 10:8521; Farajullah Munshi, "Tarikh," 445.

143. Lisan al-Mulk, *Nasikh*, 1079.

144. Lisan al-Mulk, 1079.

145. Lisan al-Mulk, 1079; Khurmuji, *Haqa'iq*, 77; Hidayat, *Tarikh*, 10:8521; Abbott, *Cities*, 127; Farajullah Munshi, "Tarikh," 445–46.

146. Farajullah Munshi, "Tarikh," 448.

147. Khurmuji, *Haqa'iq*, 77; Lisan al-Mulk, *Nasikh*, 1079; Hidayat, *Tarikh*, 10:8521–22.

148. Lisan al-Mulk, *Nasikh*, 1079.

149. Farajullah Munshi, "Tarikh," 450.

150. For a detailed discussion of the juristic discourse around this crime and its punishments, see Abou El Fadl, *Rebellion*, 100–161.

151. Lisan al-Mulk, *Nasikh*, 1080. According to Farajullah Munshi, Asadullah's attitude toward the opposition was much more ambivalent. He accused Asadullah of secretly helping the evildoers (*ashrar*) by having them released. Farajullah Munshi, "Tarikh," 452.

152. Khurmuji, *Haqa'iq*, 78.

153. Abbott, *Cities*, 127.

154. Farajullah Munshi, "Tarikh," 450.

155. Farajullah Munshi, 450.

156. Farajullah Munshi, 450–51.

157. Khurmuji, *Haqa'iq*, 78; Hidayat, *Tarikh*, 10:8522.

158. Lisan al-Mulk, *Nasikh*, 1081.

159. Hidayat, *Tarikh*, 10:8522; Lisan al-Mulk, *Nasikh*, 1081; Khurmuji, *Haqa'iq*, 78; Farajullah Munshi, "Tarikh," 451.

160. Lisan al-Mulk, *Nasikh*, 1081; Farajullah Munshi, "Tarikh," 452.

161. Farajullah Munshi, "Tarikh," 453–54.

162. Lisan al-Mulk, *Nasikh*, 1083. For a slightly different account of this episode and the Imam Jum'ah's speech, in which he calls the opposition "stirrers of sedition" (*mufsidan*), "atheists" (*mulhidan*), "rebels [*muharib*] against religion," and "traitors against the sultan of Iran," implying that they deserved a death sentence, see Farajullah Munshi, "Tarikh," 458.

163. It is unclear what type of jihad is meant here in light of multiple contemporary understandings of the term. Robert Gleave makes a distinction between a jihad in accordance with Shi'i jurisprudence, which is basically impossible in the absence of the Imam, and jihad to mean collective defense, which is possible and carries no liability for bloodshed. Gleave, "Jihad."

164. Farajullah Munshi, "Tarikh," 460.

165. Lisan al-Mulk, Nasikh, 1084. See also Khurmuji, Haqa'iq, 78.

166. Hidayat, Tarikh, 10:8523.

167. Farajullah Munshi, "Tarikh," 460.

168. Farajullah Munshi, 460.

169. Lisan al-Mulk, Nasikh, 1085–86; Khurmuji, Haqa'iq, 79.

170. Lisan al-Mulk, Nasikh, 1086; Hidayat, Tarikh, 10:8524; Khurmuji, Haqa'iq, 79. For an account of his last days before his capture that suggests he was duped into coming back to Isfahan by his host, see Sayyah Mahallati, Khatirat, 50–52.

171. Lisan al-Mulk, Nasikh, 1085.

172. Farajullah Munshi, "Tarikh," 462.

173. Khurmuji, Haqa'iq, 96.

174. Hidayat, Tarikh, 10:8524.

175. For more on Amir Kabir and his reforms, see Adamiyat, Amir, 118–68.

176. For brief biographies, see Bamdad, Sharh-i Hal, 1:300–301; Sa'adat Nuri, Rijal, 182–88; MacEoin, "Čerāğ-'Alī." Adamiyat describes Chiragh 'Ali as a trusted government servant whom Amir Kabir sent on secret missions on his behalf. Adamiyat, Amir, 72. Chiragh 'Ali was the chief negotiator sent to deal with Hasan Khan Salar's rebellion in Khurasan, which started in 1848. A. Amanat, Pivot, 115.

177. Zanganah, "Vaqayi'," 196.

178. Lisan al-Mulk, Nasikh, 1124–26.

179. Zanganah, "Vaqayi'," 195.

180. Zanganah, 194–95.

181. Zanganah, 196. For another brief account, see Lisan al-Mulk, Nasikh, 1124.

182. On the importance of forts as a means of securing autonomy for the Bahktiyaris, see Khazeni, Tribes, 51.

183. Zanganah, "Vaqayi'," 196; Lisan al-Mulk, Nasikh, 1124–25.

184. Zanganah, "Vaqayi'," 197.

185. Zanganah, 198.

186. Zanganah, 198.

187. Zanganah, 198–99.

188. Zanganah, 200.

189. Zanganah, 201. For a brief account of this episode, see Lisan al-Mulk, Nasikh, 1125.

190. Moojan Momen explores this episode using sources for Babi history rather than government sources or Chiragh 'Ali's firsthand account. Momen, "Persecution," 472. The other sources he uses are as follows: 'Abdu'l-Baha, Traveller's Narrative, 2:331; Nicolas, Seyyèd Ali, 430. Riza Quli Khan Hidayat's account provides an

important window into the shari'ah procedure used in this case: "Among the strange occurrences during these days was that in the city of Isfahan, there were two ignorant afflicted people [*majhul masru'*] from the misguided Babi sect. One claimed specific prophethood [*nubuvvat-i khassah*], and the other claimed vicegerency [*vilayat*]. The 'ulama issued *fatvas* declaring both to be infidels [*bih kufr-i har du fatva nivishtand*] and agreeing on a death sentence [*vajib al-qatland*]. Chiragh 'Ali Khan, the assistant governor, according to the *fatva* of the learned 'ulama and the jurists of Islam [*fuqaha-yi Islam*] had both of them killed in the Naqsh-i Jahan Square." Hidayat, *Tarikh*, 10:8598. A brief discussion of this episode is also available in Khurmuji, *Haqa'iq*, 95.

191. Mazandarani, *Tarikh*, 4:19.

192. Zanganah, "Vaqayi'," 202.

193. Zanganah, 202–3.

194. Mazandarani, *Tarikh*, 4:19.

195. Mazandarani, 4:20.

196. Mazandarani, 4:20; Zanganah, "Vaqayi'," 203. In the official newspaper account, the 'ulama's rulings are referred to as *fatvas*, saying that the figures in question were to be "sentenced to death" (*vajib al-qatl*). *Vaqayi'-i Ittifaqiyah*, n.48 (9 Rabi' al-Avval 1268 H. / [January 1, 1852]).

197. Mazandarani, *Tarikh*, 4:20; Zanganah, "Vaqayi'," 203.

198. Zanganah, "Vaqayi'," 203; Lisan al-Mulk, *Nasikh*, 1126. According to Fazil-i Mazandarani, the ruffians (*ashrar*) repeatedly desecrated the Babis' corpses and even dug them up after their initial burial. Mazandarani, *Tarikh*, 4:20–21. On the desecration of Baha'i burial sites, see M. Amanat, "Set in Stone."

199. *Vaqayi'-i Ittifaqiyah*, no. 48.

200. For accounts of the meeting between the Bab and Manuchihr Khan, see Nabil Zarandi, *Dawn-Breakers*, 199–216; 'Abdu'l-Baha, *Traveller's Narrative*, 2:264–68; Lisan al-Mulk, *Nasikh*, 1010–11. For a scholarly treatment of the episode, see A. Amanat, *Resurrection*, 268.

201. Zanganah, "Vaqayi'," 203.

202. Zanganah, 204. According to the official government newspaper account, it was his bloodied hat (*kulah*) that was found close to a tower (*burj*). *Vaqayi'-i Ittifaqiyah*, n.76 (27 Ramazan 1268 H. / [July 15, 1852]).

203. Zanganah, "Vaqayi'," 204.

204. *Vaqayi'-i Ittifaqiyah*, n.76.

205. *Vaqayi'-i Ittifaqiyah*, n.76.

206. Zanganah, "Vaqayi'," 204.

207. *Vaqayi'-i Ittifaqiyah*, n.76.

208. Zanganah, "Vaqayi'," 204. In the government newspaper account, the sons take part in the *qisas* as well. The accounts are consistent insofar as strangulation by rope was the manner of retaliation. *Vaqayi'-i Ittifaqiyah*, n.76.

209. Zanganah, "Vaqayi'," 204. For a brief account of this episode, see Lisan al-Mulk, *Nasikh*, 1126.

FIVE   Policing Vice in Shiraz

1. Sa'idi Sirjani, *Vaqayi'*, 582 (10 Jumada al-Avval 1317 H. / September 17, 1899).

2. Sa'idi Sirjani, 583 (20 Jumada al-Avval 1317 H. / September 27, 1899).

3. Hafiz, *Divan*, 100. For a recent study of Hafiz's verse, one that calls into question the reduction of his libertine verses to Sufi metaphors, see Brookshaw, *Hafiz*.

4. For case studies of policing and surveillance in Muslim societies, see Petry, *Criminal*, 123–64; Zarinebaf, *Crime*, 125–40; Başaran, *Selim III*; K. Fahmy, "Police"; Ileri, "Rule."

5. Cook, *Commanding*.

6. Stilt, *Islamic*.

7. Ja'fariyan, *Din*, 434, 439, 442–44; Cook, *Commanding*, 300.

8. Lambton, "Hisba," 491.

9. For more on Falasiri, see Falasiri and Shirazi, *Durnama'i*; Rahmati, Shakuri, and Sha'bani, *Naqsh*.

10. Cook, *Commanding*, 252–300.

11. Lange, "Legal."

12. Peters, *Crime*, 59–61. For a discussion of the function of *hudud* penalties in the Ottoman context, see Katz, "Ḥadd."

13. Rabb, "Islamic Rule," 1332.

14. Prostitution in nineteenth-century Iran has received relatively little attention. For twentieth-century studies, see Gahan, "Red-Light"; Hosseini, "Zoned."

15. For a book-length discussion of sexual violation in Islamic law, see Azam, *Sexual*. In fact, there is no single term for rape in Persian and Arabic sources of the time. A commonly used Islamic legal term for rape was *ghasb*, a form of forced property appropriation or, in some contexts, a form of property damage.

16. For thoughtful discussions of similar issues in the Ottoman context, see Tuğ, *Politics*; Semerdjian, *Straight*.

17. According to Heinrich Brugsch, it was located a mere fifty steps away from the grave of Sa'di. Brugsch, *Sarzamin*, 328. See also Curzon, *Persia*, 107; Sykes, *Ten Thousand*, 322. Binning's informant claimed that the well was no longer being used for this purpose during his time. Binning, *Journal*, 1:300. For a detailed discussion, see Betteridge, "Ziarat," 305.

18. This event had taken place seventeen years before Wills visited Shiraz, meaning sometime between the late 1840s and the early 1860s. Wills, *Land*, 275–76.

19. Najafi, *Jawahir*, 41:400–401.

20. Foucault, *Discipline*, 32–72.

21. Wills, *Land*, 276.

22. See Leviticus 20:10; Deuteronomy 22:22.

23. *Jewish Chronicle*, April 10, 1896, in Yeroushalmi, *Jews*, 229.

24. For concerns with moral pollution, or moral contagion, and the politics of space, see Hamadeh, "Mean." For broader discussions of contagion and law, see Stearns, *Infectious*.

25. Saʿidi Sirjani, *Vaqayiʿ*, 73 (7 Jumada al-Sani–13 Rajab 1294 H. / July 19–24, 1877).

26. Al-Hallaq, "Barber," 568.

27. Perhaps this also signified that his hair sparked the sexual arousal of his patrons.

28. *Farhang*, n.449 (1 Shaʿban 1304 H. / [April 25, 1887]). For banishment as a punishment for prostitution and sexual vice, see Hamadeh, "Mean," 266; Semerdjian, *Straight*, 99, 128.

29. Why he did so was not immediately clear, but it might have been that he was sexually attracted to a woman who resembled a man and that he was excited by the idea of appearing with a barefaced and unveiled woman in public. For an important study of shifting gender norms during the Qajar period and the anxieties surrounding it, see Najmabadi, *Women*.

30. Saʿidi Sirjani, *Vaqayiʿ*, 602 (20 Zi Qiʿdah 1317 H. / March 22, 1900).

31. According to *fiqh* manuals, individuals (especially those who were in a subordinate position) who witnessed their relatives committing misdeeds were dissuaded from reporting it to the authorities; instead, they were to gently advise their relatives to change their behavior. Alshech, "'Do Not Enter," 300–301. Al-Ghazali similarly encouraged concealing the sins of fellow Muslims, presumably witnessed in private. Reza, "Islam's," 742. Within the domicile, Islamic scholars "enabled people to conceal information about themselves that society considered degrading, such as information about immoral behavior, illegal acts, intimate body parts, etc." Alshech, "Out of Sight," 268. In the aforementioned case, the sister may have reported it to the *biglarbigi* and asked him only to punish the prostitute and not her brother. She was seeking to "publicize" the existence of the prostitute while protecting the misdeeds of her brother.

32. Saʿidi Sirjani, *Vaqayiʿ*, 609 (1 Safar 1318 H. / May 30, 1900).

33. K. Fahmy, *Quest*, 199–200.

34. Mottahedeh and Stilt, "Public," 740.

35. Saʿidi Sirjani, *Vaqayiʿ*, 466 (16 Rabiʿ al-Sani 1312 H. / October 16, 1894).

36. For an anthropological study of temporary marriage in Iran, see Haeri, *Law*.

37. Saʿidi Sirjani, *Vaqayiʿ*, 671 (28 Muharram 1320 H. / May 7, 1902).

38. Some people believed that the *karguzar* wrote the anonymous text in order to profit from it, perhaps by extorting the Christian merchant. The governor, Asif al-Dawlah, seems to have believed this, since he met with the *karguzar* and addressed him harshly. Saʿidi Sirjani, 673 (28 Safar 1320 H. / June 4, 1902).

39. This was different from the eighteenth-century Ottoman Empire, where urban residents were collectively punished if prostitution occurred in their neighborhood. Wishnitzer, "Into the Dark," 516; Marcus, *Middle East*, 117.

40. Saʿidi Sirjani, *Vaqayiʿ*, 686 (12 Rajab 1320 H. / October 11, 1902). The continued consideration of wells to punish deviant women suggests that this association did not entirely disappear.

41. Al-Ghazali believed that individual Muslims could act as *muhtasibs* and that *muhtasibs* could seek the help of armed individuals (not necessarily government officials) in commanding good and forbidding wrong. Reza, "Islam's," 740, 742. For a fuller treatment of his views, see Cook, *Commanding*, 427–68.

42. *Ruznamah-i Dawlat-i 'Illiyah-i Iran*, n.475 (2 Rabi' al-Sani 1277 H. / [October 17, 1860]).

43. "Guzarish az Dar al-'Ilm-i Shiraz," in Bayani, *Panjah*, 367. The undated document is from the Iranian Ministry of Foreign Affairs Archive.

44. This is a slightly different name for the Military Code discussed in chapter 3.

45. Sa'idi Sirjani, *Vaqayi'*, 578–79 (22 Rabi' al-Sani 1317 H. / August 30, 1899).

46. *Ruznamah-i Dawlat-i 'Illiyah-i Iran*, n.604 (17 Safar 1284 H. / [June 20, 1867]).

47. Sa'idi Sirjani, *Vaqayi'*, 363–64 (1 Muharram 1308 H. / August 17, 1890).

48. Sa'idi Sirjani, 444 (14 Jumada al-Sani 1311 H. / December 23, 1893).

49. *Farhang*, n.412 (20 Rabi' al-Avval 1303 H. / [December 16, 1886]). This is yet another reference to the Military Code.

50. Sa'idi Sirjani, *Vaqayi'*, 584 (28 Jumada al-Avval 1317 H. / October 5, 1899).

51. Sa'idi Sirjani, 602 (20 Zi Qi'dah 1317 H. / March 22, 1900).

52. Note that this was consistent with what happened to the Jewish woman in the aforementioned case of adultery.

53. Sa'idi Sirjani, *Vaqayi'*, 602 (20 Zi Qi'dah 1317 H. / March 22, 1900).

54. For a discussion of the case of Jews converting to Islam in order to take sanctuary at the Imam Riza Shrine in Mashhad, see M. Amanat, *Jewish*, 47–56; Tsadik, *Foreigners*, 34–36.

55. The use of the bridle could be seen as a means of bestialization and dehumanization. For a discussion of this process, see Lange and Fierro, "Spatial," 7.

56. Sa'idi Sirjani, *Vaqayi'*, 638 (19 Muharram 1319 H. / May 8, 1901).

57. Sa'idi Sirjani, 609 (1 Safar 1318 H. / May 30, 1900).

58. Sa'idi Sirjani, 707 (12 Rabi' al-Avval 1321 H. / June 9, 1903).

59. Marcus has made this point forcefully in the case of eighteenth-century Aleppo. Marcus, "Privacy," 170–71, 177.

60. Sa'idi Sirjani, *Vaqayi'*, 582 (10 Jumada al-Avval 1317 H. / September 17, 1899).

61. Ussher, *Journey*, 512.

62. "Report," 29 Safar 1284 H. / [July 3, 1867], SAKM, no. 295/7245, folio 12.

63. "Report," 7 Rabi' al-Avval 1284 H. / [July 9, 1867], SAKM, no. 295/7245, folio 48.

64. Tsadik, *Foreigners*, 11.

65. The Pact of 'Umar mentions that Jews should cut their forelocks as part of this differentiation. See Rooijakkers, "Luscious," 44–45.

66. Sa'idi Sirjani, *Vaqayi'*, 139 (5 Ramazan–20 Ramazan 1298 H. / August 1–16, 1881).

67. For a discussion of Shafti's views, see chapter 1.

68. Sa'idi Sirjani, *Vaqayi'*, 139 (5 Ramazan–20 Ramazan 1298 H. / August 1–16, 1881).

69. Sa'idi Sirjani, 139–40 (5 Ramazan–20 Ramazan 1298 H. / August 1–16, 1881); Matthee, *Pursuit*, 195–96.

70. "Telegram from the Minister of Foreign Affairs to Sahib Divan," 18 Sha'ban 1299 H. / [July 4, 1882], SAKM, no. 295/7679, folios 356–57.

71. "Telegram from Fath 'Ali Sahib Divan to the Minister of Foreign Affairs," 22 Sha'ban 1299 H. / [July 8, 1882], SAKM, no. 295/7679, folio 357.

72. Sa'idi Sirjani, *Vaqayi'*, 470 (17 Jumada al-Avval 1312 H. / November 16, 1894); Matthee, *Pursuit*, 196.

73. Sa'idi Sirjani, *Vaqayi'*, 470 (17 Jumada al-Avval 1312 H. / November 16, 1894); Matthee, *Pursuit*, 196.

74. Sa'idi Sirjani, 470 (17 Jumada al-Avval 1312 H. / November 16, 1894).

75. Sa'idi Sirjani, 714–15 (3 Jumada al-Avval 1321 H. / July 28, 1903).

76. The *na'ib* seems to be the same figure as the Muslim *kadkhuda* of the Jewish neighborhood.

77. Sa'idi Sirjani, *Vaqayi'*, 728 (4 Zi Qi'dah 1321 H. / January 22, 1904).

78. Sa'idi Sirjani, 229 (18 Zi Hijjah 1301 H. / October 19, 1884); Matthee, *Pursuit*, 196.

79. *Farhang*, n.454 (18 Sha'ban 1304 H. / [May 12, 1887]).

80. For discussions of this prohibition and its importance in *hisbah* manuals, see Stilt, *Islamic*, 96–97; Reza, "Islam's," 723–28; Cook, *Commanding*, 80; Klein, "Public," 48–49.

81. Badi'i, *Guzarishha*, 39 (15 Zi al-Hijjah 1307 H. / August 2, 1890).

82. Sa'idi Sirjani, *Vaqayi'*, 186 (14 Rajab 1300 H. / May 2, 1883).

83. Sa'idi Sirjani, 280–81 (25 Jumada al-Avval 1304 H. / February 19, 1887). The Sahib Divan was fond of frequenting the Dilgusha Garden, which he built on the hillside of Tang-i Allah Akbar. For this, he was mocked in a popular song (*tasnif*). See Browne, *Year*, 283–84.

84. Lange, "On That Day."

85. "Report on Events Occurring in Fars Province," Ramazan 1306 H. / [May/June 1889], SAKM, no. 295/7650, folio 110.

86. Faruqi, "Music," 22; Klein, "Music," 215–16; Shiloah, "Music," 147–48.

87. For a productive study of soundscapes in Egypt and its significance in everyday life, see Z. Fahmy, *Street Sounds*.

88. The accounts of this episode found in Iranian and British archives are largely consistent. For the latter, I have relied on C. E. Davies's excellent dissertation on Fars province. "Letter from Minister of Foreign Affairs to Nasir al-Din Shah," 14 Jumada al-Avval 1284 H. / [September 13, 1867], SAKM, no. 295/7245, folio 287; Davies, "History," 80–81.

89. "Report on Events Occurring in Fars Province," Ramazan 1306 H. / [May/June 1889], SAKM, no. 295/7650, folio 110.

NOTES TO PAGES 206–19

90. Sa'idi Sirjani, *Vaqayi'*, 338 (28 Zi Qi'dah 1306 H. / July 27, 1889).

91. Sa'idi Sirjani, 339 (28 Zi Qi'dah 1306 H. / July 27, 1889).

92. The use of the term *hadd* is strange because the playing of music did not constitute one of the recognized *hadd* offenses.

93. Badi'i, *Guzarishha*, 37–38 (17 Zi Qi'dah 1307 H. / July 5, 1890).

94. Sa'idi Sirjani, *Vaqayi'*, 339 (28 Zi Hijjah 1306 H. / August 28, 1889).

95. Sa'idi Sirjani, 409 (29 Zi Hijjah 1309 H. / July 25, 1892).

96. Sa'idi Sirjani, 588 (11 Rajab 1317 H. / November 16, 1899).

97. Sa'idi Sirjani, 616 (19 Rabi' al-Sani 1319 H. / August 16, 1900).

98. Sa'idi Sirjani, 597 (20 Shaval 1317 H. / February 21, 1900).

99. Sa'idi Sirjani, 597–98 (20 Shaval 1317 H. / February 21, 1900).

100. Sa'idi Sirjani, 719 (6 Rajab 1321 H. / September 28, 1903).

101. Weber, "Politics," 78.

SIX Murder in Shiraz

1. For scholarship on homicide in Muslim societies, see Anderson, "Homicide"; Peters, *Crime*, 38–53; K. Fahmy, *Quest*, 93–154; Petry, *Criminal*, 203–52; Zarinebaf, *Crime*, 112–24.

2. For honor killing, see Bulunur, "Honour."

3. Shafti, *Maqalah*, 59–129. See also Peters, *Crime*, 31.

4. Sa'idi Sirjani, *Vaqayi'*, 179 (17 Rabi' al-Sani 1300 H. / February 25, 1883).

5. *Farhang*, n.188 (22 Rabi' al-Avval 1300 H. / [February 1, 1883]).

6. Badi'i, *Guzarishha*, 37 (12 Zi Qi'dah 1307 H. / June 30, 1890).

7. *Ruznamah-i Dawlat-i 'Illiyah-i Iran*, n.501 (12 Rabi' al-Sani 1278 H./ [October 17, 1861]). Given that this case predates Sipahsalar's Military Code of 1865, this is probably a reference to the earlier 1857/58 (1274 H.) version of the code.

8. *Vaqayi'-i Ittifaqiyah*, n.257 (24 Rabi' al-Sani 1272 H. / [January 3, 1856]).

9. For the sovereign or judge acting as the heir of someone without family members, see Anderson, "Homicide," 814.

10. Sa'idi Sirjani, *Vaqayi'*, 537 (21 Jumada al-Avval 1315 H. / November 17, 1897).

11. Majlisi, *Hudud*, 63.

12. *Ruznamah-i Dawlat-i 'Illiyah-i Iran*, n.504 (10 Jumada al-Avval 1278 H. / [November 13, 1861]). For a reproduction of this image and a discussion of how this visual depiction was rare, see A. Amanat, *Pivot*, plate 15.

13. *Vaqayi'-i Ittifaqiyah*, n.204 (7 Rabi' al-Sani 1271 H. / [December 27, 1854]).

14. *Vaqayi'-i Ittifaqiyah*, n.264 (12 Jumada al-Sani 1274 H. / [January 28, 1858]).

15. On the insanity defense for homicide in Islamic law, see Dols, *Majnun*, 442–43. For the legal culpability of the insane, see also Anderson, "Homicide," 825. In Qajar Iran, as in Khedival Egypt, the use of medical specialists in homicide cases became more common. See K. Fahmy, *Quest*, 6, 21, 110.

16. *Vaqayi'-i Ittifaqiyah*, n.383 (20 Shaval 1274 H. / [June 3, 1858]).

17. Sa'idi Sirjani, *Vaqayi'*, 74 (14 Rajab–13 Sha'ban 1294 H. / July 25, 1877–August 23, 1877).

18. In another murder case, the head of the Shiraz troops, Ahmad Khan Sarhang, was reprimanded for allowing his troops to interfere with the investigation and trial of a fellow soldier who had been murdered by trying to storm the residence of the *biglarbigi* to lay hands on the murderer. The summary suggested that they were to be punished according to the Military Code (*qanun-i nizami*) and by the judgment of the head of the Fars Military Court (Divankhanah-i Nizami-i Fars). This indicates the presence of Military Courts alongside the Divankhanah in the provinces. *Ruznamah-i Dawlat-i 'Illiyah*, no. 524 (21 Zi Hijjah 1278 H. / [June 19, 1862]).

19. Sa'idi Sirjani, *Vaqayi'*, 327–28 (21 Rabi' al-Sani 1306 H. / December 25, 1888).

20. Sa'idi Sirjani, 607 (3 Muharram 1318 H. / May 3, 1900). For more on women poisoning their husbands to escape harsher liability in the Ottoman Empire, see Imber, "Why"; Aykut, "Toxic."

21. For a discussion of this category, see Najmabadi, "Types."

22. For the use of the amicable settlement more broadly, see Othman, "'Amicable."

23. For doubt in homicide cases in Islamic legal theory, see Rabb, *Doubt*, 2–3, 31, 34–35. When several people were involved in homicide, Muslim jurists typically said that the talion did not apply unless there was a conspiracy to murder. See Anderson, "Homicide," 827–28.

24. Sa'idi Sirjani, *Vaqayi'*, 327 (21 Rabi' al-Sani H. / December 25, 1888). For a similar settlement (*sulh*) document outlining terms in another unproven homicide case, dated 1881, see Rajabzadah, Eura, and Morimoto, *Asnad*, 189–90.

25. For the Islamic legal rules for homicides in which it is unclear who delivered the death blow, see Anderson, "Homicide," 827.

26. The mother's role as the decision-maker in *qisas* cases is consistent with current practice in the Islamic Republic of Iran. See Osanloo, *Forgiveness*.

27. Sa'idi Sirjani, *Vaqayi'*, 329 (24 Jumada al-Avval 1306 H. / January 27, 1889).

28. Badi'i, *Guzarishha*, 132 (23 Safar 1307 H. / October 17, 1889).

29. Anderson, "Homicide," 815.

30. Sa'idi Sirjani, *Vaqayi'*, 208–9 (30 Rabi' al-Avval 1301 H. / January 29, 1884).

31. Sa'idi Sirjani, 209 (22 Rabi' al-Sani 1301 H. / February 25, 1884).

32. Sa'idi Sirjani, 209.

33. Sa'idi Sirjani, 228 (18 Zi Hijjah 1301 H. / October 9, 1884). The blood price of a slave murdered by a Muslim was, at most, their market value. See Peters, *Crime*, 51; Anderson, "Homicide," 815.

34. The Hanafis were the only school to consider *qisas* as a possible punishment for a Muslim who murdered a non-Muslim *zimmi*. All other schools (including the Imami school) only allowed for compensation, which was less than the compensa-

tion for a murdered Muslim. See Amanullah, "Juristic," 187–88; Anderson, "Homicide," 815; Peters, *Crime*, 47.

35. *Vaqayi'-i Ittifaqiyah*, n.116 (12 Rajab 1269 H. / [April 21, 1853]).

36. For intentional versus accidental deaths, see Peters, *Crime*, 43; Anderson, "Homicide," 818–23; Powers, *Intent*, 171–76.

37. Anderson, "Homicide," 815–16. In a case of intentional homicide in the summer of 1876, the murderer, Muhammad Khan, harassed and tortured a Jewish man to death over a debt owed to him. The case similarly remained unresolved. Sa'idi Sirjani, *Vaqayi'*, 61 (22 Rabi' al-Sani–24 Jumada al-Avval 1293 H. / May 17, 1876–June 17, 1876).

38. Sa'idi Sirjani, *Vaqayi'*, 68 (28 Safar–2 Rabi' al-Sani 1294 H. / March 14, 1877–April 16, 1877).

39. Hallaq, "'God,'" 71.

40. Foucault, *Discipline*, 32–72.

41. Flandin and Coste, *Safarnamah*, 333–34.

42. *Ruznamah-i Iran*, n.315 (13 Rabi' al-Avval 1294 H. / [March 29, 1877]).

43. Sayyah Mahallati, *Khatirat*, 17.

44. Browne, *Year*, 266.

45. Browne, 274.

46. *Vaqayi'-i Ittifaqiyah*, n.97 (27 Safar 1269 H. / [December 9, 1852]).

47. Sa'idi Sirjani, *Vaqayi'*, 223 (28 Ramazan 1301 H. / July 22, 1884); "Telegram from Sadr-i A'zam to Sahib Divan," 4 Zi Qi'dah 1301 H. / [August 26, 1884], SAKM, no. 295/7411, folios 316–17.

48. "Telegraphic Response from Fath 'Ali [Sahib Divan] to Sadr-i A'zam," 5 Zi Qi'dah 1301 H. / [August 27, 1884], SAKM, no. 295/7411, folio 317.

49. Sa'idi Sirjani, *Vaqayi'*, 223 (28 Ramazan 1301 H. / July 22, 1884).

50. Sa'idi Sirjani, 223.

51. Sa'idi Sirjani, 224.

52. Sahib Divan claimed in his correspondence with the prime minister that the evidence for conviction was confession (*iqrar*), although he left out the use of judicial torture. "Telegraphic Response from Fath 'Ali [Sahib Divan] to Sadr-i A'zam," 5 Zi Qi'dah 1301 H. / [August 27, 1884], SAKM, no. 295/7411, folio 317.

53. Among early Muslim jurists, the head, face, and genitals were considered to be off-limits in all types of punishments (*hadd*, *ta'zir*, and *qisas*). Some even argued that blackening the face and shaving beards were similarly mutilations (*muthlah*). Medieval Muslim governments, however, did not necessarily adhere to these restrictions. Lange and Fierro, "Spatial," 6–7.

54. "Telegraphic Response from Fath 'Ali [Sahib Divan] to Sadr-i A'zam," 5 Zi Qi'dah 1301 H. / [August 27, 1884], SAKM, no. 295/7411, folio 317. Sahib Divan also used the term *muslah* to refer to the initial mutilation of the Tabrizi *darvish*.

55. Sa'idi Sirjani, *Vaqayi'*, 224 (28 Ramazan 1301 H. / July 22, 1884). Sahib Divan indicated that he did not mete out the same punishment on him "since he was a sayyid." "Telegraphic Response from Fath 'Ali [Sahib Divan] to Sadr-i A'zam," 5 Zi Qi'dah 1301 H. / [August 27, 1884], SAKM, no. 295/7411, folio 317. The Shi'i punishment

for an accomplice who held down a person who was murdered, based on one well-known hadith, was life imprisonment and fifty lashes per year. Majlisi, *Hudud*, 117. Both the actual punishment and the Shiʻi juridical punishment had an underlying logic of equivalences: in the first, it was the hands that held down the person that were severed, and in the second, it was the restriction on freedom that was re-created.

56. *Vaqayiʻ-i Ittifaqiyah*, n.100 (18 Rabiʻ al-Avval 1269 H. / [December 30, 1852]).

57. *Farhang*, n.147 (2 Jumada al-Akhar 1299 H. / [April 20, 1882]).

58. Powers, *Intent*, 175–76; Anderson, "Homicide," 826.

59. *Farhang*, n.187 (15 Rabiʻ al-Avval 1300 H. / [January 25, 1883]).

60. Saʻidi Sirjani, *Vaqayiʻ*, 177–78 (9 Safar 1300 H. / December 25, 1882).

61. "Telegram from Fath ʻAli [Sahib Divan] to Mustawfi al-Mamalik," 4 Rabiʻ al-Sani 1300 H. / [February 12, 1883], SAKM, no. 295/7421, folio 271.

62. Saʻidi Sirjani, *Vaqayiʻ*, 293 (22 Zi Qiʻdah 1304 H. / August 14, 1887).

63. Saʻidi Sirjani, 562 (25 Shaval 1316 H. / March 8, 1899); Saʻidi Sirjani, 563 (25 Zi Qiʻdah 1316 H. / April 6, 1899).

64. Saʻidi Sirjani, 563 (25 Zi Qiʻdah 1316 H. / April 6, 1899).

65. Saʻidi Sirjani, 567 (1 Muharram 1317 H. / May 11, 1899).

66. Islam brought an end to the cycle of violence among pre-Islamic Arabian tribes, in which retaliation against the family of a murderer was common. See Peters, *Crime*, 40.

67. Saʻidi Sirjani, *Vaqayiʻ*, 598–99 (28 Shaval 1317 H. / February 27, 1900).

68. For studies of multiple legal jurisdictions in the Ottoman Empire, see Barkey and Benton, "Aspects"; Boogert, *Capitulations*.

69. This may be found in article 12 of the Agreement. "Iran-ʻUsmani," 398.

70. Crews, "Muslim," 176–78.

71. Saʻidi Sirjani, *Vaqayiʻ*, 631 (8 Zi Qiʻdah 1318 H. / February 27, 1901).

72. Saʻidi Sirjani, 631–32.

73. Saʻidi Sirjani, 660 (5 Shaval 1319 H. / January 16, 1902).

74. Saʻidi Sirjani, 662 (3 Zi Hijjah 1319 H. / March 13, 1902).

SEVEN   Seeking Refuge in the Shrine City of Qum, "The Abode of Faith"

1. Momen, *Introduction*, 41, 182.

2. A. Amanat, "Between," 104–5; Algar, *Religion*, 46–47.

3. Mounsey, *Journey*, 175.

4. Brugsch, *Sarzamin*, 195.

5. ʻAyn al-Saltanah, *Ruznamah*, 1:305; Feuvrier, *Sih sal*, 253. According to Reza Sheikholislami, she was appointed the deputy governor of Qum in 1888. In 1890, she was named the replacement for Mirza Muhammad Khan Sipahsalar. On the basis of Amin al-Sultan's telegraphic exchange with her, she was not to collect taxes for the first two months of her tenure since this belonged to Sipahsalar by custom. Sheik-

holeslami, *Structure*, 124, 142, 201–2. Contrary to Sheikholislami's characterization of her as a "deputy" governor, I'timad al-Saltanah described her as the female governor (*hakamah*) of Qum. I'timad al-Saltanah, *Ruznamah*, 938.

6. She was referred to as the Na'ib al-Iyalah, or assistant governor. Afzal al-Mulk, *Tarikh*, 192–93.

7. A. Amanat, *Pivot*, 136.

8. For examples of people taking sanctuary at the Ma'sumah Shrine from the thirteenth century to the early Qajar period, see Eshaghi, "Quietness," 497–99.

9. Fowler, *Three*, 1:36–37.

10. Fowler, 1:37–38; Binning, *Journal*, 2:197. Derrida has discussed the concept of the "city of refuge" in the Jewish tradition and its relevance for contemporary refugees. See Derrida, *Cosmopolitanism*, 17–18.

11. Binning, *Journal*, 2:197–98.

12. Dieulafoy, *Perse*, 182; Curzon, *Persia*, 2:11–12; De Windt, *Ride*, 118; Binning, *Journal*, 2:195–6; Arnold, *Persia*, 283–84; Vámbéry, *Arminius*, 93; Serena, *Safarnamah*, 145.

13. Ussher, *Journey*, 608.

14. Ironically, Adib al-Mulk's father, Hajj Ali Khan Muqaddam Maragha'i, had taken refuge in Qum after being stripped of his position as court inspector (*nazir*) and chief of the royal household (*khansalar*) for supposedly stealing from the royal treasury in 1845. Muhammad Shah and his prime minister, Mirza Aqasi, ordered the governor of Qum to detain him anyway and send him to Tehran in chains. Kia, "Inside," 105.

15. Adib al-Mulk, "Khatirat," 467.

16. Adib al-Mulk, 472.

17. Adib al-Mulk, 472. Note the blurring of *hadd* and *siyasat* punishments in discussing the punishment of the thief. While cutting off the hand was clearly inspired by *hadd* punishment (albeit in Sunni rather than Shi'i form), it was referred to here as a *siyasat* and was supplemented with other fines and punishments not found in Islamic jurisprudence.

18. Adib al-Mulk, 472.

19. Adib al-Mulk, 473.

20. This is precisely the point made by Marxist-oriented political ecologists. See Peluso and Watts, *Violent*.

21. Adib al-Mulk, "Khatirat," 473.

22. Adib al-Mulk, 474.

23. Nasir al-Din Shah, *Safarha*, 275. Beyond Nasir al-Din Shah's travelogues, this work includes a number of very valuable primary sources about the social history of Qum that are cited throughout.

24. Nasir al-Din Shah, 276.

25. Nasir al-Din Shah, 276.

26. Amir Kabir and Mirza Aqa Khan Nuri previously intervened in conflicts over water sharing in Qum. Shimamoto, "Society," 132.

27. Nasir al-Din Shah, *Safarha*, 276–77.

28. Adib al-Mulk, "Khatirat," 474.

29. Adib al-Mulk, 474. The Nasiri Qanat was founded sometime between 1859 and 1861 by royal decree in response to local complaints of a lack of water. Nasir al-Din Shah tasked the governor to establish a *qanat*, and the governor, in turn, appointed Muhammad Taqi Arbab for the task. The *qanat* was an endowment (*vaqf*) for the people of the city. Shimamoto, "Society," 132, 140; Lambton, "Qanats," 164–65. For the text of the original endowment document (*vaqfnamah*), see Modarressi, "Vaqfnamah," 575–76.

30. Adib al-Mulk, "Khatirat," 474–75.

31. Nasir al-Din Shah, *Safarha*, 276–77.

32. Nasir al-Din Shah, 278.

33. Nasir al-Din Shah, 277.

34. Adib al-Mulk, "Khatirat," 468.

35. Adib al-Mulk, 476.

36. Adib al-Mulk, 470.

37. Adib al-Mulk, 469.

38. Adib al-Mulk, 469.

39. Adib al-Mulk, 476.

40. Adib al-Mulk, 476.

41. Adib al-Mulk, 478.

42. Throughout the 1850s–60s, the term "Divankhanah" was used interchangeably for governor's court because governors were closely associated with the shah's court and appointed to restore imperial authority. Later, the head of the Divankhanah came to represent the shah's judicial authority in provincial cities alongside the governor's court.

43. Adib al-Mulk, "Khatirat," 478.

44. Adib al-Mulk, 496.

45. Adib al-Mulk, 479.

46. Adib al-Mulk, 470.

47. Adib al-Mulk, 479.

48. For community policing in early modern Cairo, see Raymond, "Role."

49. Adib al-Mulk, "Khatirat," 470.

50. Adib al-Mulk, 479. See also Pargari and Bitarafian, "Qum," 217.

51. Adib al-Mulk, "Khatirat," 480.

52. Adib al-Mulk, 480.

53. Adib al-Mulk, 489.

54. Adib al-Mulk, 490.

55. Adib al-Mulk, 491.

56. Adib al-Mulk, 492.

57. Adib al-Mulk, 475.

58. Adib al-Mulk, 482.

59. Adib al-Mulk, 482.

60. Adib al-Mulk, 469. *Ma'man* and *mustajir* both refer to Islamic notions of protection. Shoukri, *Refugee*; Zaman, "Jiwār."

61. Qummi, *Tuhfat*, 2:91–92.

62. Adib al-Mulk, "Khatirat," 475.

63. Adib al-Mulk, 476.

64. Hajj Mirza Sayyid Husayn was the *mutavallibashi* between 1856/57 (1273 H.) and 1900 (1317 H.). Modarressi and Mar'ashi, *Turbat*, 1:248; Qurayshi-Karin, *Qum*, 176. He had tremendous material wealth, which included revenues from his various properties and agricultural lands, gardens, *qanat*s, the Ma'sumah Shrine, the shrines of Safavid shahs, shops, hammams, workshops, and caravansarais. Najm al-Mulk, *Safarnamah*, 3–4; 'Ayn al-Saltanah, *Ruznamah*, 1:306, 310, 447; Arbab, *Tarikh*, 31–32; Qurayshi-Karin, *Qum*, 177; Shimamoto, "Society," 130.

65. For a brief discussion of this episode, see Qurayshi-Karin, *Qum*, 140.

66. Adib al-Mulk, "Khatirat," 483.

67. Adib al-Mulk, 484.

68. Adib al-Mulk, 484–85.

69. Adib al-Mulk, 485.

70. Adib al-Mulk, 486.

71. This technique of cutting off water and food was found in Shi'i jurisprudence. Najafi, *Jawahir*, 41:314, 42:299–300.

72. Adib al-Mulk, "Khatirat," 486.

73. Adib al-Mulk, 487.

74. Adib al-Mulk, 488.

75. Adib al-Mulk, 489.

76. Adib al-Mulk, 492.

77. Adib al-Mulk, 493.

78. Adib al-Mulk, 494.

79. Adib al-Mulk, 495. He seems to have been echoing the efforts of Muhammad Shah and Mirza Aqasi to restrict the *bast* to these shrines, as well as later Nasiri *farman*s to that effect. Eshaghi, "Quietness," 500–501.

80. Adib al-Mulk, "Khatirat," 496.

81. Adib al-Mulk, 477.

82. Adib al-Mulk, 477.

83. Adib al-Mulk, 476.

84. Adib al-Mulk, 476.

85. *Ruznamah-i Dawlat-i 'Illiyah-i Iran*, n.537 (23 Sha'ban 1279 H. / [February 12, 1863]); Adib al-Mulk, "Khatirat," 477. The inclusion of this episode in the official newspaper allows us to date some of the cases mentioned by Adib al-Mulk.

86. Adib al-Mulk, "Khatirat," 477.

87. Adib al-Mulk, 477.

88. Adib al-Mulk, 488.

89. Adib al-Mulk, 490.

90. Adib al-Mulk, 490.

91. Gulistan, "Safar."

92. "Nasir al-Din Shah's Imperial Order to 'Ala al-Dawlah" (n.d.), SAKM, no. 296/1604. Internal evidence suggests that this decree was issued between 1867 and 1869.

93. Adib al-Mulk, "Khatirat," 490.

94. "Nasir al-Din Shah's Imperial Order" (n.d.), SAKM, no. 296/1676.

95. Majlisi, Hudud, 24.

96. Okazaki, "Great"; Melville, "Persian"; Majd, Victorian.

97. Fayz, "Vaqayi'," 112–14.

98. Fayz's stated purpose of writing such an account was that "future generations may learn a lesson." Fayz, 112.

99. Reza, "Islam's," 753, 756; Kamali, "Right," 269.

100. Çiğdem, "Cannibalism," 292–93; Szombathy, "Eating," 217.

101. Çiğdem, "Cannibalism," 292; Szombathy, "Eating," 218. For a study of cannibalism as ritual and public punishment, see Bashir, "Shah Isma'il."

102. Szombathy, "Eating," 219.

103. Hajji Sayyid Javad, who was quite wealthy, was known for his charismatic and judicial authority. He often mobilized followers against the government if he felt the shari'ah had been violated. Afzal al-Mulk, Safarnamah, 76; I'tisam al-Mulk, Safarnamah, 60; Arbab, Tarikh, 30, 82–83, 93, 103; Shimamoto, "Society," 129, 140.

104. Fayz, "Vaqayi'," 125.

105. For the actions of Moroccan butchers in a similar context of famine, see Holden, Politics, 76.

106. Fayz, "Vaqayi'," 127.

107. Fayz, 124.

108. Fayz, 130. In other cases, it was unclear what punishment was given, such as in the case of a butcher who confessed to selling dog meat. Fayz, 136.

109. Fayz, 122–23.

110. Fayz, 123.

111. For an analysis of the scapegoat figure, see Girard, Violence.

112. Fayz, "Vaqayi'," 116. In Shi'i jurisprudence, stoning was a hadd punishment reserved for certain forms of zina. In practice, ordinary people stoned religious deviants and apostates. Katz, "Hadd," 369.

113. Fayz, "Vaqayi'," 128.

114. Fayz, 136.

115. Ruznamah-i Iran, n.7 (3 Safar 1288 H. / [April 23, 1871]); Majd, Victorian, 48.

116. Fayz, "Vaqayi'," 131–32.

117. Arbab, Tarikh, 60, cited in Shimamoto, "Society," 132–33.

118. Fayz, "Vaqayi'," 120–21. This appears to have been consistent with certain hudud penalties for people engaging in zina, which included having a wall demolished on the convicted. See El-Rouayheb, Homosexuality, 118.

119. Fayz, "Vaqayi'," 130.

120. Presumably, Lab-i Chal was a reference to the Alvandiyah neighborhood.

121. Fayz, "Vaqayi'," 122.

122. A series of telegrams from the Iranian provinces provide a similarly detailed picture of Qum for 1889–90 under the governorship of Muhammad 'Ali Khan Sipahdar, who notably made the seat of his government outside the *bast* zone. Badi'i, *Guzarishha*, 40.

123. Nasir al-Din Shah, *Safarha*, 282.

124. Nasir al-Din Shah, 298.

125. Nasir al-Din Shah, 278–79.

126. "Telegram from Husayn Sipahsalar to the Mutavallibashi," 11 Rabi' al-Avval 1296 H. / [April 3, 1879], SAKM, no. 295/8102, folio 8; Nasir al-Din Shah, *Safarha*, 291.

127. "Telegram from the Mutavallibashi to Husayn Sipahsalar," 14 Rabi' al-Sani 1296 H. / April 6, 1879], SAKM, no. 295/8102, folio 8; "Telegram from Husayn Sipahsalar to the Mutavallibashi," 15 Rabi' al-Sani, 1296 H. / [April 7, 1879], SAKM, no. 295/8102, folio 9; Nasir al-Din Shah, *Safarha*, 292. A shorter account of this incident is found in Eshaghi, "Quietness," 502.

128. "Telegram from Na'ib al-Saltanah to I'tizad al-Dawlah," 14 Jumada al-Avval 1296 H. / [May 6, 1879], SAKM, no. 295/8102, folios 14–5.

129. "Telegram from I'tizad al-Dawlah to Na'ib al-Saltanah," 15 Jumada al-Avval 1296 H. / [May 7, 1879], SAKM, no. 295/8102, folio 15.

130. "Telegram from Na'ib al-Saltanah to I'tizad al-Dawlah," 22 Jumada al-Avval 1296 H. / [May 14, 1879], SAKM, no. 295/8102, folio 18.

131. "Telegram from I'tizad al-Dawlah to Na'ib al-Saltanah," 24 Jumada al-Avval 1296 H. / [May 16, 1879], SAKM, no. 295/8102, folio 18.

132. Najm al-Mulk, *Safarnamah*, 4.

133. "Telegram from Na'ib al-Saltanah to I'tizad al-Dawlah," 12 Sha'ban 1296 H. / [August 1, 1879], SAKM, no. 295/8102, folio 29; "Telegram from I'tizad al-Dawlah," 13 Sha'ban 1296 H. / [August 2, 1879], SAKM, no. 295/8102, folio 30; Nasir al-Din Shah, *Safarha*, 299. For *qatl-i laws*, see Peters, *Crime*, 17, 18, 193.

134. "Telegram from Sadr-i A'zam to the Mutavallibashi," 15 Muharram 1303 H. / [August 24, 1885], SAKM, no. 295/8164, folios 20–21; Nasir al-Din Shah, *Safarha*, 314.

135. "Telegram from Sadr-i A'zam to the Mutavallibashi," 15 Muharram 1303 H. / [August 24, 1885], SAKM, no. 295/8164, folios 20–21; Nasir al-Din Shah, *Safarha*, 314.

136. "Telegram from the Mutavallibashi to the Sadr-i A'zam," 17 Muharram 1303 H. / [October 26, 1885], SAKM, no. 295/8164, folio 21; Nasir al-Din Shah, *Safarha*, 314.

137. "Telegram from Sadr-i A'zam to the Mutavallibashi," 19 Muharram 1303 H. / [October 28, 1885], SAKM, no. 295/8164, folio 21; Nasir al-Din Shah, *Safarha*, 315.

138. Sadr, *Khatirat*, 50–51.

139. Sadr, 53–54.

140. Sadr, 53.

141. Sadr, 54.

142. I'timad al-Saltanah, *Ruznamah*, 219.

143. Sadr, *Khatirat*, 55.

144. "Telegram from Mustawfi al-Mamalik to I'tizad al-Dawlah and Muta-vallibashi," 9 Rabi' al-Avval 1300 H. / [January 19, 1883], SAKM, no. 295/7679, folio 36; "Telegram from Mustawfi al-Mamalik to I'tizad al-Dawlah," 10 Rabi' al-Avval 1300 H. / [January 20, 1883], SAKM, no. 295/7679, folio 37.

145. "Telegram from [Nasir al-Din Shah] to I'tizad al-Dawlah," 13 Jumada al-Avval 1300 H. / [March 23, 1883], SAKM, no. 295/7421, folio 8.

146. "Telegram from Mustawfi al-Mamalik to I'tizad al-Dawlah and Muta-vallibashi," 6 Jumada al-Avval 1300 H. / [March 16, 1883], SAKM, no. 295/7421, folio 10. See also Sadr, *Khatirat*, 55–56.

147. Sadr, *Khatirat*, 56.

148. Sadr, 57.

149. "Nasir al-Din Shah's Imperial Decree," 5 Jumada al-Sani 1300 H. / [April 13, 1883], SAKM, no. 295/7421, folio 17.

150. "Telegram from [I'tizad al-Dawlah] to Nasir al-Din Shah," 6 Jumada al-Sani 1300 H. / April 14, 1883], SAKM, no. 295/7421, folio 17; "Telegram on behalf of Na-sir al-Din Shah to I'tizad al-Dawlah and Mutavallibashi," 6 Jumada al-Sani 1300 H. / [April 14, 1883], SAKM, no. 295/7421, folios 18–19. Sadr al-Ashraf suggests that 'Abdul-lah Sultan paid a bribe to the *mutavallibashi*, who then influenced the governor to say that the *bast* is sacred and violating it would cause a general tumult. Sadr, *Khatirat*, 58.

151. Sadr, *Khatirat*, 58.

152. "Telegram from I'tizad al-Dawlah to Nasir al-Din Shah," 6 Jumada al-Sani 1300 H. / [April 14, 1883], SAKM, no. 295/7421, folio 19.

153. Sadr, *Khatirat*, 59. For a brief note mentioning that 'Abdullah Sultan's ex-ecution was carried out "by order of the shah" (*bih hukm-i shah*) despite the opposi-tion of the *mutavallibashi*, see I'timad al-Saltanah, *Ruznamah*, 228.

154. "Telegram from Nasrullah to I'tizad al-Dawlah," 7 Jumada al-Sani 1300 H. / [April 15, 1883], SAKM, no. 295/7421, folio 21.

155. Sayyah Mahallati, *Khatirat*, 277, 301.

156. Sayyah Mahallati, 329.

157. Kondo, "Non-Muslims"; Peirce, *Morality*.

158. For notable exceptions from early Babi history, see A. Amanat, *Resurrec-tion*, 385–94; Momen, "Trial"; MacEoin, *Messiah*, 409–50.

159. The category of "soundness of belief(s)" was also employed in the Otto-man Empire as a way to promote Sunni orthodoxy against forms of Islam deemed to be apostacies, such as the Alawis. In the nineteenth-century Ottoman Empire, this was a form of missionary correction (*tashih*) of deviant forms of Islam. See Alkan, *Non-Sunni*, 97; Deringil, *Conversion*, 242.

160. Mazandarani, *Tarikh*, 5:261. Note that in government sources, Baha'is are referred to as Babis.

161. Mazandarani, 8:655.

162. "Telegram from I'tizad al-Dawlah to Mustawfi al-Mamalik," 10 Sha'ban 1299 H. / [June 26, 1882], SAKM, 295/7679, folios 13–14.

163. "Telegram from Iʻtizad al-Dawlah to Naʼib al-Saltanah," 10 Zi Hijjah 1299 H. / [October 23, 1882], SAKM, no. 295/7679, folio 27; "Telegram from Iʻtizad al-Dawlah to Mustawfi al-Mamalik," 2 Jumada al-Avval 1299 H. / [March 22, 1882], SAKM, no. 295/7679, folios 37–38.

164. Mazandarani, *Tarikh*, 5:261.

165. "Telegram from Iʻtizad al-Dawlah to Mustawfi al-Mamalik," 2 Jumada al-Avval 1299 H. / [March 22, 1882], SAKM, no. 295/7679, folio 37; "Telegram from Iʻtizad al-Dawlah to Mustawfi al-Mamalik," 20 Jumada al-Avval 1300 H. / [March 30, 1883], SAKM, no. 295/7421, folio 9; Mazandarani, *Tarikh*, 5:262.

166. "Telegram from Iʻtizad al-Dawlah to Naʼib al-Saltanah," 10 Zi Hijjah 1299 H. / [October 23, 1882], SAKM, no. 295/7679, folio 27; "Telegram from Iʻtizad al-Dawlah to Mustawfi al-Mamalik," 2 Jumada al-Avval 1299 H. / [March 22, 1882], SAKM, no. 295/7679, folio 37; "Telegram from Iʻtizad al-Dawlah to Mustawfi al-Mamalik," 20 Jumada al-Avval 1300 H. / [March 30, 1883], SAKM, no. 295/7421, folio 9.

167. "Telegram from Mustawfi al-Mamalik to Iʻtizad al-Dawlah," 9 Shaʻban 1299 H. / [June 25, 1882], SAKM, no. 295/7679, folio 13; "Telegram from Naʼib al-Saltanah to Iʻtizad al-Dawlah," 9 Zi Hijjah 1299 H. / [October 22, 1882], SAKM, no. 295/7679, folio 27.

168. "Telegram from Iʻtizad al-Dawlah to Mustawfi al-Mamalik," 10 Shaʻban 1299 H. / [June 26, 1882], SAKM, no. 295/7679, folio 14; "Telegram from Iʻtizad al-Dawlah to Mustawfi al-Mamalik," 20 Jumada al-Avval 1300 H. / [March 30, 1883], SAKM, no. 295/7421, folios 9–10.

169. "Telegram from Iʻtizad al-Dawlah to Mustawfi al-Mamalik," 20 Jumada al-Avval 1300 H. / [March 30, 1883], SAKM, no. 295/7421, folio 9. Elsewhere, this is referred to as a *fatva-yi qatl*, suggesting that it was a legal responsum rather than a ruling. "Telegram from Mustawfi al-Mamalik to Iʻtizad al-Dawlah," 9 Shaʻban 1299 H. / [June 25, 1882], SAKM, no. 295/7679, folio 13.

170. "Telegram from Iʻtizad al-Dawlah to Mustawfi al-Mamalik," 10 Shaʻban 1299 H. / [June 26, 1882], SAKM, no. 295/7679, folio 14.

171. "Telegram from Iʻtizad al-Dawlah to Mustawfi al-Mamalik," 10 Shaʻban 1299 H. / [June 26, 1882], SAKM, no. 295/7679, folio 14; "Telegram from Iʻtizad al-Dawlah to Naʼib al-Saltanah," 10 Zi Hijjah 1299 H. / [October 23, 1882], SAKM, no. 295/7679, folio 28.

172. "Telegram from Iʻtizad al-Dawlah to Naʼib al-Saltanah," 10 Zi Hijjah 1299 H. / [October 23, 1882], SAKM, no. 295/7679, folio 28.

173. Mazandarani, *Tarikh*, 5:261–62.

174. Mazandarani, 5:262. Elsewhere, it is stated that it took Naʼib al-Saltanah ten months to secure Ghulam Riza's release after this episode. Mazandarani, 6:621.

175. "Telegram from Mustawfi al-Mamalik to Iʻtizad al-Dawlah," 9 Shaʻban 1299 H. / [June 25, 1882], SAKM, no. 295/7679, folio 13.

176. "Telegram from Iʻtizad al-Dawlah to Naʼib al-Saltanah," 10 Zi Hijjah 1299 H. / [October 23, 1882], SAKM, no. 295/7679, folio 27.

177. "Telegram from Mustawfi al-Mamalik to I'tizad al-Dawlah," 8 Rabi' al-Sani 1300 H. / [February 16, 1883], SAKM, no. 295/7679, folio 37.

178. "Telegram from Mustawfi al-Mamalik to I'tizad al-Dawlah," 16 Jumada al-Avval 1300 H. / [March 26, 1883], SAKM, no. 295/7421, folio 9.

179. "Telegram from Mustawfi al-Mamalik to Ghulam Riza," 24 Jumada al-Avval 1300 H. / [April 3, 1883], SAKM, no. 295/7421, folios 11–12.

180. Mazandarani, Tarikh, 5:263, 6:621, 8:655.

181. Mazandarani, 6:600–601; Muhammad Husayni, Tarikh, 59–61. I have relied on Nusratullah Muhammad Husayni's community history because it also includes long and previously unpublished passages from the memoirs of Muhammad Ibn Naddaf. Both this and Mazandarani's account include telegrams from shahs and prime ministers that I was otherwise unable to locate, thus making them unique sources for reconstructing the legal history of Baha'is during the period.

182. European travelers claimed that non-Muslims were not allowed to live in Qum for this reason. Curzon, Persia, 2:11; Stewart, Persia, 236. Eugène Flandin claimed that he was chased away from the shrine by an "angry mullah" because a Christian's presence would be polluting. Flandin and Coste, Safarnamah, 123. For evidence of Jews residing in the city, see Dieulafoy, Perse, 182.

183. This account is from the memoirs of Muhammad Ibn Naddaf, which is reproduced in Muhammad Husayni, Tarikh, 89.

184. Muhammad Husayni, 89.

185. Mazandarani, Tarikh, 6:601; Muhammad Husayni, Tarikh, 85.

186. Mazandarani, Tarikh, 6:601–2; Muhammad Husayni, Tarikh, 85. For ritual cursing in Safavid Iran, see Stanfield-Johnson, "Tabarra'iyan."

187. Mazandarani, Tarikh, 6:602–3; Muhammad Husayni, Tarikh, 85, 90–91.

188. Mazandarani, Tarikh, 6:603–5; Muhammad Husayni, Tarikh, 92, 94.

189. Mazandarani, Tarikh, 6:605; Muhammad Husayni, Tarikh, 92–93.

190. Mazandarani, Tarikh, 6:605; Muhammad Husayni, Tarikh, 93.

191. Mazandarani, Tarikh, 6:605–6; Muhammad Husayni, Tarikh, 113.

192. Mazandarani, Tarikh, 6:606–8; Muhammad Husayni, Tarikh, 116. The phrase tajassus-i batin appeared in al-Ghazali's work of Islamic ethics and also in a similar work by the early nineteenth-century Shi'i jurist Ahmad Naraqi. Ghazali, Kimiya, 250; Naraqi, Mi'raj, 327.

193. Mazandarani, Tarikh, 6:606–8; Muhammad Husayni, Tarikh, 116.

194. Mazandarani, Tarikh, 6:608–9; Muhammad Husayni, Tarikh, 116–17.

195. They may not have been given asylum in the Ma'sumah Shrine itself, since granting passage to suspected apostates would have led to further conflict.

196. Mazandarani, Tarikh, 6:611–13; Muhammad Husayni, Tarikh, 118–19.

197. For a similar dynamic elsewhere in Iran, see Vejdani, "Urban," 1196–97.

198. Muhammad Husayni, Tarikh, 120.

199. This is all the more surprising because Nuri was anti-Babi and anti-Baha'i during the Constitutional Revolution.

200. Mazandarani, Tarikh, 6:614–16; Muhammad Husayni, Tarikh, 120–21.

Epilogue

1. For overviews of the Constitutional Revolution, see Afary, *Iranian*; Bayat, *Iran's*.

2. The scholarship on the Islamic Revolution is vast. See Arjomand, *Turban*; Keddie and Richard, *Modern*.

3. For a survey of prevailing explanations of the revolution and their short-comings, see Kurzman, *Unthinkable*.

4. A. Amanat, "From *ijtihād*."

5. Manoukian, *City*, 194. Manoukian questions the veracity of the reports by speculating that it may have been a translation from English into Persian, despite the fact that Saʻidi-Sirjani reproduces facsimiles of the contemporary primary source in Persian. The reports were definitely composed in Persian by the two Indo-Iranian Navvab brothers, Mirza Hasan ʻAli Khan and Mirza Haydar ʻAli, who served as the English agent (Vakil) in Shiraz in succession. C. E. Davies has addressed the issue of authorship of these reports in his well-researched history of Fars province. Davies, "History," 26, 36.

6. Arjomand, *Turban*.

7. Khomeini, *Hukumat*.

8. Ervand Abrahamian and Amin Banani both erroneously claim that the early Pahlavi penal code was inspired by the Italian penal code. Abrahamian, *Iran*, 148; Banani, *Modernization*, 74. Hadi Enayat has demonstrated why these claims are false. Enayat, *Law*, 106–10, 222–23.

9. For an exception, see Keshavarzian, *Bazaar*.

10. Gahan, "Sovereign."

11. Afshari, *Human*, 64–67; Mahdavi, *Passionate*.

12. Ghobadi, *No One*. For a discussion of contemporary Iranian Shiʻi jurists' debate about music's legal status, its dissemination as an alternative public sphere, and the "semi-secret" public sphere facilitated by technological innovations, see Siamdoust, *Soundtrack*, 7–8, 15–17, 215–17.

13. Asad, *Formations*; Hallaq, *Impossible*.

14. Emon, "Codification."

15. For a book-length treatment of how some ʻulama viewed constitutionalism as compatible with Shiʻism, see Hairi, *Shiʻism*.

16. Enayat, *Law*, 91, 105–10.

17. For a succinct overview of penal developments in Iran, including codification, since the 1979 Revolution, see Peters, *Crime*, 160–64. For more detailed studies, especially of codification, see Tellenbach, "Principle"; Tavana, "Three"; Entessar, "Criminal."

18. Osanloo, *Forgiveness*.

19. For a discussion of the concept of *ghayrat*, its justification for honor killings in Pakistan, and the broader philosophical and ethico-legal significance of honor, see Appiah, *Honor*, 147–72.

20. Schneider, "Concept."

21. Osanloo provides a nuanced perspective on honor, in both Islamic and non-Islamic terms, as it pertains to whether the family of a murdered person seeks retribution. Osanloo, *Forgiveness*, 44–45, 49–55. For a broader discussion of the term *hurmah* and its ethical and legal implications, see Asad, "Reflections," 417.

22. Hoexter, "Huquq Allah," 134.

23. Mayer, "Universality"; Emon, Ellis, and Glahn, *Islamic.*

24. Eshaghi, "Quietness," 505; Chehabi, "Banning."

25. Nikpour, "Prison," 1–4.

26. Amir 'Ala'i, *Mujazat*, 32–33.

27. Foucault, *Discipline.*

28. Schayegh, "Serial"; Tafrishi, *Pulis*, 148–56.

29. "Jani-i Bi Nazir: I'dam-i 'Ali Asghar Burujirdi," *Kushish*, June 28, 1934. A picture of the hanging and the placard is reproduced alongside other pictures pertinent to the serial murder case in *Namah-i Shahrbani*, y.1, n.1 (December 1935–January 1936): 2.

30. For the debate over Foucault's initial support for the Islamic Revolution and its implications, see Afary and Anderson, *Foucault*; Ghamari-Tabrizi, *Foucault.* What has not been addressed, however, is what implications the Iranian Islamic Revolution had for his work on prisons.

31. Abrahamian, *Tortured*, 124.

32. Abrahamian, 126.

Bibliography

Archival Sources

Ayatullah Burujirdi Library (Qum)
Muhammad Baqir Shafti, "Su'al va Javab," manuscript, n.d., no. 424.

Kakh-i Gulistan (Tehran)
Hajj Mullah 'Ali Shari'atmadar, "Jami'-i Nasiri," manuscript, 1884 (1301 H.), no. 2973.

Majlis Library (Tehran)
Conte di Monteforte, "Kitabchah-i Qanun-i Jaza-yi Kunt du Munt-i Furt," printed, 1879 (1296 H.), no. 2-20359.
"Kurrasat al-Ma'i," manuscript, 1896/97 (1314 H.), no. 9451.
"Kurrasat al-Ma'i," manuscript, 1896/97 (1314 H.), no. 9452.
Mirza Muhammad Khan Qajar Sipahsalar, "Kitabchah-i Qanun-i Nizamiyah," manuscript, 1865 (1282 H.), no. IR 10-49188.
Muhammad 'Ali Jarrah-i Nizam, "Qanun-i Qushun," manuscript, 1861 (1277 H.). no. 11-9884.
Muhammad Baqir Shafti, "Su'al va Javab," manuscript, n.d., no. 11-01179.
Muhammad Baqir Shafti, "Su'al va Javab," printed, 1831 (1247 H.), no. 07-01311.
"Qanun-i Jaza," manuscript, 1881, no. 10-32094.

Malik Library (Tehran)
"Vaqayi'-i Dar al-Saltanah-i Isfahan I," manuscript, 1840 (1256 H.), no. 2256133.
"Vaqayi'-i Dar al-Saltanah-i Isfahan II," manuscript, 1841 (1257 H.), no. 1080902.
"Vaqayi'-i Dar al-Saltanah-i Isfahan III," manuscript, 1841 (1257 H.), no. 1080909.

Pazhuhishkadah-i Tarikh-i Mu'asir (Tehran)
"Tihran, Maydan-i Tupkhanah, I'dam-i Asghar-i Qatil," photograph, no. 'ayn-1-424.

SAKM (Tehran)

"Dastkhatt-i Nasir al-Din Shah bih 'Ala al-Dawlah: Luzum-i Vujud dar Ruznamahjat Risandan-i har gunah akhbar-i dakhili va khariji Ikhraj-i Malik Tarkah," no. 296/1604.

"Guzarishat va Tiligrafat Marbut bih Vaqayi'-i Dar al-Khilafah-i Tihran va Sa'ir-i Vilayat," no. 295/7650.

"Guzarish-i Dastgiri-i Chand Tan az Qumarbazha Islah-i Ravabit Bayn-i Sadr al-'Ulama va Imam Jum'ah Dastkhatt-i Nasir al-Din Shah Luzum-i Qatl-i Malik Tarkah," no. 296/1676.

"Majmu'ah-i 'Ara'iz va Nivishtijat ba Tawshih-i Nasir al-Din Shah Qajar," no. 295/7428.

"Majmu'ah-i Tiligrafha-yi Irsali az Tihran bih Qum Kashan Kirman Shiraz va Bush-ihr," no. 295/7411.

[Mirza Yusuf Khan Mustawfi al-Mamalik], "Takalif-i Hukkam-i Vilayat," no. 295/7491, folios 75–85.

"Namahha-i Maqamat va Ahl-i Haram Ruznamah-i Vilayat Madrasah-i Dar al-Funun Imarat-i Saltanati va Ghayrihi bih Nasir al-Din Shah dar Bazgasht az Safar-i Khuzistan," no. 295/7245.

"Tawqif-i Shikanjah va Musadarah-i Amval-i Mirza Husayn Tavassut-i Zabit-i Baraz-jan va Dastur-i Sadr-i 'Azam Bar Tahqiq-i Amr va Guzarish-i an bih u 1302 H." no. 295/6456.

"Tiligrafati az Dar al-Khilafah-i Tihran bih Hukkam-i Vilayat-i Qum va Kashan Isfa-han Fars va Kirman," no. 295/8102.

"Tiligrafha'i az Tihran bih Qum Kashan Isfahan Shiraz Bushihr Kirman," no. 295/8164.

"Tiligrafha-yi Irsali va Daryafti az Tihran bih Isfahan Kirman Fars Yazd Kirmansha-han Luristan 1300 H.," no. 295/7421.

"Tiligrafha-yi Shah Na'ib al-Saltanah Mustawfi al-Mamalik Amin al-Sultan Amin al-Mulk Vazir-i Kharijah bih maqamat-i kishvari va kashkari Kirman Isfahan Shiraz Bushihr," no. 295/7679.

Victoria and Albert Museum, South Kensington (London, England)
Eugène Flandin, "Meidan-i-Chah ou Place Royale, Ispahan."

Newspapers and Journals

Al-Muntabi'ah Fi al-Fars
Asiatic Journal
Farhang
Kushish
Namah-i Shahrbani
Oriental Herald
Ruznamah-i Dawlat-i 'Illiyah-i Iran
Ruznamah-i Iran
Vaqayi'-i Ittifaqiyah

Published Primary Sources

Abbott, Keith Edward. *Cities and Trade: Consul Abbott on the Economy and Society of Iran, 1847–1866*. Edited by Abbas Amanat. London: Ithaca, 1983.

'Abdu'l-Baha. *A Traveller's Narrative Written to Illustrate the Episode of the Báb*. Edited and translated by Edward Granville Browne. 2 vols. Cambridge: Cambridge University Press, 1891.

———. *Risalah-i Madaniyah*. Langenheim, Germany: Lajnah-i Nashr-i Asar-i Amri, 1984.

Adib al-Mulk, 'Abd al-'Ali Khan. "Khatirat-i Adib al-Mulk Hukmran-i Qum." In *Miras-i Islami-i Iran*, edited by 'Ali Rafi'i 'Alamru Dashti, vol. 10, 449–96. Qum: Kitabkhanah-i Hazrat Ayatullah al-'Uzma Marashi Najafi, 1999.

Afzal al-Mulk, Ghulam Husayn. *Safarnamah-i Qum*. Qum: Za'ir, 2006.

———. *Tarikh va Jughrafiya-yi Qum*. Tehran: Vahid, 1976.

Akbar, and Abū al-Faẕl ibn Mubārak. *Mukātabāt-i-'Allāmī (Inshā'i Abu'l Faẕl): Letters of the Emperor Akbar in English Translation*. Edited by Mansura Haidar. New Delhi: Munshiram Manoharlal, 1998.

Akhundzadah, Mirza Fath 'Ali. *Maqalat-i Farsi*. Edited by H. Siddiq. Tabriz: Savalan, 1978.

Al-Hallaq, Ahmad al-Budayri. "The Barber of Damascus: Ahmad Budayri al-Hallaq's Chronicle of the Year 1749." In *The Modern Middle East: A Sourcebook for History*, edited by Camron Michael Amin, Benjamin C. Fortna, and Elizabeth Brown Frierson, translated by Steve Tamari, 562–68. Oxford: Oxford University Press, 2006.

Al-i Davud, Sayyid 'Ali. *Nukhustin Kushishha-yi Qanun Guzari-i Iran*. Tehran: Duktur Mahmud Afshar, 2018.

Amin al-Sultan, Mirza 'Ali Asghar. "Dastur al-'Amal-i Hukkam-i Vilayat [1305]." In *Afkar-i Ijtima'i va Siyasi va Iqtisadi dar Asar-i Muntashir Nashudah-i dawran-i Qajar*, edited by Faridun Adamiyat and Huma Natiq, 454–71. Tehran: Agah, 1989.

Ansari, Mirza Sa'id Khan. "Qanun-i Nasiri." In *Siyasatnamahha-yi Qajari: Si va Yak Andarznamah-i Siyasi-i 'Asr-i Qajar*, edited by Ghulam Husayn Zargarinizhad, 3:303–85. Tehran: Nigaristan-i Andishah, 2016.

Arbab, Muhammad Taqi Big. *Tarikh-i Dar al-Iman-i Qum*. Edited by Husayn Mudarrisi Tabataba'i. Qum: Hikmat, 1974.

Arnold, Arthur. *Through Persia by Caravan*. London: Tinsley, 1877.

'Ayn al-Saltanah, Mas'ud Salur. *Ruznamah-i Khatirat-i 'Ayn al-Saltanah*. Edited by Iraj Afshar. 10 vols. Tehran: Intisharat-i Asatir, 1995.

Badi'i, Parviz, ed. *Guzarishha-yi awza'-i Siyasi Ijtima'i-i Vilayat-i 'Asr-i Nasiri 1307 H.Q.* Tehran: Sazman-i Asnad-i Milli-i Iran, 1994.

Bayani, Khanbaba. *Panjah Sal Tarikh-i Iran dar Dawrah-i Nasiri: Mustanad bih Asnad-i Tarikhi va Arshivi*. Vols. 4–6. Tehran: Nashr-i 'Ilm, 1996.

Bihbahani, Abu Talib. "Minhaj al-'Ali." In *Siyasatnamahha-yi Qajari: Si va Yak Andarznamah-i Siyasi-i 'Asr-i Qajar*, edited by Ghulam Husayn Zargarinizhad, 3:145–241. Tehran: Nigaristan-i Andishah, 2016.

Binning, Robert B. M. *A Journal of Two Year's Travel in Persia*. 2 vols. London: Allen, 1857.

Bore, Eugene. "Missions of Persia." *Annals of the Propagation of the Faith* 2 (November 1841): 318–34.

Browne, Edward Granville. *A Year amongst the Persians*. London: Adam and Charles Black, 1893.

Brugsch, Heinrich. *Dar Sarzamin-i Aftab: Duvvumin Safarnamah-i Haynrish Birugish*. Translated by Majid Jalilvand. Tehran: Nashr-i Markaz, 1996.

Ceza Kanunname-yi Hümayunudur. Istanbul: Takvimhane-yi Amire, 1858.

Chamich, Michael. *History of Armenia*. Translated by John Audall. Calcutta: H. Townsend, 1827.

Chodźko, Alexander. *Specimens of the Popular Poetry of Persia*. London: Oriental Translation Fund of Great Britain and Ireland, 1842.

Curzon, George Nathaniel. *Persia and the Persian Question*. 2 vols. London: Longmans, Green, 1892.

Damavandi, Muhammad Husayn Nasrullah. "Tuhfat al-Nasiriyah fi Ma'rifat al-Ilahiyah." In *Siyasatnamahha-yi Qajari: Si va Yak Andarznamah-i Siyasi-i 'Asr-i Qajar*, edited by Ghulam Husayn Zargarinizhad, 2:35–79. Tehran: Nigaristan-i Andishah, 2016.

De Bode, C. A. *Travels in Luristan and Arabistan*. 2 vols. London: Maden, 1845.

De Windt, Harry. *A Ride to India across Persia and Baluchistán*. London: Chapman and Hall, 1891.

Dieulafoy, Jane. *La Perse, la Chaldée et la Susiane*. Paris: Hachette et Cie, 1887.

Farajullah Munshi. "Tarikh-i Vaqayi'-i Dar al-Saltanah-i Isfahan." In *Mazdaknamah*, edited by Turan Tulabi and Ghulam Husayn Zargarinizhad, 435–68. Tehran: Asatir, 2015.

Fasa'i, Hasan. *Farsnamah-i Nasiri*. Edited by Mansur Rastigar. 2 vols. Tehran: Amir Kabir, 1999.

Fayz, 'Ali Akbar. "Vaqayi'-i Sal-i Qaht-i Yakhizar va Divist va Hashtad va Hasht kih dar Dar al-Iman-i Qum Ru'i dadah bidunah Ighraq-i Munshiyanah." In *Qum dar Qahti-i Buzurg-i 1288 Qamari*, edited by John David Gurney and Mansur Sifatgul, 108–38. Qum: Kitabkhanah-i Hazrat Ayatullah al-'Uzma Marashi Najafi, 2008.

Feuvrier, Jean Baptiste. *Sih sal dar darbar-i Iran: Khatirat-i Duktur Furiyah, Pizishk-i Vizhah-i Nasir al-Din Shah Qajar*. Edited by Humayun Shahidi. Translated by 'Abbas Iqbal. Tehran: Dunya-yi Kitab, 1983.

Flandin, Eugène, and Pascal Coste. *Safarnamah-i Uzhin Filandan bih Iran*. Translated by Husayn Nur Sadiqi. Tehran: Ishraqi, 1977.

———. *Voyage en perse*. 8 vols. Paris: Gide et J. Baudry, 1851–54.

Fowler, George. *Three Years in Persia; with Travelling Adventures in Koordistan*. 2 vols. London: Henry Colburn, 1841.

Fraser, James Baillie. *Travels in Koordistan, Mesopotamia, &c.* London: R. Bentley, 1840.

Ghazali, Abu Hamid Muhammad. *Kimiya-yi Sa'adat*. Tehran: Kitabkhanah va Chapkhanah-i Markazi, 1954.

Gulistan, Ibrahim. "Safar-i 'Ismat." In *Ju'i va Divar va Tishnah: Dah Dastan*, 71–78. Tehran: Gulistan, 1967.

Hafiz, Khwajah Shams al-Din Muhammad. *Divan-i Hafiz*. Edited by Parviz Natil Khanlari. Tehran: Khwarazmi, 1984.

Hajj Mirza Aqasi. "Chahar Fasl-i Sultani." In *Siyasatnamahha-yi Qajari: Si va Yak Andarznamah-i Siyasi-i 'Asr-i Qajar*, edited by Ghulam Husayn Zargarinizhad, 1:233–55. Tehran: Nigaristan-i Andishah, 2016.

Hidayat, Riza Quli Khan. *Fihris al-Tavarikh*. Edited by 'Abd al-Husayn Nava'i and Mir Hashim Muhaddis. Tehran: Pazhuhishgah-i 'Ulum-i insani va mutali'at-i farhangi, 1995.

———. *Tarikh-i Rawzat al-Safa*. Edited by Jamshid Kianfar. Tehran: Asatir, 2001.

"Iran-'Usmani 'Ahdnamah-i Muvaddat." In *Mu'ahadat va Qarardadha-yi Tarikhi dar Dawrah-i Qajar*, edited by Ghulam Riza Tabataba'i Majd, 393–98. Tehran: Bunyad-i Mawqufat-i Duktur Mahmud Afshar Yazdi, 1994.

Isfahani, Muhammad ibn Sabz 'Ali. *Vajizat al-Tahrir: dar chigunagi-i tanzim-i asnad-i shar'i milli va huquqi dar dawrah-i Safavi va Qajar*. Edited by Rasul Ja'fariyan. Qum: Nashr-i Muvarrikh, 2014.

I'timad al-Saltanah, Muhammad Hasan Khan. *Al-Ma'asir va al-Asar*. Edited by Iraj Afshar. 3 vols. Tehran: Asatir, 1984.

———. *Ruznamah-i Khatirat-i I'timad al-Saltanah*. Edited by Iraj Afshar. Tehran: Amir Kabir, 2000.

———. *Tarikh-i Muntazam-i Nasiri*. Edited by Muhammad Isma'il Rizvani. Tehran: Dunya-yi Kitab, 1984.

I'tisam al-Mulk, Mirza Khanlar Khan. *Safarnamah-i Mirza Khanlar Khan*. Edited by Manuchihr Mahmudi. Tehran: Firdawsi, 1972.

Jabiri Ansari, Hasan. *Tarikh-i Isfahan*. Edited by Jamshid Mazahiri. Isfahan: Mash'al, 1999.

———. *Tarikh-i Isfahan va Ray*. Isfahan: Mihr, 1942.

"Kanun-i Cedid." In *Mirat-ı Adalet, yahut, Tarihçe-yi adliye-yi Devlet-i Aliye*, edited by Ahmet Lütfi, 150–76. Istanbul: Kitapçı Ohannes, 1888.

Kashfi, Ja'far ibn Abi Ishaq. "Mizan al-Muluk va Tava'if va Sirat al-Mustaqim fi Suluk al-Khala'if." In *Siyasatnamahha-yi Qajari: Si va Yak Andarznamah-i Siyasi-i 'Asr-i Qajar*, edited by Ghulam Husayn Zargarinizhad, 2:81–237. Tehran: Nigaristan-i Andishah, 2016.

———. *Tuhfat al-Muluk: Guftarha'i dar barah-i Hikmat-i Siyasi*. Edited by 'Abd al-Vahhab Farati Farati. Qum: Bustan-i Kitab, 2002.

Kashif al-Ghita', Shaykh Ja'far. *Kashf Al-Ghita'*. Qum: Bustan-i Kitab, 2009.

Khomeini, Ruhollah. *Hukumat-i Islami*. n.p., 1970.

Khurmuji, Muhammad Ja'far. *Haqa'iq al-Akhbar: Tarikh-i Qajar*. Edited by Husayn Khidiv-jam. Tehran: Zavvar, 1965.

Lisan al-Mulk, Muhammad Taqi Sipihr Kashani. *Nasikh al-Tavarikh*. Edited by Jamshid Kianfar. Tehran: Asatir, 1998.

Maftun Dunbuli, 'Abd al-Razzaq. *Ma'asir-i Sultaniyah: Tarikh-i Jangha-yi Iran va Rus*. Edited by Ghulam Husayn Sadri Afshar. Tehran: Ibn Sina, 1972.

Majlisi, Muhammad Baqir. *Hudud va Qisas va Diyat*. Edited by 'Ali Fazil. Qum: Nashr-i Asar-i Islami, 198[?].

Malkam Khan, Mirza. "Daftar-i Qanun." In *Majmu'ah-i Asar-i Mirza Malkam Khan*, edited by Muhammad Muhit Tabataba'i, 119–66. Tehran: 'Ilmi, 1948.

———. "Kitabchah-i Ghaybi ya Daftar-i Tanzimat." In *Majmu'ah-i Asar-i Mirza Malkam Khan*, edited by Muhammad Muhit Tabataba'i, 1–52. Tehran: 'Ilmi, 1948.

Mazandarani, Asadullah Fazil. *Tarikh-i Zuhur al-Haqq*. 8 vols. n.p., n.d.

"Mishkat-i Muhammadiyah." In *Siyasatnamahha-yi Qajari: Si va Yak Andarznamah-i Siyasi-i 'Asr-i Qajar*, edited by Ghulam Husayn Zargarinizhad, 2:13–34. Tehran: Nigaristan-i Andishah, 2016.

Modarressi, Hossein, ed. "Vaqfnamah-i Du Qanat Dar Qum." *Vahid* 5, no. 54 (1968): 575–76.

Mounsey, Augustus Henry. *A Journey through the Caucasus and the Interior of Persia*. London, 1872.

Mushir al-Dawlah, Mirza Ja'far Khan. "Kitabchah-i Mirza Ja'far Khan Mushir al-Dawlah." In *Mu'ahadat va Qarardadha-yi Tarikhi dar Dawrah-i Qajariyah*, edited by Ghulamriza Tabataba'i Majd, 484–92. Tehran: Bunyad-i Mawqufat-i Duktur Mahmud Afshar Yazdi, 1994.

Mustashar al-Dawlah, Mirza Yusuf Khan. *One Word: Yak Kaleme: 19th-Century Persian Treatise Introducing Western Codified Law*. Translated by Sen McGlinn and A. A. Seyed-Gohrab. Leiden: Leiden University Press, 2010.

———. *Yak Kalimah*. Edited by Baqir Mu'mini. Tehran, 1980.

Mustawfi, 'Abdullah. *Sharh-i Zindigani-i Man ya Tarikh-i Ijtima'i va Idari-i Dawrah-i Qajariyah*. 3 vols. Tehran: Zuvvar, 2005.

Mustawfi al-Mamalik, Muhammad Yusuf. "Dastur al-'Amal-i Hukkam-i Vilayat 1293." In *Afkar-i Ijtima'i va Siyasi va Iqtisadi dar Asar-i Muntashir Nashudah-i dawran-i Qajar*, edited by Faridun Adamiyat and Huma Natiq, 449–53. Tehran: Intisharat-i Agah, 1989.

Muzahhab Isfahani, Muhammad 'Ali. *Muqaddamah-i Tazkirah-i Madayih al-Mu'tamidiyah: bih zamimah-i sharh-i hal va naqd-i manabi'-i Manuchihr Khan-i Mu'tamid al-Dawlah*. Edited by Husayn Majidi. Isfahan: Intisharat-i Danishgah-i Isfahan, 1390.

Nabil Zarandi. *The Dawn-Breakers: Nabil's Narrative of the Early Days of the Baha'i Revelation*. Translated by Shoghi Effendi. Wilmette, IL: Bahá'í Publishing Trust, 1999.

Najafi, Muhammad Hasan. *Jawahir al-Kalam*. 43 vols. Beirut: Dar Ihya' al-Turath al-'Arabi, 1981.

Najm al-Mulk, 'Abd al-Ghaffar. *Safarnamah-i Khuzistan*. Edited by Muhammad Dabir Siyaqi. Tehran: 'Ilmi, 1963.

Naraqi, Ahmad ibn Muhammad Mahdi. *Kitab-i Mi'raj al-Sa'adah.* Tehran: 'Ilmiyah Islamiyah, 1969.

Nasir al-Din Shah. *Safarha-yi Nasir al-Din Shah bih Qum 1266–1309 H.Q.* Edited by Fatimah Qaziha. Tehran: Sazman-i Asnad-i Milli, 2003.

Nazim al-Islam Kirmani. *Tarikh-i Bidari-i Iraniyan.* Edited by 'Ali Akbar Sa'idi Sirjani. 2 vols. Tehran: Intisharat-i Bunyad-i Farhang-i Iran, 1978.

"Qanun-i Hukumat-i Iran." In *Siyasatnamahha-yi Qajari: Si va Yak Andarznamah-i Siyasi-i 'Asr-i Qajar,* edited by Ghulam Husayn Zargarinizhad, 3:125–43. Tehran: Nigaristan-i Andishah, 2016.

Qazvini, Muhammad Shafi'. *Qanun-i Qazvini: Intiqad-i Awza'-i Ijtima'i-i Iran-i Dawrah-i Nasiri.* Edited by Iraj Afshar. Tehran: Talayah, 1991.

Qummi, Husayn bin Muhammad. *Tuhfat al-Fatimiyin fi zikr ahval Qum va al-Qummiyin.* Edited by 'Ali Rafi'i. 4 vols. Qum: Nur-i Mataf, 2012.

Qummi, Mirza Abu al-Qasim. *Jami' al-Shatat.* Edited by Murtaza Razavi. 4 vols. Tehran: Kayhan, 1371.

Rajabzadah, Hashim, Kinji Eura, and Kazuo Morimoto, eds. *Asnad-i 'Ibadi va Aini-i Shi'ah va asnad-i qaza'i-i dawrah-i Qajar.* Japan: Institute for Advanced Studies on Asia, 2016.

Raja'i, 'Abd al-Mahdi, ed. *Tarikh-i Ijtima'i-i Isfahan dar 'Asr-i Zill al-Sultan: Az Nigah-i ruznamah-i Farhang-i Isfahan.* Isfahan: Danishgah-i Isfahan, 2004.

"Ruh al-Islam va Sirat al-Mustaqim 'Ala al-Anam." In *Siyasatnamahha-yi Qajari: Si va Yak Andarznamah-i Siyasi-i 'Asr-i Qajar,* edited by Ghulam Husayn Zargarinizhad, 2:325–86. Tehran: Nigaristan-i Andishah, 2016.

Rustam al-Hukama, Muhammad Hashim. *Rustam al-Tavarikh.* Edited by Muhammad Mushiri. 3rd ed. Los Angeles: Ketab, 2007.

———. "Shams al-Anvar." In *Siyasatnamahha-yi Qajari: Si va Yak Andarznamah-i Siyasi-i 'Asr-i Qajar,* edited by Ghulam Husayn Zargarinizhad, 1:299–393. Tehran: Nigaristan-i Andishah, 2016.

Sadr, Muhsin. *Khatirat-i Sadr al-Ashraf.* Tehran: Intisharat-i Vahid, 1985.

Sa'idi, Huriyah, ed. *Shah va Jinab Aqa: Mukatibat Nasir al-Din Shah va Mirza Yusuf Khan Mustawfi al-Mamalik.* Tehran: Nashr-i Tarikh-i Iran, 2009.

Sa'idi Sirjani, 'Ali Akbar, ed. *Vaqayi'-i Ittifaqiyah: Majmu'ah-i guzarishha-yi khufyah nivisan-i Inglis dar vilayat-i junubi-i Iran az sal-i 1291 ta 1322 H.Q.* Tehran: Nashr-i Naw, 1982.

Sartip, Mirza Karim Khan. "Nazm-i Qaravulkhanahha." *Miras-i Maktub* 2, nos. 19–20 (2008): 27–29.

Savuji, Hajj Mirza Musa bin 'Ali bin Riza. "Siyasat-i Mudun." In *Siyasatnamahha-yi Qajari: Si va Yak Andarznamah-i Siyasi-i 'Asr-i Qajar,* edited by Ghulam Husayn Zargarinizhad, 2:239–324. Tehran: Nigaristan-i Andishah, 2016.

Sayyah Mahallati, Muhammad 'Ali. *Khatirat-i Hajj Sayyah, ya, Dawrah-i khawf va vahshat.* Edited by Hamid Sayyah and Sayfullah Gulkar. Tehran: Amir Kabir, 1980.

Sercey, Édouard. *Iran dar 1839–1840 M (1255–1256 H.Q.): Sifarat-i fawq al-'Adah-i Kunt du Sirsay.* Translated by Ihsan Ishraqi. Tehran: Sitad-i Inqilab-i Farhangi, 1983.

Serena, Carla. *Safarnamah-i Karla Sirna.* Translated by 'Ali Asghar Sa'idi. Tehran: Naqsh-i Jahan, 1983.

Shafti, Muhammad Baqir. *Maqalah fi Tahqiq Iqamat al-Hudud fi Hadhihi al-A'sar.* Qum: Bustan-i Kitab, 2007.

Shaykh Baha'i, Muhammad bin Husayn. *Jami'-i 'Abbasi.* 2 vols. Isfahan: Hasab al-Amr-i Nizam al-Saltanah, 1895.

Shirazi, Mirza Fazlullah. *Tarikh-i Zu al-Qarnayn.* Edited by Nasir Afsharfar. Tehran: Vizarat-i Farhang va Irshad-i Islami, 2001.

Sipihr, 'Abd al-Husayn Lisan al-Saltanah, and 'Ali Quli Khan Sardar As'ad. *Tarikh-i Bakhtiyari.* Tehran: Yasavuli, 1982.

Stewart, Charles Edward. *Through Persia in Disguise with Reminiscences of the Indian Mutiny.* London: Routledge, 1911.

Sykes, Percy Molesworth. *Ten Thousand Miles in Persia, or Eight Years in Irán.* London: J. Murray, 1902.

Tahvildar Isfahani, Husayn ibn Muhammad Ibrahim. *Jughrafiya-yi Isfahan: Jughrafiya-yi Tabi'i va Insani va Amar-i Asnaf-i Shahr.* Edited by Manuchihr Sutudah. Tehran: Intisharat-i Mu'assasah-i Mutali'at va Tahqiqat-i Ijtima'i, 1963.

Tēr Hovhaneants', Harut'iwn T'. *Tarikh-i Julfa-yi Isfahan.* Edited by Muhammad 'Ali Musavi Faridani. Translated by L. G. Minasean. Isfahan: Nashr-i Zindah Rud, 2001.

Tihrani, Mahdi Navvab. *Dastur al-A'qab: Risalah-i Intiqadi va Siyasi az Avayil-i 'Asr-i Qajar.* Edited by 'Ali Al-i Davud. Tehran: Tarikh-i Iran, 1997.

Tunakabuni, Mirza Muhammad. *Qisas Al-'Ulama.* Edited by Muhammad Salihi Mujarrad. Tehran: Muhammad Salihi Mujarrad, 2011.

Tusi, Muhammad ibn al-Hasan. *Tahdhib al-Ahkam fi sharh al-Muqni'ah l'il-Shaykh al-Mufid.* 10 vols. Beirut: Dar al-Ta'aruf, 1992.

Ussher, John. *A Journey from London to Persepolis.* London: Hurst and Blackett, 1865.

Vámbéry, Ármin. *Arminius Vambéry: His Life and Adventures.* London: T. Fisher Unwin, 1884.

Wills, Charles James. *In the Land of the Lion and Sun, or Modern Persia.* London: Ward, Lock, 1891.

Wolff, Joseph. *Missionary Journal and Memoir.* London: J. Duncan and L. B. Seeley and Son, 1827.

Yeroushalmi, David, ed. *The Jews of Iran in the Nineteenth Century: Aspects of History, Community, and Culture.* Leiden: Brill, 2009.

Zanganah, Chiragh 'Ali. "Vaqayi'-i Isfahan." In *Rijal-i Dawrah-i Qajar,* edited by Husayn Sa'adat Nuri, 182–205. Tehran: Vahid, 1985.

Zhukovskii, V. A. *Ash'ar-i 'Ammiyanah-i Iran: dar 'Asr-i Qajari.* Translated by 'Abd al-Husayn Navai. Tehran: Asatir, 2003.

Zill al-Sultan, Mas'ud Mirza. *Tarikh-i Sarguzasht-i Mas'udi: Zindaginamah va khatirat-i Zill al-Sultan.* 3 vols. Tehran: Dunya-yi Kitab, 1983.

Published Secondary Sources

Abou El Fadl, Khaled. *Rebellion and Violence in Islamic Law*. Cambridge: Cambridge University Press, 2006.

Abrahamian, Ervand. *Iran between Two Revolutions*. Princeton, NJ: Princeton University Press, 1982.

———. *Tortured Confessions: Prisons and Public Recantations in Modern Iran*. Berkeley: University of California Press, 2008.

Abu-Mannah, Butrus. "The Islamic Roots of the Gülhane Rescript." *Die Welt Des Islams* 34, no. 2 (1994): 173–203.

Adamiyat, Faridun. *Amir Kabir va Iran*. Tehran: Intisharat-i Khwarazmi, 1982.

———. *Andishahha-yi Mirza Fath ʿAli Akhundzadah*. Tehran: Khwarazmi, 1970.

Adamiyat, Faridun, and Huma Natiq. *Afkar-i Ijtimaʿi va Siyasi va Iqtisadi dar Asar-i Muntashir Nashudah-i dawran-i Qajar*. Tehran: Intisharat-i Agah, 1989.

Afary, Janet. "From Outcastes to Citizens: Jews in Qajar Iran." In *Esther's Children: A Portrait of Iranian Jews*, edited by Houman Sarshar, 139–74. Beverly Hills, CA: Jewish Publication Society, 2002.

———. *The Iranian Constitutional Revolution, 1906–1911: Grassroots Democracy, Social Democracy and the Origins of Feminism*. New York: Columbia University Press, 1996.

Afary, Janet, and Kevin B. Anderson. *Foucault and the Iranian Revolution: Gender and the Seductions of Islamism*. Chicago: University of Chicago Press, 2010.

Afshar, Iraj. "Aghaz-i Tarjumah-i Kitabha-yi Farangi bih Farsi." *Majallah-i Iran Shinasi* 14, no. 53 (2002): 79–110.

Afshari, Reza. *Human Rights in Iran: The Abuse of Cultural Relativism*. Philadelphia: University of Pennsylvania Press, 2011.

Aghaie, Kamran. *The Martyrs of Karbala: Shiʿi Symbols and Rituals in Modern Iran*. Seattle: University of Washington Press, 2004.

Ahmed, Faiz. *Afghanistan Rising: Islamic Law and Statecraft between the Ottoman and British Empires*. Cambridge: Cambridge University Press, 2017.

Ahmed, Shahab. *What Is Islam? The Importance of Being Islamic*. Princeton, NJ: Princeton University Press, 2017.

Al-Azmeh, Aziz. *Muslim Kingship: Power and the Sacred in Muslim, Christian and Pagan Polities*. London: I. B. Tauris, 1997.

Albrecht, Sarah. *Dār Al-Islām Revisited: Territoriality in Contemporary Islamic Legal Discourse on Muslims in the West*. Leiden: Brill, 2018.

Algar, Hamid. "An Introduction to the History of Freemasonry in Iran." *Middle Eastern Studies* 6, no. 3 (October 1, 1970): 276–96.

———. *Mirzā Malkum Khān: A Study in the History of Iranian Modernism*. Berkeley: University of California Press, 1973.

———. *Religion and State in Iran, 1785–1906: The Role of the Ulama in the Qajar Period*. Berkeley: University of California Press, 1969.

Alkan, Necati. *Non-Sunni Muslims in the Late Ottoman Empire State and Missionary Perceptions of the Alawis*. London: I. B. Tauris, 2022.

Alshech, Eli. "'Do Not Enter Houses Other than Your Own': The Evolution of the Notion of a Private Domestic Sphere in Early Sunnī Islamic Thought." *Islamic Law and Society* 11, no. 3 (2004): 291–332.

———. "Out of Sight and Therefore Out of Mind: Early Sunnī Islamic Modesty Regulations and the Creation of Spheres of Privacy." *Journal of Near Eastern Studies* 66, no. 4 (2007): 267–90.

al-Tihrani, Muhammad Muhsin Agha Buzurg. *al-Dhari'ah ila Tasanif al-Shi'ah*. Edited by Ja'far Murtada 'Amili. 29 vols. Beirut: Dar al-Adwa', 1983.

Amanat, Abbas. "Amīn-al-Dawla, 'Abdallāh Khan." *EIr*.

———. "Constitutional Revolution i. Intellectual Background." *EIr*.

———. "From *ijtihād* to *wilāyat-i faqīh*: The Evolution of the Shiite Legal Authority to Political Power." In *Shari'a: Islamic Law in the Contemporary Context*, edited by Abbas Amanat and Frank Griffel, 120–36. Stanford, CA: Stanford University Press, 2007.

———. "In Between the Madrasa and the Marketplace: The Designation of Clerical Leadership in Modern Shi'ism." In *Authority and Political Culture in Shi'ism*, edited by Saïd Amir Arjomand, 98–132. Albany: State University of New York Press, 1988.

———. *Iran: A Modern History*. New Haven, CT: Yale University Press, 2017.

———. *Pivot of the Universe: Nasir al-Din Shah and the Iranian Monarchy, 1831–1896*. Berkeley: University of California Press, 1997.

———. *Resurrection and Renewal: The Making of the Babi Movement in Iran, 1844–1850*. Ithaca, NY: Cornell University Press, 1989.

Amanat, Mehrdad. *Jewish Identities in Iran: Resistance and Conversion to Islam and the Baha'i Faith*. London: I. B. Tauris, 2010.

———. "Set in Stone: Homeless Corpses and Desecrated Graves in Modern Iran." *International Journal of Middle East Studies* 44, no. 2 (2012): 257–83.

Amanullah, Muhammad. "Juristic Differences over the Implementation of Qiṣāṣ against a Muslim Who Kills a Non-Muslim." *Arab Law Quarterly* 32, no. 2 (2018): 185–203.

Amir 'Ala'i, Shams al-Din. *Mujazat-i I'dam*. Tehran: Chapkhanah-i Majlis, 1950.

Ammann, Ludwig. "Private and Public in Muslim Civilization." In *Islam in Public: Turkey, Iran, and Europe*, edited by Nilüfer Göle and Ludwig Ammann, 77–126. Istanbul: İstanbul Bilgi University Press, 2006.

Anderson, J. N. D. "Homicide in Islamic Law." *Bulletin of the School of Oriental and African Studies, University of London* 13, no. 4 (1951): 811–28.

Appiah, Anthony. *The Honor Code: How Moral Revolutions Happen*. New York: Norton, 2010.

Arjomand, Saïd Amir. "Perso-Islamicate Political Ethic in Relation to the Sources of Islamic Law." In *Mirror for the Muslim Prince: Islam and the Theory of Statecraft*, edited by Mehrzad Boroujerdi, 82–106. Syracuse, NY: Syracuse University Press, 2013.

———. "Political Ethic and Public Law in the Early Qajar Period." In *Religion and Society in Qajar Iran*, edited by Robert Gleave, 21–40. New York: Routledge, 2005.

———. *The Shadow of God and the Hidden Imam: Religion, Political Order, and Societal Change in Shi'ite Iran from the Beginning to 1890*. Chicago: University of Chicago Press, 1984.

———. "The Shi'ite Hierocracy and the State in Pre-Modern Iran: 1785–1890." *European Journal of Sociology* 22, no. 1 (1981): 40–78.

———. *Sociology of Shi'ite Islam*. Leiden: Brill, 2018.

———. *The Turban for the Crown: The Islamic Revolution in Iran*. New York: Oxford University Press, 1988.

Asad, Talal. *Formations of the Secular: Christianity, Islam, Modernity*. Stanford, CA: Stanford University Press, 2003.

———. "Reflections on Violence, Law, and Humanitarianism." *Critical Inquiry* 41, no. 2 (2015): 390–427.

Ashraf, Assef. "Copied and Collected: Firmans, Petitions, and the Political History of Qajar Iran." *Journal of the Economic and Social History of the Orient* 62, nos. 5–6 (2019): 963–97.

———. "From Khan to Shah: State, Society, and Forming the Ties That Made Qajar Iran." PhD diss., Yale University, 2016.

Aykut, Ebru. "Toxic Murder, Female Poisoners, and the Question of Agency at the Late Ottoman Law Courts, 1840–1908." *Journal of Women's History* 28, no. 3 (2016): 114–37.

Ayoub, Mahmoud. "Repentance in the Islamic Tradition." In *Repentance: A Comparative Perspective*, edited by Amitai Etzioni and David E. Carney, 96–121. New York: Rowman and Littlefield, 1997.

Ayoub, Samy. "The Mecelle, Sharia, and the Ottoman State: Fashioning and Refashioning of Islamic Law in the Nineteenth and Twentieth Centuries." In *Law and Legality in the Ottoman Empire and Republic of Turkey*, edited by Kent Schull, M. Safa Saracoğlu, and Robert W. Zens, 129–55. Bloomington: Indiana University Press, 2016.

Azam, Hina. *Sexual Violation in Islamic Law: Substance, Evidence, and Procedure*. Cambridge: Cambridge University Press, 2015.

Bakhash, Shaul. *Iran, Monarchy, Bureaucracy, and Reform under the Qajars, 1858–1896*. London: Ithaca Press for the Middle East Centre St. Antony's College, 1978.

Baldwin, James E. *Islamic Law and Empire in Ottoman Cairo*. Edinburgh: Edinburgh University Press, 2017.

Bamdad, Mahdi. *Sharh-i Hal-i Rijal-i Iran Dar Qarn-i 12 va 13 va 14 Hijri*. 6 vols. Tehran: Zuvvar, 1992.

Banani, Amin. *The Modernization of Iran, 1921–1941*. Stanford, CA: Stanford University Press, 1961.

Barkey, Karen, and Lauren Benton. "Aspects of Legal Pluralism in the Ottoman Empire." In *Legal Pluralism and Empires, 1500–1850*, 83–108. New York: New York University Press, 2013.

Başaran, Betül. *Selim III, Social Control and Policing in Istanbul at the End of the Eighteenth Century: Between Crisis and Order*. Leiden: Brill, 2014.

Bashir, Shahzad. "Shah Isma'il and the Qizilbash: Cannibalism in the Religious History of Early Safavid Iran." *History of Religions* 45, no. 3 (February 1, 2006): 234–56.

Bayat, Mangol. *Iran's First Revolution: Shi'ism and the Constitutional Revolution of 1905–1909*. New York: Oxford University Press, 1991.

Beccaria, Cesare. *Beccaria: "On Crimes and Punishments" and Other Writings*. Edited by Richard Bellamy and Richard Davies. Cambridge: Cambridge University Press, 1995.

Bedau, Hugo Adam. "Bentham's Utilitarian Critique of the Death Penalty." *Journal of Criminal Law and Criminology* 74, no. 3 (1983): 1033–65.

Belhaj, Abdessamad. "Law and Order According to Ibn Taymiyya and Ibn Qayyim Al-Jawziyya." In *Islamic Theology, Philosophy and Law: Debating Ibn Taymiyya and Ibn Qayyim al-Jawziyya*, edited by Birgit Krawietz and Georges Tamer, 400–421. Berlin: De Grutyer, 2013.

Benjamin, Walter. *Reflections: Essays, Aphorisms, Autobiographical Writings*. Translated by Peter Demetz. New York: Schocken Books, 1986.

Berberian, Houri. "'Unequivocal Sole Ruler': The Lives of New Julfan Armenian Women and Early Modern Laws." *Journal of the Society of Armenian Studies* 23 (2014): 83–112.

Betteridge, Anne H. "Ziarat: Pilgrimage to the Shrines of Shiraz." PhD diss., University of Chicago, 1985.

Bigdeli, Sadeq. "Legal Positivism in the Pre-Constitutional Era of Late Nineteenth-Century Iran." *Waikato Law Review* 19, no. 2 (2011): 174–87.

Boogert, Maurits H. van den. *The Capitulations and the Ottoman Legal System: Qadis, Consuls, and Beratlis in the 18th Century*. Leiden: Brill, 2005.

Brookshaw, Dominic Parviz. *Hafiz and His Contemporaries: Poetry, Performance and Patronage in Fourteenth Century Iran*. London: I. B. Tauris, 2019.

Bucknill, John, Alexander Strachey, and Haig Apisoghom S. Utidjian, trans. *The Imperial Ottoman Penal Code*. London: Oxford University Press, 1913.

Bulunur, Kerim İlker. "An Honour Killing in Aintab: The Issue of Killing Fornicators in the Ottoman Empire." *Acta Orientalia* 69, no. 3 (2016): 231–48.

Cahen, Claude. "Himaya." *EI2*.

Calhoun, Craig, ed. *Habermas and the Public Sphere*. Cambridge, MA: MIT Press, 1992.

Calmard, Jean. "Moḥammad Shah Qājār." *EIr*.

Campo, Juan Eduardo. *The Other Sides of Paradise: Explorations into the Religious Meanings of Domestic Space in Islam*. Columbia: University of South Carolina Press, 1991.

Chehabi, H. E. "The Banning of the Veil and Its Consequences." In *The Making of Modern Iran: State and Society under Riza Shah 1921–1941*, edited by Stephanie Cronin, 203–21. London: RoutledgeCurzon, 2003.

Çiğdem, Recep. "Cannibalism as Highlighted by a Case from the Ottoman Law Court of Sofia, 1027/1618." *Acta Orientalia* 64, no. 3 (2011): 287–303.

Cohen, Esther. *The Crossroads of Justice: Law and Culture in Late Medieval France*. Leiden: Brill, 1993.

Cohen, Mark. "What Was the Pact of 'Umar? A Literary-Historical Study." *Jerusalem Studies in Arabic and Islam*, no. 23 (1999): 100–157.

Cole, Juan Ricardo. *Modernity and the Millennium: The Genesis of the Baha'i Faith in the Nineteenth-Century Middle East*. New York: Columbia University Press, 1998.

Cook, Michael. *Commanding Right and Forbidding Wrong in Islamic Thought*. Cambridge: Cambridge University Press, 2010.

Cormack, Bradin. *A Power to Do Justice: Jurisdiction, English Literature, and the Rise of Common Law*. Chicago: University of Chicago Press, 2009.

Crews, Robert. "Muslim Networks, Imperial Power, and the Local Politics of Qajar Iran." In *Asiatic Russia: Imperial Power in Regional and International Contexts*, edited by Tomohiko Uyama, 174–88. New York: Routledge, 2012.

Crone, Patricia. *God's Rule: Government and Islam*. New York: Columbia University Press, 2004.

Cronin, Stephanie. "Importing Modernity: European Military Missions to Qajar Iran." *Comparative Studies in Society and History* 50, no. 1 (January 1, 2008): 197–226.

———. *Social Histories of Iran: Modernism and Marginality in the Middle East*. New York: Cambridge University Press, 2021.

Dakake, Maria. "Hiding in Plain Sight: The Practical and Doctrinal Significance of Secrecy in Shi'ite Islam." *Journal of the American Academy of Religion* 74, no. 2 (2006): 324–55.

Danishpazhuh, Muhammad Taqi. "Jami'-i Nasiri va Qanun-i Nasiri." In *Sukhanranihayi Duvvumin Kungrah-i Tahqiqat-i Irani*, edited by Hamid Zarrinkub, 2:503–25. Mashhad: Danishkadah-i Adabiyat va 'Ulum-i Insani, 1973.

Davies, C. E. "A History of the Province of Fars during the Later Nineteenth Century." PhD diss., University of Oxford, 1984.

Deringil, Selim. *Conversion and Apostasy in the Late Ottoman Empire*. Cambridge: Cambridge University Press, 2012.

Derrida, Jacques. *On Cosmopolitanism and Forgiveness*. London: Routledge, 2001.

Dols, Michael Walters. *Majnun: The Madman in Medieval Islamic Society*. Edited by Diana E. Immisch. Oxford, UK: Clarendon, 1992.

Dorsett, Shaunnagh, and Shaun McVeigh. *Jurisdiction*. London: Routledge-Cavendish, 2012.

Douzinas, Costas. "The Metaphysics of Jurisdiction." In *Jurisprudence of Jurisdiction*, edited by Shaun McVeigh, 21–32. London: Routledge-Cavendish, 2016.

Duby, Georges. "Introduction: Private Power, Public Power." In *A History of Private Life: Revelations of the Medieval World*, edited by Philippe Ariès and Georges

Duby, translated by Arthur Goldhammer, 3–31. Cambridge, MA: Harvard University Press, 1988.

Duindam, Jeroen. *Dynasties: A Global History of Power, 1300–1800.* Cambridge: Cambridge University Press, 2016.

Durkheim, Émile. *The Elementary Forms of Religious Life.* Edited by Mark S. Cladis. Translated by Carol Cosman. Oxford: Oxford University Press, 2001.

———. "Two Laws of Penal Evolution." Translated by William Jeffrey. *University of Cincinnati Law Review* 38, no. 1 (1969): 32–60.

Ebrami, Hooshang. "The Impure Jew." In *Esther's Children: A Portrait of Iranian Jews*, edited by Houman Sarshar, 95–102. Beverly Hills, CA: Jewish Publication Society, 2002.

El-Awa, Mohammed S. "Ta'azir in the Islamic Penal System." *Journal of Islamic and Comparative Law* 6 (1976): 41–59.

Elias, Norbert. *The Civilizing Process: Sociogenetic and Psychogenetic Investigations.* Edited by Eric Dunning, Johan Goudsblom, and Stephen Mennell. Translated by Edmund Jephcott. Oxford, UK: Blackwell, 2000.

El-Rouayheb, Khaled. *Before Homosexuality in the Arab-Islamic World, 1500–1800.* Chicago: University of Chicago Press, 2005.

El Shamsy, Ahmed. "Shame, Sin, and Virtue: Islamic Notions of Privacy." In *Public and Private in Ancient Mediterranean Law and Religion*, edited by Clifford Ando and Jörg Rüpke, 237–50. Berlin: De Gruyter, 2015.

Emon, Anver M. "Codification and Islamic Law: The Ideology behind a Tragic Narrative." *Middle East Law and Governance* 8, no. 2–3 (2016): 275–309.

———. "Huqūq Allāh and Huqūq Al-'Ibād: A Legal Heuristic for a Natural Rights Regime." *Islamic Law and Society* 13, no. 3 (2006): 325–91.

———. "The Quadrants of Sharī'a: The Here and Hereafter as Constitutive of Islamic Law." In *Roads to Paradise: Eschatology and Concepts of the Hereafter in Islam*, edited by Todd Lawson and Sebastian Günther, 1099–1126. Leiden: Brill, 2017.

Emon, Anver M., Mark S. Ellis, and Benjamin Glahn, eds. *Islamic Law and International Human Rights Law: Searching for Common Ground?* Oxford: Oxford University Press, 2015.

Enayat, Hadi. *Law, State, and Society in Modern Iran: Constitutionalism, Autocracy, and Legal Reform, 1906–1941.* New York: Palgrave Macmillan, 2013.

Entessar, Nader. "Criminal Law and the Legal System in Revolutionary Iran." *Boston College Third World Law Journal* 8 (1988): 91–102.

Ergin, Nina. "Ottoman Royal Women's Spaces: The Acoustic Dimension." *Journal of Women's History* 26, no. 1 (March 20, 2014): 89–111.

Eshaghi, Peyman. "Quietness beyond Political Power: Politics of Taking Sanctuary (Bast Neshini) in the Shi'ite Shrines of Iran." *Iranian Studies* 49, no. 3 (2016): 493–514.

Fahmy, Khaled. "The Anatomy of Justice: Forensic Medicine and Criminal Law in Nineteenth-Century Egypt." *Islamic Law and Society* 6, no. 2 (1999): 224–71.

———. *In Quest of Justice: Islamic Law and Forensic Medicine in Modern Egypt.* Oakland: University of California Press, 2018.

———. "The Police and the People in Nineteenth-Century Egypt." *Die Welt des Islams* 39, no. 3 (1999): 340–77.

———. "Towards a Social History of Modern Alexandria." In *Alexandria, Real and Imagined*, 281–306. Aldershot, UK: Ashgate, 2004.

Fahmy, Ziad. *Street Sounds: Listening to Everyday Life in Modern Egypt.* Stanford, CA: Stanford University Press, 2020.

Falasiri, Fakhr al-Din, and Nasir Makarim Shirazi. *Durnama'i az sima-yi yak mujahid: Sharhi az zindagani-i Sayyid 'Ali Akbar Mujtahid Falasiri va mubarazat-i u ba Isti'mar va istibdad-i 'asr-i khud.* Qum: Falasiri, 1992.

Farridnejad, Shervin. "The Royal Farman and the Abolition of Zoroastrian Poll Tax in Qajar Iran." *Himalayan and Central Asian Studies* 25, nos. 1–3 (2021): 105–31.

Faruqi, Lois Ibsen al. "Music, Musicians and Muslim Law." *Asian Music* 17, no. 1 (1985): 3–36.

Fath-'Alizadah, Muhandis 'Ali. "Vazhah-i Qanun va Vurud-i An Bih Huquq-i Iran." *Majallah-i Kanun-i Vukala*, no. 177 (2003): 166–74.

Fleischer, Cornell. "The Lawgiver as Messiah: The Making of the Imperial Image in the Reign of Süleyman." In *Soliman le Magnifique et son temps: Actes du colloque de Paris, Galeries Nationales du Grand Palais, 7–10 mars 1990*, edited by Gilles Veinstein, 159–77. Paris: Documentation française, 1992.

Floor, Willem. "Change and Development in the Judicial System of Qajar Iran (1800–1925)." In *Qajar Iran: Political, Social, and Cultural Change, 1800–1925*, edited by Clifford Edmund Bosworth and Carole Hillenbrand, 113–47. Edinburgh: Edinburgh University Press, 1983.

———. "Judicial and Legal Systems iv. Judicial System from the Advent of Islam through the 19th Century." *EIr.*

———. "The Marketpolice in Qājār Persia: The Office of Dārūgha-yi Bāzār and Muḥtasib." *Die Welt des Islams* 13, no. 3/4 (1971): 212–29.

———. "The Office of Muhtasib in Iran." *Iranian Studies* 18, no. 1 (1985): 53–74.

———. "The Police in Qâjâr Persia." *Zeitschrift der Deutschen Morgenländischen Gesellschaft* 123 (1973): 293–315.

Ford, Richard T. "Law's Territory (A History of Jurisdiction)." *Michigan Law Review* 97, no. 4 (1999): 843–930.

Foucault, Michel. *Discipline and Punish: The Birth of the Prison.* Translated by Alan Sheridan. New York: Vintage, 2012.

Fragner, Bert. "Farmān." *EIr.*

Friedland, Paul. *Seeing Justice Done: The Age of Spectacular Capital Punishment in France.* Oxford: Oxford University Press, 2014.

Gahan, Jairan. "Red-Light Tehran: Prostitution, Intimately Public Islam, and the Rule of the Sovereign, 1910–1980." PhD diss., University of Toronto, 2017.

———. "The Sovereign and the Sensible." *Comparative Studies of South Asia, Africa and the Middle East* 41, no. 2 (2021): 222–35.

Garland, David. *Punishment and Modern Society: A Study in Social Theory*. Chicago: University of Chicago Press, 2014.

Ghamari-Tabrizi, Behrooz. *Foucault in Iran: Islamic Revolution after the Enlightenment*. Minneapolis: University of Minnesota Press, 2017.

Ghobadi, Bahman. *No One Knows about Persian Cats*. Film. New York: IFC Films, 2010.

Girard, René. *Violence and the Sacred*. Baltimore: Johns Hopkins University Press, 1979.

Gleave, Robert. "Crimes against God and Violent Punishment in Al-Fatawa al-'Alamgiriyya." In *Religion and Violence in South Asia: Theory and Practice*, edited by John R. Hinnells and Richard King, 83–106. London: Routledge, 2007.

———. "Jihad and the Religious Legitimacy of the Early Qajar State." In *Religion and Society in Qajar Iran*, edited by Robert Gleave, 41–70. London: Routledge, 2004.

———. "Public Violence, State Legitimacy: The Iqāmat al-Ḥudūd and the Sacred State." In *Public Violence in Islamic Societies: Power, Discipline, and the Construction of the Public Sphere, 7th–19th Centuries C.E.*, edited by Christian Lange and Maribel Fierro, 255–75. Edinburgh: Edinburgh University Press, 2009.

———. "Two Classical Shi'i Theories of Qada." In *Studies in Islamic and Middle Eastern Texts and Traditions in Memory of Norman Calder*, edited by Gerald R. Hawting, A. Samely, and J. A. Mojaddedi, 105–21. Oxford: Oxford University Press, 2000.

Graeber, David. *Debt: The First 5,000 Years*. New York: Melville House, 2014.

Graeber, David, and Marshall Sahlins. *On Kings*. Chicago: Hau Books, 2017.

Grehan, James. *Everyday Life and Consumer Culture in 18th-Century Damascus*. Seattle: University of Washington Press, 2007.

Gulbun, Muhammad. "Lughat-i Ruznamah va Nukhustin Ruznamah-i Chapi-i Farsi dar Iran." *Barrisiha-yi Tarikhi* 5, no. 5 (1970): 75–114.

Habermas, Jürgen. *The Structural Transformation of the Public Sphere: An Inquiry into a Category of Bourgeois Society*. Translated by Thomas Burger and Frederick Lawrence. Cambridge, MA: MIT Press, 1989.

Haeri, Shahla. *Law of Desire: Temporary Marriage in Shi'i Iran*. Syracuse, NY: Syracuse University Press, 2014.

Hairi, 'Abd al-Hadi. "The Legitimacy of the Early Qajar Rule as Viewed by the Shi'i Religious Leaders." *Middle Eastern Studies* 24, no. 3 (1988): 271–86.

———. *Shi'ism and Constitutionalism in Iran: A Study of the Role Played by the Persian Residents of Iraq in Iranian Politics*. Leiden: Brill, 1977.

Hallaq, Wael. "'God Cannot Be Harmed': On Huquq Allah/Huquq al-'Ibad Continuum." In *Routledge Handbook of Islamic Law*, edited by Khaled Abou El Fadl, 67–81. London: Routledge, 2019.

———. *The Impossible State: Islam, Politics, and Modernity's Moral Predicament*. New York: Columbia University Press, 2013.

———. *Sharī'a: Theory, Practice, Transformations*. New York: Cambridge University Press, 2009.

Hamadeh, Shirine. "Mean Streets: Space and Moral Order in Early Ottoman Istanbul." *Turcica* 44 (2013): 249–77.

Hambly, Gavin. "Farmānfarmā, Ḥosayn-ʿAlī Mīrzā." *EIr.*

Hamoudi, Haider Ala. "Sex and the Shariʿa: Defining Gender Norms and Sexual Deviancy in Shiʿi Islam." *Fordham International Law Journal* 39, no. 1 (2015): 25–100.

Han, Byung-Chul. *Topology of Violence.* Cambridge, MA: MIT Press, 2018.

Hasanzadah, Parvanah, Ghulam Husayn Zargarinizhad, and Riza Shaʿbani Samaghabadi. "Dar al-Tarjumah-i Humayuni Nukhustin Iqdam-i Vizarat-i Intibaʿat dar Bab-i Tarjumah." *Faslnamah-i Anjuman-i Irani Mutalaʿat-i Farhangi va Irtibati* 16, no. 58 (2020): 58–80.

Heern, Zackery M. *The Emergence of Modern Shiʿism: Islamic Reform in Iraq and Iran.* London: Oneworld, 2015.

Heyd, Uriel. *Studies in Old Ottoman Criminal Law.* Edited by V. L. Ménage. Oxford, UK: Clarendon, 1973.

Hillenbrand, Carole. "A Little-Known Mirror for Princes by al-Ghazali." In *Words, Texts and Concepts Cruising the Mediterranean Sea*, edited by Rudiger Arnzen and Jorn Thielmann, 593–601. Leuven: Peeters, 2004.

Hoexter, Miriam. "Huquq Allah and Huquq Al-ʿIbad as Reflected in the *Waqf* Institution." *Jerusalem Studies in Arabic and Islam* 19 (1995): 133–56.

Holden, Stacy E. *The Politics of Food in Modern Morocco.* Gainesville: University Press of Florida, 2009.

Hosseini, Fatemeh. "Zoned Desires: Prostitution, Family Politics, and Sexual Ideology in 20th Century Iran." PhD diss., University of Maryland, 2014.

Ileri, Nurcin. "Rule, Misconduct, and Dysfunction The Police Forces in Theory and Practice in Fin-de-Siècle Istanbul." *Comparative Studies of South Asia, Africa and the Middle East* 34, no. 1 (2014): 147–59.

Imber, Colin. "Why You Should Poison Your Husband: A Note on Liability in Hanafi Law in the Ottoman Period." *Islamic Law and Society* 1, no. 2 (1994): 206–16.

Iqbal, ʿAbbas. "Hujjat Al-Islam Hajj Sayyid Muhammad Baqir Shafti." *Majallah-i Yadigar* 10 (1948): 28–43.

Jackson, Peter. "Beglerbegī." *EIr.*

Jaʿfariyan, Rasul. *Din va Siyasat dar Dawrah-i Safavi.* Qum: Ansariyan, 1991.

———. *Kilk va Kitab: Shamil-i 532 Maqalah-i Kutah-i Tarikhi Siyasi va Ijtimaʿi.* Qum: Nashr-i Muʾarrikh, 2014.

Johansen, Baber. "The Claims of Men and the Claims of God: The Limits of Government Authority in Hanafite Law." In *Pluriformiteit En Verdeling van de Macht in Het Midden-Oosten*, 60–104. Nijmegen: Vereniging voor de Studie van het Midden-Oosten en de Islam, 1980.

———. *Contingency in a Sacred Law: Legal and Ethical Norms in the Muslim Fiqh.* Leiden: Brill, 1999.

———. "La découverte des choses qui parlent La légalisation de la torture judiciaire en droit musulman (xiiie–xive siècles)." *Enquête*, no. 7 (1999): 175–202.

———. "Sacred and Religious Element in Hanafite Law: Function and Limits of the Absolute Character of Government Authority." In *Islam et politique au Maghreb:*

Travaux de la table ronde du Centre de recherches et d'études sur les sociétés Médi-terranéennes, Aix-en-Provence, Juin 1979, edited by Jean-Claude Vatin and Jean-Claude Vatin, 281–303. Paris: Editions du Centre national de la recherche scientifique, 1981.

———. "Secular and Religious Elements in Hanafite Law: Function and Limits of the Absolute Character of Government Authority." In *Contingency in a Sacred Law: Legal and Ethical Norms in the Muslim Fiqh*, 189–218. Leiden: Brill, 1999.

———. "Signs as Evidence: The Doctrine of Ibn Taymiyya (1263–1328) and Ibn Qayyim al-Jawziyya (d. 1351) on Proof." *Islamic Law and Society* 9, no. 2 (2002): 168–93.

———. "The Valorization of the Human Body in Muslim Sunni Law." *Interdisciplinary Journal of Middle Eastern Studies* 4 (1996): 71–112.

Kadivar, Mohsen. "An Introduction to the Public and Private Debate in Islam." *Social Research* 70, no. 3 (2003): 659–80.

Kafadar, Cemal. "Janissaries and Other Riffraff of Ottoman Istanbul: Rebels without a Cause?" In *Identity and Identity Formation in the Ottoman World: A Volume of Essays in Honor of Norman Itzkowitz*, edited by Baki Tezcan and Karl K. Barbir, 113–34. Madison: University of Wisconsin Press, 2007.

Kamali, Mohammad Hashim. *Principles of Islamic Jurisprudence*. Cambridge, UK: Islamic Texts Society, 1991.

———. "The Right to Personal Safety and the Principle of Legality in the Sharī'ah." *Islamic Studies* 39, no. 2 (2000): 249–89.

Karny, Azriel. "Mirza Hosein Khan Moshir Od-Dowle and His Attempts at Reform in Iran, 1871–1873." PhD diss., UCLA, 1976.

———. "The Premiership of Mirza Hosein Khan and His Reforms in Iran, 1872–1873." *Asian and African Studies* 10 (1975): 127–56.

Kashani-Sabet, Firoozeh. *Frontier Fictions: Shaping the Iranian Nation, 1804–1946*. Princeton, NJ: Princeton University Press, 1999.

Kashifi, Husayn Va'iz. *Akhlaq-i Muhsini*. Edited by Sayyid Hasan Naqibi. Qum: Za'ir, 2014.

Katz, Marion Holmes. *Body of Text: The Emergence of the Sunnī Law of Ritual Purity*. Albany: SUNY Press, 2002.

———. "The Ḥadd Penalty for Zinā: Symbol or Deterrent? Texts from the Early Sixteenth Century." In *The Lineaments of Islam: Studies in Honor of Fred McGraw Donner*, edited by Paul Cobb, 351–76. Leiden: Brill, 2012.

Kazemi, Ranin. "Doctoring the Body and Exciting the Soul: Drugs and Consumer Culture in Medieval and Early Modern Iran." *Modern Asian Studies* 54, no. 2 (2020): 554–617.

Kazemi Moussavi, Ahmad. *Religious Authority in Shi'ite Islam: From the Office of Mufti to the Institution of Marja'*. Kuala Lumpur: International Institute of Islamic Thought and Civilization, 2007.

Keddie, Nikki R., and Yann Richard. *Modern Iran: Roots and Results of Revolution*. New Haven, CT: Yale University Press, 2003.

Keshavarzian, Arang. *Bazaar and State in Iran: The Politics of the Tehran Marketplace.* New York: Cambridge University Press, 2007.

Khalisi, 'Abbas. *Tarikhchah-i Bast va Bastnishini: Hamrah ba Shavahid-i tarikhi.* Tehran: Intisharat-i 'Ilmi, 1987.

Khan, Ruqayya Yasmine. *Self and Secrecy in Early Islam.* Columbia: University of South Carolina Press, 2008.

Khazeni, Arash. *Tribes and Empire on the Margins of Nineteenth-Century Iran.* Seattle: University of Washington Press, 2010.

Kia, Mehrdad. "Inside the Court of Naser Od-Din Shah Qajar, 1881–96: The Life and Diary of Mohammad Hasan Khan E'temad Os-Saltaneh." *Middle Eastern Studies* 37, no. 1 (2001): 101–41.

Kister, M. J. "'Do Not Assimilate Yourselves . . .': Lā Tashabbahū." *Jerusalem Studies in Arabic and Islam* 12 (1989): 321–71.

Klein, Yaron. "Between Public and Private: An Examination of Ḥisba Literature." *Harvard Middle Eastern and Islamic Review* 7 (2006): 41–62.

———. "Music, Rapture and Pragmatics: Ghazali on Sama' and Wajd." In *No Tapping around Philology: A Festschrift in Honor of Wheeler McIntosh Thackston Jr.'s 70th Birthday,* edited by Alireza Korangy and Daniel Sheffield, 215–41. Wiesbaden: Harrassowitz Verlag, 2014.

Kohlberg, E. "Bahā'-al-Dīn 'Āmelī." *EIr.*

Kondo, Nobuaki. *Islamic Law and Society in Iran: A Social History of Tehran.* London: Routledge, 2017.

———. "Non-Muslims at the Shari'a Court in Qajar Tehran." In *Human Mobility and Multiethnic Coexistence in Middle Eastern Urban Societies 2: Tehran, Cairo, Istanbul, Aleppo, and Beirut,* edited by Hidemitsu Kuroki, 7–21. Tokyo: Research Institute for Languages and Cultures of Asia and Africa, 2018.

Kurzman, Charles. *The Unthinkable Revolution in Iran.* Cambridge, MA: Harvard University Press, 2004.

Lafi, Nora. "Policing the Medina: Public Order in Tunis at the Time of the Tanzimat (1857–1864)." *Journal of the Ottoman and Turkish Studies Association* 4, no. 1 (2017): 55–71.

Lambton, A. K. S. "The Evolution of the Office of the Darugheh." *Majallah-i Mardum Shinasi* 111 (1338): 1–10.

———. "Hisba iii.-Persia." *EI2.*

———. "Hukuma ii.-Persia." *EI2.*

———. "Islamic Political Thought." In *The Legacy of Islam,* edited by Clifford Bosworth, 2nd ed., 404–24. Oxford: Oxford University Press, 1974.

———. *Islamic Society in Persia: An Inaugural Lecture Delivered on 9 March 1954.* London: SOAS, 1954.

———. *Landlord and Peasant in Persia: A Study of Land Tenure and Land Revenue Administration.* London: I. B. Tauris, 1991.

———. "Mahkama 3. Iran." *EI2.*

——. "The Qanats of Qum." In *Qanat, Kariz, and Khattara: Traditional Water Systems in the Middle East and North Africa*, edited by Peter Beaumont and Michael E Bonine, 151–75. London: Middle East & North African Studies Press, 1989.

——. "Some New Trends in Islamic Political Thought in Late 18th and Early 19th Century Persia." *Studia Islamica*, no. 39 (1974): 95–128.

Lange, Christian. *Justice, Punishment and the Medieval Muslim Imagination*. Cambridge: Cambridge University Press, 2013.

——. "Legal and Cultural Aspects of Ignominious Parading (Tashhir) in Islam." *Islamic Law and Society* 14, no. 1 (2007): 81–108.

——. "'On That Day When Faces Will Be White or Black' (Q3:106): Towards a Semiology of the Face in the Arabo-Islamic Tradition." *Journal of the American Oriental Society* 127, no. 4 (2007): 429–45.

——. "Torture and Public Executions in the Islamic Middle Period (Eleventh–Fifteenth Centuries)." In *The Cambridge World History of Violence: 500–1500 AD*, edited by Harriet Zurndorfer, Matthew Gordon, and Richard Kaeuper, 2:164–84. Cambridge: Cambridge University Press, 2020.

Lange, Christian, and Maribel Fierro. "Spatial, Ritual and Representational Aspects of Public Violence in Islamic Societies (7th–19th Centuries C.E.)." In *Public Violence in Islamic Societies: Power, Discipline, and the Construction of the Public Sphere, 7th–19th Centuries C.E.*, edited by Christian Lange and Maribel Fierro, 1–24. Edinburgh: Edinburgh University Press, 2009.

Levy-Rubin, Milka. "Shurut 'Umar and Its Alternatives: The Legal Debate on the Status of the Dhimmis." *Jerusalem Studies in Arabic and Islam* 30 (2005): 170–207.

Loeb, Laurence D. *Outcaste: Jewish Life in Southern Iran*. New York: Gordon and Breach, 1977.

Lorentz, John H. "Iran's Great Reformer of the Nineteenth Century: An Analysis of Amīr Kabīr's Reforms." *Iranian Studies* 4, no. 2–3 (1971): 85–103.

MacEoin, Denis. "Čerāġ-'Alī Khan Serāj-al-Molk Zangana." *EIr*.

——. *The Messiah of Shiraz: Studies in Early and Middle Babism*. Leiden: Brill, 2009.

Maghen, Ze'ev. "Close Encounters: Some Preliminary Observations on the Transmission of Impurity in Early Sunni Jurisprudence." *Islamic Law and Society* 6, no. 3 (1999): 348–92.

Mahdavi, Pardis. *Passionate Uprisings: Iran's Sexual Revolution*. Stanford, CA: Stanford University Press, 2008.

Majd, Mohammad Gholi. *A Victorian Holocaust: Iran in the Great Famine of 1869–1873*. Lanham, MD: Hamilton Books, 2017.

Makdisi, Ussama Samir. *Culture of Sectarianism: Community, History, and Violence in Nineteenth-Century Ottoman Lebanon*. Berkeley: University of California Press, 2000.

Mangeneh-Nourai, Fereshteh. "The Life and Thought of Mirza Malkam Khan, 1833/4–1908: A Contribution to the History of Iranian Liberal Ideas." PhD diss., University of Colorado at Boulder, 1970.

Manoukian, Setrag. *City of Knowledge in Twentieth Century Iran: Shiraz, History and Poetry*. New York: Routledge, 2012.

Mansfield, Mary. *The Humiliation of Sinners: Public Penance in Thirteenth-Century France*. Ithaca, NY: Cornell University Press, 2018.

Marcus, Abraham. *The Middle East on the Eve of Modernity: Aleppo in the Eighteenth Century*. New York: Columbia University Press, 1989.

——. "Privacy in Eighteenth-Century Aleppo: The Limits of Cultural Ideals." *International Journal of Middle East Studies* 18, no. 2 (1986): 165–83.

Martin, Vanessa. "An Evaluation of Reform and Development of the State in the Early Qājār Period." *Die Welt des Islams* 36, no. 1 (March 1, 1996): 1–24.

——. *The Qajar Pact: Bargaining, Protest and the State in Nineteenth-Century Persia*. London: I. B. Tauris, 2005.

Marzolph, Ulrich. *Narrative Illustration in Persian Lithographed Books*. Leiden: Brill, 2001.

Matthee, Rudi. *The Pursuit of Pleasure: Drugs and Stimulants in Iranian History, 1500–1900*. Princeton, NJ: Princeton University Press, 2005.

Mayer, Ann Elizabeth. "The Universality of Human Rights: Lessons from the Islamic Republic." *Social Research* 67, no. 2 (2000): 519–36.

Melville, Charles. "The Persian Famine of 1870–1872: Prices and Politics." *Disasters* 12, no. 4 (1988): 309–25.

Mirzai, Behnaz A. *A History of Slavery and Emancipation in Iran, 1800–1929*. Austin: University of Texas Press, 2017.

Modarressi, Hossein. "Circumstantial Evidence in the Administration of Islamic Justice." In *Justice and Leadership in Early Islamic Courts*, edited by Intisar A. Rabb and Abigail Krasner Balbale, 16–22. Cambridge, MA: Harvard University Press, 2017.

Modarressi, Hossein, and Mahmud Mar'ashi. *Turbat-i Pakan: Asar va Banaha-yi Qadim-i Mahdudah-i Kununi-i Dar al-Mu'minin-i Qum*. 2 vols. Qum: Chapkhanah-i Mihr, 1976.

Momen, Moojan. "Bahá'í Influence on the Reform Movements of the Islamic World in the 1860s and 1870s." *Bahá'í Studies Bulletin* 2, no. 2 (September 1983): 47–65.

——. *An Introduction to Shi'i Islam: The History and Doctrines of Twelver Shi'ism*. New Haven, CT: Yale University Press, 1987.

——. "Persecution and Resilience: A History of the Baha'i Religion in Qajar Isfahan." *Journal of Religious History* 36, no. 4 (2012): 471–85.

——. "The Trial of Mullā 'Alī Basṭāmī: A Combined Sunnī-Shī'ī Fatwā against the Bāb." *Iran* 20 (1982): 113–43.

Mottahedeh, Roy, and Kristen Stilt. "Public and Private as Viewed through the Work of the Muhtasib." *Social Research: An International Quarterly* 70, no. 3 (2003): 735–48.

Mu'allim Habibabadi, Muhammad 'Ali. *Makarim al-Asar dar Ahval-i Rijal-i Dawrah-i Qajar*. 5 vols. Isfahan: Intisharat-i Kamal, 1983.

Muhammad Husayni, Nusratullah. *Tarikh-i Amr-i Baha'i dar Shahr-i Qum*. Darmstadt: 'Asr-i Jadid, 2005.

Müller, Christian. "Crimes without Criminals? Legal Documents on Fourteenth-Century Injury and Homicide Cases from the Haram Collection in Jerusalem."

In *Legal Documents as Sources for the History of Muslim Societies*, edited by Maaike van Berkel, Léon Buskens, and Petra Sijpesteijn, 129–79. Leiden: Brill, 2017.

Munt, Harry. *The Holy City of Medina: Sacred Space in Early Islamic Arabia*. New York: Cambridge University Press, 2014.

Musallam, Basim. "The Ordering of Muslim Societies." In *The Cambridge Illustrated History of the Islamic World*, edited by Francis Robinson, 164–207. Cambridge: Cambridge University Press, 1996.

Najmabadi, Afsaneh. "Types, Acts, or What? Regulation of Sexuality in Nineteenth-Century Iran." In *Islamicate Sexualities: Translations Across Temporal Geographies of Desire*, edited by Kathryn Babayan and Afsaneh Najmabadi, 275–96. Cambridge, MA: Harvard Center for Middle Eastern Studies / Harvard University Press, 2008.

———. *Women with Mustaches and Men without Beards: Gender and Sexual Anxieties of Iranian Modernity*. Berkeley: University of California Press, 2005.

Nashat, Guity. *The Origins of Modern Reform in Iran, 1870–80*. Urbana: University of Illinois Press, 1982.

Nasiri, Muhammad Riza, Daryush Rahmanian, and Sayyid Husayn Razavi Khurasani. "Lutiyan va Naqsh-i Anan dar Ashubha-yi Isfahan Bayn-i Salha-yi 1240 ta 1265 H.Q. barabar ba 1824 ta 1849." *Du Faslnamah-i Pazuhishnamah-i Tarikhha-yi Mahalli-i Iran* 3, no. 3/6 (2015): 98–121.

Newman, Andrew J. "Clerical Perceptions of Sufi Practices in Late Seventeenth-Century Persia: Arguments over the Permissibility of Singing (Ghina)." In *The Heritage of Sufism*, vol. 3, *Late Classical Persianate Sufism: The Safavid and Mughal Period (1501–1750)*, edited by Leonard Lewisohn, 135–64. London: Oneworld, 1999.

Nicolas, A.-L.-M. *Seyyèd Ali Mohammed dit Le Bab*. Paris: Dujarric, 1905.

Nielsen, Jorgen S. *Secular Justice in an Islamic State: Mazalim under the Bahri Mamluks 662/1264–789/1387*. Istanbul: Nederlands historisch-archaeologisch instituut, 1985.

Nikpour, Golnar. "Prison Days: Incarceration and Punishment in Modern Iran." PhD diss., New York University, 2015.

Okazaki, Shoko. "The Great Persian Famine of 1870–71." *Bulletin of the School of Oriental and African Studies* 49, no. 1 (1986): 183–92.

Opwis, Felicitas Meta Maria. *Maṣlaḥa and the Purpose of the Law: Islamic Discourse on Legal Change from the 4th/10th to 8th/14th Century*. Leiden: Brill, 2010.

Osanloo, Arzoo. *Forgiveness Work: Mercy, Law, and Victims' Rights in Iran*. Princeton, NJ: Princeton University Press, 2020.

Othman, Aida. "'And Amicable Settlement Is Best': Sulh and Dispute Resolution in Islamic Law." *Arab Law Quarterly* 21, no. 1 (2007): 64–90.

Pargari, Salih, and Muhammad Bitarafian. "Qum dar Dawrah-i Nasiri: Yak barrisi-i Jughrafiya-yi Tarikhi." *Du Faslnamah-i Pazuhishnamah-i Tarikhha-yi Mahalli-i Iran* 3, no. 2 (2015): 208–26.

Peirce, Leslie. "Domesticating Sexuality: Harem Culture in Ottoman Imperial Law." In *Harem Histories: Envisioning Places and Living Spaces*, edited by Marilyn Booth, 104–35. Durham, NC: Duke University Press, 2010.

———. *Morality Tales: Law and Gender in the Ottoman Court of Aintab.* Berkeley: University of California Press, 2003.

Peluso, Nancy Lee, and Michael Watts, eds. *Violent Environments.* Ithaca, NY: Cornell University Press, 2001.

Perry, John R. *Karim Khan Zand: A History of Iran, 1747–1779.* Chicago: University of Chicago Press, 1979.

Peters, Rudolph. *Crime and Punishment in Islamic Law: Theory and Practice from the Sixteenth to the Twenty-First Century.* Cambridge: Cambridge University, 2005.

———. "Murder in Khaybar: Some Thoughts on the Origins of the 'Qasāma' Procedure in Islamic Law." *Islamic Law and Society* 9, no. 2 (2002): 132–67.

———. "Murder on the Nile: Homicide Trials in 19th Century Egyptian Shariʿa Courts." *Die Welt des Islams* 30, no. 1–4 (1990): 98–116.

———. *Shariʿa, Justice and Legal Order: Egyptian and Islamic Law: Selected Essays.* Leiden: Brill, 2020.

Petry, Carl F. *The Criminal Underworld in a Medieval Islamic Society: Narratives from Cairo and Damascus under the Mamluks.* Chicago: Middle East Documentation Center, 2016.

Piacentini, Laura. "Punishment and Parade: The Cultural Form of Penal Exile in Russia." In *Transnational Penal Cultures,* edited by Vivien Miller and James Campbell, 127–43. Abingdon, UK: Routledge, 2014.

Powers, Paul R. *Intent in Islamic Law: Motive and Meaning in Medieval Sunnī Fiqh.* Leiden: Brill, 2006.

———. "Offending Heaven and Earth: Sin and Expiation in Islamic Homicide Law." *Islamic Law and Society* 14, no. 1 (2007): 42–80.

Qaraguzlu, Hasan. *Qum-i Qadim az Safaviyah ta Qajar 1057–1331.* Qum: Hasan Qaraguzlu, 2014.

Qurayshi-Karin, Hasan. *Qum az Ibtidaʾi-i Dawrah-i Qajar ta Mashrutah.* Qum: Zaʾir, 2011.

Rabb, Intisar. *Doubt in Islamic Law: A History of Legal Maxims, Interpretation, and Islamic Criminal Law.* Cambridge: Cambridge University Press, 2017.

———. "The Islamic Rule of Lenity: Judicial Discretion and Legal Canons." *Vanderbilt Journal of Transnational Law* 44, no. 5 (2011): 1299–1351.

———. "Society and Propriety: The Cultural Construction of Defamation and Blasphemy as Crimes in Islamic Law." In *Accusations of Unbelief in Islam: A Diachronic Perspective on Takfīr,* edited by Camilla Adang, Hassan Ansari, Maribel Fierro, and Sabine Schmidtke, 434–64. Leiden: Brill, 2015.

Rabben, Linda. *Sanctuary and Asylum: A Social and Political History.* Seattle: University of Washington Press, 2016.

Rabi, Uzi, and Nugzar Ter-Oganov. "The Military of Qajar Iran: The Features of an Irregular Army from the Eighteenth to the Early Twentieth Century." *Iranian Studies* 45, no. 3 (2012): 333–54.

Rahmati, Muhammad Riza, Abu al-Fayz Shakuri, and Riza Shaʿbani. *Naqsh-i mujtahid-i Fars dar nahzat-i tanbaku: Zindaginamah-i siyasi, ijtimaʿi-i Sayyid ʿAli Akbar Falasiri.* Qum: Bunyad-i Tarikh-i Inqilab-i Islami-i Iran, 1992.

Ra'in, Isma'il. *Iraniyan-i Armani*. Tehran: Mu'assasah-i Ra'in, 1970.

Rapoport, Yossef. "Royal Justice and Religious Law: Siyāsah and Shari'ah under the Mamluks." *Mamluk Studies Review* 16, no. 71 (2012): 71–102.

Raymond, André. "The Role of Communities (Tawa'if) in the Administration of Cairo in the Ottoman Period." In *The State and Its Servants: Administration in Egypt from Ottoman Times to the Present*, edited by Nelly Hanna, 32–43. Cairo: American University in Cairo Press, 1995.

Reinhart, A. Kevin. "Impurity/No Danger." *History of Religions* 30, no. 1 (1990): 1–24.

Rejali, Darius M. *Torture and Modernity: Self, Society, and State in Modern Iran*. Boulder, CO: Westview, 1994.

Reza, Sadiq. "Islam's Fourth Amendment: Search and Seizure in Islamic Doctrine and Muslim Practice." *Georgetown Journal of International Law* 40, no. 3 (2009): 703–806.

———. "Torture and Islamic Law." *Chicago Journal of International Law* 8, no. 1 (2007): 21–42.

Richards, John F. *The Mughal Empire*. Cambridge: Cambridge University Press, 2012.

Richland, Justin B. "Jurisdiction: Grounding Law in Language." *Annual Review of Anthropology* 42, no. 1 (October 2013): 209–26.

Rizvi, Sajjad. "Shi'i Political Theology and Esotericism in Qajar Iran: The Case of Sayyid Ja'far Kashfi." In *L'ésotérisme shi'ite: Ses racines et ses prolongements = Shi'i esotericism: Its Roots and Developments*, edited by Maria De Cillis, Daniel De Smet, and Orkhan Mir-Kasimov. Turnhout: Brepols, 2016.

Rooijakkers, Christina Thérèse (Tineke). "The Luscious Locks of Lust: Hair and the Construction of Gender in Egypt from Clement to the Fāṭimids." *Al-Masāq* 30, no. 1 (2018): 26–55.

Rosenthal, Franz. "Gambling in Islam." In *Man versus Society in Medieval Islam*, edited by Dimitri Gutas, 335–516. Leiden: Brill, 2015.

———. "The Herb: Hashish versus Medieval Muslim Society." In *Man versus Society in Medieval Islam*, edited by Dimitri Gutas, 131–334. Leiden: Brill, 2015.

Sa'adat Nuri, Husayn. *Rijal-i Dawrah-i Qajar*. Tehran: Vaḥid, 1985.

Savory, R. M. "Bast." *EI2*.

Schacht, J. "Aman." *EI2*.

Schayegh, Cyrus. "Serial Murder in Tehran: Crime, Science, and the Formation of Modern State and Society in Interwar Iran." *Comparative Studies in Society and History* 47, no. 4 (October 1, 2005): 836–62.

———. *Who Is Knowledgeable, Is Strong: Science, Class, and the Formation of Modern Iranian Society, 1900–1950*. Berkeley: University of California Press, 2009.

Schmitt, Carl. *The Concept of the Political*. Chicago: University of Chicago Press, 2008.

———. *Dictatorship*. New York: Wiley, 2015.

Schneider, Irene. "The Concept of Honor and Its Reflection in the Iranian Penal Code." *Journal of Persianate Studies* 5, no. 1 (2012): 43–57.

———. "Imprisonment in Pre-Classical and Classical Islamic Law." *Islamic Law and Society* 2, no. 2 (1995): 157–73.

———. "Muḥammad Bāqir Šaftī (1180–1260/1766–1844) und die Isfahaner Gerichts-barkeit." *Der Islam* 79, no. 2 (2002): 240–73.

———. *The Petitioning System in Iran: State, Society and Power Relations in the Late 19th Century.* Wiesbaden: Harrassowitz, 2006.

———. "Religious and State Jurisdiction during Nāsir Al-Dīn Shāh's Reign." In *Religion and Society in Qajar Iran*, edited by R. M. Gleave, 84–110. London: RoutledgeCurzon, 2004.

Schull, Kent. "Criminal Codes, Crime, and the Transformation of Punishment in the Late Ottoman Empire." In *Law and Legality in the Ottoman Empire and Republic of Turkey*, edited by Kent Schull, M. Safa Saracoğlu, and Robert W. Zens, 156–78. Bloomington: Indiana University Press, 2016.

Semerdjian, Elyse. *"Off the Straight Path": Illicit Sex, Law, and Community in Ottoman Aleppo.* Syracuse, NY: Syracuse University Press, 2008.

Sheikholeslami, A. Reza. *The Structure of Central Authority in Qajar Iran, 1871–1896.* Atlanta: Scholars, 1997.

Shiloah, Amnon. "Music and Religion in Islam." *Acta Musicologica* 69, no. 2 (1997): 143–55.

Shimamoto, Takamitsu. "Society and Economy of Qum in the Latter Half of the 19th Century Iran." *Orient* 24 (1988): 124–40.

Shoemaker, Karl. *Sanctuary and Crime in the Middle Ages, 400–1500.* New York: Fordham University Press, 2011.

Shoukri, Arafat Madi. *Refugee Status in Islam: Concepts of Protection in Islamic Tradition and International Law.* London: I. B. Tauris, 2011.

Siamdoust, Nahid. *Soundtrack of the Revolution: The Politics of Music in Iran.* Stanford, CA: Stanford University Press, 2017.

Singha, Radhika. *A Despotism of Law: Crime and Justice in Early Colonial India.* New Delhi: Oxford University Press, 2000.

Smith, Philip. *Punishment and Culture.* Chicago: University of Chicago Press, 2008.

Sohrabi, Nader. *Revolution and Constitutionalism in the Ottoman Empire and Iran, 1902–1910.* Cambridge: Cambridge University Press, 2011.

Soroudi, Sorour. "The Concept of Jewish Impurity and Its Reflection in Persian and Judeo-Persian Traditions." *Irano-Judaica: Studies Relating to Jewish Contacts with Persian Culture throughout the Ages* 3 (1994): 142–70.

Spierenburg, Pieter. *The Spectacle of Suffering: Executions and the Evolution of Repression from a Preindustrial Metropolis to the European Experience.* Cambridge: Cambridge University Press, 2008.

Stanfield-Johnson, Rosemary. "The Tabarra'iyan and the Early Safavids." *Iranian Studies* 37, no. 1 (2004): 47–71.

Stearns, Justin K. *Infectious Ideas: Contagion in Premodern Islamic and Christian Thought in the Western Mediterranean.* Baltimore: Johns Hopkins University Press, 2011.

Steingass, Francis. *A Comprehensive Persian-English Dictionary.* Beirut: Librairie du Liban, 1975.

Stilt, Kristen. *Islamic Law in Action: Authority, Discretion, and Everyday Experiences in Mamluk Egypt.* Oxford: Oxford University Press, 2012.

Stilt, Kristen, and M. Safa Saraçoğlu. "Hisba and Muhtasib." In *The Oxford Handbook of Islamic Law,* edited by Anver M. Emon and Rumee Ahmed, 327–56. Oxford University Press, 2018.

Szombathy, Zoltan. "Eating People Is Wrong: Some Eyewitness Reports of Cannibalism in Arabic Sources." In *Violence in Islamic Thought from the Qur'an to the Mongols,* edited by Robert Gleave and István Kristó-Nagy, 200–224. Edinburgh: Edinburgh University Press, 2015.

Tafrishi, Murtaza Sayfi Fami. *Pulis-i Khufyah-i Iran 1299–1320: Mururi bar rukhdadha-yi siyasi va tarikhchah-i Shahrbani.* Tehran: Qaqnus, 1989.

Tavana, Mohammad H. "Three Decades of Islamic Criminal Law Legislation in Iran: A Legislative History Analysis with Emphasis on the Amendments of the 2013 Islamic Penal Code." *Electronic Journal of Islamic and Middle Eastern Law* 2 (2014): 24–38.

Tellenbach, Silvia. "The Principle of Legality in the Iranian Constitutional and Criminal Law." In *The Rule of Law, Islam, and Constitutional Politics in Egypt and Iran,* edited by Saïd Amir Arjomand and Nathaniel Brown, 101–22. Albany: SUNY Press, 2013.

Thompson, E. P. "The Moral Economy of the English Crowd in the Eighteenth Century." In *Customs in Common: Studies in Traditional Popular Culture,* 185–258. New York: New Press, 1993.

———. "Rough Music." In *Customs in Common: Studies in Traditional Popular Culture,* 467–538. New York: New Press, 1993.

Thompson, Elizabeth. "Public and Private in Middle Eastern Women's History." *Journal of Women's History* 15, no. 1 (2003): 52–69.

Tillier, Mathieu. "The Mazalim in Historiography." In *The Oxford Handbook of Islamic Law,* edited by Rumee Ahmed and Anver M. Emon, 357–80. Oxford: Oxford University Press, 2019.

Tilly, Charles. "War Making and State Making as Organized Crime." In *Bringing the State Back In,* edited by Peter B. Evans, Dietrich Rueschemeyer, and Theda Skocpol, 169–87. Cambridge: Cambridge University Press, 1985.

Tor, D. G. "The Islamisation of Iranian Kingly Ideals in the Persianate Fürstenspiegel." *Iran* 49 (2011): 115–22.

Tsadik, Daniel. *Between Foreigners and Shi'is: Nineteenth-Century Iran and Its Jewish Minority.* Stanford, CA: Stanford University Press, 2007.

———. "The Legal Status of Religious Minorities: Imāmī Shī'ī Law and Iran's Constitutional Revolution." *Islamic Law and Society* 10, no. 3 (2003): 376–408.

Tuğ, Başak. *Politics of Honor in Ottoman Anatolia: Sexual Violence and Socio-Legal Surveillance in the Eighteenth Century.* Leiden: Brill, 2017.

Tulabi, Turan, and Ghulam Husayn Zargarinizhad. "Daramad: Tarikh-i Vaqayi'-i Dar al-Saltanah-i Isfahan." In *Mazdaknamah,* edited by Turan Tulabi and Ghulam Husayn Zargarinizhad, 435–42. Tehran: Asatir, 2015.

Turna, Nalan. "Pandemonium and Order: Suretyship, Surveillance, and Taxation in Early Nineteenth-Century İstanbul." *New Perspectives on Turkey* 39 (September 2008): 167–89.

Ueno, Masayuki. "'For the Fatherland and the State': Armenians Negotiate the Tanzimat Reforms." *International Journal of Middle East Studies* 45, no. 1 (2013): 93–109.

Vejdani, Farzin. "Urban Violence and Space: Lutis, Seminarians, and Sayyids in Late Qajar Iran." *Journal of Social History* 52, no. 4 (2019): 1185–1211.

Vikør, Knut S. "Muslim Subjects and the Rights of God." In *The Crisis of Citizenship in the Arab World*, edited by Nils Butenschøn and Roel Meijer, 271–95. Leiden: Brill, 2017.

Walcher, Heidi. *In the Shadow of the King: Zill al-Sultān and Isfahān under the Qājārs*. London: I. B. Tauris, 2008.

———. "Isfahan viii. Qajar Period." *EIr*.

Warner, Michael. *Publics and Counterpublics*. New York: Zone Books, 2002.

Watt, W. Montgomery. "Idjara." *EI2*.

Weber, Max. *Basic Concepts in Sociology*. New York: Citadel, 1966.

———. "Politics as a Vocation." In *Essays in Sociology*, edited by H. H. Garth and C. Wright Mills, 77–128. New York: MacMillan, 1946.

Wensinck, A. J. "Al-Masjid al-Haram." *EI2*.

Werner, Christoph. *An Iranian Town in Transition: A Social and Economic History of the Elites of Tabriz, 1747–1848*. Wiesbaden: Harrassowitz, 2000.

Westermarck, Edward. "Asylum." In *Encyclopaedia of Religion and Ethics*, vol. 2, 161–64. Edinburgh: T. & T. Clark, 1909.

Wishnitzer, Avner. "Into the Dark: Power, Light, and Nocturnal Life in 18th-Century Istanbul." *International Journal of Middle East Studies* 46, no. 3 (2014): 513–31.

Wyers, Marc David. *"Wicked" Istanbul: The Regulation of Prostitution in the Early Turkish Republic*. Istanbul: Libra Kitap, 2012.

Yilmaz, Huseyin. *Caliphate Redefined: The Mystical Turn in Ottoman Political Thought*. Princeton, NJ: Princeton University Press, 2020.

Zaman, Tahir. "Jiwār: From a Right of Neighbourliness to a Right to Neighbourhood for Refugees." In *Migration and Islamic Ethics: Issues of Residence, Naturalization and Citizenship*, edited by Ray Jureidini and Said Fares Hassan, 47–66. Leiden: Brill, 2019.

Zargarinizhad, Ghulam Husayn. "Daramad." In *Siyasatnamahha-yi Qajari: Si va Yak Andarznamah-i Siyasi-i 'Asr-i Qajar*, edited by Ghulam Husayn Zargarinizhad, vol. 1, 13–137. Tehran: Nigaristan-i Andishah, 2016.

Zarinebaf, Fariba. *Crime and Punishment in Istanbul: 1700–1800*. Berkeley: University of California Press, 2010.

Index

Page numbers in *italics* refer to figures.